"A very thoughtful, deeply personal and practical application of Stephen (and clearly Sandra) Covey's principles about what matters most—one's family."
—John E. Pepper, Chairman and CEO, Procter & Gamble

"Stephen Covey extends his life's work on organizations to society's most challenging area, the family, with practical examples of how to strengthen the most vital relationship of all."
—Tom Curley, President and Publisher, *USA Today*

"Family relationships require commitment, humility, patience, and the ability to forgive one another. Stephen Covey's book reminds us that the most important work we do each day is what we do for our families."
—Greg Coleman, Publisher, *Reader's Digest*

"The ever-present conflict between professional life and family life is addressed in *The 7 Habits of Highly Effective Families* through an excellent blend of principle, common sense, and example. Success is possible in both with the proper sense of priority and balance."
—Donald G. Soderquist, Vice Chairman and COO, Wal-Mart Stores, Inc.

"An outstanding book on principle-centered family relationships. It couldn't have come at a more opportune time, when lack of family ties is destroying relationships and causing excessive violence."
—Arun Gandhi, grandson of Mahatma Gandhi and Founder/Director,
    Gandhi Institute

"*The 7 Habits of Highly Effective Families* inspires us to create extraordinary family relationships and provides the practical insight to do it."
—John Gray, author of *Men Are from Mars, Women Are from Venus*

THE 7 HABITS OF HIGHLY EFFECTIVE FAMILIES

Also by Stephen R. Covey

THE 7 HABITS OF HIGHLY EFFECTIVE PEOPLE

PRINCIPLE-CENTERED LEADERSHIP

FIRST THINGS FIRST
(With A. Roger Merrill and Rebecca R. Merrill)

THE 7 HABITS OF HIGHLY EFFECTIVE FAMILIES

BUILDING A BEAUTIFUL FAMILY CULTURE IN A TURBULENT WORLD

Stephen R. Covey

FranklinCovey™

SIMON & SCHUSTER
A VIACOM COMPANY

First published in Great Britain by Simon & Schuster UK Ltd, 1998
This paperback edition first published by Simon & Schuster UK Ltd, 1999
A Viacom company

Copyright © 1997 by Franklin Covey Company

1 3 5 7 9 10 8 6 4 2

Simon & Schuster UK Ltd
Africa House
64-78 Kingsway
London WC2B 6AH

Simon & Schuster Australia
Sydney

A CIP catalogue record for this book is available
from the British Library

ISBN 0-684-86008-2

Printed and bound in Great Britain by
The Bath Press, Bath

ACKNOWLEDGMENTS

This book is truly the synergistic product of a team of people. Without their tireless, wholehearted, unique contributions it never would have come about. Each of their names could easily be listed on the cover alongside mine, and I express my deep appreciation to them:

—my beloved wife, Sandra, for many of the ideas and stories in this book, for her constant support and encouragement, for her intuitive wisdom and her education in child development, and above all for her sacrificial dedication over four decades in raising nine marvelous children.

—my dear children Cynthia, Maria, Stephen, Sean, David, Catherine, Colleen, Jenny, and Joshua, and their spouses and children, for their revealing and often embarrassing stories and for the quality of their lives and contributions.

—Boyd Craig, for his superb management of the whole three-year team production process, his unflagging positive energy, his remarkable judgment and counseling on many key issues, and his work hand in glove with Rebecca in the editing process.

—Rebecca Merrill, for her unusual editorial ability in weaving the ideas, stories, transcripts, and research together in a way that truly sings. Never have I had such a faithful translator.

—my dear brother, John M. R. Covey, for his lifelong loyalty and friendship, his inspiration to me in the development of the ideas in this book, his gifted ability to model and present these family principles, and his excellent work as a content leader in Franklin Covey Company's home and family area. He is also my personal spokesman for this family material. Also to his wife, Jane, a wonderful mother of a lovely family, whose early work on the book team and contributions of stories and learnings from presenting this material have been invaluable.

—my friend and colleague George Durrant, whose early work on the book team and association with us has infused both the book and us with an undying spirit of hope.

—Toni Harris and Pia Jensen, for their second-mile administrative support and their ability to interview and relate with people in a way that has drawn out so many of the powerful stories in this book.

—Rick Meeves, for incredible research and documentation contributions.

—Wally Goddard, for providing the team with decades of the learnings of many scholars, himself included, in the field of family and human development.

I also express my appreciation to many others whose contributions have made all the difference:

—my associates at Franklin Covey Company for their direct and indirect help and support to this project, particularly Greg Link, Stephen M. R. Covey, Roger Merrill, Patti Pallat, Nancy Aldridge, Darla Salin, Kerrie Flygare, Leea Bailey, Christie Brzezinski, Julie Shepherd, Gloria Lees, and our outside counsel, Richard Hill.

—Randy Royter and his associates at Royter Snow Design for bringing the visual and design elements of the book alive.

—our friends at Golden Books, particularly Bob Asahina, for his splendid professional editing and for always keeping us connected to the pulse of the reader. Also my supportive and creative literary agent, Jan Miller.

—the hundreds of families who have so willingly shared their experiences in applying this material in their families.

—the many mentors, teachers, scholars, authors, and leaders who have influenced my thinking over the years.

—the spouses and children of the book team members whose constancy of support, encouragement, patience, and belief have sustained and lifted us all.

—my parents, my three sisters, Irene, Helen Jean, and Marilyn, and my brother, John, for contributing to my happy childhood.

And, finally, I express my appreciation for the goodness of an overriding Providence in my life.

For all children, our common mission

CONTENTS

A Personal Message

Dear Reader,

Never in all my life have I had such a passion for a project as I have for writing this book—because family is what I care the most about, as I imagine you do also.

Applying the 7 Habits material to the family is an absolute natural. It fits. In fact, it's where it was really learned. You'll sense this when you read the marvelous stories of how families of every kind share how they applied the 7 Habits and what resulted.

I'm also sharing a lot about me and our family—how we've tried to apply it and also how we've blown it. Every family situation is unique and different. So is ours. But in many ways every family is similar. My guess is that we struggle with many of the same kinds of problems and day-to-day challenges you do.

One of the personal dilemmas I have in writing the book is just how much to share of our family stories, mistakes, and achievements. On the one hand, I don't want to sound as if we think we have all the answers. On the other hand, I don't want to hold back from sharing where my heart is and where I have really learned the remarkable power of the 7 Habits.

I've asked Sandra and the children to share also—the good and the bad. Their stories are set off with their names in bold. Perhaps we've gone overboard; about a fifth of the stories are about us. But the stories are only illustrations of principles, which are universal. You may not relate to the stories, but I believe you will relate to the principles. And I hope the stories will trigger new ideas that work in your situation.

With all this material, I want, above all, to instill a sense of hope that this way of thinking can really be helpful and can work for you. I know you want to prioritize your family, and I want to share with you a powerful way of doing this in our crazy, turbulent, often family-unfriendly world.

Finally, I firmly believe that family is the building block of society and that our greatest fulfillment lies there. I also believe the most important work we will ever do is at home. Former First Lady Barbara Bush said it beautifully to the graduating students at Wellesley College: "As important as your obligations as a doctor, lawyer, or business leader will be, you are a human being first, and those human connections—with spouses, with children, with friends—are the most important investments you will ever make. At the end of your life, you will never regret not having passed one more test, not winning one more verdict, or not closing one more deal. You will regret time not spent with a husband, a child, a friend, or a parent. . . . Our success as a society depends not on what happens in the White House but on what happens inside your house."[1]

I am convinced that if we as a society work diligently in every other area of life and neglect the family, it would be analogous to straightening deck chairs on the *Titanic*.

Sincerely,
Stephen R. Covey

FOREWORD

At the conclusion of our son's basketball tournament, I visited with one of the mothers. She said, "I'm surprised that your husband has been here for almost every game Joshua has played. I know he's on the run—writing, consulting, traveling. How has he managed?" The first thought that flashed into my mind was that he has a great wife and a full-time assistant. But putting that aside, I replied, "He makes it a priority." And he does.

Stephen once told a group of high-powered businessmen, "If your company were falling apart, you know you'd do whatever you had to do to save it. Somehow you'd find a way. The same reasoning applies to your family." Most of us know what we need to do, but do we want to do it?

Stephen and I both had happy childhoods and wanted the same for our children. Life was much simpler then. I still remember the long summer evenings as a child playing night games with all the neighborhood children: kick the can; hide-and-seek; red rover, red rover; run, sheepie, run. Our parents watched us from lawn chairs or sat on their porches, chatting and visiting. Often, my mom and dad walked hand in hand to Fernwood's Ice Cream Parlor to get a double-decker cone. As children we took time to lie on the cool green grass and watch the clouds make pictures in the sky. Sometimes we slept outside on summer nights, after gazing in wonder at the billions of stars in the Milky Way. This was the picture in my mind, the ideal of a happy, secure family.

Stephen and I often discussed the kind of home and family life we wanted to create. As our family grew and our lives became busier and more complicated, we realized that successful families don't just happen. It takes every bit of combined energy, talent, desire, vision, and determination you can muster. Things you really care about take time, thought, planning, and prioritizing. You have to work at it and make sacrifices; you have to want it and pay the price.

People have often remarked to me, "You have nine kids. How wonderful. You must be patient." I never could follow that line of reasoning. Why would I be patient because I had nine kids? Why wouldn't I be a raving maniac? Or they'd say, "If you have that many kids, I guess one more doesn't matter." They say that because they never had one more.

Raising a large family has been hard work. I wanted life to be simple, the way I had remembered my own childhood, but Stephen kept reminding me that our life together would never be like that. It was more complicated. There was more pressure. The world has changed. Those days are gone—but they can still be remembered and treasured.

As Stephen was building his reputation as a consultant, speaker, and author, he had to travel a lot. This meant planning ahead so as not to miss important events such as football games, school productions, and junior proms. Whenever he was gone, he would call nightly to talk to each child and touch base.

"Somebody get the phone," you'd hear. "You know it's going to be Dad again. I talked to him last night. It's your turn!" "Oh, brother! Tell him to call back when the movie is over." "Is there no respect?" we'd ask.

When he was home, he was totally there. He was so much a part of their lives and so involved that I don't think anyone remembers his being gone. Stephen has always been a great listener, a continual learner, and a perpetual student. He's always asking questions—picking people's brains as if he's devouring the last of a Thanksgiving turkey, hoping to hear opinions different from his own. He values the differences. I admire him for trying to walk his talk. He truly tries to live all the principles he teaches and believes in. This is not easy to do. He is a man without guile. He has an uncommon sense of humility that touches, changes, and softens his heart, thus making me want to do likewise.

He is an idealist (which is a blessing and a curse). His idealism inspires and motivates me, the people he teaches, and our children; it makes us want to achieve and lift ourselves and others. He is also a struggler, as I am (and as most of us are).

When we're trying to live what we believe, struggling but moving in the right direction, our children will usually accept our values. Our hearts and intentions are good—we have the vision and desire—but we often blow it. Our temper can put us in a compromised situation, and our pride can keep us there. We often get off track, but we keep coming back.

I remember an experience I had when our oldest daughter, Cynthia, was three years old. We had just moved into our first house—a tiny, new, three-bedroom tract house that we were crazy about. I loved decorating and worked hard to make it charming and attractive.

My literary club was meeting there, and I had spent hours cleaning so that every room looked perfect. I was anxious to show my friends around, hoping they would be impressed. I put Cynthia down for the night and thought she would be sleeping when they peeked in to see her—noticing, of course, her darling room with the bright yellow tied quilt and matching curtains and the cute, colorful animals I had made and hung on the walls. But when I opened her door to show off my daughter and her room, I discovered to my dismay that she had hopped out of bed, pulled all of her toys out of her toy chest, and scattered them all over the floor. She had emptied the clothes from her dresser drawers and thrown them all over the floor. She had dumped out her Tinker Toys, puzzles, and crayon box—and she was still going at it! Her room was a disaster. It looked as if a tornado had hit it. In the midst of all this, she looked up with a mischievous smile on her face and said sweetly, "Hi, Mummy!"

I was furious that she had disobeyed me and gotten out of bed; I was upset that her room was all messed up and that no one could see how cute it was decorated; and I was annoyed that she had put me in this embarrassing situation in front of my friends.

I spoke sharply to her, spontaneously spanked her little bottom, and put her back to bed with a warning not to get up again. Her lower lip started to quiver. She looked shocked at my response, and her eyes filled with tears. She started sobbing, not understanding what she had done wrong.

I closed the door and immediately felt terrible for overreacting. I was ashamed at my behavior, realizing that it was my pride—not her actions—that had set me off. I was angry at myself for such an immature response and shallowness. I was sure I had ruined her for life. Years later I asked her if she remembered the incident, and I breathed a sigh of relief when she said no.

Faced with the same situation today, I think my response would be to laugh. "That's easy for you to say!" my daughters respond as they struggle with their toddlers. But what once seemed important to me has shifted and matured.

We all go through stages. Concern about appearances, making good impressions, being popular, comparing yourself to others, having unbridled ambition, wanting to make money, striving to be recognized and noticed, and trying to establish yourself—all fade as your responsibilities and character grow.

Life's tests refine you. Genuine friendships sustain you. Being unaffected and genuine, having integrity, and facing problems squarely help as you try to reach out, make a difference, touch a life, be an example, do the right thing. You become motivated as you struggle to become a better person.

The struggles are ongoing. After raising nine kids, I think I'm just beginning to get some perspective. Many times I blew it, lost my temper, misunderstood, judged before understanding, didn't listen, and acted unwisely. But I also tried to learn from my mistakes. I apologized, grew up, shifted my values, recognized growth stages, didn't overreact, rolled with the punches, learned to laugh at myself, had fewer rules, enjoyed life more, and realized that raising kids is hard work—physically and emotionally. It's draining as well as fulfilling. You fall into bed at night, totally exhausted, and like Scarlett O' Hara murmur, "Tomorrow is another day." Oh, to be half as smart as your child thinks you are and half as dumb as your teenager sees you!

Through it all I've learned that parenting is basically a life of sacrifice. I have a sign in my kitchen to remind me: "Motherhood is not for wimps." Along with your children you go through lessons and practicing, carpools and braces, tears and tantrums, ages and stages, traumas and triumphs, homework, table manners, puberty, pimples, puppy love, driver's licenses, fighting, and teasing.

But in the end (as in childbirth) you don't remember the pain. You remember the joy of being a parent, of worrying and sacrificing for that remarkable son or daughter you love with all your soul. You remember the expressions on your children's faces through the years—how they looked in that special dress or outfit they wore. You remember your pride in their success, your pain in their struggles. You remember the wonderful times, the fun of it all, the quiet moments of bonding as you gazed at the baby you were nursing, filled with the awe and wonder of your stewardship and your fulfillment in being a parent and nurturing a family.

It wasn't until we had our seventh baby, Colleen, that I felt as though I was really putting it all together. I finally learned how to say no to the unimportant. As I sat in my rocking chair, looking out the window, nursing, bonding, glad to be there, savoring the moment rather than thinking I should be doing something else, a sense of joy and balance filled me. Finally I knew that for me this is what it was all about.

So I only remember the good times. But then, only seven of our children are married. We still have two at home. And Joshua, our seventeen-year-old high school junior, often reminds me (with a twinkle in his eye), "We could ruin you guys!"

Each of you has a very different and very personal family life, one that is unlike anyone else's. You've probably discovered, as I did, that life isn't simple anymore. Society doesn't support families as it used to. Life is more technological, faster, more sophisticated, scarier.

The theories and principles put forth in this book were not invented by Stephen. He noticed them, observed them, put them together in some workable order. These are universal principles that you already know in your heart to be true. That's why they seem so familiar. You've seen them in action. They've worked in your own life. You've even used them yourself—often.

What is helpful, however, is giving you a framework, a way of thinking about and looking at your own unique situation and finding a way to deal with it. It's a starting point, a way to examine where you are right now and where you want to go, and ways that might help you get there.

A few years ago Carol, one of my best and dearest friends, developed cancer. After months of radiation, chemotherapy, and operations, she realized what her fate would be. She never asked, "Why me?" There was no bitterness or feeling of despair. Her whole perspective on life changed dramatically. "I don't have any time for things that don't matter," she told me. "I know what's important and where to put my priorities." Her courage touched my heart as I watched her strengthen her relationship with her husband, children, and loved ones. Her utmost desire was to serve, contribute, and somehow make a difference. Her death made all of us who loved her want to become better and stronger people—more willing to love, care, and serve. In a sense she wrote her mission statement for life on her deathbed. You can begin writing yours now.

No one will ever really understand your situation, your uniqueness—the rocks or baggage you carry or the idealism you hope for. You can take from this book what you will, what feels right for you. Some story or example might hit home and you'll be able to stand back, stand apart, and look at your own life and gain insight or perspective.

We want to give hope to those who feel they've made a lot of mistakes, blown it, or not prioritized their families and are feeling the repercussions of that decision—or even those who may have lost a child along the way. You can reclaim a lost child. It is never too late. You should never give up or stop trying.

I believe this book will help you become that agent of change, that transition person who will make a difference.

Every good wish in your efforts,
Sandra Merrill Covey

YOU'RE GOING TO BE "OFF TRACK" 90 PERCENT OF THE TIME. SO WHAT?

Good families—even great families—are off track 90 percent of the time! The key is that they have a sense of destination. They know what the "track" looks like. And they keep coming back to it time and time again.

It's like the flight of an airplane. Before the plane takes off, the pilots have a flight plan. They know exactly where they're going and start off in accordance with their plan. But during the course of the flight, wind, rain, turbulence, air traffic, human error, and other factors act upon that plane. They move it slightly in different directions so that *most of the time* that plane is not even on the prescribed flight path! Throughout the entire trip there are slight deviations from the flight plan.

Weather systems or unusually heavy air traffic may even cause major deviations. But barring anything too major, the plane will arrive at its destination.

Now how does that happen? During the flight, the pilots receive constant feedback. They receive information from instruments that read the environment, from control towers, from other airplanes—even sometimes from the stars. And based on that feedback, they make adjustments so that time and time again, they keep returning to the flight plan.

The hope lies not in the deviations but in the vision, the plan, and the ability to get back on track.

The flight of that airplane is, I believe, the ideal metaphor for family life. With regard to our families, it doesn't make any difference if we are off target or even if our family is a mess. The hope lies in the vision and in the plan and in the courage to keep coming back time and time again.

Sean (our son):

In general, I'd say that our family had as many fights as other families when we were growing up. We had our share of problems, too. But I am convinced that it was the ability to renew, to apologize, and to start again that made our family relationships strong.

On our family trips, for example, Dad would have all these plans for us to get up at 5:00 A.M., have breakfast, and get ready to be on the road by 8:00. The problem was that when the day arrived, we'd all be sleeping in and no one wanted to help. Dad would lose his temper. When we'd finally get off, about twelve hours after the time we were supposed to go, no one would even want to talk to Dad because he was so mad.

But what I remember the most is that Dad always apologized. Always. And it was a humbling thing to see him apologize for losing his temper—especially when you knew deep inside that you were one of the ones who had provoked him.

As I look back, I think what made the difference in our family was that both Mom and Dad would always keep coming back, keep trying—even when we were goofing off, even when it seemed that all their new plans and systems for family meetings and family goals and family chores were never going to work.

As you can see, our family is no exception. I'm no exception. I want to affirm at the very outset that whatever your situation—even if you are having many difficulties, problems, and setbacks—there is tremendous hope in moving toward your destination. The key is in having *a destination, a flight plan,* and *a compass.*

> *The key is in having a destination, a flight plan, and a compass.*

This metaphor of the airplane will be used continuously throughout this book to communicate a sense of hope and excitement around the whole idea of building a beautiful family culture.

The Three Purposes of This Book

My desire in writing this book is to help you keep this sense of hope first and fore-most in your mind and heart, and to help you develop these three things that will help you and your family stay on track: a destination, a flight plan, and a compass.

1. A clear vision of your destination. I realize that you come to this book with a unique family situation and unique needs. You may be struggling to keep your marriage together or to rebuild it. Or you may already have a good marriage but want a great one—one that is deeply satisfying and fulfill-ing. You may be a single parent and feel overwhelmed by the relentless crush of demands and pressures put upon you. You may be struggling with a wayward child or a rebellious teenager who is under the control of a gang or drugs or some other negative influence in society. You may be trying to blend two families together who "couldn't care less."

Perhaps you want your children to do their jobs and their homework cheerfully, without being reminded. Or you're feeling challenged trying to fulfill combined (and apparently conflicting) roles in your family life, such as parent, judge, jury, jailer, and friend. Or you're bouncing back and forth between strictness and per-missiveness, not knowing how to discipline.

You may be struggling simply to make ends meet. You may be "robbing Peter to pay Paul." Your economic worries may almost overwhelm you and consume all your time and your emotions so that there is hardly anything left for relationships. You may have two or more jobs, and you and your loved ones just pass one another like ships in the night. The idea of a beautiful family culture may seem ever so remote.

It could be that the feeling and spirit in your family is contentious, that you have people quarreling, fighting, yelling, screaming, demanding, snarling, sniping, sneer-ing, blaming, criticizing, walking out, slamming doors, ignoring, withdrawing, or whatever. It could be that some older kids won't even come home, that there seems to be no natural affection left. It could be that the feeling in your marriage has died or is dying, or that you're feeling empty and alone. Or it could be that you're work-ing your heart out to make everything nice, and nothing seems to improve. You're exhausted, and you have a sense of futility and "what's the use?"

Or you may be a grandparent who cares deeply but doesn't know how to help without making things worse. Perhaps your relationship with a son or daughter-in-law has become soured, and there's nothing but surface politeness and a deep cold war inside, which occasionally erupts into a hot one. It could be that you've been a victim of abuse for many years—in your upbringing or in your marriage—and you're desirous and determined to stop that cycle, but you can't seem to find any pattern or example to follow and keep falling back into the same tendencies and practices you abhor. Or it could be you're a couple that wants desperately to have children but can't, and you feel the sweetness in your marriage beginning to slip away.

You may even be experiencing a combination of many of these stresses, and you have no sense of hope at all. Whatever your situation, it is vitally important that you do not compare your family to any other family. No one will ever know the full reality of your situation, and until you feel that they do, their advice is worthless. Similarly, you will never know the full reality of another family or another person's family situation. Our common tendency is to project our own situation onto others and try to prescribe what is right for them. But what we see on the surface is usually only the tip of the iceberg. Many people think that other families are just about perfect while theirs is falling apart. Yet every family has its challenges, its own bag of rocks.

The wonderful thing is that vision is greater than baggage. This means that a sense of what you can envision for the future—a better situation, a better state of being—is more powerful than whatever ugliness has accumulated in the past or whatever situation you are confronting in the present.

So I would like to share with you the way that families throughout the world have created a sense of shared vision and values through the development of a "family mission statement." I'll show you how you can develop such a statement and how it will unify and strengthen your family. A family mission statement can become your family's unique "destination," and the values it contains will represent your guidelines.

The vision of a better, more effective family will probably start with you. But to make it work well, others in the family must also feel involved. They must help to form it—or at least understand it and buy into it. And the reason is simple. Have you ever done a jigsaw puzzle or seen someone doing one? How important is it that you have the final scene in mind? How important is it that all who are working on it have the same final scene in mind? Without a sense of shared vision, people would be using different criteria to make their decisions, and the result would be total confusion.

Vision is greater than baggage.

The idea is to create a vision that is shared by everyone in the family. When your destination is clear, you can keep coming back to the flight plan time and time again. In fact, the journey is really part of the destination. They are inseparably connected. How you travel is as important as where you arrive.

2. A flight plan. It's also vital that you have a flight plan based on the principles that will enable you to arrive at your destination. Let me share with you a story to illustrate.

I have a dear friend who once shared with me his deep concern over a son he described as being "rebellious," "disturbing," and "an ingrate."

"Stephen, I don't know what to do," he said. "It's gotten to the point where if I come into the room to watch television with my son, he turns it off and walks out. I've tried my best to reach him, but it's just beyond me."

At the time I was teaching some university classes around the 7 Habits. I said, "Why don't you come with me to my class right now? We're going to be talking about Habit 5—how to listen empathically to another person before you attempt to explain yourself. My guess is that your son may not feel understood."

"I already understand him," he replied. "And I can see problems he's going to have if he doesn't listen to me."

"Let me suggest that you assume you know nothing about your son. Just start with a clean slate. Listen to him without any moral evaluation or judgment. Come to class and learn how to do this and how to listen within his frame of reference."

So he came. Thinking he understood after just one class, he went to his son and said, "I need to listen to you. I probably don't understand you, and I want to."

His son replied, "You have never understood me—ever!" And with that, he walked out.

The following day my friend said, "Stephen, it didn't work. I made such an effort, and this is how he treated me! I felt like saying, 'You idiot! Don't you realize what I've done and what I'm trying to do now?' I really don't know if there's any hope."

I said, "He's testing your sincerity. And what did he find out? He found out you don't really want to understand him. You want him to shape up."

"He should, the little whippersnapper!" he replied. "He knows full well what he's doing to mess things up."

I replied, "Look at the spirit inside you now. You're angry and frustrated and full of judgments. Do you think you can use some surface-level listening technique with your son and get him to open up? Do you think it's possible for you to talk to him or even look at him without somehow communicating all those negative things you're feeling deep inside? You've got to do much more private work inside your own mind and heart. You'll eventually learn to love him unconditionally just the way he is rather than withholding your love until he shapes up. On the way, you'll learn to listen within his frame of reference and, if necessary, apologize for your judgments and past mistakes or do whatever it takes."

My friend caught the message. He could see that he had been trying to practice the technique at the surface but was not dealing with what would produce the power to practice it sincerely and consistently, regardless of the outcome.

So he returned to class for more learning and began to work on his feelings and motives. He soon started to sense a new attitude within himself. His feelings about his son turned more tender and sensitive and open.

He finally said, "I'm ready. I'm going to try it again."

I said, "He'll test your sincerity again."

"It's all right, Stephen," he replied. "At this point I feel as if he could reject every overture I make, and it would be all right. I would just keep making them because it's the right thing to do, and he's worth it."

That night he sat down with his son and said, "I know you feel as though I haven't tried to understand you, but I want you to know that I am trying and will continue to try."

Again, the boy coldly replied, "You have never understood me." He stood up and started to walk out, but just as he reached the door, my friend said to his son, "Before you leave, I want to say that I'm really sorry for the way I embarrassed you in front of your friends the other night."

His son whipped around and said, "You have no idea how much that embarrassed me!" His eyes began to fill with tears.

"Stephen," he said to me later, "all the training and encouragement you gave me did not even begin to have the impact of that moment when I saw my son begin to tear up. I had no idea that he even cared, that he was that vulnerable. For the first time I *really* wanted to listen."

And he did. The boy gradually began to open up. They talked until midnight, and when his wife came in and said, "It's time for bed," his son quickly replied, "We want to talk, don't we, Dad?" They continued to talk into the early morning hours.

The next day in the hallway of my office building, my friend, with tears in his eyes, said, "Stephen, I found my son again."

As my friend discovered, there are certain fundamental principles that govern in all human interactions, and living in harmony with those principles or natural laws is absolutely essential for quality family life. In this situation, for example, the principle my friend had been violating was the basic principle of respect. The son also violated it. But this father's choice to live in harmony with that principle—to try to genuinely and empathically listen to and understand his son—dramatically changed the entire situation. You change one element in any chemical formula and everything changes.

Exercising the *principle* of respect and being able to genuinely and empathically listen to another human being are among the habits of highly effective people in any walk of life. Can you imagine a truly effective individual who would not respect and honor others or who would not deeply listen and understand? Incidentally, that is how you can tell if you have found a principle that is truly *universal* (meaning that it applies everywhere), *timeless* (meaning that it applies at any time), and *self-evident* (meaning that arguing against it is patently foolish, such as arguing that you could build a strong long-term relationship without respect). Just imagine the absurdity of trying to live its opposite.

The 7 Habits are based on universal, timeless, and self-evident principles that are just as true in the world of human relations as the law of gravity is in the physical world. These principles ultimately govern in all of life. They have been part of successful individuals, families, organizations, and civilizations throughout time. These habits are not tricks or techniques. They're not quick fixes. They're not a bunch of practices or "to do" lists. They are *habits*—established patterns of thinking and doing things—that all successful families have in common.

> *There are certain fundamental principles that govern in all human interactions, and living in harmony with those principles or natural laws is absolutely essential for quality family life.*

The violation of these principles virtually guarantees failure in family or other interdependent situations. As Leo Tolstoy observed in his epic novel *Anna Karenina*, "Happy families are all alike; every unhappy family is unhappy in its own way."[1] Whether we're talking about a two-parent or a single-parent family, whether there are ten children or none, whether there has been a history of neglect and abuse or a legacy of love and faith, the fact is that happy families have certain constant characteristics. And these characteristics are contained in the 7 Habits.

One of the other significant principles my friend learned in this situation concerns the very nature of change itself—the reality that all true and lasting change occurs from the *inside out*. In other words, instead of trying to change the situation or his son, he went to work on himself. And it was his own deep interior work that eventually created change in the circumstance and in his son.

This inside-out approach is at the very heart of the 7 Habits. By consistently applying the principles contained in these habits, you can bring about positive changes in any relationship or situation. You can become an *agent of change*. In addition, focusing on principles will have a far greater effect on behavior than focusing on behavior alone. This is because these principles are already intuitively known or deeply embodied in people, and seeking to understand them will help people understand more of their own true nature and possibilities, and unleash their potential.

One of the reasons this inside-out approach is so vital today is that times have changed dramatically. In the past, it was easier to successfully raise a family "outside-in," because society was an ally, a resource. People were surrounded by role models, examples, media reinforcement, and family-friendly laws and support systems that sustained marriage and helped create strong families. Even when there were problems within the family, there was still this powerful reinforcement of the whole idea of successful marriage and family life. Because of this you could essentially raise your family "outside-in." Success was much more a matter of "going with the flow."

But the jet stream has changed—dramatically. *And to "go with the flow" today is family-fatal!*

Even though we can be encouraged by efforts to return to "family values," the reality is that the trends in the wider society over the last thirty to fifty years have basically shifted from pro-family to anti-family. We're trying to navigate through what has become a turbulent, family-unfriendly environment, and there are powerful headwinds that easily throw many families off track.

> *The jet stream has changed— dramatically. And to "go with the flow" today is family-fatal!*

At a recent conference on families, one state governor shared this sobering experience:

I had a conversation recently with a man whom I consider a very good father. He told me this story:

His seven-year-old son recently seemed to have some things on his mind. He said, "Dad, I just can't quit thinking about it." And this father assumed that it was a nightmare or some kind of scary movie he had seen.

But after a lot of persuasion and some coaxing, he told of horrible, ugly hard-core pornography that he'd been exposed to. The father said, "Where did this come from?" The boy gave him the name of a nine-year-old neighbor, a trusted neighbor. He had seen it on the computer. "How many times did you see it?" the father asked. "Lots of times" was the reply.

Well, the father went to the parents of the nine-year-old. They were shocked. They were dismayed. They were sickened to think that the minds of these two little boys had been polluted at their tender age. The parents of the nine-year-old confronted him. He collapsed in tears. He said, "I know it's wrong, but I just keep looking at it."

They were concerned, of course, that there might be an adult involved. But no. It was introduced to the nine-year-old by a sixth grader who gave him the Internet address at school and said, "Look at this. It's really cool." And it spread around that neighborhood like a plague.

The father told me that they had encouraged their children, as they felt they should, to learn to use the computer. And the nine-year-old was good at it. But they kept the computer downstairs, behind a closed door. Unwittingly, they had turned that room into a porn shop.[2]

How could this happen? How could it be that we live in a society where technology makes it possible for children—who have no wisdom or experience or judgment on these matters—to become victims of such sick, deeply addictive mental poisoning as pornography?

Over the past thirty years the situation for families has changed powerfully and dramatically. Consider the following:

- Illegitimate birth rates have increased more than 400 percent.[3]
- The percentage of families headed by a single parent has more than tripled.[4]
- The divorce rate has more than doubled.[5] Many project that about half of all new marriages will end in divorce.
- Teenage suicide has increased almost 300 percent.[6]
- Scholastic Aptitude Test scores among all students have dropped 73 points.[7]
- The number one health problem for American women today is domestic violence. Four million women are beaten each year by their partners.[8]
- One-fourth of all adolescents contract a sexually transmitted disease before they graduate from high school.[9]

Since 1940 the top disciplinary problems in public school have changed from chewing gum and running in the halls to teen pregnancy, rape, and assault.[10]

Top Disciplinary Problems According to Public School Teachers

1940	1990
Talking out of turn	Drug abuse
Chewing gum	Alcohol abuse
Making noise	Pregnancy
Running in the halls	Suicide
Cutting in line	Rape
Dress code infractions	Robbery
Littering	Assault

In the midst of all this, the percentage of families with one parent at home with the children during the day has dropped from 66.7 to 16.9 percent.[11] And the average child spends seven hours a day watching television—and five minutes a day with Dad![12]

The great historian Arnold Toynbee taught that we can summarize all of history in one simple idea: Nothing fails like success. In other words, when the response is equal to the challenge, that is success; but when the challenge changes, the old response no longer works.

The challenge has changed, so we must develop a response that is equal to the challenge. The desire to create a strong family is not enough. Even good ideas are not enough. We need a new mind-set and a new skill-set. The challenge has taken a quantum leap, and if we are to respond effectively, so must we.

> Why mission statements? Why special family times? Why one-on-one bonding experiences? Because without new basic patterns or structures in place, families will be blown off course.

The 7 Habits framework represents such a mind-set and skill-set. Throughout this book I will show you how—even in the midst of the turbulent environment—many families are using the principles in the 7 Habits framework to get and stay on track.

Specifically, I'm going to encourage you to set aside a special "family time" each week that, barring emergencies or unexpected interruptions, you hold inviolate. This family time will be a time for planning, communicating, teaching values, and having fun together. It will be a powerful factor in helping you and your family stay on course. I'm also going to suggest that you have regular one-on-one bonding times with each member of your family—times when the agenda is usually written by the other person. If you do these two things, I can almost guarantee that the quality of your family life will improve dramatically.

But why mission statements? Why special family times? Why one-on-one bonding experiences? Simply because the world has changed in profound ways, and the speed of change itself is changing, is increasing. Without new basic patterns or structures in place, families will be blown off course.

As Alfred North Whitehead once said, "The habit of the active utilization of well-understood principles is the final possession of wisdom."[13] You don't have to learn a hundred new practices. You don't have to be constantly searching for newer, better techniques. All you need is a basic framework of fundamental principles that you can apply in any situation.

The 7 Habits create such a framework. The greatest power of the 7 Habits does not lie in the individual habits but in all the habits together and in the relationship between them. With this framework you can diagnose or figure out just about anything that happens in any conceivable family situation. And you can sense what the first steps are in fixing it or improving it. Millions of people who got into the original 7 Habits material can so testify. It's not that the habits tell you what to do but that they give you a way of thinking and of being so that *you* will come to know what to do—and when to do it. *How* to do it will take skill, and that involves practice.

As one family said, "We've sometimes found it hard to live these principles. *But it's much, much harder not to!*" Every action has a consequence, and actions that are not based on principles will have unhappy consequences.

So my second purpose in writing this book is to show you how, regardless of your situation, the 7 Habits framework can be an enormously useful tool in helping you diagnose your situation and create positive change from the inside out.

3. A compass. The 7 Habits framework deeply affirms that you are the creative force of your own life and that through your example and leadership you can become a creative force—an agent of change—in your family life. So the third purpose of this book is to help you recognize and develop four unique gifts you have that will enable you to become an agent of change in your family. These gifts become a compass or an inner guidance system that will help your family stay on course as you move toward your destination. They enable you to recognize and align your life with universal principles—even in the midst of turbulent social weather—and they empower you to determine and take whatever action is most appropriate and effective in your situation.

And wouldn't you agree that any contribution this book makes to you and your family would be far greater if it left you independent of me or any other author, counselor, or so-called advice giver and empowered you to figure out things for yourself and call upon other resources as you felt appropriate?

Again, no one knows your family situation as you do. *You* are the one in the cockpit. *You* are the one who has to deal with the turbulence, the weather, the forces that would blow you and your family off track. *You* are the one who is equipped to understand what needs to happen in your family and to make it happen.

Far more than techniques and practices that may have worked in other situations, you need an approach that will enable you, even empower you, to apply principles in *your* situation.

There's an expression in the Far East: "Give a man a fish, and you feed him for the day; teach him how to fish, and you feed him for a lifetime." This book is not about giving you a fish. Even though there are scores of illustrations and examples from all kinds of people in all kinds of settings showing how they applied the 7 Habits in their circum-

> *Far more than techniques and practices that may have worked in other situations, you need an approach that will enable you, even empower you, to apply principles in your situation.*

stances, the focus of this book is on teaching you how to fish. This will be done by sharing a sequenced set of principles that will help you develop your own capacity to optimize your unique situation. So look beyond the stories. Look for the principles. The stories may not apply to your situation, but *I can absolutely guarantee that the principles and the framework will.*

The End in Mind: A Beautiful Family Culture

Now this book is about the 7 Habits of *highly effective* families. So what is "effectiveness" in the family? I suggest it can be captured in four words: a beautiful family culture.

When I say *culture*, I'm talking about the spirit of the family—the feeling, the "vibes," the chemistry, the climate or atmosphere in the home. It's the character of the family—the depth, quality, and maturity of the relationships. It's the way family members relate to one another and how they feel about one another. It's the spirit or feeling that grows out of the collective patterns of behavior that characterize family interaction. And these things, like the tip of an iceberg, come out of the unseen mass of shared beliefs and values underneath.

> *Family itself is a "we" experience, a "we" mentality.*

When I talk about a *beautiful* family culture, I realize that the word "beautiful" may mean different things to different people. But I'm using it to describe a nurturing culture where family members deeply, sincerely, and genuinely enjoy being together, where they have a sense of shared beliefs and values, where they act and interact in ways that really work, based on the principles that govern in all of life. I'm talking about a culture that has moved from "me" to "we."*

Family itself is a "we" experience, a "we" mentality. And admittedly, the movement from "me" to "we"—from independence to interdependence—is perhaps one of the most challenging and difficult aspects of family life. But like the "road less traveled" spoken of in the Robert Frost poem,[14] it's the road that makes all the difference. Despite the priority that American culture clearly places on individual freedom, immediate gratification, efficiency, and control, there is literally no road laden with as much joy and satisfaction as the road of rich, interdependent family living.

When your happiness comes primarily from the happiness of others, you know you have moved from "me" to "we." And the whole problem-solving and opportunity-seizing process changes. But until family is really a priority, this movement does

*For a complimentary self-scoring survey to help you evaluate your current family culture, call (44) 0121-604-6999 or visit www.franklincovey.com on the Internet.

not usually take place. Marriage often becomes nothing more than two married singles living together, because the movement from independence to interdependence never happened.

A beautiful family culture is a "we" culture. It reflects that movement. It's the kind of culture that enables you to work together to select and move toward a "together" destination and to contribute, to make a difference—in society generally and perhaps to other families in particular. It also enables you to deal with the powerful forces that would throw you off track—including turbulent weather outside the plane (the culture we live in and things such as economic dislocation or sudden illness over which you have no control) and turbulent social weather inside the cockpit (contention, lack of communication, and the tendency to criticize, complain, compare, and compete).

Involve Your Family Now

Before you actually move into the 7 Habits, I'd like to acknowledge that the response to the original 7 Habits book and the expressed desire to apply this material to the family has been overwhelming. Based on that response, I have included a few of the family stories which "really worked" that were in the original 7 Habits book.

But most of the stories are new—many, in fact, have been shared by people who are working to apply these principles in their own families.* I suggest that you read the stories with the idea of drawing from them the fundamental principles involved as well as ideas for possible applications—even new and different applications—in your own family.

I would also like to suggest that, if at all possible, you take immediate steps to involve your family right from the beginning. I can guarantee you that the learning will be deeper, the bonding stronger, and the insight and joy greater if you can discover and share together. Also, by doing it together, you won't find yourself ahead of a spouse or your teenage children who might feel threatened by your new knowledge or your desire to create change. I'm aware of many individuals who got into self-help books on family and began to judge their spouse—so severely that a year later they found themselves "justifiably" divorced.

> *K*eep in mind that when you're working with your family, "slow" is "fast" and "fast" is "slow."

Learning together will be a powerful force in helping you build a "we" culture. So if at all possible, read the book together—perhaps even out

*Names have been changed to protect the privacy of those who have so generously shared their experiences.

loud to each other. Discuss the stories together. Talk about the ideas together as you go along. You might want to begin by simply sharing some of the stories at the dinner table. Or you may want to become more deeply involved in discussion and application. I've included some first-step suggestions at the end of each chapter on ways to teach and involve your family—and even study groups—in the material presented in that chapter. You may also want to refer to the 7 Habits diagram and definitions on page 390. Be patient. Go slowly. Respect the level of understanding of each person. Don't bulldoze through the material. Keep in mind that when you're working with your family, "slow" is "fast" and "fast" is "slow."

But again, I acknowledge that you are the expert on your family. Your situation may be such that you don't want to involve anyone else at this time. You may be dealing with sensitive issues that make doing this together unwise. Or you may simply want to see if this material makes sense to you and then involve others later. Or you may just want to begin with your spouse and some older teenage children.

That's fine. You know your situation best. All I'm saying is that after years of experience in working with the 7 Habits in many different settings, I have learned that when people go through it together—when they read it together, discuss it together, talk back and forth, and get the new insights and learnings and understandings together—it starts a bonding process that becomes truly exciting. The spirit is one of being equally yoked together: "I'm not perfect. You're not perfect. We're learning and growing together." When you share in humility what you are learning, with no intent to "shape up" someone else, it unfreezes the labels or judgments others have of you and makes it "safe," permissible, and legitimate for you to continue to grow and change.

> "*Never,
> never, NEVER
> give up!*"

I would also say this: Do not get discouraged if your initial efforts meet with resistance. Keep in mind that any time you try something new, you're going to get some flack:

"So what's wrong with us?"

"Why all the big deal about changing?"

"Why can't we just be like a normal family?

"I'm hungry. Let's eat first."

"I've got ten minutes and that's it. I'm out of here."

"Can I bring a friend?"

"I'd rather watch TV."

Just smile and keep moving forward. I promise you: It will be worth the effort!

The Miracle of the Chinese Bamboo Tree

Finally, I'd like to suggest that in everything you do in your family, you keep in mind the miracle of the Chinese bamboo tree. After the seed for this amazing tree is planted, you see nothing, absolutely *nothing*, for four years except for a tiny shoot coming out of a bulb. During those four years, all the growth is underground in a massive, fibrous root structure that spreads deep and wide in the earth. But then in the fifth year the Chinese bamboo tree grows up to eighty feet!

Many things in family life are like the Chinese bamboo tree. You work and you invest time and effort, and you do everything you can possibly do to nurture growth, and sometimes you don't see anything for weeks, months, or even years. But if you're patient and keep working and nurturing, that "fifth year" will come, and you will be astonished at the growth and change you see taking place.

Patience is faith in action. Patience is emotional diligence. It's the willingness to suffer inside so that others can grow. It reveals love. It gives birth to understanding. Even as we become aware of our suffering in love, we learn about ourselves and our own weaknesses and motives.

So, to paraphrase Winston Churchill, we must "never, *never*, NEVER give up!"

I know of one little girl who would always run out to the front porch. Her mother would go out, hug her, and invite her back. One day the little girl did this, and because her mother was busy, she forgot to go and get her. After a while the little girl went back into the house. Her mother hugged her and told her she was glad she was back. Then the little girl said, "Momma, always come after me."

Inside each of us is this deep longing for "home," for the rich, satisfying relationships and interactions of quality family life. And we must never give up. No matter how far we feel we've gotten off track, we can always take steps to correct the course. I strongly encourage you: No matter how far away a son or daughter seems to be, hang in there. Never give up. Your children are bone of your bone, flesh of your flesh, whether physically by birth or emotionally by the bonding of the family commitment you have made. Eventually, like the Prodigal son, they will return. You will reclaim them.

As the metaphor of the airplane reminds us, the destination is within reach. And the journey can be rich, enriching, and joyful. In fact, the journey is really part of the destination, because in the family, as in life, how you travel is as important as where you arrive.

As Shakespeare has written:

There is a tide in the affairs of men,
Which, taken at the flood, leads on to fortune;
Omitted, all the voyage of their life
Is bound in shallows and in miseries.
On such a full sea are we now afloat,
And we must take the current when it serves,
Or lose our ventures.[15]

We must take this tide *now*, for despite the trends in society we all know deep inside that family is supremely important. In fact, when I ask audiences worldwide what the three most important things in their lives are, 95 percent put "family" or "family relationships" on that list. Seventy-five percent put family first.

I feel the same way, and I imagine you do, too. Our greatest joys and our deepest heartaches surround what is happening in our family life. It is said that "no mother is happier than her most unhappy child." We want things to be right. We want to have the joy we somehow know deep inside is possible and natural and right in family life. But when we sense a gap between this vision of the rich, beautiful family life we want to have and the reality of our everyday family lives, we feel off track. It's easy to get discouraged, to feel a little hopeless—to feel that there is no way we can ever have the kind of family life we really want.

But there is hope, tremendous hope! The key is to remember to keep working from the inside out and keep getting back on track when we blow it.

I wish you well. I realize that your family is different from ours. Through divorce or the death of your spouse, you may be attempting to raise children alone. You may be a grandparent with all your children grown. You may be recently married and not have children yet. You may be an aunt or an uncle or a brother or a sister or a cousin. But whoever you are, you're part of a family, and family love is in a league of its own. When family relationships are good, life itself is good. It is my hope and belief that these 7 Habits will help you create a beautiful family culture in which life is really good.

SHARING THIS CHAPTER WITH ADULTS AND TEENS

Family Life Is Like an Airplane Flight

- Review the airplane illustration on pages 9–10. Ask family members: In what ways do you think family life is like an airplane flight?
- Ask: When do you feel our family is "off course?" Responses might include: during times of stress; in times of conflict when there's fighting, yelling, blaming, and criticizing; during painful times of loneliness and insecurity.
- Ask: When do you feel our family is "on course?" Responses might include: when we're taking walks, talking together, relaxing, going to the park, taking trips together, or having special dinners, "work" parties, family picnics, or barbecues.
- Encourage family members to think of a time when they knew they were off course. Ask: What caused it? What other things can you think of that impact you in negative ways?
- Review the story "I Found My Son Again" on page 13–14. Ask family members: How do we get back on track? Some ideas might include: having one-on-one time, asking for and getting feedback, listening, forgiving, apologizing, putting pride aside, becoming humble, taking responsibility, examining your thinking, connecting with what's important, respecting one another, considering consequences.
- Review Sean's recollections, "Mom and Dad would always keep coming back," on page 10. Discuss how family members can correct their course more effectively.

Learning Together

- Ask family members: How do we learn and share together as a family? Responses might include: reading stories together, sharing music, taking trips, enjoying new experiences together, gathering family photos, sharing family stories. Ask: How important is this to our family?
- Discuss how you can make reading and discussing this book together a commitment.

It's Never Too Late

- Consider the miracle of the Chinese bamboo tree as described on pages 22–23. Review the story "Momma, always come after me" on page 23. Ask family members: How does this impact the way we think about our family and the struggles we face? Are there any specific areas or relationships in which we need to allow time for growth?

SHARING THIS CHAPTER WITH CHILDREN

Play the Game

- Blindfold a family member. Lead him or her to a place in the house, the yard or a nearby park, where returning to the starting point without sight will be a little difficult. Make sure the return path is safe, with no stairs or other obstacles in the way.
- Turn the person around a few times and explain that it will be his or her job to find the way back to the designated starting point.
- Let the person try to return. After a moment ask if he or she would like some help or clues.
- Let family members direct the person back with instructions such as "turn left, go straight, turn right."
- When safely back, ask the person if it was hard to find the way when he or she couldn't see it and had no instructions. Give each child a chance to be blindfolded and try to find the way back.

Summarize the Game

- Help the children understand that you are all going through life together, but none of you can see the future. Often you will need instructions or clues and some assistance from your family to get to your destination.
- Talk about how wonderful it is to have a family to rely on.
- Help the children see that a family "flight plan" with some "help" to become a strong and happy family is just as valuable as the help and assistance they received when they were blindfolded and tried to find their way back to the designated starting point.

Action

- Decide to meet weekly as a family and talk about your family flight plan. Discuss what you can do to help one another, support one other, have fun together, and stay close all your lives.
- During the week, post little reminders here and there about the next family meeting.
- Plan fun bonding activities such as a visit to family member not living in your home, a trip to the ice cream store, a sports day, or sharing a great lesson or story that clearly shows how much you value the family and how committed you are as a parent to making it a priority.

HABIT 1
BE PROACTIVE

Stimulus ▷ **Freedom to Choose** ▷ Response

As I mentioned in the original 7 Habits book, many years ago when I was in Hawaii on a sabbatical, I was wandering through some stacks of books in the back of a college library. A particular book drew my interest, and as I flipped through the pages, my eyes fell on a single paragraph that was so compelling, so memorable, so staggering that it has profoundly influenced the rest of my life.

In that paragraph were three sentences that contained a single powerful idea:

> *Between stimulus and response, there is a space.*
> *In that space lies our freedom and power to choose our response.*
> *In our response lies our growth and our happiness.*

I cannot begin to describe the effect that idea had on me. I was overwhelmed by it. I reflected on it again and again. I reveled in the freedom of it. I personalized it. Between whatever happened to me and my response to it was a space. In that space was my freedom and power to choose my response. And in my response lay my growth and happiness.

The more I pondered it, the more I realized that I could choose responses that would affect the stimulus itself. I could become a force of nature in my own right.

This experience was forcibly brought to my mind again when I was in the middle of a taping session one evening and received a note saying that Sandra was on the phone and needed to speak to me.

"What are you doing?" she asked with impatience in her tone. "You knew we were having guests for dinner tonight. Where are you?"

I could tell she was upset, but as it happened, I had been involved all day in taping a video in a mountain setting. When we got to the final scene, the director insisted that it be done with the sun setting in the West, so we had to wait for nearly an hour to achieve this special effect.

In the midst of my own pent-up frustration over all these delays, I replied curtly, "Look, Sandra, it's not my fault that you scheduled the dinner. And I can't help it that things are running behind here. You'll have to figure out how to handle things at home, but I can't leave. And the longer we talk now, the later I'll be. I have work to do. I'll come when I can."

As I hung up the phone and started walking back to the shoot, I suddenly realized that my response to Sandra had been completely reactive. Her question had been reasonable. She was in a tough social situation. Expectations had been created, and I wasn't there to help fulfill them. But instead of understanding, I had been so filled with my own situation that I had responded abruptly—and that response had undoubtedly made things even worse.

The more I thought about it, the more I realized that my actions had really been off track. This was not the way I wanted to behave toward my wife. These were not the feelings I wanted in our relationship. If I had only acted differently, if I had been more patient, more understanding, more considerate—if I had acted out of my love for her instead of reacting to the pressures of the moment, the results would have been completely different.

But the problem was that I *didn't* think about it at the time. Instead of acting

based on the principles I knew would bring positive results, I reacted based on the feeling of the moment. I got sucked into the emotion of the situation, which seemed so overpowering, so consuming at the time that it completely blinded me to what I really felt deep inside and what I really wanted to do.

Fortunately, we were able to complete the taping quickly. As I drove home, it was Sandra—and not the taping—that was on my mind. My irritation was gone. Feelings of understanding and love for her filled my heart. I prepared to apologize. She ended up apologizing to me as well. Things worked out, and the warmth and closeness of our relationship were restored.

Creating a "Pause Button"

It is *so* easy to be reactive! Don't you find this to be the case in your own life? You get caught up in the moment. You say things you don't mean. You do things you later regret. And you think, "Oh, if only I had stopped to think about it, I never would have reacted that way!"

Obviously, family life would be a whole lot better if people acted based on their deepest values instead of reacting to the emotion or circumstance of the moment. What we all need is a "pause button"— something that enables us to stop between what happens to us and our response to it, and to choose our own response.

It's possible for us as individuals to develop this capacity to pause. And it's also possible to develop a habit right at the center of a family culture of learning to pause and give wiser responses. How to create that pause button in the family— how to cultivate the spirit of acting based on principle-centered values instead of reacting based on feelings or circumstance—is the focus of Habits 1, 2, and 3.

Your Four Unique Human Gifts

Habit 1—Be proactive—is the ability to act based on principles and values rather than reacting based on emotion or circumstance. The ability to do that comes from the development and use of four unique human gifts that animals do not have.

To help you understand what those gifts are, let me share with you how a single mother used them to become an agent of change in her family. She said:

For years I fought with my children and they fought with each other. I constantly judged, criticized, and scolded. Our home was filled with contention, and I knew my constant nagging was hurting my children's self-esteem.

Again and again I resolved to try to change, but each time I would fall back into negative habit patterns. The whole situation caused me to hate myself and take my anger out on my children, and that made me feel even more guilty. I felt that I was caught in a downward spiral which started in my childhood and which I was helpless to do anything about. I knew something had to be done, but I didn't know what.

Eventually, I decided to make my problems a matter of sustained thought, meditation, and specific and earnest prayer. I gradually came to two insights about the real motives for my negative, critical behavior.

First, I came to see more clearly the impact my own childhood experiences had on my attitude and behavior. I began to see the psychological scarring of my own upbringing. My childhood home was broken in almost every way. I can't remember ever seeing my parents talk through their problems and differences. They would either argue and fight, or they'd angrily go their separate ways and use the silent treatment. Sometimes that would last for days. My parents' marriage eventually ended in divorce.

So when I had to deal with these same issues and problems with my own family, I didn't know what to do. I had no model, no example to follow. Instead of finding a model or working it through within myself, I would take out my frustration and my confusion on the kids. And as much as I didn't like it, I found myself dealing with my children exactly as my parents had dealt with me.

The second insight I gained was that I was trying to win social approval for myself through my children's behavior. I wanted to get other people to like me because of their good behavior. I constantly feared that instead of winning approval, my children's behavior would embarrass me. Because of that lack of faith in them, I instructed, threatened, bribed, and manipulated my kids into behaving the way I wanted them to behave. I began to see that my own hunger for approval was keeping my children from growth and responsibility. My actions were actually helping to create the very thing I feared: irresponsible behavior.

Those two insights helped me realize that I needed to conquer my own problems instead of trying to find solutions by getting others to change. My unhappy, confused childhood inclined me to be negative, but it didn't force me to be that way. I could choose to respond differently. It was futile to blame my parents or my circumstances for my painful situation.

I had a very hard time admitting this to myself. I had to struggle with years of accumulated pride. But as I gradually swallowed the bitter pill, I discovered a marvelously free feeling. I was in control. I could choose a better way. I was responsible for myself.

Now when I get into a frustrating situation, I pause. I examine my tendencies. I compare them against my vision. I back away from speaking impulsively or striking out. I constantly strive for perspective and control.

Because the struggle continues, I retire frequently to the solitude of my own inner self to recommit to win my battles privately, to get my motives straight.

This woman was able to create a pause button or a space between what happened to her and her response to it. And in that space she was able to *act* instead of *react*. Now how did she do that?

Notice how she was able to step back and almost observe herself—to become aware of her own behavior. This is the first unique human gift: *self-awareness*. As humans we can stand apart from our own life and observe it. We can even observe our thoughts. We can then step in to make changes and improvements. Animals cannot do this, but we can. This mother did. And it led her to important insights.

The second gift she used was her *conscience*. Notice how her conscience—her moral or ethical sense or "inner voice"—let her know deep inside that the way she was treating her children was harmful, that it was taking her and her children down the same heartbreaking path that she had walked as a child. Conscience is another unique human gift. It enables you to evaluate what you observe about your own life. To use a computer metaphor, we could say that this moral sense of what is right and wrong is embedded in our "hardware." But because of all of the cultural "software" we pick up and because we misuse, disregard, and neglect this special gift of conscience, we can lose contact with this moral nature within us. Conscience gives us not only a moral sense but a moral power. It represents an energy source that aligns us with the deepest and finest principles contained in our highest nature. All six of the major religions of the world—in one way or another and using different language—teach this basic idea.

Now notice the third gift she used: *imagination*. This is her ability to envision something entirely different from her past experience. She could envision or imagine a far better response, one that would work in both the short and the long term. She recognized this capacity when she said, "I was in control. I could choose a better way." And because she was self-aware, she could examine her tendencies and compare them against her vision of that better way.

And what is the fourth gift? It's *independent will*—the power to take action. Listen to her language again: "I back away from speaking impulsively or striking out. I constantly strive for perspective and control" and "Because the struggle continues, I retire frequently to the solitude of my own inner self to recommit, to win

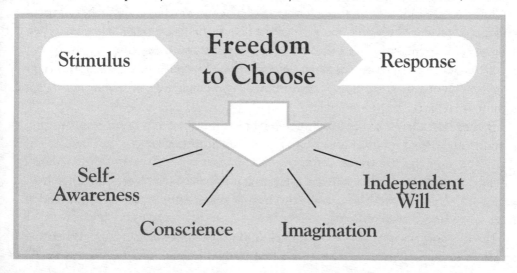

my battles privately, to get my motives straight." Just look at her tremendous intention and the willpower she's exercising! She's swimming upstream—even against deeply embedded tendencies. She's getting a grip on her life. She's willing it. She's making it happen. Of course it's hard. But that's the essence of what true happiness is: subordinating what we want now for what we want eventually. This woman has subordinated her impulse to get back, to justify herself, to win, to satisfy her ego—all in the name of the wisdom that her awareness, conscience, and imagination have given her—because what she wants eventually is something far greater, far more powerful in the spirit of the family than the short-term ego gratification she had before.

These four gifts—self-awareness, conscience, creative imagination, and independent will—reside in the space we humans have between what happens to us and our response to it.

Animals have no such space between stimulus and response. They are totally a product of their natural instincts and training. Although they also possess unique gifts we don't have, they basically live for survival and procreation.

But because of this space in human beings, there is more—infinitely more. And this "more" is the life force, the propensity that keeps us ever becoming. In fact, "grow or die" is the moral imperative of all existence.

Since the cloning in Scotland of a sheep named Dolly, there has been renewed interest in the possibility of cloning people and the question of whether it is ethical. So far, much of the discussion is based on the assumption that people are simply more advanced animals—that there is no space between stimulus and response and that we are fundamentally a product of *nature* (our genes) and *nurture* (our training, upbringing, culture, and present environment).

But this assumption does not begin to explain the magnificent heights that people such as Gandhi, Nelson Mandela, or Mother Teresa have climbed, or as many of the great mothers and fathers in the stories in this book have achieved. That is because deep in the DNA—in the chromosomal structure of the nucleus of every cell of our body—is the possibility of more development and growth and higher achievements and contribution because of the development and use of these unique human gifts.

Now as this woman learns how to develop and use her pause button, she is becoming proactive. She's also becoming a "transition person" in her family—that is, she's stopping the transmission of tendencies from one generation to another. She's stopping it with herself. She's stopping it *in* herself. She's suffering, if you will, to some degree, which helps burn out the intergenerational dross—this inherited tendency, this well-developed habit to get back, to get even, to be right. Her example is like wildfire to the seedbed of the family culture, to everyone who had entered into this retaliating, contentious, fighting spirit.

Can you imagine the good this woman is doing, the change she's bringing about, the modeling she's providing, the example she's giving? Slowly, subtly, perhaps almost imperceptibly she is bringing about a profound change in the family culture. She's writing a new script. She has become an agent of change.

We all have the ability to do this, and nothing is more exciting. Nothing is more ennobling, more motivating, more affirming, more empowering than the awareness of these four gifts and how they can combine together to bring about fundamental personal and family change. Throughout this book we will explore these gifts in depth through the experiences of people who have developed and used them.

The fact that we have these four unique gifts means no one has to be a victim. Even if you came from a dysfunctional or abusive family, you can choose to pass on a legacy of kindness and love. Even if you just want to be kinder and more patient and respectful than some of the models you've had in your life, cultivating these four gifts can nourish that seed of desire and explode it, enabling you to become the kind of person, the kind of family member you really want to be.

A "Fifth" Human Gift

As Sandra and I have looked back at our family life over the years, we've come to the conclusion that, in one sense, we could say there is a fifth human gift: a sense of humor. We could easily place humor along with self-awareness, imagination, conscience, and independent will, but it is really more of a second order human gift because it emerges from the blending of the other four. Gaining a humorous perspective requires *self-awareness*, the ability to see the irony and paradox in things and to reassert what is truly important. Humor draws upon creative *imagination*, the ability to put things together in ways that are truly new and funny. True humor also draws on *conscience* so that it is genuinely uplifting and doesn't fall into the counterfeit of cynicism or putting people down. It also involves willpower in making the choice to develop a humorous mind-set—to not be reactive, to not be overwhelmed.

Although it is a second order human gift, it is vitally important to the development of a beautiful family culture. In fact, I would say that in our own family the central element that has preserved the sanity, fun, unity, togetherness, and magnetic attraction of our family culture is laughter—telling jokes, seeing the "funny" side of life, poking holes at stuffed shirts, and simply having fun together.

I remember one day when our son Stephen was very young, we stopped at the dairy to get some ice cream. A woman came rushing in, zooming past us in a big hurry. She grabbed two bottles of milk and hurried to the cash register. In the rush, the momentum caused the heavy bottles to bang together, exploding and causing glass and milk to fly all over the floor. The whole place became totally silent. All eyes were on her in her drenched and embarrassed state. No one knew what to do or say.

Suddenly, little Stephen piped up: "Have a laugh, lady! Have a laugh!"

She and everyone else instantly broke out laughing, putting the incident into perspective. Thereafter, when any of us overreacted to a minor situation, someone would say, "Have a laugh!"

We enjoy humor even around our tendency to be reactive. For example, we once saw a Tarzan film together, and we decided to learn a little of the repertoire of the monkeys. So now when we realize we're beginning to get a little reactive, we act out this repertoire. Someone will start, and we'll all join in. We scratch our sides and shout, "Ooo! ooo! ooo! ah! ah! ah!" For us this clearly communicates "Hold it! There's no space here between stimulus and response. We've become animals."

Laughter is a great tension releaser. It's a producer of endorphins and other mood-altering chemicals in the brain that give a sense of pleasure and relief from pain. Humor is also the humanizer and equalizer in relationships. It's all of these things—but it's also much, much more! A sense of humor reflects the very essence of "We're off track—but so what?" It puts things in proper perspective so that we don't "sweat the small stuff." It enables us to realize that, in a sense, all stuff is small. It keeps us from taking ourselves too seriously and being constantly uptight, constricted, demanding, overexacting, disproportionate, imbalanced, and perfectionistic. It enables us to avoid the hazard of being so immersed in moral values or so wrapped up in moral rigidity that we're blind to our own humanness and the realities of our situation.

People who can laugh at their mistakes, stupidities, and rough edges can get back on track much faster than those perfectionistic souls who place themselves on guilt trips. A sense of humor is often the third alternative to guilt tripping, perfectionistic expectations, and an undisciplined, loosey-goosey, "anything goes" lifestyle.

As with anything else, humor can be carried to excess. It can result in a culture of sarcasm and cutting humor, and it can even produce light-mindedness where nothing is taken seriously.

But true humor is not light-mindedness; it's lightheartedness. And it is one of the fundamental elements of a beautiful family culture. Being around merry, cheerful people who are upbeat and full of good stories and good humor is the very thing that makes people want to be with others. It's also a key to proactivity because it gives you a positive, uplifting, nonreactive way to respond to the ups and downs of daily life.

Love Is a Verb

At one seminar where I was speaking on the concept of proactivity, a man came up and said, "Stephen, I like what you're saying, but every situation is different. Look at my marriage. I'm really worried. My wife and I just don't have the same feelings for each other that we used to have. I guess I just don't love her anymore, and she doesn't love me. What can I do?"

"The feeling isn't there anymore?" I inquired.

"That's right," he reaffirmed. "And we have three children we're really concerned about. What do you suggest?"

"Love her," I replied.

"I told you, the feeling just isn't there anymore."

"Love her."

"You don't understand. The feeling of love just isn't there."

"Then love her. If the feeling isn't there, that's a good reason to love her."

"But how do you love when you don't love?"

"My friend, love is a verb. Love—the feeling—is a fruit of love the verb. So love her. Sacrifice. Listen to her. Empathize. Appreciate. Affirm her. Are you willing to do that?"

Hollywood has scripted us to believe that love is a feeling. Relationships are disposable. Marriage and family are matters of contract and convenience rather than commitment and integrity. But these messages give a highly distorted picture of reality. If we return to our metaphor of the airplane flight, these messages are like static that garbles the clear direction from the radio control tower. And they get many, many people off track.

Just look around you—maybe even in your own family. Anyone who has been through a divorce, an estrangement from a companion, a child, or a parent, or a broken relationship of any kind can tell you that there is deep pain, deep scarring. And there are long-lasting

> "We do not have to love. We choose to love."

consequences that Hollywood usually doesn't tell you about. So while it may seem "easier" in the short run, it is often far more difficult and more painful in the long run to break up a relationship than to heal it—particularly when children are involved.

As M. Scott Peck has said:

The desire to love is not itself love. . . . Love is an act of will—namely an intention and an action. Will also implies choice. We do not have to love. We choose to love. No matter how much we may think we are loving, if we are in fact not loving, it is because we have chosen not to love and therefore do not love despite our good intentions. On the other hand, whenever we do actually exert ourselves in the cause of spiritual growth, it is because we have chosen to do so. The choice to love has been made.[1]

I have one friend who uses his gifts to make a powerful proactive choice every day. When he comes home from work, he sits in his car in the driveway and pushes his pause button. He literally puts his life on pause. He gets perspective. He thinks about the members of his family and what they are doing inside the walls of his house. He considers what kind of environment and feeling he wants to help create when he goes inside. He says to himself, "My family is the most enjoyable, the most pleasant, the most important part of my life. I'm going to go into my home and feel and communicate my love for them."

When he walks through the door, instead of finding fault and becoming critical or simply going off by himself to relax and take care of his own needs, he might dramatically shout, "I'm home! Please try to restrain yourselves from hugging and kissing me!" Then he might go around the house and interact in positive ways with every family member—kissing his wife, rolling around on the floor with the kids, or doing whatever it takes to create pleasantness and happiness, whether it's taking out the garbage or helping with a project or just listening. In doing these things he rises above his fatigue, his challenges or setbacks at work, his tendencies to find fault or be disappointed in what he may find at home. He becomes a conscious, positive creative force in the family culture.

Think about the proactive choice this man is making and the impact it has on his family! Think about the relationships he's building and about how that is going to impact every dimension of family life for years, perhaps for generations to come!

Any successful marriage, any successful family takes work. It's not a matter of accident, it's a matter of achievement. It takes effort and sacrifice. It takes knowing that—"for better or worse, in sickness and in health, as long as you live"—love is a verb.

Developing Your Unique Human Gifts

The four unique gifts we've talked about are common to all people except perhaps some who are sufficiently mentally handicapped that they lack self-awareness. But developing them takes conscious effort.

It's like developing a muscle. If you've ever been into muscle development, you know that the key is to push the fiber until it breaks. Then nature overcompensates in repairing the broken material, and the fiber becomes stronger within forty-eight hours. You probably also know the importance of adjusting your exercises to bring into play the weaker muscles rather than taking the course of least resistance and staying only with those muscles that are strong and developed.

Because of my own knee and back problems, I have had to learn to exercise in a way that forces me to bring into play muscles and even entire muscle groups that I would otherwise rarely use or even be aware of. I realize now that the development of these muscles is necessary for an integrated, balanced level of health and fitness, for posture, for various skill activities, and sometimes even for normal walking. For example, to compensate for my knee injuries, I used to focus on developing the quadriceps—the muscles in the front of the upper leg—but I neglected the development of the hamstrings, which are the muscles at the back of the leg. And this affected a full, balanced recovery of my knees and also my back.

So it is in life. Our tendency is to run with our strengths and leave our weaknesses undeveloped. Sometimes that's fine, when we can organize to make those weaknesses irrelevant through the strengths of others, but most of the time it isn't fine because the full utilization of our capacities requires overcoming those weaknesses.

And so it is with our unique human gifts. As we go through life interacting with external circumstances, with other people, and with our own nature, we have constant ongoing opportunities to come face-to-face with our weaknesses. We can choose to ignore them, or we can push against the resistance and break through to new levels of competence and strength.

Consider the development of your own gifts as you go through the following questionnaire:[2]

Instructions: Circle the number along the matrix that most closely represents your normal behavior or attitudes regarding the questions at the left. (0=Never, 2=Sometimes, 4=Always)

Self-awareness:

1. Am I able to stand apart from my thoughts or feelings and examine and change them?

N		S		A
x	x	x	x	x
0	1	2	3	4

2. Am I aware of the way I think about things and the impact it has on my attitudes and behaviors and the results I'm getting in my life?

N		S		A
x	x	x	x	x
0	1	2	3	4

3. Am I aware of a difference between my biological, genealogical, psychological, and sociological scripting—and my own deep inner thoughts?

N		S		A
x	x	x	x	x
0	1	2	3	4

4. When the response of other people to me—or something I do—challenges the way I see myself, am I able to evaluate that feedback against deep personal self-knowledge and learn from it?

N		S		A
x	x	x	x	x
0	1	2	3	4

Conscience:

1. Do I sometimes feel an inner prompting that I should do something or that I shouldn't do something I'm about to do?

N		S		A
x——x——x——x——x				
0	1	2	3	4

2. Do I sense the difference between "social conscience"—what society has conditioned me to value—and my own inner directives?

N		S		A
x——x——x——x——x				
0	1	2	3	4

3. Do I inwardly sense the reality of universal principles such as integrity and trustworthiness?

N		S		A
x——x——x——x——x				
0	1	2	3	4

4. Do I see a pattern in human experience—bigger than the society in which I live—that validates the reality of principles?

N		S		A
x——x——x——x——x				
0	1	2	3	4

Imagination:

1. Do I think ahead?

N		S		A
x——x——x——x——x				
0	1	2	3	4

2. Do I visualize my life beyond its present reality?

N		S		A
x——x——x——x——x				
0	1	2	3	4

3. Do I use visualization to help reaffirm and realize my goals?

N		S		A
x——x——x——x——x				
0	1	2	3	4

4. Do I look for new, creative ways to solve problems in a variety of situations and value the different views of others?

N		S		A
x——x——x——x——x				
0	1	2	3	4

Independent Will:

1. Am I able to make and keep promises to myself as well as to others?

N		S		A
x——x——x——x——x				
0	1	2	3	4

2. Do I have the capacity to act on my own inner imperatives even when it means swimming upstream?

N		S		A
x——x——x——x——x				
0	1	2	3	4

	N	S	A
3. Have I developed the ability to set and achieve meaningful goals in my life?	x——x——x——x——x		
	0 1 2 3 4		

3. Have I developed the ability to set and achieve meaningful goals in my life?

N   S   A
x——x——x——x——x
0   1   2   3   4

4. Can I subordinate my moods to my commitments?

N   S   A
x——x——x——x——x
0   1   2   3   4

Now add up your score for each of the four gifts. Measure your score in each of the sections by the following key:

0–7   Inactive gift
8–12   Active gift
13–16   Highly developed gift

I have done this questionnaire many times with thousands of people in many different settings, and the overwhelming finding is this: The gift most neglected is self-awareness. Perhaps you have heard the expression "Think outside the box," meaning to get outside the normal way of thinking, the normal assumptions and paradigms in which we operate. That's another expression for using self-awareness. Until the gift of self-awareness is cultivated, the use of conscience, imagination, and willpower will always be "within the box"—that is, within one's own life experience or one's present way of thinking or paradigm.

So in a sense the unique leveraging of the four human gifts is in self-awareness, because when you have the ability to think outside the box—to examine your own assumptions and your own way of thinking, to stand apart from your own mind and examine it, to think about your very thoughts, feelings, and even moods—then you have the basis for using imagination, conscience, and independent will in entirely new ways. You literally become transcendent. You have transcended yourself; you have transcended your background, your history, your psychic baggage.

This transcendence is fundamental to the life force in all of us and helps unleash the propensity to become, to grow, to develop. It is also fundamental in our relationships with others and in cultivating a beautiful family culture. The more the family has a collective sense of self-awareness, the more it can look in on itself and improve itself: make changes, select goals outside of tradition, and set up structures and other plans to achieve those goals that lie outside social scripting and deeply established habit patterns.

The ancient Greek saying "Know thyself"[3] is enormously significant because it reflects the understanding that self-knowledge is the basis of all other knowledge. If we don't take ourselves into account, all we are doing is projecting ourselves onto life and onto other people. We then judge ourselves by our motives—and others by their behavior. Until we know ourselves and are aware of ourselves as separate from others and from the environment—until we can be separated even from ourselves so that we can observe our own tendencies, thoughts, and desires—we have no foundation from which to know and respect other people, let alone to create change within ourselves.

Developing all four of these gifts is vital to proactivity. You cannot neglect one of them because the key is in the synergy or the relationship among them. Hitler, for example, had tremendous self-awareness, imagination, and willpower—but no conscience. And it proved to be his undoing. It also changed the course of the world in many tragic ways. Others are very principled and conscience driven, but they have no imagination, no vision. They are good—but good for what? Toward what end? Others have great willpower but no vision. They often do the same things again and again with no meaningful end in mind.

And this applies to an entire family as well. The collective sense of these four gifts—the relationship among these gifts as well as the relationship among the individuals in the family—is what enables the family to move to higher and higher levels of achievement and significance and contribution. The key lies in the proper nurturance of all four gifts in the individual and in the family culture so that there is a great sense of self- and family awareness, a highly cultivated and sensitive individual and collective conscience, the development of the creative, imaginative instincts into shared vision, and the development and use of a strong personal and social will to do whatever it takes to fulfill a mission, to achieve a vision, to matter.

The Circle of Influence and the Circle of Concern

The essence of proactivity and the use of these four unique gifts lies in taking the responsibility and the initiative to focus on the things in our lives we can actually do something about. As Saint Francis wrote in his well-known "Serenity Prayer": "God grant me the serenity to accept the things I cannot change, the courage to change the things I can, and the wisdom to know the difference."[4]

One way to make this differentiation more clear in our minds is to look at our lives in terms of what I call the Circle of Influence and the Circle of Concern. The Circle of Concern is a large circle that embraces everything in your life that you may be concerned about. The Circle of Influence is a smaller circle within the Circle of Concern that embraces the things you can actually do something about.

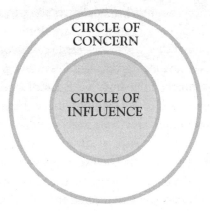

The reactive tendency is to focus on the Circle of Concern, but this only causes the inner Circle of Influence to be diminished. The nature of energy focused on the outer Circle of Concern is negative. And when you combine that negative energy with neglect of the Circle of Influence, inevitably the Circle of Influence gets smaller.

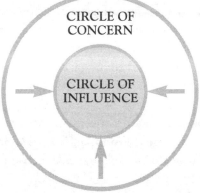

But proactive people focus on their Circle of Influence. As a result, that circle increases.

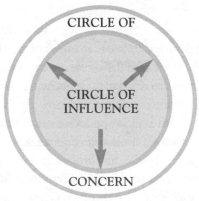

Consider the impact of one man's decision to work in his Circle of Influence:

In my later teens I noticed that Mom and Dad were becoming very critical of each other. There were arguments and tears. They would say things that hurt—and they knew what to say. There was also making up and "everything's fine." But over time the arguments increased and the hurt got deeper.

When I was about twenty-one, they finally separated. I remember at the time feeling a great sense of duty and a desire to help "fix it." I guess that's a natural response for a child. You love your parents. You want to do everything you can.

I would say to my dad, "Why don't you just go to Mom and say 'I'm sorry. I know I've done lots of things that hurt you, but please forgive me. Let's work at this. I'm committed to it.'" And he would say, "I can't. I'm not going to bare my soul like that and have it stomped on again."

I would say to my mom, "Look at everything you've had together. Isn't it worth trying to save?" And she would say, "I can't do it. I simply cannot handle this man."

There was deep unhappiness, deep anguish, deep anger on both sides. And both Mom and Dad went to unbelievable effort to get us children to see that their side was right and the other was wrong.

When I finally realized they were going to divorce, I couldn't believe it. I felt so empty and sad inside. Sometimes I would just weep. One of the most solid things in my life was gone. And I became consumed with self-focus. Why me? Why can't I do something to help?

I had a very good friend who finally said to me, "You know what you need to do? You need to stop feeling sorry for yourself. Just look at you. This is not your problem. You are connected to it, but this is your parents' problem, not yours. You need to stop feeling sorry for yourself and figure out what you can do to support and love each of your parents, because they need you more than they have ever needed you before."

When my friend said that to me, something happened inside. I suddenly realized that I was not the victim here. My inner voice said, "Your greatest responsibility as a son is to love each of your parents and to chart your own course. You need to choose your response to what has happened here."

That was a profound moment in my life. It was a moment of choice. It was realizing that I was not a victim and that I could do something about it.

So I focused on loving and supporting both my parents, and I refused to take sides. My parents did not like it. They accused me of being neutral, wimpy, not being willing to take a stand. But they both came to respect my position over time.

As I thought about my own life, it was suddenly as if I could step aside from myself, my family experience, their marriage, and become a learner. I knew that someday I wanted to be married and have a family. So I asked myself, "What does this mean to you, Brent? What are you going to learn from this? What kind of marriage are you going to build? Which of your weaknesses that you happen to share with your parents are you going to give up?"

I decided that what I really wanted was a strong, healthy, growing marriage. And I have since found that when you have that kind of resolve, it gives you the sustaining power to swallow hard in difficult moments—to not say something that will hurt feelings, to apologize, to come back to it, because you are affirming something that is more important to you than just the emotion of the moment.

I also made the resolve to always remember that it's more important to be "one" than to be right or have it your way. The tiny victory that comes from winning the argument only causes greater separation, which really deprives you of the deeper satisfaction of a marriage relationship. I count that as one of my greatest life learnings. And from that I determined that when I faced a situation where I wanted something different from what my wife wanted and I did something dumb that put a wall between us (which, even at that time, I realized I would do on a regular basis), I would not live with it or let it expand but would always apologize. I would always say, "I'm sorry," and reaffirm my love and commitment to her and work it out. I determined to always do everything in my power, not to be perfect—because I knew that was impossible— but to keep working at it, to keep trying.

It hasn't been easy. Sometimes it takes a lot of effort when there are deep issues. But I believe my resolve reflects a priority that might never have been there had I not gone through the painful experience of my parents' divorce.

Think about this man's experience. Here were the two people he loved most in the world—the people from whom he had gotten much of his own sense of identity and security over the years—and their marriage was falling apart. He felt betrayed. His own sense of security was put in jeopardy. His vision, his feelings about marriage were threatened. He was in deep pain. He later said it was the most difficult, the most challenging time in his life.

Through the help of a friend he realized that their marriage was in his Circle of Concern but not in his Circle of Influence. He decided to be proactive. He realized he couldn't fix their marriage, but there were things he could do. And his inner compass told him what those things were. So he began to focus on his Circle of Influence. He worked on loving and supporting both parents—even when it was hard, even when they reacted in negative ways. He gained the courage to act based on principle rather than reacting to his parents' emotional response.

He also started to think about his own future, his own marriage. He began to recognize values he wanted to have in his relationship with his future wife. As a result, he was able to begin his marriage with the vision of that relationship in mind. And the power of that vision has carried him through the challenges to it. It's given him the power to apologize and to keep coming back.

Can you see what a difference a Circle of Influence focus makes?

Consider another example. I'm aware of one set of parents who decided that the behavior of their daughter had deteriorated to the point where allowing her to continue to live at home would destroy the family. The father determined that when she got home that night, he would tell her that she had to do certain things or move out the next day. So he sat down to wait for her. While he was waiting, he decided to take a three-by-five card and list the changes she had to make in order to stay. When he finished the list, he had feelings that only those who have suffered a similar situation can know.

But in this emotionally pained spirit, as he continued to wait for her to come home, he turned the card over. The other side was blank. He decided to list on that side of the card the improvements he would agree to make if she would agree to her changes. He was in tears as he realized that his list was longer than hers. In that spirit he humbly greeted her when she came home, and they began a long, meaningful talk, beginning with *his* side of the card. His choice to begin with that side made all the difference—inside out.

Now just think about the word "responsible"—"response-able," able to choose your own response. That is the essence of proactivity. It is something we can do in our own lives. The interesting thing is that when *you* focus on your Circle of Influence and it gets larger, you are also modeling to others through your example. And they will tend to focus on their inner circle also. Sometimes others may do the opposite out of reactive anger, but if you're sincere and persistent, your example can eventually impact the spirit of everyone so that they will become proactive and take more initiative, more "response-ability" in the family culture.

Listen to Your Language

One of the best ways to tell whether you're in your Circle of Influence or Circle of Concern is to listen to your own language. If you're in your Circle of Concern, your language will be blaming, accusing, reactive.

"I can't believe the way these kids are behaving! They're driving me crazy!"

"My spouse is so inconsiderate!"

"Why did my father have to be an alcoholic?"

If you're in your Circle of Influence, your language will be proactive. It will reflect a focus on the things you can do something about.

"I can help create rules in our family that will enable the children to learn about the consequences of their behavior. I can look for opportunities to teach and reinforce positive behavior."

"I can be considerate. I can model the kind of loving interaction I would like to see in my marriage."

"I can learn more about my father and his addiction to alcohol. I can seek to understand him, to love and to forgive. I can choose a different path for myself, and I can teach and influence my family so that this will not be part of their lives."

In order to get a deeper insight into your own level of proactivity or reactivity, you might like to try the following experiment. You may want to ask your spouse or someone else to participate with you and give you feedback.

1. Identify a problem in your family culture.
2. Describe it to someone else (or write your description down), using completely reactive terms. Focus on your Circle of Concern. Work hard. See how completely you can convince someone else that this problem is not your fault.
3. Describe the same problem in completely proactive terms. Focus on your response-ability. Talk about what you can do in your Circle of Influence. Convince someone else that you can make a real difference in this situation.
4. Now think about the difference in the two descriptions. Which one more closely resembles your normal habit pattern when talking about family problems?

If you find that you are using essentially reactive language, you can take immediate steps to replace that kind of language with proactive words and phrases. The very act of forcing yourself to use the words will help you recognize habits of reactivity and begin to change.

Teaching responsibility for language is another way we can help even young children learn to integrate Habit 1.

Colleen (*our daughter*):

Recently, I tried to help our three-year-old be more responsible for her language. I said to her, "In our family we don't say hate or shut up or call people stupid. You have to be careful about the way you talk to people. You need to be responsible." Every now and then I would remind her, "Don't call people names, Erika. Try to be responsible for the way you talk and act."

Then the other day I happened to remark, "Oh, I hated that movie!" Erika immediately replied, "Don't say hate, Mom! You're responsible."

Erika is now like the Gestapo in our family. We all have to watch our language when we're around her.

Building the Emotional Bank Account

One very practical, useful way to understand and apply this whole idea of proactivity and this inside-out approach of focusing on the Circle of Influence is by using the analogy or metaphor of the Emotional Bank Account.

The Emotional Bank Account represents the quality of the relationship you have with others. It's like a financial bank account in that you can make "deposits," by proactively doing things that build trust in the relationship, or you can make 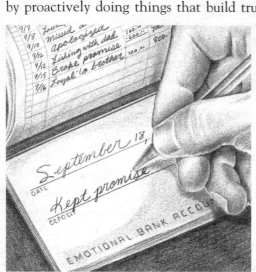 "withdrawals," by reactively doing things that decrease the level of trust. And at any given time *the balance of trust in the account determines how well you can communicate and solve problems with another person.*

If you have a high balance in your Emotional Bank Account with a family member, then there's a high level of trust. Communication is open and free. You can even make a mistake in the relationship, and the "emotional reserves" will compensate for it.

But if the account balance is low or even overdrawn, then there's no trust and thus no authentic communication. It's like walking on minefields. You're always on your guard. You have to measure every word. And even your better intentions are misunderstood.

Remember the story of my friend who "found his son again." You could say that the relationship between this father and son was $100, $200, or even $10,000 overdrawn. There was no trust, no real communication, no ability to work together to solve problems. And the harder this father pushed, the worse it got. But then my friend did something proactive that made a tremendous difference. Taking an inside-out approach, he became an agent of change. He stopped reacting to his son. He made an enormous deposit in this boy's Emotional Bank Account. He listened, really, deeply listened. And the boy suddenly felt validated, affirmed, recognized as an important human being.

One of the biggest problems in many family cultures is the reactive tendency to continually make withdrawals instead of deposits. Consider on the following page what my friend Dr. Glen C. Griffin suggests is a typical day in the life of a teenager.

What kind of impact will this kind of communication—day in and day out—have on the balance in the Emotional Bank Account?

Remember, love is a verb. One of the great benefits of being proactive is that you can choose to make deposits instead of withdrawals. No matter what the situa-

You can choose to make deposits instead of withdrawals. No matter what the situation, there are always things you can do that will make relationships better.

A Day's Input To A Teen

6:55 A.M.	Get up or you'll be late again.
7:14 A.M.	But you've got to eat breakfast.
7:16 A.M.	You look like something on punk video. Put on something decent.
7:18 A.M.	Don't forget to take out the garbage.
7:23 A.M.	Put on your coat. Don't you know it's cold outside? You can't walk to school in weather like this.
7:25 A.M.	I expect you to come straight home from school and get your homework done before going off anywhere.
5:42 P.M.	You forgot the garbage. Thanks to you we'll have garbage up to our ears for another week.
5:46 P.M.	Put this darn skateboard away. Someone's going to trip over it and break his neck.
5:55 P.M.	Come to dinner. Why do I always have to look for you when it's time to eat? You should have been helping to set the table.
6:02 P.M.	How many times do I have to tell you dinner is ready?
6:12 P.M.	Do you have to come to the table with earphones on your head, plugged into that rotten noise you call music? Can you hear what I'm saying? Take those things out of your ears.
6:16 P.M.	Things are going to have to shape up around here. Your room is a disgrace, and you're going to have to start carrying your load. This isn't a palace with servants to wait on you.
6:36 P.M.	Turn off that video game and unload the dishwasher and then put the dirty dishes in it. When I was your age, we didn't have dishwashers. We had to wash dishes in hot soapy water.
7:08 P.M.	What are you watching? It doesn't look very good to me, and it's dumb to think you can do homework better with the TV going.
7:32 P.M.	I told you to turn off the TV until your homework is finished. And why are those shoes and candy wrappers in the middle of the floor? I've told you a million times it's easier to put things away right then rather than later. Do you like to hear me yell?
9:59 P.M.	That stereo is so loud I can't hear myself think. Go to sleep or you'll be late again tomorrow.[5]

tion, there are always things you can do that will make relationships better.

One father from a blended family shared this experience:

I have always considered myself to be an honest, hardworking man. I was successful at work and in my relationships with my wife and children—with the exception of our fifteen-year-old daughter Tara.

I had made several futile attempts to mend my broken relationship with her, but every attempt had ended in a frustrating failure. She just didn't trust me. And whenever I tried to resolve our differences, I seemed to make things worse.

Then I learned about the Emotional Bank Account, and I came across a question that really hit me hard: "Ask yourself, are those around you made happier or better by your presence in the home?"

In my heart I had to answer, "No. My presence is making things worse for my daughter Tara."

That introspection almost broke my heart.

After the initial shock I came to the realization that if this sad truth were to change, it would only be because I changed myself, because I changed my own heart. I not only had to act differently toward her; I needed to commit to truly loving her. I had to quit criticizing and always blaming her, to quit thinking that she was the source of our poor relationship. I had to quit competing with her by always making my will supersede hers.

I knew that unless I acted on these feelings immediately, I would probably never act on them, so I resolved to do so. I made a commitment that for thirty days I would make five deposits daily into my Emotional Bank Account with Tara—and absolutely no withdrawals.

My first impulse was to go to my daughter and tell her what I had learned, but my better judgment told me that the time was not right for teaching with words. It was time to begin making deposits. Later that day, when Tara came home from school, I greeted her with a warm smile and asked, "How are you?" Her curt reply was "A lot you care." I swallowed hard and tried to act as if I'd not heard it. I smiled and replied, "I just wondered how you were doing.'"

During the next several days I worked hard to keep my commitment. I put reminder "stickies" everywhere, including on the rearview mirror of my car. I continued to dodge her frequent barbs, which was not easy for me because I had been conditioned to fight back. Each experience caused me to see just how cynical our relationship had become. I began to realize how often in the past I had expected her to change before I would do anything myself to make things better.

As I focused on changing my own feelings and actions rather than hers, I began to see Tara in an entirely new light. I began to appreciate her great need to be loved. And as I continued to let the negative blows glance off, I felt an increasing strength to do so without any inner resentment, but with increased love.

Almost without effort I found myself beginning to do little things for her—little favors that I knew I did not have to do. While she studied, I would quietly walk in and turn up the light. When she asked, "What's this all about?," I'd reply, "I just thought you could read better with more light."

Finally, after about two weeks, Tara looked at me quizzically and asked, "Dad, there's something different about you. What's happening? What's going on?"

I said, "I've come to recognize some things about myself that need changing, that's all. I'm so grateful that now I can express my love to you by treating you the way I know I should have treated you all along."

We began to spend more time together at home, just talking and listening to each other. More than two months have gone by now, and our relationship has been much, much deeper and more positive. It's not flawless yet, but we're getting there. The pain is gone. The trust and love increase each day, and it's due to the simple yet profound idea of making only deposits and no withdrawals in the Emotional Bank Account—and doing it consistently and sincerely. As you do you will begin to see the person differently and begin to replace self-serving motives with service motives.

I am certain that if you ask my daughter what she thinks of me now, she would quickly reply, "My dad? We're friends. I trust him."

You can see how this father used proactivity to make a real difference in his relationship with his daughter. Notice how he used all four human gifts. Look at how *self-aware* he was. Look at how he could stand apart from himself, from his daughter, from the whole situation and see what was happening. Notice how he could compare what was happening with what his *conscience* was telling him was right. Notice how he had a sense of what was possible. Through his *imagination* he could envision something different. And notice how he used his *willpower* to act.

And as he used all four gifts, look at what began to happen. Things began to improve dramatically—not only the quality of the relationship but also how he felt about himself and how his daughter felt about herself. It was like flooding a toxic culture with a healing balm. That's literally what he did. He made many deposits because he got his head out of the weaknesses of other people and focused on his own Circle of Influence—on those things he could do something about. He was truly an agent of change.

Just remember, every time you build your emotional life on the weaknesses of others, you give your power—that is, your unique human gifts—away to their weaknesses so that your emotional life is a product of how they treat you. You disempower yourself and empower the weaknesses of others.

But when you focus on your Circle of Influence and on doing what you can to build the Emotional Bank Account—to build relationships of trust and unconditional love—you dramatically increase your ability to influence others in positive ways.

Let me share with you some specific ideas—some "deposits" you can make in your own family—that may be helpful. These are practical ways that you can begin to practice Habit 1 in your family now.

Being Kind

Some years ago I spent a special evening with two of my sons. It was an organized father and sons outing, complete with gymnastics, wrestling matches, hotdogs,

orangeade, and a movie—the works.

In the middle of the movie, Sean, who was then four years old, fell asleep in his seat. His older brother, Stephen, who was six, stayed awake, and we watched the rest of the movie together. When it was over, I picked Sean up in my arms, carried him out to the car, and laid him in the backseat. It was very cold that night, so I took off my coat and gently arranged it over and around him.

When we arrived home, I quickly carried Sean in and tucked him into bed. After Stephen put on his pajamas and brushed his teeth, I lay down next to him to talk about the night out together.

"How'd you like it, Stephen?"

"Fine," he answered.

"Did you have fun?"

"Yes."

"What did you like most?"

"I don't know. The trampoline, I guess."

"That was quite a thing, wasn't it? Doing those somersaults and tricks in the air like that?"

There wasn't much response on his part. I found myself making conversation. I wondered why Stephen wouldn't open up more. He usually did when exciting things happened. I was a little disappointed. I sensed something was wrong; he had been so quiet on the way home and getting ready for bed.

Suddenly Stephen turned over on his side to face the wall. I wondered why and lifted myself up just enough to see his eyes welling up with tears.

"What's wrong, honey? What is it?"

He turned back, and I could sense he was feeling some embarrassment for the tears and his quivering lips and chin.

"Daddy, if I were cold, would you put your coat around me, too?"

Of all the events of that special night out together, the most important was a little act of kindness—a momentary, unconscious showing of love to his little brother.

What a powerful, personal lesson that was to me of the importance of kindness!

In relationships the little things are the big things. One woman told of growing up in a home where there was a plaque on the kitchen wall that read: "To do carefully and constantly and kindly many little things is *not* a little thing."

Cynthia (*daughter*):

One thing that stands out in my mind about being a teenager is the feeling of being overwhelmed. I remember the pressure of trying to do well in school and being on the debate team and involved in three or four other things all at the same time.

And sometimes I'd come home and I'd find my whole room clean and organized. There would be a note that said, "Love, the Good Fairy," and I knew Mom had just worked her head off to help me get ahead because I was so overwhelmed with what I had to do.

It really took a load off. I would come into that room and just whisper, "Oh, thank you. Thank you!"

Little kindnesses go a long way toward building relationships of trust and unconditional love. Just think about the impact in your own family of using words or phrases such as *thank you, please, excuse me, you go first,* and *may I help you.* Or performing unexpected acts of service such as helping with the dishes, taking children shopping for something that's important to them, or phoning to see if there's anything you can pick up at the store on the way home. Or finding little ways to express love, such as sending flowers, tucking a note in a lunch box or briefcase, or phoning to say "I love you" in the middle of the day. Or expressing gratitude and appreciation. Or giving sincere compliments. Or showing recognition—not just at times of special achievement or on occasions such as birthdays but on ordinary days, and just because your spouse or your children are who they are.

> "To do carefully and constantly and kindly many little things is *not* a little thing."

Twelve hugs a day—that's what people need. Hugs come physically, verbally, visually, environmentally. We all need twelve hugs a day—different forms of emotional nourishment from other people or perhaps spiritual nourishment through meditation or prayer.

I know of one woman who grew up in poverty and contention, but came to realize how important such kindness and courtesy are in the home. She learned it where she worked—at a very prestigious hotel where the entire staff had a culture of courtesy toward every guest. She knew how good it made people feel to be treated so royally. She also realized how good it made her feel to perform acts of kindness and courtesy. One day she decided to try acting this way at home with her own family. She began doing little acts of service for family members. She began using language that was positive, gentle, and kind. When serving breakfast, for example, she would say, as she did at work, "It's my pleasure!" She told me it transformed both her and her family and began a new intergenerational cycle.

One thing my brother John and his wife, Jane, do in their family is take time every morning to compliment one another. Family members take turns being the target for such compliments. And what a difference that makes!

One morning their strong, athletic son—the football hero of the high school—came bounding down the stairs with such energy, such excitement that Jane couldn't imagine why he was so animated.

"Why are you so excited?" she asked.

"It's my morning for compliments!" he replied with a smile.

One of the most important dimensions of kindness is expressing appreciation. What an important deposit to make—and to teach—in the family!

Apologizing

Perhaps there is nothing that tests our proactive capacity as much as saying "I'm sorry" to another person. If your security is based on your image or your position or on being right, to apologize is like draining all the juice from your ego. It wipes you out. It pushes every one of your human gifts to its limit.

Colleen (daughter):

Several years ago Matt and I went up to the cabin to be with the whole family for Christmas. I don't remember the details, but for some reason I was supposed to drive Mom to Salt Lake City the next day. As it happened, I already had another obligation and couldn't do it. When Dad heard my response, he just exploded—totally lost it.

"You're being selfish!" he said. "You really need to do this!" And he said a lot of other things he didn't mean.

Surprised by his abrasive response, I started crying. I was deeply hurt. I was so used to his being understanding and considerate all the time. In fact, in my whole life I can remember only about two times that he really lost his temper with me, so it took me aback. I shouldn't have taken offense, but I did. Finally, I said, "Okay, I'll do it," knowing he wouldn't listen to my conflict.

I headed home, and my husband came with me. "We're not going back tonight," I said. "I don't even care if we miss the family Christmas party!" And all the way down the canyon I was harboring bad feelings.

Shortly after we got home, the phone rang. Matt answered it. He said, "It's your dad."

"I don't want to talk to him," I said, still hurt. But I really did, so I finally picked up the phone.

"Darling," he said, "I apologize. There's really no excuse that could justify my losing

my temper with you, but let me tell you what's been going on." He told me that they had just started building the house, finances had been swelling up, things at the business were kind of shaky, and then with Christmas and the whole family there, he had felt so much pressure he blew up and I received the brunt of it. *"I just took it all out on you,"* he said. *"I'm so sorry. I apologize."* I then returned the apology, knowing I had overreacted.

Dad's apology was a big deposit in my Emotional Bank Account. And we had had a great relationship to begin with.

Matt and I went back up that night, I rearranged my schedule for the next day, took my mom to Salt Lake City, and it was as if nothing had happened. If anything, my dad and I grew closer because he could apologize immediately. I think it took a lot for him to be able to step back from the situation so quickly and say *"I'm sorry."*

Even though our temper may surface only one-hundredth of 1 percent of the time, it will affect the quality of all the rest of the time if we do not take responsibility for it and apologize. Why? Because people never know when they might hit our raw nerve, so they're always inwardly worried about it and defending themselves against it by second-guessing our behavior and curbing their own natural, spontaneous, intuitive responses.

The sooner we learn to apologize, the better. World traditions affirm this idea. The Far Eastern expression is so apt here: "If you're going to bow, bow low." A great lesson is also taught in the Bible about paying the uttermost farthing.

Agree with thine adversary quickly, whiles thou art in the way with him; lest at any time the adversary deliver thee to the judge, and the judge deliver thee to the officer, and thou be cast into prison. Verily I say unto thee, Thou shalt by no means come out thence, till thou hast paid the uttermost farthing.

There are undoubtedly a number of ways to apply this instruction in our lives, but one may be this: Whenever we disagree with others, we need to quickly "agree" with them—not on the *issue* of disagreement (that would compromise our integrity) but on the *right* to disagree, to see it the way they see it. Otherwise, to protect themselves they will put us into a mental/emotional "prison" in their own mind. And we won't be released from this prison until we pay the uttermost farthing—until we humbly and fully acknowledge our mistake in not allowing them the right to disagree. And we must do this without in any way saying, "I'll say I'm sorry if you'll say you're sorry."

If you attempt to pay the uttermost farthing by merely trying to be better and not apologizing, other people may still be suspicious and keep you behind these prison bars, behind the mental and emotional labels they have put on you that give them some feeling of security in knowing not to expect much from you.

We all "blow it" from time to time. In other words, we get off track. And when we do, we need to own up to it, humbly acknowledge it, and sincerely apologize.

Honey, I'm so sorry I embarrassed you in front of your friends. That was wrong of me. I'm going to apologize to you and also to your friends. I should never have done that. I got on some kind of an ego trip with you, and I'm sorry. I hope you will give me another chance.

Sweetheart, I apologize for cutting you off that way. You were trying to share something with me that you feel deeply about, and I got so caught up in my own agenda that I just came on like a steamroller. Will you please forgive me?

Notice again in these apologies how all four gifts are being used. First, you're aware of what's happening. Second, you consult your conscience and tap into your moral or ethical sense. Third, you have a sense of what is possible—what would be better. And fourth, you act on the other three. If any one of these four is neglected, the entire effort will break down, and you will end up trying to defend, justify, explain, or cover up the offensive behavior in some way. You may apologize, but it's superficial, it's not sincere.

Being Loyal to Those Not Present

What happens when family members are not loyal to one another, when they criticize and gossip about the others behind their backs? What does it do to the relationship, to the culture when family members make disloyal comments to other family members or to their friends:

"My husband is such a tightwad! He worries about every penny we spend."

"My wife jabbers constantly. You'd think she could shut up and let me get a word in once in a while."

"Did you hear what my son did the other day? He talked back to a teacher. They called me from the school. It was so embarrassing! I don't know what to do with that kid. He's always causing trouble."

"I can't believe my mother-in-law! She tries to control everything we do. I don't know why my wife can't just cut the apron strings and get it over with."

Comments like these are huge withdrawals not only from the person spoken *about* but also from the person spoken *to*. For example, if you were to discover that someone had made one of these comments about you, how would it make you feel?

You'd probably feel misunderstood, violated, unjustly criticized, unfairly accused. How would it affect the amount of trust in your relationship with that person? Would you feel safe? Would you feel affirmed? Would you feel you could confide in that person and your confidence would be treated with respect?

On the other hand, if someone said something like this *to* you about someone else, how would you feel? You might initially be pleased that the person had "confided" in you, but wouldn't you begin to wonder if that same person, in a different circumstance, might say something equally negative about you to someone else?

Next to apologizing, the toughest and one of the most important deposits an individual can make—or an entire family can adopt as a fundamental value and commitment—is to be loyal to family members when they are not present. In other words, talk about others as if they were present. That doesn't mean you are unaware of their weaknesses and are Pollyannaish and take the "ostrich head in the sand" approach. It means, rather, that you usually focus on the positive rather than the negative—and if you do talk about those weaknesses, you do it in such a responsible and constructive way that you would not be ashamed to have those people you're talking about overhear your conversation.

> *Always talk about others as if they were present.*

A friend of ours had an eighteen-year-old son whose habits irritated his married brother and sisters and their spouses. When he wasn't there (which was often, since he spent most hours away from home with friends), the family would talk about him. Their favorite conversation centered on his girlfriends, his habit of sleeping late, and his demands on his mother to serve him at his beck and call. This man participated in these rather gossipy conversations about his son, and the discussions caused him to believe that his son was truly irresponsible.

At one point this friend became aware of what was happening and the part he was playing in it. He decided to follow the principle of being loyal to those not present by being loyal to his son. Thereafter, when such conversations began to develop, he would gently interrupt any negative comments and say something good that he had observed his son doing. He had a good story to counteract any derogatory comments the others might make. Soon the conversation would lose its spice and shift to other, more interesting subjects.

Our friend said he soon felt that the others in the family began to connect with this principle of family loyalty. They began to realize that he would also defend them if they were not present. And in some almost unexplainable manner—perhaps because he began to see his son differently—this change also improved his Emotional Bank Account with this son, who hadn't even been aware of the family conversations about him. Bottom line: The way you treat any relationship in the family will eventually affect every relationship in the family.

I remember one time when I was running out of the house to go somewhere in a hurry. I knew that if I stopped to say good-bye to my three-year-old son Joshua, I would get caught up in his needs and questions. It would take time, and I was into efficiency. So I said to my other children, "See ya, kids. I've got to run! Don't tell Joshua I'm going."

> *The way you treat any relationship in the family will eventually affect every relationship in the family.*

I got halfway out to the car before I realized what I had just done. I turned around, went back into the house, and said to the other children, "That was wrong of me to run out on Joshua like that and not to say good-bye to him as well. I'm going to find him to say good-bye."

Sure enough, I had to spend some time with him. I had to talk with him about what he wanted to talk about before I could go. But it built the Emotional Bank Account with Joshua and with the other children as well.

I sometimes think: What would have happened if I hadn't gone back? What if I had gone to Joshua that night and tried to have a good relationship with him? Would he have been loving and open with me if he knew I had run out on him when he wanted and needed me? How would this have affected my relationship with my other sons and daughters? Would they have thought that I would run out on them, too, if interacting with them sidetracked my agenda?

The message sent to one is truly sent to all because everyone is a "one," and they know that if you treat one that way, all it takes is a change of circumstances and you'll treat them that way, too. That's why it is so important to be loyal to those not present.

Notice here, too, how all four gifts are in proactive use. To be loyal, you have to be self-aware. You have to have a sense of conscience, a moral sense of right and wrong. You have to have a sense of what's possible, what's better. And you have to have the intestinal fortitude to make it happen.

Being loyal to those not present is clearly a proactive choice.

Making and Keeping Promises

Many times over the years people have asked if I had one idea that would best help people grow so that they could better cope with their problems, seize their opportunities, and make their life successful. I've come to give a simple four-word answer: "Make and keep promises."

Although this may sound like an oversimplification, I truly believe it is profound. In fact, as you will discover, all of the first three habits are embodied in that simple four-word expression. If an entire family would cultivate the spirit of making and keeping promises to one another, it would create a multitude of other good things.

Cynthia (*daughter*):

When I was twelve years old, Dad promised to take me with him on a business trip to San Francisco. I was so excited! We talked about the trip for three months. We were going to be there for two days and one night, and we planned every detail. Dad was going to be busy in meetings the first day, so I would hang around the hotel. After his meetings, we planned to take a cab to Chinatown and have our favorite Chinese food. Then we'd see a movie, take a ride on a trolley car, and go back to our hotel room for a video and hot fudge sundaes from room service. I was dying with anticipation.

The day finally arrived. The hours dragged by as I waited at the hotel. Six o'clock came, but Dad didn't. Finally, at 6:30, he arrived with another man—a dear friend and an influential business acquaintance. I remember how my heart sank as this man said, "I'm so excited to have you here, Stephen. Tonight, Lois and I would like to take you to the wharf for a spectacular seafood dinner, and then you must see the view from our house." When Dad told him I was there, this man said, "Of course, she can come, too. We'd love having her."

Oh, great! I thought. I hate fish, and I'll be stuck alone in the backseat while Dad and his friend talk. I could see all my hopes and plans going down the drain.

My disappointment was bigger than life. This man was pressing so hard. I wanted to say, "Dad, this is our time together! You promised!" But I was twelve years old, so I only cried inside.

I will never forget the feeling I had when Dad said, "Gosh, Bill, I'd love to see you both, but this is a special time with my girl. We've already got it planned to the minute. You were kind to invite us." I could tell this man was disappointed, but—amazingly to me—he seemed to understand.

We did absolutely everything we had planned on that trip. We didn't miss a thing. That was just about the happiest time of my life. I don't think any young girl ever loved her father as much as I loved mine that night.

I'm convinced you would be hard-pressed to come up with a deposit that has more impact in the family than making and keeping promises. Just think about it! How much excitement, anticipation, and hope is created by a promise? And the promises we make in the family are the most vital and often the most tender promises of all.

The most foundational promise we ever make to another human being is the vow inside a marriage. It's the ultimate promise. And equal to it is the promise we implicitly have with our children—particularly when they're little—that we will take care of them, that we will nurture them. That's why divorce and abandonment are such painful withdrawals. Those involved often feel as though the ultimate promises have been broken. So when these things have occurred, it becomes even more important to make deposits that will help rebuild bridges of confidence and trust.

At one time a man who had helped me on a particular project described the awful divorce he had just gone through. But he spoke with a kind of glowing pride about how he had kept the promise he had made to himself and his wife many months before that no matter what happened, he would not bad-mouth her—especially in front of his kids—and that he would always speak of her in ways that were affirming, uplifting, and positive. This was during the time when the legal and emotional battles were going on, and he said it was the hardest thing he had ever done. But he also said how grateful he was that he did it because it made all the difference—not only in how his children felt about themselves but also in how they felt about both their parents and their sense of family, despite the very difficult situation. He couldn't say enough about how glad he was that he kept the promise he had made.

Even when promises have been broken in the past, you can sometimes turn the situation into a deposit. I remember a man once who didn't come through on a commitment he had made to me. Later, he asked if he could have the opportunity to do something else, and I said no. Based on my past experience with him, I wasn't sure he would follow through.

But that man said to me, "I didn't come through before. I should have acknowledged it. I just gave a halfhearted effort, and that was wrong of me. Would you please give me one more opportunity? Not only will I come through, I will come through in gangbuster style."

I agreed, and he did it. He came through in a remarkable way. And in my eyes, he rose even higher than if he had kept his first commitment. His courage in coming back, in dealing with a difficult problem and a mistake in an honorable way, made a massive deposit in my Emotional Bank Account.

Forgiving

For many people the ultimate test of the proactive muscle comes in forgiving. In fact, you will always be a victim until you forgive.

One woman shared this experience:

You will always be a victim until you forgive.

I came from a very united family. We were always together—children, parents, brothers, sisters, aunts, uncles, cousins, grandparents—and we dearly loved one another.

When my father followed my mother in death, it deeply saddened us all. The four of us children met to divide our parents' things among us and our families. What happened at that meeting was an unforeseen shock from which we thought we would never recover. We had always been an emotional family, and at times we had disagreed to the point of some arguing and temporary ill will toward one another. But this time we argued beyond anything we had ever known before. The fight became so heated that we found ourselves yelling bitterly at one another. We began to emotionally tear at each other. Without being able to settle our differences, we each determined and announced that we were going to get lawyers to represent us and that the matter would be settled in court.

Each of us left that meeting feeling bitter and deeply resentful. We stopped visiting or even phoning one another. We stopped getting together on birthdays or holidays.

The situation went on for four years. It was the hardest trial of my life. Often, I felt the pain of loneliness and the unforgiving spirit of the bitterness and accusations that divided us. As my pain deepened, I kept thinking, If they really loved me, they would call me. What's wrong with them? Why don't they call?

Then one day I learned about the concept of the Emotional Bank Account. I came to realize that not forgiving my brothers and sisters was reactive on my part and that love is a verb, an action, something that I must do.

That night, as I was sitting alone in my room, the phone seemed to cry out to be used. I mustered all my courage and dialed the number of my oldest brother. When I heard his wonderful voice say, "Hello," tears flooded my eyes, and I could scarcely speak.

When he learned who it was, his emotions matched mine. We each raced to be the first to say, "I'm sorry." The conversation turned to expressions of love, forgiveness, and memories.

I called the others. It took most of the night. Each responded just as my oldest brother had.

That was the greatest and most significant night of my life. For the first time in four years I felt whole. The pain that had quietly been ever present was gone—replaced by the joy of forgiveness and peace. I felt renewed.

Notice how all four gifts came into play in this remarkable reconciliation. Look at this woman's depth of awareness of what was happening. Observe this woman's connection with her conscience, her moral sense. Also note how the concept of the Emotional Bank Account created a vision of what is possible and how these three gifts joined in producing the willpower to forgive and connect together again, and to experience the happiness that such an emotional reunion brings.

Another woman shared this experience:

I remember as a child feeling happy and secure. I have warm memories of going on pic-nics as a family, playing games in the front room, and gardening together. I knew my parents loved each other and they loved us children.

But as I reached my mid-teens, things began to change. My dad went on occasional business trips. He began working late at night and on Saturdays. The relationship between him and my mom seemed strained. He didn't spend time with the family anymore. One night as I was returning home from the graveyard shift at the restaurant where I worked, I saw my Dad pull up at the same time. I realized then that he hadn't been home all night.

Eventually, my mother and father separated and then divorced. It was a bitter blow to all of us children, especially when we discovered that Dad had been unfaithful to Mom. His infidelity, we learned, had started on one of his business trips.

Several years later I married a wonderful young man. We loved each other deeply, and we both took our marriage vows very seriously. Everything seemed to be going very well—until one day when he told me his job would require him to leave for a few days on a business trip. Suddenly, all the pain of the past washed over me. It was on his business trips, I remembered, that my dad began being unfaithful to my mother. I had absolutely no reason to doubt my husband. There was nothing to justify my fear. But the fear was there—deep and painful.

I spent much of the time my husband was gone crying and wondering. When I tried to explain my fears, I knew he didn't really understand. He was totally committed to me and didn't see his traveling as a problem. But from my perspective he didn't seem to realize how he needed to be always on his guard. I felt he would not have nearly the discernment in these situations that I would have because no one in his family had ever done what my father had done.

My husband went on several business trips during the following months. I tried to be more positive in my interactions with him. I worked hard to control my thoughts and feelings. But every time he left, I would panic inside. The emotional stress became so intense that I had difficulty eating and sleeping whenever he was gone. And as hard as I tried, nothing seemed to make things better.

Finally, after years of dealing with deep pain, I reached a point where I was able to forgive my father. I could see his behavior for what it was: his behavior. He had hurt us all deeply, but I found I could forgive him and love him and let go of the fear and the pain.

This became a major turning point in my life. All of a sudden I discovered that the tension in my marriage was gone. I was able to say, "That was my dad, not my husband." I found I could kiss my husband good-bye as he left on his trips and shift my focus to all I wanted to get done before he got back.

I don't mean to suggest that everything became perfect overnight. Years of resentment toward my father had created deeply ingrained habits. But after that pivotal experience, when the occasional thought or feeling would surface, I was able to recognize it, address it quickly, and move on.

Again: You will always be a victim until you forgive. When you truly forgive, you open the channels through which trust and unconditional love can flow. You cleanse your own heart. You also remove a major obstacle that keeps others from changing because when you don't forgive, you put yourself between people and their own conscience. You get in the way. You become a roadblock to change. Instead of spending their energy on deep interior work with their own conscience, they spend it defending and justifying their behavior to you.

One of the greatest deposits you can make in your relationships with other family members—and in the basic quality and richness of your own life—is to forgive. Remember, it isn't the snake bite that does the serious damage; it's chasing the snake that drives the poison to the heart.

> *It isn't the snake bite that does the serious damage; it's chasing the snake that drives the poison to the heart.*

The Primary Laws of Love

In this chapter we've taken a look at five significant deposits you can proactively and immediately begin to make into the Emotional Bank Accounts of the members of your family. The reason these deposits create such a powerful difference in the family culture is that they are based on the Primary Laws of Love—laws which reflect the reality that love in its purest form is *unconditional.*

There are three such laws: acceptance rather than rejection, understanding rather than judgment, and participation rather than manipulation. Living these laws is a proactive choice that is not based on another's behavior or on social status, educational attainment, wealth, reputation, or any other factor except the intrinsic worth of a human being.

These laws are the foundation of a beautiful family culture, because only when we live the Primary Laws of Love do we encourage obedience to the Primary Laws of Life (such as honesty, responsibility, integrity, and service).

Sometimes when people are struggling with a loved one and doing everything they can to lead that person toward what they feel is a responsible course, it's very easy to fall into the trap of living the "secondary" or counterfeit laws of love— judgment, rejection, and manipulation. They love the end in mind more than they love the person. They love conditionally. In other words, they use love to manipulate and control. As a result, others feel rejected and fight to stay the same.

> *When we live the Primary Laws of Love, we encourage obedience to the Primary Laws of Life.*

But when you deeply accept and love people as they are, you actually encourage them to become better. By accepting people you're not condoning their weakness or agreeing with their opinion; you're simply affirming their intrinsic worth. You're acknowledging that they think or feel in a particular way. You're freeing them of the need to defend, protect, and preserve themselves. So instead of wasting their energy defending themselves, they're able to focus on interacting with their own conscience and unleashing their growth potential.

By loving people unconditionally, you unleash their natural power to become their better self. And you can only do this when you separate the person from the behavior and believe in the unseen potential.

Just consider how valuable this perspective would be when dealing with a family member—particularly a child—who is filled with negative energy or who has

gone off track for a period of time. What would happen if, rather than labeling this child based on current behavior, you were to affirm the unseen potential and love unconditionally instead? As Goethe said, "Treat a man as he is and he will remain as he is. Treat a man as he can and should be, and he will become as he can and should be."

I once had a friend who was dean of a very prestigious school. He planned and saved for years to provide his son with the opportunity to attend that institution, but when the time came, the boy refused to go. This deeply concerned his father. Graduating from that particular school would have been a great asset to the boy. Besides, it was a family tradition. Three generations of attendance preceded the boy's. The father talked and urged and pleaded. He also tried to listen to the boy to understand him, all the while hoping that his son would change his mind.

He would say, "Son, can't you see what this means for your life? You can't base long-range decisions on short-range emotions."

The son would respond, "You don't understand! It's my life. You just want me the way *you* want. I don't even know if I want to go to college at all."

The father would come back with "Not at all, son. *You're* the one who doesn't understand. I only want what is best for you. Stop being so foolish."

The subtle message being communicated was one of conditional love. The son felt that in a sense the father's desire for him to attend the school outweighed the value he placed on him as a person and as a son, which was terribly threatening. Consequently, he fought for and with his own identity and integrity, and he increased his resolve and his efforts to rationalize his decision not to go.

After some intense soul-searching, the father decided to make a sacrifice—to renounce conditional love. He knew that his son might choose differently from what he wished; nevertheless, he and his wife resolved to love their son unconditionally, regardless of his choice. It was an extremely difficult thing to do because the value of his educational experience was so close to their hearts and because it was something they had planned and worked for since his birth.

The father and mother went through a very difficult rescripting process, proactively using all four gifts and struggling to understand the nature of unconditional love. They eventually felt it deep inside, and they communicated to the boy what they had done and why. They told him that they had come to the point at which they could say in all honesty that his decision would not affect their feeling of unconditional love toward him. They didn't do this to manipulate him, to use backhand psychology to try to get him to "shape up." They did it as the emergent extension of their own growth in character.

The boy didn't give much of a response, but his parents had such a mind-set and heart-set of unconditional love at that point that it would have made no difference in their feelings for him. About a week later he told his parents that he had decided not to go. They were perfectly prepared for his response and continued to show unconditional love for him. Everything was settled, and life went along normally.

A short time later an interesting thing happened. Now that the boy no longer felt he had to defend his position, he searched within himself more deeply and found that he really did want to have this educational experience. He applied for admission, and then he told his father, who again showed unconditional love by fully accepting his son's decision. Our friend was happy but not excessively so, because he had truly learned to love without condition.

Because these parents lived the Primary Laws of Love, their son was able to search his own heart and choose to live in harmony with one of the Primary Laws of Life involving growth and education.

Many people who have never received unconditional love and have never developed a sense of intrinsic worth struggle all their lives for approval and recognition. To compensate for the impoverished, empty, hollow feeling they have inside, they borrow strength from a position of power, status, money, possessions, credentials, or reputation. They often become very narcissistic, interpreting everything personally. And their very behavior is so distasteful that others reject them, throwing fuel on the fire.

That's why these Primary Laws of Love are so important. They affirm the basic worth of the individual. And people who have been loved unconditionally are then free to develop their own strength through integrity to their own inner compass.

Every Problem Is an Opportunity to Make a Deposit

As we move now into the rest of the habits, notice how each grows out of the Primary Laws of Love and how each builds the Emotional Bank Account.

Proactively making deposits is something we can always do. In fact, one of the most empowering and exciting aspects of the Emotional Bank Account idea is that we can proactively choose to turn every family problem into an opportunity for a deposit.

- Someone's "bad day" becomes an opportunity to be kind.
- An offense becomes an opportunity to apologize, to forgive.
- Someone's gossip becomes an opportunity to be loyal, to quietly defend those not present.

With the image of the Emotional Bank Account in your mind and heart, problems and circumstances are no longer obstacles that get in the way of the path; they *are* the path. Everyday interactions become opportunities to build relationships of love and trust. And challenges become like inoculations that activate and boost the "immune system" of the entire family. Deep inside, everyone knows that making these deposits will make a big difference in the quality of family relationships. It comes out of our conscience, out of our connection to the principles that ultimately govern in life.

Can you see how the proactive, inside-out choice to make deposits—and not withdrawals—can help you create a beautiful family culture?

Just think about the difference it makes in your own family when:

INSTEAD OF MAKING WITHDRAWALS BY	YOU MAKE DEPOSITS BY
Speaking disrespectfully, putting people down, or acting in rude and discourteous ways	Being kind
Never saying "I'm sorry" or saying it insincerely	Apologizing
Criticizing, complaining, and talking about others in negative ways when they're not around	Being loyal to those not present
Never making commitments to anyone, or making commitments but rarely following through	Making and keeping promises
Being quick to take offense, holding grudges, throwing people's past mistakes up to them, and nurturing grievances	Forgiving

Remember the Chinese Bamboo Tree

As you begin to make deposits, you may see positive results almost immediately. More often it will take time. You'll find it easier to make and continue to make deposits if you keep in mind the miracle of the Chinese bamboo tree.

I know of one woman and her husband who made deposits into their Emotional Bank Account with her father for many years, apparently without results. After fifteen years of working in a business with her father, this woman's husband changed jobs so that he could be with his family on Sundays. This caused a schism so deep, so painful for her father that he became embittered and would not even speak to her husband or recognize him in any way. But neither this woman nor her husband would take offense. They made continual deposits of unconditional love. They frequently drove out to the farm where her father lived, some sixty miles away. Her husband would wait in the car—sometimes for more than an hour—while she visited. She often took things to her father that she had baked or she thought he might enjoy. She spent time with him at Christmas, on his birthday, and on many other occasions. Never once did she press him or even ask him to invite her husband into his home.

Whenever her father came into town, this woman would leave the office where she worked with her husband and meet him for shopping or for lunch. She did everything she could possibly think of to communicate her love and her appreciation to her father. And her husband supported her in all of this.

Then one day when she was visiting her father on the farm, he suddenly looked at her and said, "Would it be easier for you if your husband were to come inside?"

She caught her breath. "Oh, yes, it would!" she exclaimed with tears in her eyes.

"Well," he said slowly, "go and get him then."

From that point on they were able to make even greater deposits of love. This woman's husband helped her father work on projects around the farm. This became an even greater deposit as advancing years caused her father to lose some of his mental capacity. Toward the end of his life, he acknowledged that he felt as close to this son-in-law as he felt to his own son.

In all your efforts, remember that, as with the Chinese bamboo tree, you may not see results for years. But do not be discouraged. Do not be seduced by those who say, "It's useless. It's hopeless. There's nothing you can do. It's too late."

It *can* be done. It's *never* too late. Just keep working in your Circle of Influence. Be a light, not a judge; a model, not a critic. And have faith in the eventual outcome.

I've talked with many husbands and wives over the years—most of them friends—who have come to me frustrated with their spouses, feeling that they were at the end of their tether. Often, these people have been filled with a sense of their own rightness and their partner's lack of understanding and responsibility. They've been drawn into a cycle where one spouse is constantly judging, preaching, nagging, condemning, criticizing, and handing out emotional punishment, and the other is, in a sense, rebelling by ignoring, defensively resisting, and justifying every behavior by the treatment he or she is receiving.

My counsel to those who judge (who are usually the ones coming to me, hoping that I can somehow "shape up" their spouse or affirm their reasons for wanting a divorce) is to become a light, not a judge—in other words, to stop trying to change their spouse and just go to work on themselves, to get out of a judging mind-set, to stop trying to manipulate or give love conditionally.

If people take this counsel to heart and are humbled by it, and if they are patient, persistent, and non-manipulating—even when provoked—a sweet softness begins to return. The unconditional love and inside-out change become irresistible.

There are situations, of course, such as those involving real abuse, when this counsel would not be the right course. But in most cases I have found that this approach leads people to the inner wisdom that cultivates happiness in married life. Proactively setting the example and patiently making deposits of unconditional love often brings amazing results over time.

Habit 1: The Key to All the Other Habits

Habit 1—Be proactive—is the key that unlocks the door to all the other habits. In fact, you'll find that people who continually avoid taking responsibility and initiative will not be able to fully cultivate any of the other habits. Instead, they'll be out in their Circle of Concern—usually blaming and accusing other people for their situation, because when people are not true to their conscience, they typically take out their guilt on others. Most anger is merely guilt overflowing.

Habit 1 embodies the greatest gift that we as humans uniquely have: the power to choose. Next to life itself, is there a greater gift? The truth is that the basic solutions to our problems lie within us. We can't escape the nature of things. Like it or not—realize it or not—principles and conscience are within us. As educator and religious leader David O. McKay has said, "The greatest battles of life are fought out daily in the silent chambers of the soul." It's futile to fight our battles on the wrong battlefields.

> "The greatest battles of life are fought out daily in the silent chambers of the soul."

The decision to be the creative force of our own lives is the most fundamental choice of all. It is the heart and soul of being a transition person. It is the essence of becoming an agent of change. As Joseph Zinker has said, "[A person can discover that] no matter where he is right now, he is still the creator of his own destiny."[6]

Not only can an individual be proactive but an entire family can be proactive. A family can become a transition family inside their intergenerational family or extended family, or to other families with whom they come in contact. And all four gifts can be collectivized so that instead of self-awareness you have family awareness; instead of individual conscience you have a social conscience; instead of one person's imagination or vision you have a shared vision; and instead of independent will you have social will. Then all the members of the family are able to say in their own words, "This is what we are like. We are people of conscience and vision, people who act on our awareness of what's happening and what needs to happen."

How this transformation takes place and how the proactive muscle is developed and used in a marvelous way is found in Habit 2: Begin with the end in mind.

Sharing This Chapter with Adults and Teens

Increasing our Proactive Muscles

- Discuss with family members: When do you feel you are most proactive? When are you most reactive? What are the consequences?
- Review the material on the four human gifts (pages 29–33). Ask: What can we do to build our proactive muscles?

Creating a Pause Button: Stop, Think, and Choose

- Talk together about the concept of the pause button.
- Ask the family to choose something to represent a pause button for the family. It could be a body movement, such as signaling with a hand, jumping up and down, or waving an arm; an action, such as switching the lights on and off; a sound, such as blowing a whistle, ringing a bell, or mimicking an animal sound; or even a word. Each time this signal is given, everyone will know the pause button is being pushed. All activity, including conversation, arguing, debating, and so forth, should cease. This signal serves as a reminder for all to stop, think, and consider the consequences of continuing as they are. Talk together about how using this pause button gives family members the opportunity to subordinate what may seem important at the moment (winning an argument, getting their way, being "first" or "best") for what really matters most (creating strong relationships, having a happy family, or building a beautiful family culture).

Working in Your Circle of Influence

- Review the material on pages 40–44. Have family members discuss some things that they do not have direct influence over, such as other people's thoughts and actions, the weather, seasons, and natural disasters. Help everyone understand that although there are some things we cannot influence, there is much that we *can* influence. Talk about how much more effective it is to concentrate energy and effort on what you *can* influence.
- Ask family members: What are some things we can do to take good care of our bodies to help prevent illness?
- Review the material on pages 45–61. Talk together about what you can do to build Emotional Bank Accounts in the family. Encourage family members to commit to making deposits and limiting withdrawals for one week. At the end of the week discuss the difference it has made.

SHARING THIS CHAPTER WITH CHILDREN

Developing Conscience: A Treasure Hunt

- Choose a "treasure" that everyone will enjoy, making sure that there is enough for all to share.

- Choose a safe spot to hide the treasure, making sure that it is accessible to everyone.

- Develop clues that lead to the treasure. In order to obtain the clues participants must answer questions that will exercise their conscience. Positive answers lead them closer to the treasure; negative answers lead them away. Examples might include:

Question: As you are walking to school, you notice that the boy in front of you has dropped a five-dollar bill. What do you do? Positive responses could be: Pick it up and return it to the boy. Tell a teacher and hand it over. Negative responses could be: Keep it. Head to the store. Taunt the boy.

Question: Someone steals the answers to next week's math exam and offers you a copy. What do you do? Positive responses could be: Refuse a copy and study. Encourage the person to be honest. Negative responses could be: Take it; you need the A. Tell everyone else so they will like you.

Understanding the Emotional Bank Account

- Visit a local bank, open an account, and explain deposits and withdrawals.
- Make your own "EBA" box. Let the children decorate it. Put it in a special place that is noticeable and accessible to everyone. Create some "deposit slips" on three-by-five cards. Encourage the children to make "deposits" during the week to other family members. Some examples might include: "Dad, thanks for taking me golfing. I love you." Or "Brooke, I noticed how well you folded the laundry this week." Or "John made my bed today, and I didn't even ask him to." Or "Mom takes me to soccer every week. She is so nice." Find a time to talk about the deposits made during the week. Encourage family members to use this opportunity to share what a "deposit" is to them.

HABIT 2
BEGIN WITH THE
END IN MIND

One young father shared this experience of how his wife was able to be proactive in a challenging situation with their son:

I came home from work the other day, and my three-and-a-half-year-old son Brenton met me at the door. He was beaming. He said, "Dad, I am a hardworking man!"

I later found out that while my wife had been downstairs, Brenton had emptied a one-and-a-half-gallon jug of water from the fridge, most of it on the floor. My wife's initial reaction had been to yell at him and spank him. But instead she stopped herself and said patiently, "Brenton, what were you trying to do?"

"I was trying to be a helping man, Mom," he replied proudly.

"What do you mean?" she asked.

"I washed the dishes for you."

Sure enough, there on the kitchen table were all the dishes he had washed with the water from the water jug.

"Well, honey, why did you use the water from the fridge?"

"I couldn't reach the water in the sink."

"Oh!" she said. Then she looked around. "Well, what do you think you could do next time that would make less of a mess?"

He thought about it for a minute. Then his face lit up. "I could do it in the bathroom!" he exclaimed.

"The dishes might break in the bathroom," she replied. "But how about this? What if you came and got me and I helped you move a chair in front of the kitchen sink so that you could do the work there?"

"Good idea!" he exclaimed happily.

"Now what shall we do with this mess?" she asked.

"Well," he said thoughtfully, "we could use a lot of paper towels!" So she gave him some paper towels, and she went and got the mop.

As she was telling me what had happened, I realized how important it was that my wife had been able to catch herself between stimulus and response. She made a proactive choice. And she was able to do it because she thought about the end in mind. The important thing here is not having a clean floor. It's raising this boy.

It took her about ten minutes to clean up the mess. If she had been reactive, it also would have taken her about ten minutes, but the difference would have been that Brenton would have met me at the door and said, "Daddy, I am a bad boy!"

Just think about the difference it made in this family for this woman to act instead of react! This little boy could have come out of this experience feeling guilty, embarrassed, and ashamed. But instead he felt affirmed, appreciated, loved. His good intentions and his desire to help were nurtured. He learned how to help in better ways. His whole attitude about himself and about helping in his home were positively affected by this interaction.

How was this woman able to turn what could have been a very frustrating experience into an actual deposit into this little boy's Emotional Bank Account? As her husband observed, she had clear in her mind what was most important. It wasn't having a clean floor; it was raising that boy. She had a purpose that was bigger than her problem. And in that instant between what happened and her response to it, she was able to connect to that purpose. She acted with the end in mind.

The End in Mind: Your "Destination"

Habit 2—Begin with the end in mind—is to create a clear, compelling vision of what you and your family are all about. Going back to the airplane metaphor, Habit

2 defines your destination. And having your destination clearly in mind affects every decision along the way.

Habit 2 is based on the principle of vision—and vision is powerful! It's the principle that enables prisoners of war to survive.[1] Research shows it's what gives successful children the drive to succeed.[2] It's a moving power behind successful individuals and organizations in every walk of life. Vision is greater than "baggage"—greater than the negative baggage of the past and even the accumulated baggage of the present. Tapping into this sense of vision gives you the power and the purpose to rise above the baggage and act based on what really matters most.

Now there are many ways to apply this principle of vision—to begin with the end in mind—in the family culture. You can begin a year, a week, or a day with the end in mind. You can begin a family experience or activity with the end in mind. You can begin a season of dance or piano lessons, or a special family dinner, or the building of a new home, or a search for a family pet with the end in mind.

But in this chapter we're going to focus on the most profound, significant, and far-reaching application of "begin with the end in mind" in the family—the creation of a "family mission statement."

> *A* family mission statement is a combined, unified expression from all family members of what your family is all about and the principles you choose to govern your family life.

A family mission statement is a combined, unified expression from all family members of what your family is all about—what it is you really want to do and be—and the principles you choose to govern your family life. It's based on the idea that all things are created twice. First comes the idea, or the mental creation; then comes the reality, or the physical creation. It's drafting the blueprint before constructing the building, writing the script before performing the play, creating the flight plan before taking off in the airplane. It's like the carpenter's rule: "Measure twice, cut once."

Can you imagine the consequences of the opposite—of beginning with no end in mind?

Suppose you were to go to a construction site and ask the workers there, "What are you building?"

"We have no idea," one of them replies.

"Well, what does your blueprint show?" you ask.

The foreman replies, "We have no blueprint. We feel that if we build with great skill and craftsmanship, in the end we will have a beautiful building. We must get back to work now so we can complete our task. Perhaps then we will be able to determine just what it is we have built."

Or, going back to the airplane metaphor, suppose someone were to ask you as a pilot, "Where will you be flying to today?"

Would this be your reply? "I really don't know. We have no flight plan. We'll just load the passengers and take the plane up. There are a lot of air currents up there. They blow in different directions on different days. We'll just catch the current that's blowing the hardest and go wherever it takes us. When we get there, we will know where we were headed."

In my profession, if I'm working with a particular organization or client—particularly with the top executive cabinet—I often ask all the members to write a one-sentence answer to this question: "What is the essential mission or purpose of this organization, and what is its main strategy in accomplishing that purpose?" I then have them read these papers out loud to the others, and they are usually shocked at the differences. They cannot believe that everyone sees it so differently, particularly on an issue of such governing importance. And this sometimes happens even when the company mission statement is on the wall in that very room.

You might consider trying the same thing in your family. Tonight, just go and ask each member of your family individually, "What is the purpose of our family? What is this family about?" Ask your spouse, "What is the purpose of our marriage? What is its essential reason for being? What are its high priority goals?" You may be surprised by the answers you receive.

The point is that it's vital to have the entire culture aligned—to head toward a mutually agreed upon destination. It's critical to have everyone in the cockpit knowing that all are heading to the same place, rather than having the pilot thinking they're going to New York and the flight engineer thinking they're going to Chicago.

As it says in Proverbs, "Without vision the people perish." The opposite of Habit 2 in the family is to have no mental creation, no envisioning of the future—to just let life happen, to be swept along with the flow of society's values and trends without having any sense of vision or purpose. It's simply living out the scripts that have been given to you. In fact, it's really not living at all; it's being lived.

Because all things are created twice, if you don't take charge of the first creation, someone or something else will. Creating a family mission statement is taking charge of the first creation. It's deciding what kind of family you really want to be and identifying the principles that will help you get there. And that decision will give context to every other decision you make. It will become your destination. It will act like a huge, powerful magnet that draws you toward it and helps you stay on track.

Creating Our Own Family Mission Statement

I hope you'll excuse the long personal reference that follows, but we learned the power of all this not in the reading, observing, teaching, or writing but in the *doing*.

Please understand that this is a very intimate sharing of our personal and family life. It reflects our own deep values and beliefs. But know that we recognize and honor the principle of respect for all, including those who believe differently.

If you were to ask Sandra and me, "What has been the most transforming event in your own family history?", we would answer without hesitation that it was the creation of our family mission statement. Our first mission statement was created in a sacred marriage ceremony some forty-one years ago. Our second mission statement was developed in stages over a period of fifteen years and several children. Through the years these mission statements have created the common sense of destination and manner of travel that has represented the social will, the culture, in the family. And either directly or indirectly, consciously or unconsciously, almost everything else in our family has grown out of it.

On the day we were married, immediately after the ceremony, Sandra and I went to a park called Memory Grove. We sat together and talked about what that ceremony meant and how we were going to try to live our lives by it. We talked about the two families we had come from. We discussed what we wanted to continue to do in our own newly formed family and what things we wanted to do differently.

We also reaffirmed that our marriage was much more than a *contractual* relationship; it was a *covenant* relationship. And our commitment to each other was total, complete, and for always. We also recognized that our covenant was not only with each other; it was also with God. And we determined that we would be able to love each other more if we loved Him first.

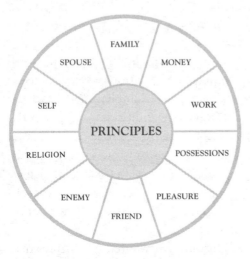

So we made the decision to put principles ahead of each other and ahead of our family. And we feel that one decision, more than any other single factor, has given us the strength to apologize, to forgive, to be kind, and to keep coming back to the flight path time and time again. We've discovered that the more we are able to center our lives on these principles, the more wisdom and strength we can access—especially in situations where it would be very easy to be centered and even controlled by other things, such as work, money, possessions, or even family itself. Without that decision, we are convinced, we would have been far more dependent on each other's moods or on our popularity with our children for our sense of security, rather than on our own inner integrity.

Putting principles first has given a sense of appropriate priority to everything else. It's been like a set of glasses through which we view all of life. It's given us a sense of "stewardship"—a sense that we are both responsible and accountable for the way in which we handle all things, including family. And it's helped us realize that family itself is a principle—universal, timeless, and self-evident.

That day as Sandra and I sat in Memory Grove, we also began to talk about the children we would have. We took seriously the words of Daniel Webster:

If we work on marble, it will perish. If we work upon brass, time will efface it. If we rear temples, they will crumble into dust, but if we work upon immortal minds, and instill into them just principles, we are then engraving upon that tablet that which no time will efface, but will brighten and brighten to all eternity.

We began to identify some of the principles we wanted to use in raising our children. Then and over the next few years as children began to come, we often asked ourselves, "What kind of strength and abilities will our children need to have in order to be successful when they're grown?" And out of these discussions came ten abilities we thought were vitally important—ten things we felt these children would need to be able to do when they became independent and started families of their own. These included the ability to work, to learn, to communicate, to solve problems, to repent, to forgive, to serve, to worship, to survive in the wilderness, and to play and have fun.

Part of our vision was to gather together at the dinner table at the end of the day and regroup, share experiences, laugh, bond, philosophize, and discuss values. We wanted our children to enjoy and deeply appreciate each other, to do things together, and to love being with each other.

As the children grew, this vision gave direction to many family discussions and activities. It caused us to plan each of our summers, our vacations, and our leisure time in a way that would help us realize our dream. For example, one of the ten things on our list was the ability to survive in adverse conditions, so to help the children develop this skill, we enrolled our family in survival programs. We were trained and led into the wilderness for several days with nothing but our wits to sustain us. We learned to survive through our ingenuity and through the knowledge we had gained about what we could and could not eat and drink. We learned techniques that would allow us to survive in freezing conditions, extremely hot conditions, and conditions where there was no water.

Another item concerned the value of education. We wanted our children to work in school and get as much education as possible, and not take shortcuts to simply get grades and diplomas. So we read together as a family. We organized our home so that our children had a time and a place to do homework. We became interested in what our children were learning in school, and we gave them opportunities to teach us what they were learning. We focused primarily on learning, not grades, and we hardly ever had to encourage the children to do their homework. We rarely saw a grade lower than an A minus.

Over the years, the focus on these and other "ends in mind" made a powerful difference in our family direction and in our family culture. But then, starting about twenty years ago, we developed a whole new level of family unity and synergy. At that time we started developing and organizing the 7 Habits material. We began to realize that successful organizations of all kinds have mission statements. Many were sincere and became the major force in all decision-making; many were written only for public relations purposes. We began to realize what more recent research clearly shows: that the sincere kind of statement is an absolutely critical ingredient of high-performance organizations—fundamental not only to the productivity and success of the organization but also to the satisfaction and happiness of the people who work in it.[3]

> *For the most part, families don't have the kind of mission statement so critical to organizational success. Yet family is the most important, fundamental organization in the world.*

We realized that even though most families begin with a sacred marriage ceremony (which represents a kind of "beginning with the end in mind"), for the most part, families don't have the kind of mission statement so critical to organizational success. Yet family is the most important, fundamental organization in the world, the literal building block of society. No civilization has ever survived its breakup. No other institution can fulfill its essential purpose. No other institution has had its impact for good or ill. Nevertheless, in most families members do not have a deep sense of shared vision around its essential meaning and purpose. They have not paid the price to develop a shared vision and value system, which is the essence of the character and culture of the family.

So we became convinced that we needed to develop a "family mission statement." We had to create a vision of what we wanted our family to be like, what we would live by, what we would stand for—even die for. It would be a vision that was shared and owned by all family members, not just the two of us.

So we began the process of creating it. We met as a family once a week to talk about it. We had different fun activities for the children that helped them tap into their four human gifts and get their ideas out on the table. We brainstormed together. Between family meetings we privately pondered these things. We sometimes discussed them one-on-one or at dinner. One night as we met, we asked the children, "How do you think we could be better parents? In what ways can we improve?" (After twenty minutes of being bombarded by the ideas and suggestions that flowed freely, we said, "Okay, we think we get the idea!")

Gradually, we began to address a whole range of deeper issues. We asked family members:

What kind of family do we really want to be?
What kind of home would you like to invite your friends to?
What embarrasses you about our family?
What makes you feel comfortable here?
What makes you want to come home?
What makes you feel drawn to us as your parents so that you are open to our influence?
What makes us feel open to your influence?
What do we want to be remembered by?

We asked all the children who could write to make their own list of things that were important to them. They brought back their ideas the following week, and we had an open discussion about why these traits were so important or desirable. Eventually, all of the children wrote their own mission statements about what they felt was important and why. Together we read and discussed each one. Each was thoughtful and special. We had to smile when we read Sean's. Coming from the teenage football frame of mind he held at the time, it read: "We're one heck of a family, and we kick butt!" Not too refined—but to the point.

It took us about eight months to develop our mission statement. Everyone participated. Even my mother was involved. Today we have grandchildren who have also become a part of it, so there are now four generations involved in our family mission statement.

A Destination and a Compass

It is almost impossible to communicate the impact that creating a family mission statement has had on our family—both directly and indirectly. Perhaps the best way to describe it is in terms of the airplane metaphor: Creating a family mission statement has given us a *destination* and a *compass*.

The mission statement itself has given us a *clear, shared vision of the destination* where we as a family want to go. It has been a guide to our family now for a decade and a half. We have it up on a wall in our family room. We look at it often and ask ourselves, "How well are we living up to what we have decided to be and to do? Is our home really a place where the sounds of love are found? Are we being cynical and critical? Do we use cutting humor? Do we walk out on each other and not communicate? Are we giving back or only taking?"

As we compare our actions to this statement, we get feedback that tells us when we're off course. In fact, it is this statement—this sense of destination—that makes feedback meaningful. Without it, feedback becomes confusing and counterproductive. There's no way to tell if it's relevant. There's nothing to measure it against. But a clear sense of shared vision and values enables us to evaluate feedback and use it to make continual course corrections so that we can eventually arrive at our destination.

Our sense of destination also allows us to better understand our present situation and to realize that the ends and means are inseparable; in other words, the destination and the manner of traveling are interwoven. When the destination represents a certain quality of family life and of love in the relationship, is it possible to imagine any separation between that destination and the manner of traveling to get there? In reality, the ends and the means—the destination and the journey—are the same.

> *In reality, the ends and the means—the destination and the journey—are the same.*

Certainly our family is not free from problems, but much of the time, at least, family members really do feel that our home is a place of faith, order, truth, love, happiness, and relaxation. We try to act in ways that are responsibly independent and effectively interdependent. We attempt to serve worthy purposes in society. And we're grateful to see these things manifest in the lives of our married children who now have families of their own and have developed their own mission statements.

The process of creating our mission statement has also enabled us to *turn our four unique human gifts into a "compass"* to help keep us on track. We had been aware of some of the *principles* we wanted to live by—principles such as those mentioned in the Emotional Bank Account deposits in Habit 1—but as we came together and talked about them as a family, we reached a whole new level of understanding and commitment to live by them.

As we interacted, *self-awareness* became *family awareness*—our ability to see ourselves as a family. *Conscience* became *family conscience*—the unity of the shared moral nature of everyone in the family and the clarity that came from discussing these things together. *Imagination* became *creative synergy* as we hammered out the issues and came to something everyone could agree on. And *independent will* became *interdependent will* or *social will* as we all worked together to make it happen.

This was one of the most exciting things that developed out of our family mission statement work—the creation of this social will, this sense of "we." This is *our* decision, *our* determination. This is what *we* have decided *we* are going to be and to do. It represented the collective awareness, the collective conscience, and the collective imagination that came together synergistically to produce this collective commitment, this collective promise or expression of collective will.

Nothing is more bonding and more binding than for everybody to be involved

in the process of synergistic interaction and communication until this social will is fashioned and formed. When you create a social will, you produce something that is much more synergistic than just a collection of individual wills. And this gives an entirely new dimension to the concept of synergy. Synergy is producing not just a third alternative solution but a third alternative spirit—the spirit of the family.

In our family, by combining our unique human gifts in this way we were able to create a *family compass* that helped us determine our direction. That compass serves as an inner guidance system to help us keep our destination clear and move continually toward it. It also enables us to interpret feedback and helps us keep coming back to the flight path time and time again.

Creating Your Own Family Mission Statement

Our own family experience—plus my experience with thousands of families worldwide—has led to the development of a simple three-step process any family can go through to create a family mission statement.

Step One: Explore What Your Family Is All About

The goal here is to get everyone's feelings and ideas out on the table. And depending on your situation, you may choose any one of a variety of ways to do this.

A Mission Statement for Two

If your family is just you and your spouse at this point, you may want to go some-place where you can be alone together for a couple of days or even just a few hours. Enjoy some time just relaxing and being together. When the atmosphere is right, you may want to try to envision together what you want your relationship to be ten, twenty-five, or fifty years down the road. You may want to seek inspiration by reflecting on the words spoken as part of your marriage ceremony. If you can't remember them, you could make it a point to listen when you attend the weddings of relatives and friends. You may hear words such as these:

Cleave unto each other and none else.
Observe all the laws, covenants, and obligations pertaining to the holy state of matrimony.
Love, honor, and cherish each other as long as you both shall live.
Be blessed with joy in your posterity.
Have a long life of happiness together.

If words such as these resonate in your heart, they can become the basis for a powerful mission statement.

Or you might find other words to inspire you. In our marriage, Sandra and I have found great inspiration in the Quaker proverb, "Thee lift me and I'll lift thee, and we will ascend together."

You might also discuss together questions such as these:

What kind of marriage partners do we want to be?
How do we want to treat each other?
How do we want to resolve our differences?
How do we want to handle our finances?
What kind of parents do we want to be?
What principles do we want to teach our children to help them prepare for adulthood and to lead responsible, caring lives?
How do we help develop the potential talent of each child?
What kind of discipline do we want to use with our children?
What roles (earning, financial management, housekeeping, and so on) will each of us have?
How can we best relate to each other's families?
What traditions do we bring with us from the families in which we were raised?
What traditions do we want to keep and create?
What intergenerational traits or tendencies are we happy or unhappy with, and how do we make changes?
How do we want to give back?

Whatever method you use, remember that the process is as important as the product. Take the time together. Build the Emotional Bank Account. Interact deeply on the issues. Make sure that the final product represents all that is in both of your minds and hearts.

One woman said this:

The process is as important as the product.

When I met my husband twenty years ago, we were both very frightened of relationships because we had both been burned in marriages before. But one of the things that really impressed me about Chuck from the beginning is that he had actually listed everything he wanted in a marriage relationship and put it on his refrigerator door. So every female who tromped through his apartment had the option of saying, "Yeah, this is what I want" or "No, that's not what I want." He was really clear and up front about it.

So right from the very beginning we were able to work from that list. I added things to it that were important to me, and we worked together at hammering out what we wanted in our relationship. We said, "We will have no secrets from each other," "We will hold no resentments," "We will be totally up front with each other about our needs," and so on.

And going through this has made a tremendous difference in our marriage. It's written in our hearts now. We don't have to go back and say, "Hey, this person isn't living up to this or that," because whenever we feel resentment or whenever we feel something going on that we don't like, we immediately talk to each other. And this has grown out of what we originally agreed to do.

The reason a mission statement is so important in a marriage is that no two people are completely alike. There are always differences. And when you put two people together in this most tender, sensitive, and intimate relationship called marriage, if you don't take the time to explore these differences and create a sense of shared vision, then these differences can drive them apart.

Consider two people we'll call Sally and Paul. Paul comes from a very supportive family. When Paul was in high school, if he had said, "Today I lost my track meet," his mother might have responded (in spirit if not in exact words), "Oh, Paul, that's too bad! You must really be disappointed. We're proud of the effort. We love you." If he had said, "Mom, I just won the school election," his mother might have replied, "Oh, Paul, I'm so happy for you! We love you. We're proud of you." Paul's success or failure made no difference. His parents were unconditionally affectionate and caring.

Sally, on the other hand, comes from a family that is not supportive. Her parents are generally disinterested, unaffectionate, and conditional in their love. If Sally had said to her mother, "Today I lost my track meet," her mother would have replied, "Well, what happened? I told you that you ought to exercise and practice more! Your sister was a tremendous track star, and she exercised and practiced a lot more than you. What am I going to tell Dad?" But if Sally had said, "Mom, I just won the student body election," her mother would have replied, "Oh, great! I'm really proud of you. I can hardly wait to tell Dad!"

Now two people have had totally different nurturing experiences. One has learned to love unconditionally. The other loves conditionally. They meet and begin dating. After a while they say to each other, "I love you." They get married. But within a few months of living together, of interacting intimately with each other on a daily basis, they're in trouble.

Based on Sally's conditional expressions of love, Paul finally says to her, "You don't love me anymore."

"What do you mean, I don't love you?" she demands. "I cook, I clean, I help earn the living. What do you mean, I don't love you?"

Can you imagine the problems that could accumulate over time if these two people never developed a common understanding of "love"?

In addition to this difference, what if the people in Paul's family never learned to discuss real problems or confront issues? What if they simply whisked them under the rug, pretending they didn't exist, essentially putting their heads in the sand? What if they never learned to really communicate because things were so positive and supportive? And what if Sally's family dealt with problems and differences either by fighting (yelling, screaming, blaming, and accusing) or "flighting" (taking off, slamming doors, or walking out)? On top of two altogether different nurturing experiences, they would have learned two altogether different approaches to solving their problems.

> *If you carefully consider the problems people face in marriage, you will find that in almost every case they arise out of conflicting role expectations and problem-solving strategies.*

Can you see why Sally and Paul could easily have struggles in their marriage? Can you see how each major difference compounds the problem? Can you see how the negative, hurt feelings produced by unsuccessfully dealing with these differences could easily feed on themselves, and how Sally and Paul's relationship could quickly deteriorate from one of attraction to one of accommodation, then to toleration, and finally to hostility?

In the midst of their conflict, society may say that they should break up, they should opt out. And in some cases where there are extreme abuses, perhaps that would be justified. But breaking up may bring about suffering that's even greater than the suffering we've just described. Can you see what a difference it would make to this couple to have a sense of shared vision, particularly if it was based on principles that provided a solid foundation for resolving and even rising above these differences?

If you carefully consider the problems people face in marriage, you will find that in almost every case they arise out of *conflicting role expectations* and are exacerbated by *conflicting problem-solving strategies*. A husband may think it's his wife's role to take care of the finances; after all, his mother did. And the wife may think that is her husband's role, since her father filled that role when she was growing up. This may not be a big problem until they try to solve it and their problem-solving scripts come to the surface. He is a "passive aggressive." He slowly boils inside and says nothing, but is continuously judging and becomes increasingly irritated. She is an "active aggressive." She wants to talk it out, thrash it out, fight it out. They get into a state of collusion, even codependency, with each other—with each needing the weaknesses of the other to validate his/her own perception and justify himself/herself. They both blame the other. Thus, a small problem becomes a large one; a molehill becomes a mountain. It may even become a mountain *range* because conflicting problem-solving scripts compound every problem and magnify every difference. Study your own marriage challenges and problems to see if they, too, are not fundamentally rooted in conflicting role expectations and compounded by conflicting problem-solving scripts.

Conflicting scripts most often reveal themselves in two closely related areas, and the gift of self-awareness is the key to understanding both. The first is in the area of values and goals—or the way things should be—and the second is in the area of assumptions about the way things are. These two areas are interrelated, since we usually define the way things are in terms of the way things should be. When we say we have a problem, we are basically saying things are not the way they should be. To one spouse the problem may be tragic; to the other, nonexistent.

> *The power of co-missioning is that it literally transcends "your way" or "my way." It creates a new way, a higher way—"our way."*

One spouse may think of "family" as a close-knit "nuclear" or two-generation family consisting only of parents and children, while to the other spouse the concept of "family" is intergenerational, involving a great deal of open communication, interaction, and activity with aunts and uncles, nieces and nephews, grandparents, and so forth. One person may be scripted into believing that love is a feeling, while the other person sees love as a verb. One may solve problems by fighting or flighting, while the other wants to communicate and talk them through. One may see differences as weaknesses, while the other sees differences as strengths. Where people stand on these issues tends to be a product of their experiences with the significant models of their lives, and in any marriage, these things need to be talked out and worked out.

This coming together—this sharing and agreeing upon role expectations, problem-solving strategies, vision and values in a relationship—is called "co-missioning." In other words, it's a commingling or joining of missions or purposes. It's binding them so that they have the same destination. And the power of it is that it literally transcends "your way" or "my way." It creates a new way, a higher way—"our way." It enables marriage partners to work together to explore differences and to resolve problems in ways that build the Emotional Bank Account and bring positive results.

This co-missioning between a husband and wife is so vital, so impactful in a relationship and in the family as a whole, you may discover—as we have—that even when you have a family mission statement that includes your children, you also want to maintain a "marriage mission statement" that reflects the unique relationship between you and your spouse.

If the two of you are older and your children are grown, you may want to ask different questions, such as these:

*What can we do to promote the growth and happiness
of our children and grandchildren?
What needs do they have that we can help fulfill?
What principles should govern our interaction with them?
In what ways can we appropriately be involved in their lives and their families?
How can we help them develop their own family mission statements?
How can we encourage them to deal with their challenges and problems within the
context of that statement?
How can we help them want to give back?*

When you raise your children, you're also raising your grandchildren. Patterns tend to persist.

You may also want to consider plans to create a three-generation mission statement. Think about activities that could include all three generations—vacations, holidays, and birthdays. Remember that it is never too late to start wise parenting of your grown children. They still need you. They will need you all their lives. When you raise your children, you're also raising your grandchildren. Patterns tend to persist. In fact, you often have a second shot at raising your children as you help raise your grandchildren.

A Mission Statement for Three or More

The importance of a mission statement becomes even more evident when there are children in the family. Now you have people who need to have a sense of belonging, who need to be taught and trained—people who will be influenced in many different ways through their growing-up years. And without some unifying sense of vision and values, they may well be bouncing off the walls with no sense of family identity or purpose. So, again, a family mission statement becomes supremely important.

When children are young, they generally love to be included in the process of creating the mission statement. They love sharing their ideas and helping to create something that gives them a sense of family identity.

Catherine (daughter):

Before my husband and I were married, we talked about what we wanted our home to be like, especially when we had children. Did we want it to be fun, relaxing, educational, etcetera? We talked about how we wanted to have honesty and integrity in our relationship, how we wanted our love to last, to never flicker and die. It was out of those discussions that we wrote our family mission statement.

We have three children now, and although our mission statement has remained fundamentally the same, it has changed a little with each child. Our first baby kind of threw us for a loop, and everything centered around her. But the next baby put us more in perspective, and we were able to step back and realize better how we wanted to raise our kids together—how we wanted them to be upstanding citizens in the community, to serve others, and so on.

The children have added things to the mission statement as well. Our oldest is only six. She says she wants to make sure we tell lots of jokes in our family, so we have added that little statement for her and for our three-year-old son.

Every New Year's Eve we sit down and work on our mission statement and write out our goals for the coming year. We find that our kids are very excited about the whole process. Then we put our mission statement on the fridge. The children continually refer to it. They say, "Mom, you're not supposed to raise your voice. Remember—happy, cheerful tones in our home." It's a big reminder.

A husband and father shared this experience:

About four years ago my wife and I, our two children, and my mother-in-law who lives with us created a family mission statement. Just recently we were reviewing that statement to see what we felt we needed to change.

In the course of the discussion, Sarah, our eleven-year-old, said something really important. She was talking about how one person can bring stress into the family, and it affects everyone else. I think she was particularly feeling this from Grandma, because Grandma is going through some things right now and tends to speak crossly to the kids when we're not around.

But when Sarah said it, she didn't say it about Grandma; she said it about the family. And Grandma caught onto it right away. She said, "You know, I really do that, and I want to improve." My wife and I quickly said, "You know, Grandma, we all do that. We all need to improve." And so one of the lines in our mission statement now reads, "We will recognize when we are experiencing stress in our lives and not pass it on to others."

I'm convinced that just going through the process itself is very healthy for a family because it provides a safe environment for people to share. And safe environments don't happen naturally in human behavior. The typical response is to be critical or defensive. But when you say, "Okay, we're going to talk about how we'd like our family to be," you create a safe space for people to express their feelings and ideas. It's non-threatening because you don't talk about people, you talk about issues.

What a wonderful experience for children—to know that their ideas and feelings are valued and that they are a vital part of making their family all that it can be!

Now, when teenagers are involved, the effort to create a family mission statement may be a little more complex. In fact, you may even initially meet with some resistance. In our own family we found that some of the older children were not really interested in the process at first. They wanted to hurry and get it over with. They didn't see the reason for taking so much time to talk about such serious things. But as we found ways to lighten it up and as we kept coming back to it, their interest grew.

Sean (son):

I think I was in high school when we did our family mission statement. I didn't really care about the words at the time. But the whole process of doing it—knowing that my parents had a vision and a target—gave me a sense of stability. I felt, Things are okay. My parents have things sorted out, and we're focused.

One father with older children shared this:

For my fiftieth birthday I decided to involve my two teenage daughters in the mission statement process by taking them with my wife and me to Hawaii for a "7 Habits Week." I thought we might spend about half of each day reading and discussing one of the 7 Habits, and the other half of the day having fun, playing on the beach, and doing other normal vacation kinds of things.

When I told my daughters what I had planned, they were less than enthusiastic.

"Oh, great! Spring break with my nose in a book. What will I tell my friends?"

"Is this another Daddy self-help kick that won't last?"

I remained undaunted. I said, "I promise to make it fun, and this is the birthday gift I really want. So are you both in?"

Two big sighs.

"Guess so," one replied. (Translation: "It won't last. We'll do the beach a lot. My tan will be a killer.")

"Guess so," the other one replied. (Translation: "Funniest thing I've ever heard. Oh, well, it's his present, so I'll humor him.")

"Great!" I replied. "I really appreciate my present." (Translation: "Oh, boy! What have I gotten myself into?")

As we boarded the plane, I handed them copies of 7 Habits and highlighters, and I settled back in my seat. It took a while, but eventually—in accordance with our agreement—copies of Glamour, Seventeen, and Sassy were put away, and they began to read. Questions began to surface.

"Uh . . . Daddy, what's a 'para-dig-em?'"

"That's pronounced 'para-dime,' and it means the way you see things—your perspective, your point of view."

"Daddy, I've read a couple of chapters, and it's really interesting. However, I wish to be 'proactive' and say that we don't need to discuss this twenty-four hours of each day."

I finally drifted off to sleep thinking there was something about all this I liked.

When we arrived on the island, we got settled and moved into a routine. We spent a certain time reading each day and a certain time playing at the beach. During meals we involved the girls in discussion about what they had read. Within three days everyone really began to sense the power of these ideas. They began to talk about them, even throughout the day.

On our final night there, we drafted our family mission statement. I gathered the important tools: pen, paper, and popcorn. "Family, time to express our mission," I began optimistically. "This mission statement must contain what each of us expects from this family. Anyone want to begin?"

They didn't hesitate. Convinced I really wanted their expectations, they openly offered suggestions. I was reminded of what usually happens when I ask what they want for Christmas. This was their creation, not merely something we dictated. No suggestion was dismissed lightly. This was important business, and we treated the process with respect.

We enjoyed talking together about what we really wanted our family to be. We worked hard to create a mission statement that truly expressed everyone's deepest values and desires. After we completed the task, I asked, "Does everyone feel this statement has in it what we want and expect?"

One daughter replied, "It's a very good family mission statement."

My other daughter said, "That was fun. Everyone's ideas are equal."

My wife said, "We nailed it!"

On the way home the girls commented on how the experience had caused them to think more deeply. One of them said, "Dad, your birthday present was a gift to us!"

Sometime later this man told me, "I do not have the words to describe the impact this has had on all of us as individuals and on our family." When I asked him to give me an illustration, he said:

Shortly after we returned home, my wife and I needed to be away for a few days. I asked the children if they would like someone to stay with them during our absence. I will never forget their response: "Put our family mission statement on the refrigerator. We'll have principles to guide us while you're gone."

He said that that was just one of a multitude of ways in which their mission statement had positively influenced their lives.

If your family includes children living at home, you may want to call a "family meeting" to introduce the idea and start the mission statement process. If so, be sure to make it fun and enjoyable. With young children, you may want to use colored markers and posters, and serve a treat. Remember that young children have a short attention span. Spending ten fun minutes together each week over a period of several weeks will be much more effective than trying to hold long, philosophical discussions.

Older children may prefer more involved discussions. But again, make it fun. Perhaps spread it out over several weeks. You may want to have notebooks and pencils on hand, or to just talk and have one person write down ideas. Whatever the situation, make sure everyone feels comfortable and free to participate.

If you feel there may be resistance from older children, you might prefer to begin by talking informally at a family dinner about what is important and not even mention the mission statement kinds of words. Or you might decide to discuss the idea privately, one on one, with family members—maybe when you're working on a project or doing something together. You might want to ask family members privately how they feel about the family and what they'd like to see happen in it. In this way you can engage their minds in thinking about the family and get the idea into both their conscious and unconscious minds. Be patient. It may take weeks of one-on-one discussions and building up to it before you feel you can all talk about it together.

When you do feel the time is right, get everyone together to talk it over. Make sure it's at a time when you feel good and you sense that your family does also. Don't try to do it when you feel emotionally wiped out, exhausted, or angry, or you're in the middle of some family crisis. Again, you could even do this at a family dinner or on a family vacation. Take time. Make it fun. And if you sense too much resistance, back off. You can talk about it another day. Be patient. Have faith in the people and in the process. Give it time.

When you do reach a point where you can discuss these family issues, be explicit about the idea that you want to come up with a mission statement to serve as a unifying and motivating influence for everyone in the family. Ask questions that will help family members engage all their unique human gifts, such as:

What is the purpose of our family?
What kind of family do we want to be?
What kinds of things do we want to do?
What kind of feeling do we want to have in our home?
What kind of relationships do we want to have with one another?
How do we want to treat one another and speak to one another?
What things are truly important to us as a family?
What are our family's highest priority goals?
What are the unique talents, gifts, and abilities of family members?
What are our responsibilities as family members?
What are the principles and guidelines we want our family to follow?
Who are our heroes? What is it about them that we like and would like to emulate?
What families inspire us and why do we admire them?
How can we contribute to society as a family and become more service-oriented?

As you discuss these questions, you will probably hear a variety of responses. Remember that *everybody in the family is important. Everybody's ideas are important.* You may have to deal with all kinds of positive and negative expressions. Don't judge them. Respect them. Let them be expressed freely. Don't try to resolve everything. All you're doing at this point is preparing minds and hearts to think reflectively. In a sense you're preparing the ground and beginning to sow a few seeds. Don't try to get the harvest yet.

You'll find that these discussions probably go better if you set up three ground rules:

First, listen with respect. Make sure everyone has a chance to give input. Remember that involvement in the process is as important as the product. Unless people feel that they have had some say in the formation of the vision and values that will govern them, guide them, lead them, and measure their progress, they will not be committed. In other words, "no involvement, no commitment." So be sure that everyone knows his or her ideas will be heard and recognized as important. Help children understand what it means to show respect while others are speaking. Assure them that others, in turn, will show respect for their ideas.

> *No involvement, no commitment.*

Second, restate accurately to show you understand. One of the best ways to show respect is to restate others' points to their satisfaction. Then encourage other family members to also restate the ideas that are expressed—particularly when there are disagreements—to the satisfaction of the other. As family members do this for each other, mutual understanding will soften hearts and release creative energies.

Third, consider writing down the ideas. Perhaps you'd like to invite someone to be the family scribe. Ask that person to write down all the ideas that are expressed. Don't evaluate the ideas. Don't judge them. Don't compare their relative worth. Those are tasks for further down the road. Just capture them so that everyone's ideas are "out on the table" and visible to all.

Then you can begin the refinement process. You'll find that the greatest struggle in doing mission statements is prioritizing destinations and values—in other words, deciding what is the highest purpose and the highest value, and then the next highest and the next. This is tough duty.

I attended a conference of Asian leaders in Bangkok, where research was presented showing the prioritization of values in the Western world compared to the Asian world. People from both areas of the world said they valued cooperation and teamwork, but it was a low value in the Western world and a high value in the Eastern world. Interestingly, the Asian leaders were very anxious not to lose that value and go the Western way, which focused primarily on independence, freedom of action, and individuality.

Now, I'm not attempting to deal with the question of which value is right or should be the highest. I'm only trying to demonstrate that the real heart of the challenge in developing mission statements is in prioritizing these things.

One way that I have seen this challenge dealt with effectively in the family is for people to write down their top five values and then eliminate them one at a time until they are down to one. This way, people are forced to think through what really matters most to them. This itself can be a great teaching process, since family members may also come to discover that integrity is greater than loyalty, honor is greater than moods, principles are greater than values, mission is greater than baggage, leadership is greater than management, effectiveness is greater than efficiency, and imagination is more powerful than conscious willpower activity.

The very process of exploring what your family is all about can bring other powerful benefits to the family culture as well. Mission statements focus on possibilities, not on limitations. Instead of arguing for your weaknesses, in a sense you're arguing for what is possible, for what you can visualize. Whatever you argue for eventually becomes yours. Notice that the great literature, the great movies, and the great art—the kind that really inspire and edify—essentially focus on vision and possibilities and on tapping into our most noble motives and impulses, our highest self.

> *Mission statements focus on possibilities, not on limitations.*

And just think about the impact on the Emotional Bank Account! If nothing else were to be gained from this process, the mere act of spending the time, of listening to one another, and of relating on such a deep level would make tremendous deposits. Think about what it communicates to family members about their individual worth and the value of their ideas.

This process can also be very enjoyable. Initially, it may feel a little uncomfortable. It may throw people a little out of their comfort zone because they've never become involved with others in such deep, reflective discussion. But as they do become involved, a kind of excitement begins to develop. The communication becomes very authentic and the bonding becomes very deep. And slowly, almost imperceptibly perhaps, within the hearts and minds of family members, the substance of the mission statement itself begins to come into focus.

Step Two: Write Your Family Mission Statement

With ideas out on the table, you're now ready to have someone in the family refine and distill and pull them all together into some kind of expression that will reflect the collective feeling of the hearts and minds of those who have contributed.

In one sense, it is extremely important to get this expression down on paper. The very process of writing brings a crystallization of thought and distills learning and insights into words. It also imprints the brain and reinforces learning, and it makes the expression visible and available to everyone in the family.

In another sense, writing a mission statement on paper is not as powerful as writing it in the hearts and minds of family members. But the two are not mutually exclusive. One can lead to the other.

Let me emphasize here that whatever you come up with at first will be a *rough draft*—possibly the first of many drafts. Family members will need to look at it, think about it, live with it, discuss it, make changes. They will need to work with it until everyone comes to agreement: "This is what this family is about. This is our mission. We believe it. We buy into it. We are ready to commit to live it."

The following are examples of family mission statements that have gone through this process—including our own, which is first. As you can tell, each statement is unique, and each reflects the values and beliefs of those who wrote it. These are not intended to be models for your mission statement. Yours would reflect your own hopes, values, and beliefs.

Perhaps you will feel—as we do—a sense of deep respect and appreciation for the very personal sharing by those who have given permission for us to print their mission statements.

The mission of our family is to create a nurturing place of faith, order, truth, love, happiness, and relaxation, and to provide opportunity for each individual to become responsibly independent, and effectively interdependent, in order to serve worthy purposes in society.

Our family mission is to:
Value honesty with ourselves and others.
Create an environment where each of us can find support and encouragement in achieving our life's goals.
Respect and accept each person's unique personality and talents.
Promote a loving, kind, and happy atmosphere.
Support family endeavors that better society.
Maintain patience through understanding.
Always resolve conflicts with each other rather than harboring anger.
Promote the realization of life's treasures.

Our family mission:
To love each other...
To help each other...
To believe in each other...
To wisely use our time, talents, and resources to bless others...
To worship together...
Forever.

Our home will be a place where our family, friends, and guests find joy, comfort, peace, and happiness. We will seek to create a clean and orderly environment that is livable and comfortable. We will exercise wisdom in what we choose to eat, read, see, and do at home. We want to teach our children to love, learn, laugh, and to work and develop their unique talents.

Our family is happy and has fun together.
We all feel secure and feel a sense of belonging.
We support each other fully in our seen and unseen potential.
We show unconditional love in our family and inspiration for each other.
We are a family where we can continually grow in mental, physical, social/emotional, and spiritual ways.
We discuss and discover all aspects of life.
We nurture all life forms and protect the environment.
We are a family that serves each other and the community.
We are a family of cleanliness and order.
We believe that diversity of race and culture is a gift.
We appreciate the grace of God.
We hope to leave a legacy of the strength and importance of families.

Keep in mind that a mission statement doesn't have to be some big, formal document. It can even be a word or a phrase, or something creative and entirely different such as an image or a symbol. I know of some families who have written a family song that embodies what matters most to them. Others have captured a sense of vision through poetry and art. I have known of families who have structured their mission statement by building phrases around each letter of their last name. There's even one family I know of that gets a powerful sense of vision from a four-foot stick! This stick goes straight for some distance and then suddenly corkscrews and gnarls at the end. This serves as a reminder to this family that "when you pick up one end of the stick, you pick up the other." In other words, the choices you make have consequences, so make your choices carefully.

So you see, it doesn't have to be some magnificent verbal expression. The only real criterion is that it represent everyone in the family and inspire you and bring you together. And whether your mission statement is a word, a page, or a document, whether it's written in poetry or prose, music or art, if it captures and gives cohesion to what is in the hearts and minds of family members, it will inspire, energize, and unify your family in ways that are so marvelous, you have to experience them in order to believe.

> *A* mission statement doesn't have to be some big, formal document. It can even be a word or a phrase, or something creative and entirely different such as an image or a symbol.

Step Three: Use It to Stay on Track

A mission statement is not some "to do" to check off your list. It's meant to be the literal constitution of your family life. And just as the United States Constitution has survived for more than two hundred sometimes turbulent years, your family constitution can be the foundational document that will unify and hold your family together for decades—even generations—to come.

We'll talk more about how to turn your mission statement into a constitution in Habit 3. But for now I just want to mention this step and to summarize all the steps by showing you how one father from a blended family applied this three-step process. He said:

> We created our family mission statement over a period of several weeks.
>
> The first week we called the four children together and said, "Look, if we're all going in different directions and we're always fighting with one another, things aren't going to go very smoothly." We told them that things would be much easier if we all shared the same value system. So we gave everyone five three-by-five cards and said, "Just write down one word on each card that you would use to describe this family."
>
> When we sorted through the cards and eliminated the duplications, that left us with twenty-eight different words. So the next week we had everybody define what those words meant so that we could understand what they really had in mind. For example, our eight-

year-old daughter had written the word "cool" on one of her cards. She wanted to have a "cool" family. So we encouraged her to explain to us what a "cool" family would be like. Eventually everyone's definitions were clarified, so there was deep understanding.

The next week we put all the words on a big flip chart and gave everyone ten votes. They could use up to three votes per item if they wished, but they could not spend more than ten votes in total. After the vote, we were left with about ten items that were important to everyone.

The following week we voted again on the ten items, and we got the list down to six. Then we broke up into three groups, and each group wrote one or two phrases about two of the words, defining what they meant. We came back together and read our phrases to the others.

The next week we discussed the phrases. We clarified them. We made sure they said what we wanted to say. We made them grammatically correct. And we turned them into our mission statement:

> Our family mission:
> To always be kind, respectful, and supportive of each other,
> To be honest and open with each other,
> To keep a spiritual feeling in the home,
> To love each other unconditionally,
> To be responsible to live a happy, healthy, and fulfilling life,
> To make this house a place we want to come home to.

It was really great because from start to finish we had involvement. The mission statement was their words and their sentences, and they could see that.

We put the statement in a beautiful frame and hung it over the fireplace. We said, "Okay, now anyone who can memorize this statement gets the big candy bar of their choice."

Every week we have somebody share what one of those words or sentences means to him or her. It only takes two or three minutes, but it makes the mission statement come alive. We're also setting goals around the mission statement, making it a central part of our lives.

This mission statement process has been tremendously helpful to us. In a normal family you tend to assume certain behaviors. But when you're blending a family, you're coming in with two sets of ideas about how to raise children in the first place. Our mission statement has really given us some structure, some common values and a common focus on where we're going.

Two of the most powerful psychological forces that imprint the brain are writing and visualizing, both of which are involved in this mission statement process. When these activities are consciously done, the content rapidly translates itself into the subconscious mind and to the deeper parts of the heart, helping you to stay on track.

Both processes cause people to crystallize their thinking. And if all the senses are employed in the processes, this crystallization becomes laserlike. It literally imprints the brain or etches into the brain the content and feeling embodied in the writing or the visualizing. And this enables you to translate the mission to the moments of daily living.*

The Power of a Family Mission Statement

Many families talk about how, over time, the mission statement has a profound impact on children—particularly when they feel their input is welcome and genuinely affects the direction the family will take.

And it has a profound impact on parents as well. With proper involvement in the process of creating a mission statement, you'll find that it will overcome the fear of parenting, of being decisive. You won't fall into the trap of trying to win a popularity contest with your kids. You also won't take rebellion or rejection personally simply because you're emotionally dependent on your children's acceptance. You won't get into the state of collusion that many parents do wherein they feel validated by the weaknesses of their children and look about for friendly, sympathetic allies who will agree with them and massage their hearts and make them feel that they're okay and it's their "bratty kids" who aren't.

With a clear sense of shared vision and values, you can be very demanding when it comes to standards. You can have the courage to hold your children accountable and to let them experience the consequences of their actions. Ironically, you will also become more loving and empathic as you respect the individuality of each child and allow your children to be self-regulating, to make their own decisions within the scope of their experience and wisdom.

> *With proper involvement in the process of creating a mission statement, you'll find that you won't fall into the trap of trying to win a popularity contest with your kids.*

In addition, a mission statement will create a powerful bonding between parents and children, between husbands and wives, that simply does not exist when there's no sense of shared vision and values. It's like the difference between a diamond and a piece of graphite. They are both made of the same material, but a diamond is the hardest of all substances while graphite can be split apart. The difference lies in the depth of bonding in the atoms.

*For additional examples of family mission statements and a worksheet to help you develop your own, call (44) 0121-604-6999 or visit www.franklincovey.com on the Internet.

A father shared this experience:

Some time ago I was thinking about my role as a father and envisioning how I wanted to be remembered by my kids. So when we planned our vacation that summer, I decided to apply the principle of vision to the family. We came up with a sort of family mission statement for the event. We called it the "Smith Team." It described for us the perspective we wanted to take when we went off together on our trip.

We each took a particular role that would help contribute to building the Smith Team. My six-year-old daughter chose the role of family cheerleader. Her goal was to be an influence to dispel any contention in the family, particularly while we were traveling together in the car. She made up several cheers, and whenever there was a problem, she would break into one of them: "Smiths! Smiths! Driving down the street! When we stick together, we can't be beat!" Whether or not we felt like it, we'd all have to join in, and it was very helpful in dispelling the bad feeling that might have been there.

We also had matching T-shirts. At one point we went into a service station, and the attendant wasn't paying much attention. But when he looked up and we were all standing there with our matching shirts, he did a double take and said, "Hey, you guys look like a team!" That just kind of cemented it. We looked at one another and felt an incredible high. We got back in the car and took off, windows down, radio cranked up, ice cream melting in the backseat. We were a family!

About three months after we got back from our vacation, our three-year-old son was diagnosed with leukemia. This threw our family into months of challenge. The interesting thing was that whenever we took our son to the hospital for his chemotherapy treatments, he would always ask if he could wear his shirt. Maybe it was his way of connecting with the team and feeling the support and the memories he had around the experiences of being together on that family vacation.

After his sixth treatment he caught a serious infection that put him in intensive care for two weeks. We came very close to losing him, but he pulled through. He wore that T-shirt almost nonstop through those days, and it was covered with stains of vomit, blood, and tears. When he finally did pull through and we brought him home, we all wore our family T-shirts in his honor. We all wanted to connect to that family mission feeling we had created on our vacation.

That vision of the Smith Team helped us through what was the greatest challenge our family had ever faced.

A divorced mother of four shared this experience:

Twenty years ago my husband moved out, and I was left with four children—ages four, six, eight, and ten. For a while I absolutely lost it. I was devastated. For several days I just lay in bed and cried all day. The pain was so deep. And I was so frightened of what lay ahead for us. I didn't know how I was going to do it. There were times I would just go from one hour to the next and think, "Well, I didn't cry in this hour. Let's see if I can not cry the next hour." And this was very hard on the children because their dad had just moved out of the house and for a while they thought their mom was "gone," too.

It was the children that finally gave me the strength to pull through. I realized that if I didn't get my act together, not only was I going down the tubes but I would be taking four precious people with me. And so they were my real motivation, the reason for my conscious choice.

I began to realize that I needed a new vision. We were no longer a "traditional" family. And since our family no longer "looked" the same—it no longer looked like the family we had been and had thought we were always going to be—I needed to change the "look."

So we talked together about this new family structure. We made some fundamental decisions. It was okay if we went to church meetings or to school plays. We were missing an integral part—there was no denying that—but that was okay. We could still do the good things. We could still have the values, the principles, the happy things in life almost as well.

I had to come to a place with my own personal feelings about the children's dad where I could value his goodness and still allow those things I didn't agree with. I didn't want to forgive him. I didn't want to allow the children to go with him and do things with him. But my higher conscience, my better self, told me that that kind of attitude wasn't going to work out in the end. I knew that my hatred and anger would eat away at me and destroy my family. And so I prayed for courage. I prayed for the desire to want to do what was right, because if I could at least want to do it, then it wouldn't be so hard.

It wasn't easy. There were times when I was so angry I actually wanted to kill the man—especially when his choices kept hurting the children. But over the years I was able to work through my anger, and I finally reached the point where I could care for this man almost like a brother. I began to look at him not as my former husband, not as the father of my children, but as a man who made some really tragic mistakes.

Now each of the children has had crises with their dad, and each has come to the point of letting go of having the dad he or she had always wanted and envisioned. They've all come to the point where they can value the goodness and still allow him to have his imperfections that are so painful. They know now that they have to deal with their dad as he is, not how they wish he would be, because he's not that person—not now, maybe never.

What helped us most was in coming up with a new end in mind. We created a new vision of what our family would be.

> The family mission statement literally becomes the DNA of family life.

In both of these situations, notice the power this sense of shared vision and values had in keeping the family focused and together—even in the midst of challenge. That's the power of a family mission statement. It literally becomes the DNA of family life. It's like the chromosomal

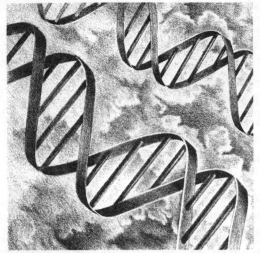

structure inside each cell of the body that represents the blueprint for the operation of the entire body. Because of this DNA, every cell is, in a sense, a hologram of the entire body. And the DNA defines not only the function of that cell but also how it relates to every other cell as well.

Creating shared vision creates deep bonding, a sense of unity in purpose, a deep, burning "yes!" that is so powerful, so cohesive, so motivating that it literally pulls people together with a purpose strong enough to transcend the obstacles, the challenges of daily living, the negative scripting of the past, and even the accumulated baggage of the present.

"Love" Is a Commitment

Now why does a family mission statement have that kind of power? A forty-three-year-old woman who married for the first time said this:

To me the family mission statement gives a practical, concrete, and doable aspect to what love really is. Love is certainly the roses and the dinners out and the romantic vacations. But it's also the hugs and the bathrobes and getting the morning paper for each other or making the coffee or feeding the guinea pigs. It's in the details as well as the symphony.

I think the mission statement is a way of making that commitment real. And I think the process of doing it can be as valuable as the ultimate product, because it's the working together to create that vision and make it real that defines and refines and grows love.

A wife and mother in a blended family shared this:

I think the difference in having a family mission statement is that you have a set of rules or principles that commit you, that don't make it easy for you to cop out. Had I had this kind of grounding, I probably would have dealt with my first relationship differently. There just wasn't a sense of shared vision and commitment that I could put my arms around and say, "Why should I stay in this marriage? What can I do to make it work?" Instead it was, "I've had it. I'm done. I'm out of here." And it was over. There was never that sense of real commitment to a common vision.

But things are different now. Take my relationship with Bonnie, for example. She's not my "stepdaughter," she's my daughter. The only "steps" we have in our family are out the back door and up to the second floor. We made an agreement: "There are no steps in this family. We are all one. We were all created equal. We all have equal say in this family. Whether you are here full-time or part-time is insignificant."

With our personalities and our working styles, I think it would be very easy for a family like ours to disintegrate, to become dysfunctional. But this sense of shared vision has given us the strength and commitment to stay together as a family, to act like a family, to be a family.

Again, remember: Love is a verb. It's also a commitment. A family mission statement makes explicit what that commitment means.

As we observed in Habit 1, the most fundamental promises we make to other human beings are those we make to the members of our family—in our marriage vows, in our implicit promises to care for and nurture our children. Through a family mission statement you can let your children know that you are totally committed to them, that you have been from the very moment of their birth or adoption, that the bond has never been broken and never will be broken, and that nothing can happen that will ever break it. You can say to them, "My commitment is not a function of your behavior or attitude or commitment to me. It is total and complete. My love will always be there. You will always be in my heart. I will never betray you. I will never leave you. I will always be true to you no matter what you do. This is something I want you to know, and I will continue to tell you this through both my words and my actions. My commitment is total, and my love is unconditional."

> *Through a family mission statement you can let your children know that you are totally committed to them, that you have been from the very moment of their birth or adoption.*

When children feel this level of commitment—and when it's communicated consistently through words and actions—they are then willing to live with limits, to accept responsibility and be accountable for their actions. But when the price has not been paid in making the deep decisions that are contained in these mission statements, parents can easily be uprooted by the social forces and by the pressures they will continually get against taking the responsible course, moving toward interdependency, maintaining standards in the home, and carrying out agreed upon consequences.

Creating a family mission statement enables you and your family to examine, clarify, and renew those promises—and to keep them constantly before you so that those commitments become written in your mind and your heart, and affect the way you live your life every day.

Strengthening the Extended Family

As you can tell from the stories we've shared, family mission statements provide strength and direction for families of every configuration: two-parent families, single-parent families, blended families, and so on. They can also provide purpose and strength to relationships in the extended and intergenerational family as well. One husband and father said this:

As I worked on a personal mission statement, one important thing that emerged was how I felt about my extended family—about my brother and my sisters and their children. I remember as a child watching some of the major wars between my mom and dad. There were times when my dad broke everything in the house—just threw everything he could find, shattering things against walls. It seemed that there were hundreds of nights that my mom would stand at the window crying. And that really left some impressions on me.

I don't know exactly what influence that had in my sisters' lives, but they've married either very dominant or very passive men—no middle-of-the-road, regular-type men—and some of the marriages haven't worked out.

So as I thought about my mission statement, I felt a real sense of responsibility concerning their children and a great desire to give them a good role model. And every week when I review my mission statement, I think very seriously about what I could be doing for a nephew or a niece.

His wife added:

This has helped him become a real transition person in his family. Not only has he stopped a culture of alcoholism and emotional abuse, but he has also set a really high standard of education and contribution for his nieces and nephews. He will go to them and say, "Okay, you don't have the grades you need to get into college, so what are you going to do about it?"

We try to have nieces and nephews over often, and they notice what we do in our family. We don't watch TV at night. School is really important. We have our kids in music and sports. They see us working toward long-range goals, and it has an effect.

Notice how this man's sense of vision and values enabled him to take a positive, proactive role in his extended family. He has become an agent of change. He's working from the inside out. And what kind of difference is this going to make in the lives of his nephews and nieces?

There's no end to the good you can do in your family when you have a clear vision of your destination, your role, and your opportunity. Just think about the opportunity for grandparents, for example. Grandparents can take a vital and active role in unifying their children and grandchildren. My brother John and his wife Jane were both parents and grandparents when they developed their mission statement. They had married children living in different parts of the country as well as some children living at home. They spent eighteen months communicating with them in various ways, and they finally came up with this single phrase that embodies the essence of all they were thinking and feeling: "No empty chairs."

> "No empty chairs."

Those three simple words have profound meaning to them. They are code words. Behind them are many deep discussions and interactions concerning the spirit of unconditional love and commitment that family members have for one another. "We're going to help each other. We're not going to let anyone fail. We're going to pray for each other. We're going to serve each other. We're going to forgive each other. We're not going to hold grudges. We're not going to be offended."

Just think of the power of that kind of commitment in the intergenerational family! Think of the impact those words are going to have on aunts, uncles, and cousins as the family continues to grow.

But you don't have to be a parent or a grandparent to initiate an intergenerational family mission statement. Grown-up siblings can also become agents of change.

One man shared this:

Some time ago my dad called and suggested that our entire family get together and take a vacation. My parents were in Virginia, one sister and her husband were in Ohio, and another sister and brother were in Utah, so we were pretty spread out.

At that time I was deep into the 7 Habits material and thought it would be great if we could write an extended family mission statement. So before the vacation, I wrote to everyone. I explained what a mission statement was and included some material on how to write one. I asked each of them to come with a draft in hand.

One of the things I was really excited about in writing this mission statement was to redefine our relationships with each other. I was convinced that we had assigned labels to everyone that were not valid anymore. "Oh, Johnny—he's the happy-go-lucky guy. He's really nice, but you can't always depend on him. Jenny is the complainer. She's always going to be whining about this or that. David's going to whine, but he'll do whatever it is he's whining about." On and on it went with everyone in the family. These labels may have been true when we were twelve or thirteen, but they didn't fit anymore. And so the first night we were together, we talked about it.

It was an incredible night. We made copies of everyone's mission statement drafts and distributed them. As each person read his or her draft, we marked our favorite lines. It was really amazing how different the approaches were. My brother had written his as a beautiful poem. My father's was a paragraph. Mine was three pages. Every one was unique.

Out of the twelve drafts we came up with a family motto and had it printed on T-shirts. We didn't complete the mission statement at that point, but we did make significant progress.

Probably the most amazing thing about the whole experience was the impact of the process itself. One of the most immediate benefits came later during that vacation when the beautiful, luxurious-looking motel Mom had picked out from a brochure turned out to be a "dive." Before, this would have sent everyone into a tailspin of silent misery. But the mission statement experience allowed us to communicate openly, and in a matter of thirty minutes we saved the vacation. I'm convinced it was a result of the family togetherness we felt.

Also, as a result of that mission statement work, several families ended up moving back to be close to Mom and Dad. We decided that family was more important than money or location. In fact, we even decided that we would love to run a business together. We realized there are a lot of challenges that come along with that, but we felt it would give us the chance to know one another better. So we packed up our things and moved hundreds of miles to be together.

Before this mission statement experience, it was like "Hey, we'll see you at Christmas!" But now we realize we want our kids to grow up close to one another. We want them to know their grandparents. It's begun a new era in our family.

Notice how, even though he wasn't the parent in this family, this man accepted a proactive leadership role. Notice how he worked in his Circle of Influence and created an experience that bonded and unified the entire family. Now what kind of difference is this going to make to the entire family in years to come?

The reality is that it all comes back to you—what's going on inside your mind and heart and the proactive choices you're making to create family change.

I will never forget an experience I had with a group of parents on the East Coast of the United States. These parents were also presidents of companies, and they had brought their spouses and teenage children with them to attend this family conference. The whole purpose of the three-day conference was to learn how to develop a family mission statement.

For the first day and a half we focused almost entirely on building relationships. We worked on learning to listen to one another and expressing ourselves in ways that affirm and show value to others, rather than belittling them or making them feel put down or embarrassed.

As we moved into the afternoon of the second day, I began to focus on creating a family mission statement. They had already done a great deal of work and reading on the subject prior to the conference. But as we came to the question and answer session at the end of the day, I could tell that these people were really struggling.

They were bright—very bright. They had tremendous talent and capacity. They had accomplished great things in their professions. But they had an underlying problem: Despite their expressions to the contrary, many of them simply did not assign high priority to marriage and family in their own lives. They had a deep habituation and commitment to a working style where the family was essentially a sideshow to the main tent of career. They had basically come to the conference expecting to learn quick-fix techniques that would enable them to rebuild their family relationships and create a great family culture so that they could check "family" off their "to do" list and get back to focusing on their professions.

I tried to connect with them on a different level. I confronted them as forcefully and directly as I felt I could with this question: "Suppose you had a new product you wanted to introduce that you felt had great potential, and you wanted to carry on a nationwide marketing program to do it. Would that excite you? Would you do what was necessary to accomplish the task? Or what if you had a competitor move in on your territory and take away a sizable hunk of your business. Would you be determined to take immediate steps to remedy the situation? Or what if one of your services or products was being unusually accepted in one test market, and you had a two-year lead time on your competitors. Would that turn your talents and energies on? How would you organize yourself to capitalize on that situation as far as you possibly could?"

Almost to a person, they knew what they needed to do—or if they didn't know, they indicated that they would soon find out. It would become a high-priority item, and they would organize their life to do whatever was necessary to accomplish the desired result. They would make sacrifices. They would put aside lesser projects. They would enlist others to give them help. They would bring to bear their full talent, expertise, experience, skill, wisdom, and dedication in doing whatever was necessary to make a success out of the project.

I then changed this line of reasoning and questioning to their marriages and families. If there had been any doubt before, there was none now. It became clear—almost embarrassingly obvious to virtually everyone there—that the fundamental problem and the source of almost every other problem was the fact that they had never really come to grips with the priority of family in their personal lives.

These men and women became sobered and very thoughtful. Their failure to succeed in this family effort drove them to really examine their own personal lives. As they did so, they came to the realization that family was not just some sideshow. It was tremendously important to them. And they began to realize that "success" in this area of their lives was not a matter of technique and a quick fix; it was based on the long-term principles that govern in every dimension of life.

It was at this point that the entire nature of the meeting changed. They began to really tap into their talents and creativity and apply them to their marriage and family life. They began to look to solid, even long-term principles instead of quick fixes and techniques for the solutions to their problems. They began to think of organizing around the things that really mattered.

Notice how their failure to pull their families together in this mission statement experience drove these people back into their own minds and hearts. Until they had their own priorities straight deep inside, they were not able to work effectively on the family level. But once they had their priorities clear, their own inner victory led to victory in the family.

There's no way around the fact that in Habit 2—as in every other effort to improve the family—success comes from the inside out. You may well find that the challenge of creating your family mission statement will drive you to the need to develop your own personal mission statement because this is where, in your own heart and mind, you really hammer out the jugular issues of life. As it says in Proverbs, "Keep thy heart with all diligence, for out of it [are] the issues of life."

A clear sense of personal vision can be an enormous help to you—or any member of your family, including even young children—in knowing and doing what really matters most.

I had one counselor share with me the success he had in using mission statements to work with a nine-year-old boy who was having severe behavioral problems. This boy was of the opinion that he could get anything he wanted by bullying people. He would throw other children around the playground, and he created a lot of problems with other children and their parents who were understandably upset by this boy's behavior.

But instead of telling this boy what to do, this counselor taught him the principle of proactivity. He tapped into this boy's unique human gifts. He helped him come up with a personal mission statement of how he wanted to live his life and what he wanted to do. This sense of purpose and vision became so powerful in this nine-year-old boy's life that he turned around 180 degrees. He was able to see the bigger picture and how his behavior affected others. Within a couple of months the counselor said this boy had became a "model citizen."

One father said this:

I used to find myself being quite loud, abrupt, stark, and a little bit gruff. But when I wrote my mission statement, I realized that I needed to create more of a calming, reassuring tone in the home. And this has made such a difference! Now I try to use a softer tone of voice, and I try not to dominate the conversation.

My mission statement helps me maintain perspective. It's so easy to react when you have small children. And it's so easy not to take time to think about how that's going to affect them.

But now when I'm in the middle of a situation, I try to stop and think: Is this something that really matters? I find I can justify being strong with the children only if it's some-

thing that really affects their life. I realize now that when I overreact to a cup of spilled milk or crayon on the wall, it doesn't do them any good.

As Benjamin Franklin said so beautifully:

We stand at the crossroads, each minute, each hour, each day, making choices. We choose the thoughts we allow ourselves to think, the passions we allow ourselves to feel, and the actions we allow ourselves to perform. Each choice is made in the context of whatever value system we've selected to govern our lives. In selecting that value system, we are, in a very real way, making the most important choice we will ever make.[4]

In summary, you may well find that the challenge of creating a family mission statement will drive you to do the inner work you need to do to have your own vision and values clear. You may also discover that this challenge will drive you back into your relationship with your spouse—this very fundamental relationship out of which everything else in the family grows. If you don't have shared vision and values there, it's going to be very difficult to create them in the family. So you may also want to spend time creating a "marriage mission statement" to make certain that you and your spouse are headed down the same path.

Three "Watch Outs"

As you work on your family mission statement, you will want to keep three important "watch outs" in mind:

1. Don't "announce" it. Involving everyone on the level we're talking about takes time and patience. You may be tempted to just write a mission statement yourself or create it with your spouse and then announce it to your children. But *don't do it!* If the members of your family don't feel that the mission statement represents them, they won't support it. As one mother said, "Everyone has to feel a sense of ownership in the mission statement. Otherwise, it's like when you ask people, 'When was the last time you washed a rental car?' If it's not yours, you don't take care of it the same." So take the time to make sure that everyone is involved and committed. Except for little children, remember: "No involvement, no commitment." With little children, identification (emotional bonding) is even more powerful than involvement.

It's like when you ask people, "When was the last time you washed a rental car?" If it's not yours, you don't take care of it the same.

2. Don't rush it. If you try to rush your family through this, they'll let you have your way just to get it done so that they can get on to other things. But the finished statement will not reflect their feelings, and they'll have little allegiance to it. Again, *the process is as important as the product*. It requires deep and genuine involvement, listening to one another, and working together to make sure the mission statement represents the thoughts and feelings of everyone involved.

3. Don't ignore it. Remember, "Begin with the end in mind" is a *habit* of effective families, not an *event*. The actual writing of a mission statement is only the beginning. The richest fruits come as you translate that mission into the very fabric of your family life, into the moments of your day-to-day living. And to do that you must keep it constantly before you, reflect upon it, and use it as the literal constitution of your family life. You might want to print it up and give everyone a copy, keep a copy in your purse or wallet, or frame it and put it on the wall. One family made a plaque and hung it by their doorbell. It read: "Inside this house are the sounds of love and the spirit of service." With all the frequent comings and goings, this acted as a constant reminder to everyone of the kind of family they were striving to be.

Remember the Chinese Bamboo Tree

You'll also want to remember the Chinese bamboo tree. One father shared this fascinating account of the difference a mission statement and the 7 Habits framework made as he and his wife worked with a difficult daughter for many years.

About five years ago our bright, musically talented daughter had just gone into the seventh grade. She began hanging around with kids who had failed a few grades and were into drugs. At that time, we tried to get her to buy into a family mission statement with no effect.

In an effort to help her, we took her out of public school and put her into Catholic school through the eighth grade. We didn't allow her to hang out with kids from the old school. We even went as far as moving to another part of town. But despite heavy day-to-day teacher and parent involvement and holding her accountable for her behavior, her grades continued to deteriorate. She began to call her old friends and occasionally meet with them. She became very disrespectful toward her mother. We tried all forms of giving and taking away privileges for behavior without any effect. We finally sent her to Outward Bound with a group of kids sponsored by a local church.

During this time my wife and I wrote a marriage mission statement. We spent about an hour a day listening to each other, and we got serious about our personal mission statements. We kept coming back to the principle of choice and to the core values we would live by—come what may with our daughter.

When she refused to go to private school for high school, we moved from Texas to New Jersey, where we had relatives. We moved from a suburb community to a five-acre country environment in a wealthy part of the state with excellent public schools and very few drug problems. She began the ninth grade there and almost immediately had problems at school. Under pressure from others that we "weren't doing enough," we tried various forms of "tough love" with no positive effect. Our daughter began to cut herself and threatened to run away and commit suicide.

The school recommended that she join a group with the school counselor, where she immediately found friends who were drinking, using pot, and being sexually promiscuous. She became destructive at times, and my wife was afraid for her own safety. We put her in therapy, but with no positive effect.

During the tenth grade she began to fail everything. She refused further therapy and was kicked out of the counseling group at school. She began staying away from home with boyfriends. My wife and I felt we had exhausted all reasonable ideas. We were not willing to let her run away or to call the police on her, but we felt we had tried everything else.

At that point we decided to put our faith in principles instead of in all the popular advice we were receiving. We continued to have our daily talks, and even though I traveled a lot, we never missed a day. We began to separate our problems from those of our daughter and to believe that we were making more of a difference than we could see.

We focused on working from the inside out. We got very serious about being trustworthy. No matter what our daughter's behavior was, we never used it as an excuse to break our word. We focused on building trust in every interaction with her. We demonstrated our unconditional love for her while expressing explicitly what behavior was against our values and what the consequences would be.

We were scrupulous about keeping all consequences in our Circle of Influence. If she ran away, we would not try to find her, but we would go and get her when she called. We would express our love and concern and listen to understand, but we would not disrupt our plans or lives or hide what she was doing from our relatives. We would not trust her unconditionally. We explained to her that she—like us—had to earn trust.

We treated her as a proactive person. We affirmed her talents and allowed her levels of initiative to be equal to her trustworthiness in that area.

We developed a family mission statement even though she did not participate. We included only what we knew she also believed in. We constantly looked at our formal and informal systems of rewards, decision making, and information exchange. At her request we put her in ALC (Alternative Learning Center) classes at school and had weekly meetings with her and key school personnel to just talk.

During the eleventh grade she slowly began to respond, but she continued to use pot and LSD with her friends. She began to respect our not allowing drugs or smoking on the property. She was just passing at school, but life at home was improving dramatically.

Over the next year our relationships strengthened immensely. We gained a deeper understanding of one another and began to have family dinners together. Her "friends" began coming over to our house to hang out, and we were always present when they were around. Drugs remained part of her life, though we continued to express our disapproval and not trust her in any areas where drugs could be a factor.

She became pregnant, and although we did not approve, we allowed her to make her own decision to have an abortion. We continued to affirm her potential and express our unconditional love, and we were always there for her when she needed us—in stark contrast to her "friends."

At the beginning of the twelfth grade she had a bad experience with drugs and immediately called her mom, who took her to the hospital. She suddenly stopped all drugs and alcohol, and began to improve her performance at school.

A year later, relationships at home exceeded our wildest expectations. She began to want to demonstrate how responsible she was. She went back for an extra half year to finish high school and got all A's for the first time since grade school. She got a part-time job and began paying her own way as much as she could. She asked if she could live at home for two more years to go to community college and qualify to attend the university.

My wife and I know that there are no guarantees, but we feel that by aligning our lives with correct principles, we dramatically increased our chances for success with this daughter. The 7 Habits gave us a framework to look for principles in our situation and the confidence that, regardless of how things turned out, we could sleep at night and live with ourselves. Most unexpectedly, we both grew personally and changed as much as our daughter, if not more.

"Growing" children and relationships and all the good things we want in our families takes time. And sometimes, the forces that would throw us off course are powerful and strong—even within the family itself.

I've had some parents—particularly in blended families—tell me that their efforts to create a family mission statement have met with resistance from teenage children. There are some who say, "We didn't choose this family. This wasn't our idea. Why should we choose to cooperate?"

To these parents—and to any who meet with resistance—I would say this: One of your greatest strengths will be in having your personal mission statement and your marriage mission statement firmly in place. These teenagers may feel traumatized and insecure in their own lives and in the family. They may be bouncing off the walls. You have the potential of being the only really solid thing in their lives. If you have your direction and principles clear, and you consistently respond to them based on that direction and those principles, they will gradually come to feel the sense of that unchanging core. You will feel the strength of it also as you interact with them in principle-centered ways through the storm.

I would also say: Don't give up on a family mission statement. Do what work you can as a family. Do what you can, one-on-one, with these resistant children. Love them unconditionally. Make continual deposits into their Emotional Bank Accounts. Continue to work with your other children as well. You may even have to come up with some kind of statement that reflects the hearts and minds of those who will cooperate and just keep reaching out to the others in unconditional love.

Over time, the hearts of these resistant children may soften. It may be hard to imagine now, but I have seen it happen, time and time again. As you keep your vision clear, as you act based on principles and love unconditionally, children slowly begin to develop trust in that principle-centeredness and unconditional love.

Almost always, the strength of the destination and the compass will pull you through—as long as you have the patience and the faith to hold fast to what you know and stay the course.

SHARING THIS CHAPTER WITH ADULTS AND TEENS

All Things Are Created Twice

- Discuss the statement on page 73: "Because all things are created twice, if you don't take charge of the first creation, someone or something else will." Ask: In what ways are we taking charge of the first creation?

- Discuss examples of the first and second creations (making blueprint plans before building, creating flight plans before making a flight). In everyday life, what mental creation is required: At work? At school? At home? In sports? Gardening? Cooking?

The Power of Vision

- Review the airplane metaphor in Chapter One. Explore the significance of an airplane having a clear destination and a compass.

- Discuss the importance of vision and clear purpose in the experience related in "Creating Our Own Family Mission Statement." Discuss as parents: What abilities do we want our children to develop to be successful when they are grown?

- Identify some of the benefits that flow from developing vision. Ideas might include: a deeper sense of purpose and meaning, a sense of hope or of future possibilities, and a focus on opportunities rather than on problems.

Creating Your Own Family Mission Statement

- Discuss and apply the three-step process described on pages 79–95.

- Discuss the three suggested guidelines and "watch outs."

- Identify the four human gifts. Discuss how developing a family mission statement also develops these gifts.

SHARING THIS CHAPTER WITH CHILDREN

Planning Makes Things Better

- Ask: If we were taking a trip tomorrow, what would you pack? Don't tell family members where you are going or how long you will be gone. When they are finished packing or making a list of what they would pack, ask what difference it would have made if you had told them the destination was the North Pole and the plan was to live for a month in an igloo.

- Ask: Does it make sense to sew a dress without a pattern in mind? To cook a meal without a recipe or a plan? To build a house without a blueprint? Help the family to understand that a family also needs a plan to succeed.

- Ask children to imagine what they would like to see happen in their future. Help them translate that vision into words or pictures you can hang on their wall. The ideas expressed could be most helpful as you start developing a family mission statement.

Exploring What Each Child Is All About

- Set aside a time when each family member tells one strength he or she has noticed about a designated child. Write them down. Keep these in mind as you develop your family mission statement. Continue until everyone has had a turn.

- Encourage your children to contribute to your family mission statement. Distribute three-by-five cards to the children and ask them to write down or draw things in their family life that make them happy, activities they love to do with the family, or any good thing they see in other homes that they would like to be doing. Keep the cards as you develop your family mission statement.

- Go outside on a clear night, look at the stars, and talk about the universe. Or locate where you live on a map of the world and discuss the size of the world. Talk about what it means to be part of the human family. Consider different ways each person and each family can contribute. Ask family members what they think they can do to help the world. Write down their ideas and keep them in mind when you develop your mission statement.

- Make a family flag, select a family motto, or write a family song.

HABIT 3
PUT FIRST
THINGS FIRST

Okay, now, I know what you're going to hear from people is "We don't have the time."
But if you don't have the time for one night or at least one hour during the week where
everybody can come together as a family, then the family is not the priority.

—*Oprah Winfrey*

In this chapter we're going to take a look at two organizing structures that will help you prioritize your family in today's turbulent world and turn your mission statement into your family's constitution.

One of these structures is a weekly "family time." And as television talk show host Oprah Winfrey told her audience when she talked with me about this book on her show, "If you don't have the time for one night or at least one hour during the week where everybody can come together as a family, then the family is not the priority."

The second structure is one-on-one bonding times with each member of your family. I suggest that these two structures create a powerful way to prioritize your family and keep "first things first" in your life.

When First Things Aren't First

One of the worst feelings in the world is when you realize that the "first things" in your life—including your family—are getting pushed into second or third place, or even further down the list. And it becomes even worse when you realize what's happening as a result.

I vividly remember the painful feeling I had one night as I went to bed in a hotel in Chicago. While I had been presenting that day, my fourteen-year-old daughter Colleen had had her final dress rehearsal for a play she was in—*West Side Story*. She had not been selected to play the lead but was the understudy. And I knew that for most of the performances—possibly all—she would not play the leading role.

But tonight was her night. Tonight she was going to be the star. I had called her to wish her well, but the feeling in my heart was one of deep regret. I really wanted to be there with Colleen. And, although this is not always the case, this time I could have arranged my schedule to be there. But somehow Colleen's play had gotten lost in the press of work and other demands, and I simply didn't have it on my calendar. As a result, here I was, alone, some thirteen hundred miles away, while my daughter sang and acted her heart out to an audience that didn't include her dad.

I learned two things that night. One was that it doesn't matter whether your child is in the leading role or in the chorus, is starting quarterback or third string. What matters is that you're there for that child. And I was able to be there for several of the actual performances where Colleen was in the chorus. I affirmed her. I praised her. And I know she was glad I had come.

But the second thing I learned is that if you really want to prioritize your family, you simply have to plan ahead and be strong. It's not enough to say your family is important. If "family" is really going to be top priority, you have to "hunker down, suck it up, and make it happen!"

> *"Things which matter most must never be at the mercy of things which matter least."*

The other night after the ten o'clock news there was an advertisement on television that I have often seen. It shows a little girl approaching her father's desk. He's hassled, has papers scattered all over, and is diligently writing in his planner. She stands by him—unnoticed until she finally says, "Daddy, what are you doing?"

Without even looking up, he replies, "Oh, never mind, honey. I'm just doing some planning and organizing. These pages have the names of all the people I need to visit and talk with and all the important things I have to do."

The little girl hesitates and then asks: "Am I in that book, Daddy?"

As Goethe said, "Things which matter most must never be at the mercy of things which matter least." There is no way we can be successful in our families if we don't prioritize "family" in our lives.

And this is what Habit 3 is about. In a sense, Habit 2 tells us what "first things" are. Habit 3, then, has to do with our discipline and commitment to live by those things. Habit 3 is the test of the depth of our commitment to "first things" and of our *integrity*—whether or not our lives are truly integrated around principles.

So Why Don't We Put First Things First?

Most people clearly feel that family is top priority. Most would even put family above their own health, if it came to it. They would put family ahead of their own life. They would even die for their family. But when you ask them to really look at their lifestyle and where they give their time and their primary attention and focus, you almost always find that family gets subordinated to other values—work, friends, private hobbies.

In our surveys of over a quarter of a million people, Habit 3 is, of all the habits, the one where people consistently give themselves the lowest marks. Most people feel there's a real gap between what really matters most to them—including family—and the way they live their daily lives.

Why is this happening? What is the reason for the gap?

After one of my presentations I was visiting with a gentleman who said, "Stephen, I really don't know if I'm happy with what I've done in my life. I don't know if the price I've paid to get where I am has been worth it. I'm in line now for the presidency of my company, and I'm not sure I even want it. I'm in my late fifties, and could easily be the president for several years, but it would consume me. I know what it takes.

"What I missed most was the childhood of my kids. I just wasn't there for them, and even when I was there, I wasn't really 'there.' My mind and my heart were focused on other things. I tried to give quality time because I knew I didn't have quantity, but often it was disorienting and confusing. I even tried to buy my kids off by giving them things and providing exciting experiences, but the real bonding never took place.

"And my kids feel the enormous loss themselves. It's just as you talk about, Stephen—I have climbed the ladder of success, and as I'm getting near the top rung, I realize that the ladder is leaning against the wrong wall. I just don't have this feeling in our family—this beautiful family culture you've been talking about. But I feel as if that's where the riches are. It's not in money; it's not in positions. It's in this family relationship."

Then he began to open his briefcase. "Let me show you something," he said as he pulled out a large piece of paper. "This is what excites me!" he exclaimed, spreading it out between us. It was a blueprint of a home he was building. He called it his "three-generation home." It was designed to be a place where children and grandchildren could come and have fun and enjoy interacting with their cousins and other relatives. He was building it in Savannah, Georgia, right on the beach. As he went over the plans with me, he said, "What excites me most about this is the way it excites my kids. They also feel as though they lost their childhood with me. They miss that feeling, and they want and need it.

"In this three-generation home, we have a common project to work on together. And as we work on this project, we think about their children—my grandchildren. In a sense I am reaching my children through their children, and they love it. My children want my involvement with their children."

As he rolled the paper up and put it back into his briefcase, he said, "This is so important to me, Stephen! If accepting this position means that we have to move or that I won't have the time to really invest in my children and grandchildren, I've decided I'm not going to take it."

Notice how, for many years, "family" was not this man's most important priority. And he and his family lost many years of precious family experience because of it. But at this time in his life he had come to realize the importance of the family. In fact, family had become so important to him that it eclipsed even the presidency of a major international firm—the last rung on the ladder of "success."

Clearly, putting family first doesn't necessarily mean that you have to buy a new home or give up your job. But it does mean that you "walk your talk"—that your life really reflects and nurtures the supreme value of family.

In the midst of pressures—particularly regarding work and career—many people are blind to the real priority of family. But think about it: Your professional role is temporary. When you retire from being a salesman, banker, or designer, you will be replaced. The company will go on. And your life will change significantly as you move out of that culture and lose the immediate affirmation of your work and your talent.

> *In the end, life teaches us what is important, and that is family.*

But your role in the family will never end. You will never be replaced. Your influence and the need for your influence never ends. Even after you are gone, your children and grandchildren and great-grandchildren will still look to you as their parent or grandparent. Family is one of the few permanent roles in life, perhaps the only truly permanent role.

So if you're living your life around a temporary role and allowing your treasure chest to remain barren in terms of your only real permanent role, then you're letting yourself be seduced by the culture and robbed of the true richness of your life—the deep and lasting satisfaction that only comes through family relationships.

In the end, life teaches us what is important, and that is family. Often for people on their deathbed, things not done in the family are a source of greatest regret. And hospice volunteers report that in many cases unresolved issues—particularly with family members—seem to keep people holding on, clinging to life until there is a resolution—an acknowledging, an apologizing, a forgiving—that brings peace and release.

So why don't we get the message of the priority of family when we're first attracted to someone, when our marriage is new, when our children are small? And why don't we remember it when the inevitable challenges come?

For many of us, life is well described by Rabindranath Tagore when he said, "The song that I came to sing remains unsung. I have spent my days in stringing and unstringing my instrument."[1] We're busy—incredibly busy. We're going through the motions. But we never seem to reach the level of life where the music happens.

The Family: Sideshow or Main Tent?

The first reason we don't put family first goes back to Habit 2. We're not really connected to our deepest priorities. Remember the story about the businessmen and -women and their spouses in Habit 2 who had difficulty creating their family mission statements? Remember how they were unable to achieve the victory they wanted in their families until they really, deeply prioritized "family" in their own hearts and minds—inside out?

Many people have the feeling that family should be first. They may really want to put family first. But until that deep priority connection is there—and a commitment is made to it that is stronger than all the other forces that play on our everyday lives—we will not have what it takes to prioritize the family. Instead, we will be driven or enticed or derailed by other things.

In April 1997, *U.S. News & World Report* published a hard-hitting article entitled "Lies Parents Tell Themselves About Why They Work" that really challenged parents to do some serious soul searching and conscience work in this area. Authors Shannon Brownlee and Matthew Miller claim that few topics are as important—and involve as much self-deception and dishonesty—as finding the proper balance between child-rearing and work. They list five lies that parents tell themselves to *rationalize* (create rational lies) around their work-preference decisions. In summary, their findings were as follows:

Lie #1: We need the extra money. (But research shows that better-off Americans are nearly as likely to say they work for basic necessities as those who live near the poverty line.)

Lie #2: Day care is perfectly good. ("The most recent comprehensive study conducted by researchers at four universities found that while 15 percent of day care facilities were excellent, 70 percent were 'barely adequate,' and 15 percent were abysmal. Children in that vast middle category were physically safe but received scant or inconsistent emotional support and little intellectual stimulation.")

Lie #3: Inflexible companies are the key problem. (The truth is that family-friendly policies now in place are usually ignored. Many people want to spend more time at the office. "Home life has become more like an efficiently run but joyless workplace, while the actual workplace, with its new emphasis on empowerment and teamwork, is more like a family.")

Lie #4: Dads would gladly stay home if their wives earned more money. (In reality, few men ever seriously contemplate such a thing. "Men and women define 'masculinity' not in terms of athletic or sexual prowess but by the ability to be a 'good provider' for their families.")

Lie #5: High taxes force both of us to work. (Even recent tax cuts have sent well-off spouses rushing into the job market.)

It's easy to get addicted to the stimulation of the work environment and a certain standard of living, and to make all other lifestyle decisions based on the assumption that both parents have to work full-time. As a result, parents are held hostage by these lies—violating their conscience but feeling that they really have no choice.

> The place to start is not with the assumption that work is non-negotiable; it's with the assumption that *family* is non-negotiable. That one shift of mind-set opens the door to all kinds of creative possibilities.

The place to start is not with the assumption that work is non-negotiable; it's with the assumption that *family* is non-negotiable. That one shift of mind-set opens the door to all kinds of creative possibilities.

In her bestselling book *The Shelter of Each Other*, psychologist Mary Pipher shares the story of a couple who were caught up in a hectic lifestyle.[2] Both husband and wife worked long hours, trying to make ends meet. They felt they had no time for personal interests, for each other, or for their three-year-old twins. They anguished over the fact that it was day care providers who had seen their boys' first steps and heard their first words, and that they were now reporting problems in behavior. This couple felt they had essentially fallen out of love, and the wife also felt torn apart by her unfulfilled desire to help her mother who was ill with cancer. They seemed trapped in what appeared to them to be an impossible situation.

But through counseling they were able to make some changes that created a dramatic difference in their lives. They began by setting aside Sunday nights to spend with their family and paying attention to each other—giving back rubs and expressing words of affection. The husband told his employers he would no longer be able to work on Saturdays. The wife eventually quit her job and stayed home with the boys. They asked her mother to move in with them, pooling their financial resources and providing a built-in storyteller for the boys. They cut back in many areas. The husband carpooled to work. They quit buying things except for essentials. They stopped eating out.

As Mary Pipher said, "The family had made some hard choices. They had realized that they could have more time or more money but not both. They had chosen time."[3] And that choice made a profound difference in the quality of their personal and family lives. They were happier, more fulfilled, less stressful, and more in love.

Of course, this may not be the solution for every family that's feeling hassled and out of sync. But the point is that there are options, there are choices. You can consider cutting back, simplifying your lifestyle, changing jobs, shifting from full- to part-time work, cutting commuting time by having fewer, longer workdays or working closer to home, participating in job sharing, or creating a virtual office in your home. The bottom line is that there is no need to be held hostage by these lies if family is really your top priority. And making the family priority will push you into creative exploration of possible alternatives.

Parenthood: A Unique Role

There's no question that more money can mean a better lifestyle not only for yourself but for your kids. They may be able to go to a finer school, have educational computer software, and even better health care. And recent studies also confirm that a child whose father or mother stays home and resents it is worse off than if the parents go to work.

But there's also no question that the role of parents is a unique one, a sacred stewardship in life. It has to do with nurturing the potential of a special human being entrusted to their care. Is there really anything on any list of values that would outweigh the importance of fulfilling that stewardship well—socially, mentally, and spiritually, as well as economically?

There is no substitute for the special relationship between a parent and a child. There are times when we would like to believe there is. When we choose to put a child in day care, for example, we want to believe it's good, and so we do. If someone seems to have a positive attitude and a caring disposition, we easily believe they have both the character and the competence to help raise our child. But that which we desire most earnestly, we believe most easily. This is all part of the rationalization process. The reality is that most day care is inadequate. To paraphrase child development expert Urie Bronfenbrenner, "You can't pay someone to do for a child what a parent will do for free." [4] Even excellent child care can never do what a good parent can do.

> *The role of parents is a unique one, a sacred stewardship in life. Is there really anything that would outweigh the importance of fulfilling that stewardship well?*

So parents need to make their commitment to their children—to their family—before they make their commitment to work. And if they do need day care assistance, they need to shop for that care far more carefully than they ever would for a house or a car. They need to examine the track record of the person being considered to ensure that both character and competence are present and the person can pass the "smell test"—the sense of intuition and inspiration that parents can get regarding caregiving for their children. They need to build a relationship with the caregiver so that correct expectations and accountability are established.

Good faith is absolutely insufficient. Good intentions will never replace bad judgment. Parents need to give trust, but they also need to verify competence.

Many people are trustworthy in terms of character, but they are simply not competent—they lack knowledge and skill, and often are absolutely unaware of their incompetence. Others may be very competent but lack the character—the maturity and integrity, sincere caring, and the ability to be both kind and courageous.

And even with good care, the question each parent has to ask is "How often is such proxy caregiving right in my situation?" Sandra and I have some friends who have said that when their children were little, they felt they had all kinds of options and freedoms to do whatever they wanted. Their children were subject to them and dependent on them, and essentially they could have surrogate parenting in the form of day care and sitters whenever they wanted. So both parents became very involved in other things. But now, as their children are getting older, they are beginning to reap the whirlwind. They have no relationship. The children are getting into destructive lifestyles, and the parents have become greatly alarmed. "If we had it to do over," they've said, "we would put a higher priority on our family, on these children—particularly when they were little. We would have made a greater investment."

> *If we had it to do over, we would put a higher priority on our family, on these children—particularly when they were little. We would have made a greater investment.*

As John Greenleaf Whittier wrote, "For of all sad words of tongue or pen, the saddest are these: 'It might have been!'"[5]

On the other hand, we have another friend who said, "I've learned that for these years when I am raising these children, my other interests—professional interests, development interests, social interests—are to become secondary. My most important focus is to be there for my children, to invest myself in them at this critical stage." She went on to say that this is difficult for her because she has so many interests and capabilities, but she is committed to it because she knows how vitally important it is.

What is the difference in these two situations? Priority and commitment—a clear sense of vision and the commitment to live with integrity to it. So if we're not really prioritizing the family in daily life, the first place to look for answers is back in Habit 2: Is the mission statement really deep enough?

"When the Infrastructure Shifts, Everything Rumbles"

Assuming that we do have our Habit 2 work done, the next place we need to look is at the turbulent environment we're trying to navigate through.

We took a brief look at a few major trends in Chapter 1. But now let's take a closer look at the society we're living in. Let's examine a few of the changes over the past forty to fifty years in four dimensions—culture, laws, economy, and technology—and see how these changes impact you and your family. These facts I'm going to share come from surveys done in the United States, but they reflect growing trends worldwide.

Popular Culture

In the 1950s in the United States, the average child watched little or no TV, and what he saw on television was stable, two-parent families who generally interacted with respect. Today, the average child watches seven hours of television per day. By the end of grade school he's seen over eight thousand murders and one hundred thousand acts of violence.[6] During this time he's spent an average of five minutes a day with his father and twenty minutes with his mother, and most of that time was spent either eating or watching TV![7]

Just think about it: seven hours of TV a day and five minutes with Dad. Unbelievable!

He also has increasing access to videos and music that portray pornography, illicit sex, and violence. As we noted in Chapter 1, he goes to schools where the major concerns have shifted from chewing gum and running in the halls to drug abuse, teen pregnancy, suicide, rape, and assault.

In addition to these influences, many homes have actually begun to take on the tone of the business world. In her groundbreaking analysis *The Time Bind*, sociologist Arlie Hochschild points out how, for many people, home and office have changed places. Home has become a frantic exercise in "beat the clock," with family members having fifteen minutes to eat before rushing off to a soccer game, and trying to bond in the half hour before bed so they don't waste time. At work, on the other hand, you can socialize and relax on a break. By comparison, work seems like a refuge—a haven of grown-up sociability, competence, and relative freedom. And as a result, some people even allow their workday to lengthen because they enjoy work more than home. Hochschild writes, "In this new model of family-and-work life, a tired parent flees a world of unresolved quarrels and unwashed laundry for the reliable orderliness, harmony, and managed cheer of work."[8]

> *Just think about it: The average child spends seven hours a day watching TV and five minutes with Dad. Unbelievable!*

And it's not just the changing tone of the home environment. There is enormous affirmation on the job. There are many extrinsic rewards—including recognition, compensation, and promotion—that feed our sense of self-worth, exhilarate us, and exert a powerful pull away from family and home. They create a seductive vision of a different destination, an idyllic, warm-climated Utopia that combines the satisfaction of hard work with the apparent justification—in the "busy-ness" of meeting the unbelievable schedules and demands—for neglecting what really matters most.

The rewards of home and family, on the other hand, are almost all intrinsic. In today's world society is not on the sidelines giving praise and affirmation in your role as a father or mother. You're not paid to do it. You don't get prestige out of doing it. No one cheers you on in the role. As a parent your compensation is the satisfaction that comes from playing a significant role in influencing a life for good that no one else can fill. It's a proactive choice that can only come out of your own heart.

> *The rewards of home and family are almost all intrinsic. You're not paid to do it. You don't get prestige out of doing it. No one cheers you on in the role.*

Laws

These changes in the popular culture have driven profound changes in the political will and in resulting law. For example, throughout time, "marriage" has been recognized as the foundation of a stable society. Years ago the U.S. Supreme Court called it "the foundation of society, without which there would be neither civilization nor progress."[9] It was a commitment, a covenant among three parties—a man, a woman, and society. And for many it included a fourth: God.

Author and teacher Wendell Berry has said:

If they had only themselves to consider, lovers would not need to marry, but they must think of others and of other things. They say their vows to the community as much as to one another, and the community gathers around them to hear and to wish them well, on their behalf and on its own. It gathers around them because it understands how necessary, how joyful, and how fearful this joining is. These lovers, pledging themselves to one another "until death," are giving themselves away, and they are joined by this as no law or contract could ever join them. Lovers, then, "die" into their union with one another as a soul "dies" into its union with God. And so here, at the very heart of community life, we find not something to sell as in the public market but this momentous giving. If the community cannot protect this giving, it can protect nothing. . . .

The marriage of two lovers joins them to one another, to forebears, to descendants, to the community, to Heaven and earth. It is the fundamental connection without which nothing holds, and trust is its necessity.[10]

But today, marriage is often no longer a covenant or a commitment. It's simply a contract between consenting adults—a contract that's sometimes considered unnecessary, is easily broken when no longer seen as convenient, and is sometimes even set up with the anticipation of possible failure through a prenuptial agreement. Society and God are often no longer even part of it. The legal system no longer supports it; in some instances, in fact, it discourages it by penalizing responsible father-hood and encouraging mothers on welfare not to marry.

As a result, according to noted Princeton University family historian Lawrence Stone, "The scale of marital breakdowns in the West since 1960 has no historical precedent that I know of, and seems unique. . . . There has been nothing like it for the last 2,000 years, and probably longer." And in the words of Wendell Berry, "If you depreciate the sanctity and solemnity of marriage, not just as a bond between two people but as a bond between those two peo-ple and their forebears, their children, and their neighbors, then you have prepared the way for an epidemic of divorce, child neglect, community ruin, and loneliness."[11]

Economy

Since 1950 the median income in the United States has increased by ten times, but the cost of the average home has increased by fifteen times and inflation has risen by 600 percent. These changes alone are forcing more and more parents out of the home just to make ends meet. In a critical review of *The Time Bind* (referred to on page 121), Betsy Morris takes exception to Hochschild's view that parents spend more time at work because they find it more pleasant than dealing with the challenges of home life. "More likely," she says, "is that parents are killing them-selves because they have to keep their jobs."[12]

> *Today, marriage is often no longer a covenant or a commitment. It's simply a contract between consenting adults—a contract that's sometimes considered unnecessary and is easily broken.*

To make ends meet and for other reasons—including the desire to maintain a certain lifestyle—the percentage of families where there is one parent working and one at home with the children has dropped from 66.7 percent in 1940 to 16.9 percent in 1994. And today some 14.6 million children live in poverty—90 percent of whom live in one-parent homes.[13] There is simply much less parental involvement with children, and the reality is that for many, family gets "second shift."

The very structure of the economic world in which we live has been redefined. When the government took over the responsibility of caring for the aged and destitute in response to the Great Depression, the economic link between family generations was broken. And this has had a reverberating effect on every other link of the family. Economics define survival, and when this economic sense of respon-sibility between generations is broken, it begins to cut into the other tendons and sinews that hold the generations together, including the social and the spiritual. As a result, the short-term solution has become the long-range problem. In most cases "family" is no longer seen as an intergenerational and extended family unit that cares for itself. It has become reduced to the nuclear family of parents and children at home, and even that is being threatened. The government is seen as the first resource rather than last.

We now live in a world that values personal freedom and independence more than responsibility and interdependence—in a world with tremendous mobility in which creature comforts (especially television) enable social isolation and independent entertainment. Social life is being fractured. Families and individuals are becoming increasingly isolated. Escape from responsibility and accountability is available everywhere.

Technology

Changes in technology have accelerated the impact of changes in every other dimension. In addition to global communication and instant access to vast sources of valuable information, today's technology also provides immediate, graphic, and often unfiltered access to a full spectrum of highly impactful visual images—including pornography and vivid scenes of bloodshed and violence. Supported by and saturated with advertising, technology puts us into materialistic overload. It has caused a revolution in expectations. Certainly it increases our ability to reach out to others, including family members, and establish connections to people around the globe. But it also diverts us and keeps us from interacting with and relating in meaningful ways to members of our family in our own home.

> *What does your own heart tell you? Does watching television make you kinder? More thoughtful? More loving? Does it help you build strong relationships in your home?*

We can look to research for these answers, but there may be an even better source. What does your own heart tell you about the effects of television on you and your children? Does watching television make you kinder? More thoughtful? More loving? Does it help you build strong relationships in your home? Or does it make you feel numb? Tired? Lonely? Confused? Mean? Cynical?

When we think about the effects of the media on our families, we must realize that the media can literally drive the culture in the home. In order to take seriously what is going on in the media (unlikely romance, promiscuity, battling robots, cynical relationships, fighting, and violent brutality), we must be willing to engage in a "suspension of disbelief." We must be willing to suspend our disbelief in actions we know as adults are not real—to desensitize our adult wisdom—and for thirty or sixty minutes allow ourselves to be taken on a journey to see how we like it.

What happens to us? We begin to believe that even TV news is normal life! Children especially believe. For example, one mother told me that after watching the six o'clock news on TV, her six-year-old said to her, "Mommy, why is everybody killing everybody?" This child believed what she was seeing was normal life!

It is true that there is so much good on TV—good information and enjoyable, uplifting entertainment. But for most of us and for our families, the reality is more like digging a lovely tossed salad out of the garbage dump. There may be some great salad there, but it's pretty hard to separate out the trash, the dirt, and the flies.

Low-grade, gradual pollution can desensitize us not only to how awful the pollution but also to what we are trading off for it. It would take an enormous amount of benefit from television to trade off the time that could be spent with family members learning, loving, working, and sharing together!

A recent *U.S. News & World Report* poll reported that 90 percent of those polled felt that the nation is slipping deeper into moral decline. That same poll found that 62 percent felt TV was hostile toward their moral and spiritual values.[14] So why are so many watching so much TV?

As the societal indicators of crime, drug use, sexual pleasuring, and violence go on their upward climb with few plateaus, we should not forget that the most important indicator in any society is the commitment to loving, nurturing, and guiding the most important people in our lives—our children. Children learn the most important lessons not from Power Rangers or even Big Bird but from a loving family who reads with them, talks to them, works with them, listens to them, and spends happy time with them. When children feel loved, really loved, they thrive!

> Suppose you were on your deathbed. Would you really wish you'd spent more time watching TV?

Reflect for one moment: What were the most memorable family times in your own life? Suppose you were on your deathbed. Would you really wish you'd spent more time watching TV?

In their book *Time for Life*, sociologists John Robinson and Geoffrey Godbey reported that on the average, Americans spend fifteen of their forty hours of free time every week watching television. They suggest that maybe we are not as "busy" as we seem to be.[15]

As Marilyn Ferguson said in her landmark book *The Aquarian Conspiracy*, "Before we choose our tools and technology, we must choose our dreams and values, for some technologies serve them, while others make them unobtainable."[16]

It becomes increasingly apparent that the shifts in these meta-structures are dislocating everything. Almost all businesses are being reinvented and restructured to make them more competitive. Globalization of technology and markets is threatening the very survival not only of businesses but of governments, hospitals, health care, and educational systems as well. Every institution—including the family—is being impacted today as never before.

These changes represent a profound shift in the infrastructure, the underlying framework of our society. As Stanley M. Davis, a friend and colleague in various leadership development conferences, has said, "When the infrastructure shifts, everything else rumbles."[17] These meta-structure shifts represent the turning of a major gear, which in turn turns a smaller gear and then a smaller one, and eventually the tiny ones at the other end are whizzing. Every organization is being affected—including the family.

As we're moving from the industrial to the informational infrastructure, everything is being dislocated and must find its bearing again. And yet many people are completely unaware of all this happening. Even though they see it and it creates anxiety, they don't know what is happening or why, or what they can do about it.

A High Trapeze Act . . . with No Safety Net!

Where this infrastructure shift affects us all most personally and profoundly is in our families, our homes. Trying to successfully raise a family today is like trying to perform a high trapeze act—a feat that requires tremendous skill and almost unparalleled interdependence—*and there's no safety net!*

There used to be a safety net. There were laws that supported the family. The media promoted it, upheld it. Society honored it, sustained it. And the family, in turn, sustained society. But there is no safety net anymore. The culture, the economics, and the law have unraveled it. And technology is accelerating the disintegration.

In a 1992 statement, the U.S. Juvenile Justice and Delinquency Prevention Department summarized literally hundreds of research studies of environmental changes over recent years:

Unfortunately, economic circumstances, cultural norms, and federal legislation in the last two decades have helped to create an environment that is less supportive to strong, stable families . . . [and] at the same time these economic changes have occurred, the extended family support system has eroded.[18]

And all of this has happened so gradually that many are not even aware of it. It's like the story that author and commentator Malcolm Muggeridge tells about some frogs that were killed without resistance by being boiled alive in a cauldron of water. Normally, a frog thrown into boiling water will immediately jump out, saving his life. But these frogs didn't jump out. They didn't even resist. Why? Because when they were put into the cauldron, the water was tepid. Then little by little the temperature was raised. The water became warm . . . then warmer . . . then hot . . . then boiling. The change was so gradual that the frogs accommodated themselves to their new environment until it was too late.

This is exactly what happens with all of these forces in the world. We get used to them and they become our comfort zone—even though they're literally killing us and our families. In the words of Alexander Pope:

> Vice is a monster of so frightful mien,
> As to be hated needs but to be seen;
> Yet seen too oft, familiar with her face,
> We first endure, then pity, then embrace.[19]

It's a process of gradual desensitization. And this is exactly what happens when we gradually subordinate principles to social values. These powerful cultural forces fundamentally alter our moral or ethical sense of what is, in fact, right. We even begin to think of social values as principles and call "bad" "good" and "good" "bad." We lose our moral bearings. The airwaves get polluted with filth. The static makes it difficult to get a clear message from radio control.

And—to use the airplane metaphor again—we experience vertigo. This is what sometimes happens to a pilot who is flying without the use of instruments and goes through a sloping cloud bank, for example. He can no longer perceive ground references, and he may not even be able to tell from the "seat of the pants" sensation (the response of nerve endings in the muscles and joints) or from the tiny balance organs that are part of the inner ear, which way is up—because these feedback mechanisms are both dependent on a correct orientation to the pull of gravity. So as the brain struggles to decipher the messages sent from the senses without the clues normally supplied by vision, incorrect or conflicting interpretation may result. And the result of such sensory confusion is this dizzy, whirling sensation known as vertigo.

Similarly in life, when we encounter extremely powerful influence sources, such as a powerful social culture, charismatic people, or group movements, we experience a kind of conscience or spiritual vertigo. We become disoriented. Our moral compass is thrown off, and we don't even know it. The needle that in less turbulent times pointed easily to "true north"—or the principles that govern in all of life—is being jerked about by the powerful electric and magnetic fields of the storm.

> When we encounter extremely powerful influence sources . . . we literally experience a kind of conscience or spiritual vertigo. We become disoriented. Our moral compass is thrown off.

The Metaphor of the Compass

To demonstrate this phenomenon in my teaching—and to make five important points related to it—I will often get up in front of an audience and ask them to close their eyes. I say, "Now without peeking, everyone point north." There is a little confusion as they all try to decide and point in the direction they think is north.

I then ask them to open their eyes and see where people are pointing. At that point there's usually a great deal of laughter because they see that people are pointing in all directions—including straight up.

I then bring out a compass and show the north indicator, and I explain that north is always in the same direction. It never changes. It represents a natural magnetic force on the earth. I have used this demonstration in places throughout the world—including on ships at sea and even on satellite broadcasts with hundreds of thousands of people participating in different locations around the globe. It is one of the most powerful ways I have ever found to communicate that there is such a thing as magnetic north.

I use this illustration to make the first point: *Just as there is a "true north"—a constant reality outside ourselves that never changes—so there are natural laws or principles that never change. And these principles ultimately govern all behavior and consequences.* From that point on I use "true north" as a metaphor for principles or natural law.

I then proceed to show the difference between "principles" and behavior. I lay the see-through compass on an overhead so they can see the north indicator as well as the arrow that stands for the direction of travel. I move the compass around on the overhead so they can see that while the direction of travel changes, the north indicator never does. So if you want to go due east, you can put the arrow ninety degrees to the right of north and then follow that path.

I then explain that "direction of travel" is an interesting expression because it communicates essentially what people *do*; in other words, their behavior comes out of their basic values or what they think is important. If going east is important to them, they value that; therefore, they behave accordingly. People can move about based on their own desire and will, but the north indicator is totally independent of their desire and will.

I make the second point: *There is a difference between principles (or true north) and our behavior (or direction of travel).*

This demonstration enables me to introduce the third point: *There is a difference between natural systems (which are based on principles) and social systems (which are based on values and behavior).* To illustrate, I ask, "How many have ever 'crammed' in school?" Almost the entire audience raises their hands. I then ask, "How many got good at it?" Almost the same number raises their hands again. In other words, "cramming" worked.

I ask, "How many have ever worked on a farm?" Usually 10 to 20 percent raise their hands. I ask those people, "How many of you ever crammed on the farm?" There's always extensive laughter because people immediately recognize that you can't cram on the farm. It simply won't work. It is patently absurd to think you can forget to plant in the spring and goof off all summer, then hit it hard in the fall and expect to bring in the harvest.

I ask, "How come cramming works in school and not on the farm?" And people come to realize that a farm is a natural system governed by natural laws or principles, but a school is a social system—a social invention—that is governed by social rules or social values.

I ask, "Is it possible to get good grades and even credentials out of school and not get an education?" And almost everyone acknowledges this is possible. In other words, when it comes to the natural system of developing your mind, it is governed more by the law of the farm than the law of the school—by a natural rather than a social system.

Then I proceed with this analysis into other areas that people can relate to, such as the body. I ask, "How many of you have tried to lose weight a thousand times in your life?" A good percentage raise their hands. I ask them, "What really is the whole key to weight loss?" Eventually, everyone comes to see that in order to achieve permanent and healthy weight loss, you must align the direction of travel—your habits and your lifestyle—with the natural laws or the principles that bring the desired result, with principles such as proper nutrition and regular exercise. The social value system may reward immediate weight loss through some crash diet program, but the body eventually outsmarts the strategy of the mind. It will slow down the metabolism processes and turn on the fat thermostat. And eventually the body returns to where it was—or perhaps even worse. So people begin to see that not only the farm but also the mind and the body are governed by natural laws.

I then apply this line of reasoning to relationships. I ask, "In the *long* run, are relationships governed more by the law of the farm or the law of the school?" People all acknowledge they're governed by the law of the farm—that is, natural laws or principles rather than social values. In other words, you can't talk yourself out of problems you behave yourself into, and unless you are trustworthy, you cannot produce trust. They come to acknowledge that the principles of trustworthiness, integrity, and honesty are the foundation of any relationship that endures over time. People may fake it for a period of time or cosmetically impress others, but eventually "the hens come home to roost." Violated principles destroy trust. And it doesn't make any difference if you're dealing with relationships between people, or relationships between organizations, or relationships between society and government or between one nation and another. Ultimately, there is a moral law and a moral sense—an inward knowing, a set of principles that are universal, timeless, and self-evident—that control.

I then apply this level of thinking to issues in our society. I ask, "If we were really serious about health reform, what would we primarily focus on?" Almost everyone acknowledges that we would focus on prevention—on aligning people's behavior, their value system, their direction of travel with natural law or principles. But the social value system regarding health care—which is in the direction of travel of society—focuses primarily on the diagnosis and treatment of disease rather than on prevention or lifestyle alteration. In fact, more money is often spent in the last few weeks or days of a person's life in heroic efforts to keep that person alive than was spent on prevention during the person's entire life. This is where society's value system is, and it has essentially assigned medicine this role. That's why almost all medical dollars are spent on diagnosis and treatment of disease.

I then carry this analysis into education reform, welfare reform, political reform—actually, any reform movement. Ultimately people come to realize the fourth point: *The essence of real happiness and success is to align the direction of travel with natural laws or principles.*

Finally, I show the tremendous impact that the traditions, trends, and values of the culture can have on our sense of true north *itself*. I point out that often even the building we're in can distort our sense of true north because it has a magnetic pull of its own. When you go outside the building and stand in nature, the north indicator shifts slightly. I compare this pull to the power of the wider culture—the mega traditions, trends, and values that can slightly warp our conscience so that we're not even aware of it until we get out into nature alone where the "compass" really works, where we can slow down, reflect, and go deep inside ourselves to listen to our conscience.

> *This is perhaps the greatest role of parenting. More than directing and telling children what to do, it's helping them connect with their own gifts— particularly conscience.*

I show the compass north shifting when I put it on the overhead projector, because the machine itself represents a magnetic force. I compare this to a person's subculture—which could be the culture of the family or a business organization or a gang or a group of friends. There are many levels of subculture, and the illustration of how a machine can throw off the compass is very powerful. It's easy to see how people lose their moral bearings and get uprooted by the need for acceptance and belonging.

Then I take my pen and put it up against the compass, and I show how I can make the compass needle jump all over the place; how I can totally reverse it so that north looks south. I use this to explain how people can actually come to define "good" as "bad" and "bad" as "good," because of an extremely powerful personality they come in contact with or an extremely powerful emotional experience—such as abuse or parental betrayal—or profound conscience betrayal. These traumas may be so shaking and devastating as to undermine their whole belief system.

I use this demonstration to make the fifth and final point: *It's possible for our deep, inward sense of knowing—our own moral or ethical sense of natural laws or principles—to become changed, subordinated, even eclipsed, by traditions or by repeated violation of one's own conscience.*

In spite of the work we do on mission statements, if we don't internalize them in our hearts and minds and inside the culture of the family, these cultural forces will confuse and disorient us. They will stagger our sense of morality so that "wrong" is defined more by getting caught than by doing wrong.

This is also why it's so important that pilots be trained in the use of instruments—whether or not they actually fly in instrument conditions. And that's why it's so important that children be trained to use the instruments—the four human gifts that help keep them on track. This is perhaps the greatest role of parenting. More than directing and telling children what to do, it's helping them connect with their own gifts—particularly conscience—so that they are well trained and have immediate access to the lifesaving connection that will keep them oriented and on track. Without such a lifesaving connection, people crash. They become seduced by the culture.

Striking at the Root

I once attended a conference entitled "Religions United Against Pornography" in which leaders of religious organizations as well as women's groups, ethnic groups, and educators joined together, united by the fight against this pernicious evil that victimizes primarily women and children. It became clear that although the subject was repugnant to people's sense of decency and virtue and they would rather not discuss it, they knew it must be discussed because it is a reality in our culture.

At this conference we were shown video clips of interviews with people off the street, including many young men and young couples. These were not violent gang members, druggies, or criminals; they were normal, everyday people who looked on pornography as entertainment. Some said they watched it daily, sometimes several times a day. As we viewed these clips it became clear to us that pornography had become deeply embedded in the culture of many of the youth in the country today.

I gave a presentation on how to bring about culture change. I then attended a session where women leaders addressed this issue. They related how Mothers Against Drunk Driving (MADD) had become a compelling force in society when enough women became so alarmed about the issue of alcohol abuse that their involvement created a serious impact on the cultural norms in American society. They gave us booklets that described rather than showed the kind of pornography that was out there. And as I read about it, I became physically ill.

In my second and final presentation I told of this experience and how convinced I was that the key to culture change is to get people so immersed in the reality of what's happening that they can truly feel its full pernicious, sinister impact on the ethical and moral nature of people's minds and hearts and how this affects our whole society. The key is to *make people sick* the way I had been made sick, involve them in the data until they become thoroughly repulsed and motivated, and then *give them hope*. Get them involved in coming up with solutions and identifying what has happened elsewhere that has been successful. Work on awareness and conscience before you work on imagination and will. Stir up the first two human gifts before releasing the energy of the next two. Then search together for models and mentoring people or organizations that can influence for good and develop laws that promote the good and protect the innocent.

But above all—above legislation, above every effort to influence popular culture—strengthen the home. As Henry David Thoreau put it, "For every thousand hacking at the leaves of evil, there is one striking at the root." The home and family are the root. This is where the moral armament is developed in people to deal with these pernicious influences that technology has made available and to turn the technology into something that enables and facilitates good virtues and values and standards to be maintained throughout society.

For laws to be effective there has to be a social will (a set of mores) to enforce those laws. The great sociologist Émile Durkheim said, "When mores are sufficient, laws are unnecessary. When mores are insufficient, laws are unenforceable." Without social will, there will always be legal loopholes and ways to break the law. And children can quickly lose their innocence and become callous and eroded inside—sarcastic and cynical and far more vulnerable as prey to violent gang behavior, to adoption into a new "family" that gives acceptance and social approbation. So the key is to nurture the four gifts inside each child and to build relationships of trust and unconditional love so that you can teach and influence the members of your family in principle-centered ways.

> "For every thousand hacking at the leaves of evil, there is one striking at the root."

Interestingly, one other significant outcome of the conference was the change in the very culture and feeling among the leaders of the various faiths. In just two days it moved from courteous respect and exchange of pleasantries to genuine love, profound unity, and open, authentic communication because of a common, transcendent mission. As the leaders discovered, in these perilous times we must focus on what unites us, not on what divides us!

Who's Going to Raise Our Children?

In the absence of an inner connection with the four human gifts and a strong family influence, what impact is the kind of culture we've described in this chapter—

power boosted by technology—going to have on a child's thinking? Is it realistic to think that children are going to be impervious to the murder and killing and cruelty they watch seven hours a day on TV? Can we really believe the TV program directors who claim there is no hard scientific evidence to show a correlation between violence and immorality in our society and the graphic scenes they choose to show on the television screen—and then quote hard scientific evidence to show how much a twenty-second advertisement will impact the behavior of the viewers?[20] Is it reasonable to think that young adults exposed to a visual and emotional TV diet of sexual pleasuring can grow up with anywhere near a realistic or holistic sense of the principles that create good, enduring relationships and a happy life?

In such a turbulent environment, how can we possibly think that we can continue with "business as usual" inside our families? If we don't build better homes, we'll have to build more prisons because surrogate parenting will nurture gangs. Then the social code will surround drugs, crime, and violence. Jails and courts will become even more overcrowded. "Catch and release" will become the order of the day. And emotionally starved children will turn into angry adults, plowing through life for love, respect, and "things."

In an epic historical study, one of the world's greatest historians, Edward Gibbon, identified five main causes of the decline and fall of Roman civilization:

1. the breakdown of the family structure
2. the weakening of a sense of individual responsibility
3. excessive taxes and government control and intervention
4. seeking pleasures that became increasingly hedonistic, violent, and immoral
5. the decline of religion.[21]

His conclusions provide a stimulating and instructive perspective through which we might well look at the culture of today. And this brings us to the pivotal question on which our future and the future of our children depends:

*Who's going to raise my children—
today's alarmingly destructive culture or me?*

As I said in Habit 2, if we don't take charge of the first creation, someone or something else will. And that "something" is a powerful, turbulent, amoral, family-unfriendly environment.

This is what will shape your family if you do not.

"Outside in" No Longer Works

As I said in Chapter 1, forty years ago you could successfully raise a family "outside-in." But outside-in no longer works. We cannot rely on societal support of our families as we used to. Success today can only come from the inside out. We can and we must be the agent of change and stability in creating the supporting structures

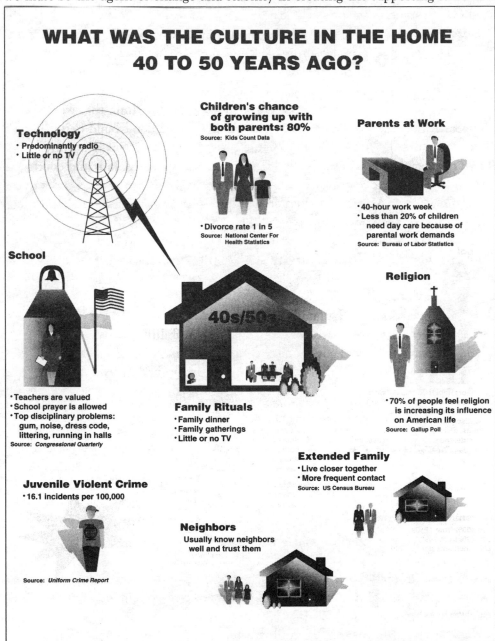

WHAT WAS THE CULTURE IN THE HOME 40 TO 50 YEARS AGO?

Technology
· Predominantly radio
· Little or no TV

Children's chance of growing up with both parents: 80%
Source: Kids Count Data

· Divorce rate 1 in 5
Source: National Center For Health Statistics

Parents at Work

· 40-hour work week
· Less than 20% of children need day care because of parental work demands
Source: Bureau of Labor Statistics

School

· Teachers are valued
· School prayer is allowed
· Top disciplinary problems: gum, noise, dress code, littering, running in halls
Source: Congressional Quarterly

40s/50s

Family Rituals
· Family dinner
· Family gatherings
· Little or no TV

Religion

· 70% of people feel religion is increasing its influence on American life
Source: Gallup Poll

Extended Family
· Live closer together
· More frequent contact
Source: US Census Bureau

Juvenile Violent Crime
· 16.1 incidents per 100,000

Source: Uniform Crime Report

Neighbors
Usually know neighbors well and trust them

for our families. We must be highly proactive. We must create. We must reinvent. We can no longer depend on society or most of its institutions. We must develop a new flight plan. We must rise above the turbulence and chart a "true north" path.

Just consider the effects of these changes in the culture of the home and the environment as represented in the chart on these pages. Think about the impact these changes are having on your own family. The point of comparing today to the past is

WHAT IS THE CULTURE IN YOUR HOME TODAY?
WHO IS RAISING YOUR CHILDREN?

Children's chance of growing up with both parents: less than 50%
Source: Kids Count Data

Technology

Parents at Work

• Divorce rate 1 in 2
• Single parent families increase 350%
Source: National Center For Health Statistics

• 45- to 50-hour work week
• More than 60% of children need day care because of parental work demands
Source: Bureau of Labor Statistics

School

90s

Religion

Source: National Commission on Children

• Parents' time with kids:
—5 minutes with Dad
—20 minutes with Mom

• Computer games
• Internet

• TV larger than life

• Teachers' moral voice is silenced
• Assaults on teachers up 700% since 1978
• Top disciplinary problems: drugs, alcohol, pregnancy, suicide, rape, robbery, and assault
Source: Congressional Quarterly

Family Rituals
• Each week a school-age child spends
—1.8 hours reading
—5.6 hours doing homework
—21 hours watching TV
Source: Learn to Discern

• Adults watch TV 15 hours/week
Source: Time for Life

• 60% of people feel religion is losing its influence on American life
• 90% feel the U.S. is slipping deeper into moral decline
Source: Gallup Poll

Extended Family
• Live farther apart
• Less frequent contact and involvement
Source: US Census Bureau

Juvenile Violent Crime
• Up 500% from 1950s
• Up 22% from 1990
• 75.8 incidents per 100,000

Neighbors
• Most Americans know well only 3 in 5 neighbors
Source: US Census Bureau

Source: Uniform Crime Report

not to suggest that we return to some idealized notion of the 40s and 50s. It is to recognize that because things have changed so much, and because the impact on the family is so staggering, we must respond in a way that is equal to the challenge.

History clearly affirms that family is the foundation of society. It is the building block of every nation. It is the headwaters of the stream of civilization. It is the glue by which everything is held together. And family itself is a principle built deeply into every person.

But the traditional family situation and the old family challenge are gone. We must understand that, more than at any other time in history, the role of parenting is absolutely vital and irreplaceable. We can no longer depend on role models in society to teach our children the true north principles that govern in all of life. We are grateful if they do, but we cannot depend on it. We must provide leadership in our families. Our children desperately need us. They need our support and advice. They need our judgment and experience, our strength and decisiveness. More than ever before they need us to provide family leadership.

So how do we do it? How do we prioritize and lead our families in significant, productive ways?

Creating Structure in the Family

Think once again about the words of Stanley M. Davis: "When the infrastructure shifts, everything else rumbles."

The profound technological and other changes we've talked about have impacted organizations of all kinds in our society. Most organizations and professions are being reinvented and restructured to accommodate this new reality. But this same kind of restructuring has not happened in the family. Despite the fact that outside-in no longer works, and despite the astounding report that today only 4 to 6 percent of American households are made up of the "traditional" working husband, wife at home, and no history of divorce for either partner,[22] most families are not effectively restructuring themselves. They're either trying to carry on in the old way—the way that worked with the challenges of the past—or they're trying to reinvent in ways that are not in harmony with the principles that create happiness and enduring family relationships. As a whole, families are not rising to the level of response the challenge demands.

So we must reinvent. The only truly successful response to structural change is structure.

When you consider the word "structure," think carefully about your response to it. As you do, be aware that you are trying to navigate through an environment where the popular culture rejects the idea of structure as being limiting, confining.

But consult your own inner compass. Think about the words of Winston Churchill: "For the first twenty-five years of my life I wanted freedom. For the next twenty-five years of my life I wanted order. For the next twenty-five years of my life I realized that order is freedom." It is the very structure of marriage and family that gives stability to society. The father in a popular family television show during the outside-in era said this: "Some men see the rules of marriage as a prison; others—the happy ones—see them as boundary lines that enclose all the things they hold dear." It is the commitment to structure that builds trust in relationships.

Think about it: When your life is a mess, what do you say? "I have to get organized. I have to put things in order!" This means creating both structure and priority or sequencing. If your room is a mess, what do you do? You organize your things in closets and dresser drawers. You organize within structure. When we say about someone, "He has his head screwed on straight," what do we mean? We basically mean that his priorities are in order. He's living by what's important. When we say to a person with a terminal disease, "Get your affairs in order," what do we mean? We mean, "Make sure your finances, insurance, relationships, and so forth, are attended to."

In a family, order means that the family is prioritized and that some kind of structure is in place to make that priority happen. In the mega sense, Habit 2—the creation of a family mission statement—provides the foundational structure for the inside-out approach to family living. In addition, there are two major organizing structures or processes that will help you put the family first in a meaningful way in your daily life: a weekly "family time" and one-on-one bonding times.

> *"Ultimately, we must decide either to steer or to go where the river takes us. The key to successful steering is to be intentional about our family rituals."*

As prominent marriage and family therapist William Doherty said, "The forces pulling on families are just too strong in the modern world. Ultimately, we must decide either to steer or to go where the river takes us. The key to successful steering is to be intentional about our family rituals."[23]

Weekly Family Time

Outside of making and honoring the basic marriage covenant, I have come to feel that probably no single structure will help you prioritize your family more than a specific time set aside every week just for the family. You could call it "family time," "family hour," "family council," or "family night" if you prefer. Whatever you call it, the main purpose is to have one time during the week that is focused on being a family.

A thirty-four-year-old woman from Oregon shared this:

My mother was the instigator of a weekly family activity time where we children got to pick whatever we wanted to do. Sometimes we went ice skating. At other times we went bowling or to a movie. We absolutely loved it! We always topped it off with a visit to our favorite restaurant in Portland. Those activity days always left me with a feeling of great closeness and that we really were part of a family unit.

I have such fond memories of these times. My mother passed away when I was a teenager, and this had a very traumatic impact on me. But my dad has made sure that every year since her death we all get together for at least one week—in-laws, children, everyone—to rekindle those same feelings.

When family members all leave to go to their homes in different states, I feel sad and yet so rich. There is such strength in a family that has lived together under the same roof. And the new members of our family have in no way detracted from this feeling—they have only enriched it.

My mother left quite a legacy. I have not married, but my brothers and sisters faithfully have their own weekly family times with their children. And that particular restaurant in Portland is still a gathering spot for us all.

Notice the feelings this woman is expressing about her memories of these family times. And look at the impact it has on her life now, on her relationships with her brothers and sisters, and on their relationships with the members of their families. Can you begin to see the kind of bonding a weekly family time creates? Can you see the way it builds the Emotional Bank Account?

A woman from Sweden shared this story:

When I was about five or six years old, my parents talked to someone who told them of the value of having regular meetings with their family. So they began to do it in our home.

I remember the first time my dad shared with us a principle of life. It was very powerful to me, because I had never seen him in the role of formal teacher, and I was impressed. My dad was a busy and successful businessman and had not had very much time for us children. I remember how special and important it made me feel that he valued us enough to take time out of his busy schedule and sit down and explain how he felt about life.

I also recall an evening when my parents invited a famous surgeon from the United States to join us for our family time. They asked him to share his experiences of medicine with us and how he had been able to help people all over the world.

This surgeon told us how decisions he had made in life eventually led him to reaching his goals and becoming more than he had imagined. I never forgot his words and the importance of taking each challenge "one step at a time." But more important, his visit left me with the feeling that it was really neat that my parents wanted to invite visitors home to share their experiences with us.

Today I have five children, and almost monthly we bring some "outsider" to our home to get acquainted with, share with, and learn from. I know it is a direct result of what I saw in my parents' home. In our jobs or at school, we have an opportunity to be exposed to people from other countries, and their visits have enriched our lives and have resulted in close friendships worldwide.

This woman was profoundly influenced by a regular family time as she was growing up and has passed the legacy on to her children. Think about the difference this will make to her children as their family tries to navigate through a turbulent, family-unfriendly environment.

A weekly family night is something we've had as part of our own family from the very beginning. When the children were very small, we used it as a time of deep communication and planning for the two of us. As they got older, we used the time to teach them, to play with them, and to involve them in fun and meaningful activities and family decisions. There have been times when one of us or one of the children could not be there. But for the most part we've tried to always set aside at least one evening a week as family time.

On a typical family night we would review our calendar on upcoming events so everyone would know what was going on. Then we'd hold a family council and discuss issues and problems. We'd each give suggestions, and together we'd make decisions. Often we would have a talent show where the kids would show us how they were coming along with their music or dance lessons. Then we'd have a short lesson and a family activity and serve refreshments. We would also always pray together and sing one of our family's favorite songs, "Love at Home" by John Hugh McNaughton.

In this way we would accomplish what we have come to feel are the four main ingredients of a successful family time: *planning, teaching, problem-solving,* and *having fun.*

Notice how this one structure can meet all four needs—physical, social, mental, and spiritual—and how it can become a major organizing element in the family.

But family time doesn't have to be that involved—especially at first. If you want, you can just begin to do some of these things at a special family dinner. Use your imagination. Make it fun. After a while, family members will begin to realize they are receiving nourishment in more ways than one, and it will be easier to hold a more involved family time. People—particularly little children—long for family experiences that make them feel close to one another. They want a family in which people demonstrate that they care about one another. Also, the more often you do things like this in your family, the easier it will become.

And you cannot begin to imagine the positive impact this will have on your family. A friend of mine did his doctoral dissertation on the effect of holding family meetings on the self-image of children. Although his research showed the positive effect was significant, one unanticipated and surprising result was the positive effect that holding such meetings had on the fathers. He tells of one father who felt very inadequate and was initially reluctant to try to hold such meetings. But after three months the father said this:

Growing up, my family didn't talk much except to put each other down and to argue. I was the youngest, and it seemed as if everyone in the family told me that I couldn't do anything right. I guess I believed them, so I didn't do much in school. It got so I didn't even have enough confidence to try anything that took any brains.

I didn't want to have these family nights because I just didn't feel I could do it. But after my wife led a discussion one week and my daughter another week, I decided to try one myself.

It took a lot of courage for me to do it, but once I got started, it was like something turned loose in me that had been tied up in a painful knot ever since I was a little boy. Words just seemed to flow out of my heart. I told the members of my family why I was so glad to be their dad and why I knew they could do good things with their lives. Then I did something I had never done before. I told them all, one by one, how much I loved them. For the first time I felt like a real father—the kind of father I wished my father had been.

Since that night I have felt much closer to my wife and kids. It's hard to explain what I mean, but a lot of new doors have opened for me and things at home seem different now.

Weekly family times provide a powerful, proactive response to today's family challenge. They provide a very practical way to prioritize the family; the time commitment itself tells the children how important the family is. They build memories. They build Emotional Bank Accounts. They help you create your own family safety net. They also help you meet several fundamental family needs: physical, economic, social, mental, aesthetic, cultural, and spiritual.

I have taught this idea now for over twenty years, and many couples and single parents have said that family time is an enormously valuable and practical "take home" idea. They say it has had the most profound effect on family prioritization, closeness, and enjoyment of any family idea they have ever heard.

Turning Your Mission Statement into Your Constitution Through "Family Time"

Family time provides a great opportunity to discuss and create your family mission statement. And once you have the mission statement, it can help you meet the need for a practical way to turn it into the constitution of your family life and to meet four everyday needs: spiritual (to plan), mental (to teach), physical (to solve problems), and social (to have fun).

Sandra:

On one of our family nights, we were talking about the kind of family we wanted to be as we had described in our mission statement. We got into a discussion about service and how important it is to serve one another—the family, neighbors, and the larger community.

So for the next family night I decided to prepare a lesson on service. We rented the video Magnificent Obsession. It tells the story of a rich playboy who became involved in a car accident that resulted in a girl's becoming blind. It showed how he felt guilty and terrible about it and realized that his careless actions had changed her life forever. In some way he wanted to make this up to her and help her deal with her new life situation, so he consulted a friend—an artist—who tried to teach him how to give anonymous service and help other people. At first he struggled with it and had difficulty understanding the reasons he should do this. But eventually he learned how to look for needs in people and situations and step into their lives and anonymously create positive change.

As we discussed this movie, we talked about what a great neighborhood we lived in—how caring and responsible the people were and how much we appreciated them. We all agreed that we wanted them to know that, and we wanted to be of some service or do something for them. We created what we called the "Phantom Family." For about three months at every family night we made a special treat—popcorn balls, candy apples, cupcakes, or something similar. We decided which family we were going to spotlight. Then we put the treat on their porch, along with a note that told how we admired their family and appreciated them. We ended the note with "the Phantom Family strikes again!" We rang the doorbell and ran like wildfire.

Each week we did the same thing. We never did get caught, although on one occasion we were reported to the police because someone thought we were trying to break in!

Pretty soon all the neighbors were talking about the Phantom Family. We acted as if we didn't know anything about it, but were also wondering who in the world the Phantom Family could be. People eventually had their suspicions, and one night we were left a treat with a note that said, "To the Phantom Family—from Your Suspicious Neighbors."

The plotting, drama, and mystery made a great adventure. It also enabled us all to learn more about the principle of anonymous service and to more fully integrate an important part of our family mission statement into our lives.

We've found that every idea in our mission statement provides a great basis for family time discussions and activities—things that help us translate the mission into moments of family living. And as long as we make it fun and exciting, everyone learns and enjoys.

By creating and living by a mission statement, families are gradually able to build moral authority in the family itself. In other words, principles get built right into the very structure and culture of the family, and everyone comes to realize that principles are at the center of the family and are the key to keeping the family strong, together, and committed to its destination. Then the mission statement becomes like the Constitution of the United States—the ultimate arbiter of every law and statute. The principles upon which it is based and the value systems that flow out of those principles create a social will that is filled with moral or ethical authority.

A Time to Plan

One husband and father shared the following:

A couple of years ago my wife and I noticed that our summers were getting increasingly busy, and we were not spending as much time with the kids as we wanted while they were out of school. So right after school let out, we had a family night where we asked the children to tell us their favorite summer things to do. They mentioned everything from the little everyday things like swimming and going out for ice cream to daylong activities such as hiking up a nearby mountain and going to the water park. It was fun because each of them got to share what he or she really enjoyed doing.

Once we got all these activities out on the table, we worked on narrowing down the list. Obviously, we couldn't do everything, so we tried to come up with those activities that everyone thought would be the most fun. Then we pulled out a huge calendar and planned when we would do them. We set aside some Saturdays for major daylong activities. We reserved some weeknights for those that didn't take as much time. We also marked out a week for our family vacation at Lake Tahoe.

The children were very excited to see that we had actually planned to do the things that were important to them. And we found over the summer that this planning made a big difference in their happiness and in ours. No longer were they constantly asking when we were going to do something because they knew when we were going to do it. It was on the family calendar. And we held to our plan. We all made it a big priority in our lives. It helped us form a collective commitment, and this sense of commitment greatly strengthened and bonded us.

This planning also made a big difference to me because it helped me commit to do what I really wanted to do but often didn't do because of the pressure of the moment. There were times when I was tempted to work late to finish a particular project, but I realized that to miss keeping the commitment I'd made to my family would be a big withdrawal. I had to follow through, so I did. And I didn't feel guilty because that's what I had planned to do.

> By creating and living by a mission statement, families are gradually able to build moral authority in the family itself.

As this man discovered, family time is a wonderful time to plan. Everyone's there and involved. You can decide together how to best spend your family time. And everyone knows what's happening.

Many families do some kind of weekly planning during their family time. One mother said:

Planning is a big part of our family time together each week. We try to go over each person's goals and activities, and put them on a magnetic chart that hangs on the door. This enables us to plan family activities together and helps us know what others in the family are doing during the week so that we can support them. It also gives us the information we need to arrange necessary transportation and baby-sitting, and resolve scheduling conflicts.

One of the best things about our calendar it is that it's by the phone, so when someone calls for a family member, any of us can say, "Oh, I'm sorry, she's not here. She's at a play practice. She should be home by five o'clock." We feel good knowing where family members are and being able to communicate easily with their friends when they call. And we feel good knowing that the kids can respond to our calls effectively as well.

Having a family calendar enables you to plan quality time together, including weekly family time and one-on-ones. It also helps everyone feel invested in the family. The calendar isn't just Mom's or Dad's; it reflects the priorities and decisions of everyone.

With specific time set aside each week for the family, you can begin to feel more peace of mind. You know that your most important stewardship is attended to. You can more fully give yourself to your family—and to work and other activities as well, because you know that you have time set aside for the things that matter most. And this can all be accomplished with as simple a tool as a wall calendar and a process of regularly meeting together to plan.*

A Time to Teach

We're also found that family time is a great time to teach basic principles of life. Sandra and I have had some wonderful family times teaching our children the principles behind the 7 Habits.

Sandra:
Some years ago a huge shopping mall complex was being built in the center of Salt Lake City. The intent was to draw people back to the city by providing excellent shop-

*For information about the 7 Habits of Highly Effective Families calendar, call (44) (0)870 600 0226 or visit www.franklincovey.com on the Internet.

ping, theaters, restaurants, and other features. One family night Stephen explained that he had met one of the architects. He said that he had arranged for us to go on the construction site so that the architect could explain to us the details and complexities of such a project.

He took all of us up to the rooftop of an adjacent building where we surveyed the massiveness of this project. We were awed by the size, the planning, the vision, the technology, and the building expertise that went into such a development. The architect explained the concept of beginning with the end in mind. Everything had to be created twice. He had to meet with the owners and builders and other architects, and explain in minute detail the size, floor space, function, design, purpose, and cost of every area.

We watched breathlessly as he scanned each section of the building with a TV monitor while explaining what would be here and what would be there. Then we followed him to a large room where he showed us hundreds and hundreds of blueprints. Some were for the heating and air-conditioning systems. Some were for the interior and exterior lighting. Some were for the staircases, exits, elevators, wiring, cement, columns, windows, sound systems, and so on.

He went on to explain the interior design—the plans for painting, wallpaper, color schemes, flooring, tiles, and ambiance. We were amazed at the detail, forethought, imagination, and planning.

As the sun set, the city became alive with shadows and lights, and we were able to make out landmarks and familiar sites around us. It was then that Stephen and I took the opportunity to talk with the children about how the principle of "begin with the end in mind" applies to the decisions and plans we make in our lives every day.

If we plan to go to college, for example, we must attend school. We must study, prepare for tests, turn in papers, learn to express ourselves in writing, complete the course. If we want to excel in music, we must have the desire and the talent. We must practice. We must give up other things in order to concentrate and progress and improve. To excel in athletics we must develop our natural talents. We must practice and participate in sports camps. We must push ourselves, believe we can do it, sustain injuries, and glory in the wins but learn from the losses. We said that things don't just happen by chance. You have to envision your goals. Make a blueprint. Count the cost. Pay the price to make it all happen.

That family night gave us a wonderful opportunity to share an important principle with our children. It was a night we will all remember.

Family time is a great time to teach competence in practical matters. One woman related this experience:

One of the family times our children remember the most was when we played a game to teach them some principles of financial management.

We set up several signs in different places in the room that said such things as "Bank,"

"Store," "Credit Card Company," and "Charity." Then we gave each of the children some object to represent work they could do to earn money. Our eight-year-old had some hand towels she could fold. Our ten-year-old had a broom to sweep the floor. Everyone had work to do so that they could earn.

When the game began, everyone started to work. After a few minutes we rang a bell, and everyone got "paid." We gave them each ten dimes for their labor. Then they had to decide what to do with their money. They could put it in the bank. They could donate some to charity. They could buy something at the "store" where we had a lot of bright-colored balloons with the names of different toys and the price written on them. In fact, if they really wanted something badly from the store and didn't have enough money to buy it, they could go to the credit card company and borrow enough to get it.

We went through the sequence several times: work, earn, spend; work, earn, spend. And then we blew a whistle. "Interest time!" we said. Those who had put money in the bank got money added. Those who had "borrowed" from the credit card company had to pay interest. After several rounds they quickly became convinced that it was much smarter to earn interest than to pay it.

As the game progressed, the children also saw that those who chose to donate to charity were helping to provide food, clothes, and other basic necessities for people throughout the world. And as we popped some of the balloons when the "interest" whistle blew, they also realized that many of the material things we work so hard for and even go into debt for don't last.

When we've asked our children to tell us about family times they remember, this one was at the top of the list. And it's made a tremendous difference when as grown-ups they've received mail containing the empty promise of "buy now, pay later." Of our four married children, not one of them carries a credit card balance requiring the payment of interest. And the only money they've borrowed has been for homes, transportation, and education.

Just think of the difference it's made to these children to learn some of the basic principles of finance in their home—especially when problems in financial management is one of the major factors linked to divorce.[24]

Family time is a great time to teach about the family itself. One woman shared this:

One of the best family nights we've had was when we brought a new baby home from the hospital. It provided a perfect teaching moment.

We had talked with them about sex on other family nights. We had explained to them that it was an important part of marriage and not something to be treated lightly.

But there in the quiet circle of family love, we were able to say to them, "This is what it's all about. It's about the love between a husband and wife. It's about bringing a new *little person into a family where he'll be loved and cherished and cared for. It's about the commitment to protect and take care of this little person until he's grown up and ready to create a family of his own."*

I don't think there's anything we could have done that would have touched their hearts more deeply or influenced their attitude more powerfully about intimacy in human relationships.

> *If we do not teach our children, society will. And they—and we—will live with the results.*

As you can see, family time provides a wonderful time to teach. And the dramatic change in society makes it even more imperative that we really teach our families in our homes. If we do not teach our children, society will. And they—and we—will live with the results.

A Time to Solve Problems

A woman from Denmark shared this experience:

In our home we have tried to get together almost weekly since our children were small. We have used the meetings for many different purposes. Occasionally these meetings have been the forum for us to lay our cards on the table and tell the kids about struggles in our lives and how we tackle them.

One time my husband lost his job, so we used the time in our family meeting to explain what had happened. We showed them the money we had in the bank, and we explained that it usually took six months to find a new job. We showed them how we needed to divide the money into six groups—one for each month. We divided each month's money into what would be needed for food, house payment, gas, electricity, and so on.

In this way they could clearly see where the money was going and how little was left. They could have panicked if it wasn't for the fact that we told them it was going to be a challenge, and we could make it. But we wanted them to see where the money would go. We wanted to avoid breaking their hearts over and over again because we couldn't afford new clothes or entertainment.

We then discussed how stressful this responsibility was for their dad and what we could do at home to de-stress him. We decided to remove all irritation spots, such as leaving schoolbags, coats, and shoes on the floor—and keep the house clean. They all agreed, and we felt very united in this difficult process that was ahead of us.

During the following six months we baked a lot of cakes to cheer us up. We didn't participate in anything that cost money or purchase things other than bare necessities. The kids continually tried to cheer up their dad, telling him they knew he would get a job soon. They went out of their way to show their confidence in him because we all knew from experience that this would be an area he would struggle with.

When he finally got a new job, the children's joy was almost greater than ours, and the celebration was one we won't soon forget. I cannot even begin to list the headaches we avoided because we took the time to sit down with them and explain our situation and what it would take to get through it.

Family time is a wonderful time for problem-solving. It's a time to address fundamental needs and work together to find ways to meet them. It's an opportunity to involve family members in the problems and work out solutions together so that we all understand, so that we all feel the solution represents us and we are committed to it.

Maria (daughter):

I remember one family night, Dad went through the list of all the responsibilities that needed to be taken care of in the home. And then he went down the list and asked who wanted to do each one.

He said, "Okay, who wants to earn the money?" No one volunteered, so he said, "Well, I guess I'll have to do that one. Okay, who wants to pay the taxes?" Again, nobody volunteered, so he said he'd do that, too. "Okay, who wants to feed the new baby?" Well, Mom was the only one qualified for that job. "So who wants to take care of the lawn?"

He went on and on with all the things that needed to be done, and it became very clear that he and Mom were both doing so much for the family. It was a great way to put our jobs as kids in perspective. It also really made us realize that everyone needed to take part.

We know of one mother who has taken into her home many foster children that the state has considered "incorrigible." These kids have had a wide variety of problems. Almost all have been in trouble with the police. As this woman has discovered, family times are great for airing and sharing. She said:

As we have dealt with these foster kids and our own kids over the years, we've found that kids really need close relationships. And these can be nurtured during family time. The kids really like to be involved. They like being in charge of something—games or treats or activities. And they appreciate a "safe" environment where they can express their concerns.

Just recently we had a foster boy who was going through very difficult challenges— physically, emotionally, and mentally. While he was in the hospital, we used a family time to update the kids on what to expect when he returned. They had concerns about his behavior—about his teasing and so on—and we let them air those concerns. We made it safe for them to be very honest, and it helped put them at ease so that they were not so apprehensive. One of the kids didn't even want him to come back at all, and knowing that, we were better able to handle it.

Creating a family forum where problems can be openly discussed builds trust in the relationship and in the family's ability to solve them.

A Time to Have Fun

Sandra:

I think everyone's favorite family nights in our home were the times when we would go on a series of adventures. Stephen would usually make them up as we went along, and none of us knew what to expect. It might be playing a game of volleyball in the back-yard, then having a swim at the high school gym followed by a visit to the pizza parlor. Or it could be going to the driving range and letting everyone hit a bucket of golf balls, and then going to a movie and finishing up with a root beer float at home. We might play a game of miniature golf at the rec center, then jump on the backyard trampoline, share some ghost stories as it got dark, and then sleep out in the backyard. Or we might join another family for a hike up Rock Canyon, build a fire and roast marshmallows, and then go bowling. Sometimes we'd take trips to a museum—the art museum, the science museum, the dinosaur museum. Sometimes we'd rent videos or show home movies and pop popcorn.

In the summer we might go swimming or floating down the Provo River in an inner tube. In the winter we might go skiing or sledding, have a snowball fight, or go ice skating on the lake. We never knew what the adventures would be, and that was half the fun.

Sometimes another family or aunts and uncles and cousins would join us. Then we might have an all-day marathon, including horseshoes, archery, Ping-Pong games, tennis, and basketball.

One of the most important ingredients of any family time is fun. This is what unites and bonds family members. This is what creates joy and pleasure in being together. As one father said:

Family time gives us the opportunity to do something that often doesn't get done in the hubbub of life—to just spend time together having fun. It seems as if there's always so much to do—work at the office, work at home, fixing dinner, getting kids ready for bed—that you don't take the time to just relax and enjoy being together. And this is so impor-tant, especially when the stress is high.

We've found that just wrestling with the kids, telling jokes, and laughing together is very therapeutic. It creates an environment where it's safe for them to tease Mom and Dad—or for Mom and Dad to tease them. It makes them feel liked.

When thing are too serious all the time, I think they wonder, "Do Mom and Dad really like me? Do they like being with me?" But when we have this regular time together and we just let go and really enjoy one another, they know we like to be with them. They associate "being liked" with having fun.

And it's almost as if this family time structure helps us—gives us the time—to be spontaneous. The kids look forward to it more than anything else during the week. Because we have so much fun together, they are the ones who always make sure we have it.

Even if nothing else happens during family time, just the joy of being together and doing things together will have tremendous positive effect on the Emotional Bank Accounts in the family. And when you add the other dimensions, family time truly becomes one of the most effective organizing structures in the family.

Making the Commitment

Perhaps you remember—or have seen in a more recent video or movie—the film clips showing the lunar voyage of Apollo 11. Those of us who witnessed it were absolutely transfixed. We could hardly believe our eyes when we saw men walking on the moon. Superlatives such as "fantastic" and "incredible" were inadequate to describe those eventful days.

Where do you think the most power and energy was expended on that heavenly journey? Going a quarter of a million miles to the moon? Returning to the earth? Orbiting the moon? Separating and redocking the lunar and command modules? Lifting off from the moon?

No, not in any of these. Not even in all of these together. It was lifting off from the Earth. More energy was spent in the first few minutes of liftoff from the earth—in the first few miles of travel—than was used in half a million miles for several days.

The gravity pull of those first few miles was enormous. The Earth's atmosphere was compressingly heavy. It took an internal thrust greater than both the pull of gravity and the resistance of atmosphere to finally break out into orbit. But once they did break out, it took almost no power to do all those other things. In fact, when one of the astronauts was asked how much power was expended when the lunar module separated from the command module to go down and survey the moon, he answered, "Less than the breath of a baby."[25]

This lunar voyage provides a powerful metaphor for describing what it takes to break out of old habits and create new ones, such as having weekly family times. The gravity force of the Earth could be compared to deeply embedded habits, tendencies programmed by genetics, environment, parents, and other significant figures. The weight of the Earth's atmosphere could be compared to the turbulent family-unfriendly environment of the wider culture, the wider society. These are two powerful forces, and you must have a collectivized social will that is stronger than both of these forces in order to make liftoff happen.

But once it does happen, you will be amazed at the freedom it gives you and your family. During liftoff, astronauts have no freedom, no power; all they can do is carry out the program. But as soon as they pull away from the gravity of the Earth and the atmosphere surrounding the Earth, they experience an unbelievable surge of freedom. And they have many, many options and alternatives.

> The most important thing is to make the commitment: "Once a week, no matter what, we will have family time together."

As the great American philosopher and psychologist William James suggested, when you are attempting to make a change, you need to make the resolve deep, seize the first moment of initiative to act on that resolve, and allow no exceptions. The most important thing is to make the commitment to do it: "Once a week, no matter what, we will have family time together." If you can, set aside a specific night to do it. Schedule it on your family calendar. You may have to change that night occasionally if something really urgent comes up, but if this happens, immediately reschedule it for another time during the week. You'll have a much better chance of doing this on a regular basis if you set aside a specific night of the week. Furthermore, you want to communicate to your children the importance of a specific family time when they're little, before the onslaught of the teenage social agenda.

And no matter what happens in your family meeting, don't get discouraged. We've had family meetings where two of our nine children (teenage sons, of course) were sprawled out on the couch asleep, and some of the others were climbing the walls. We've had meetings that basically started out as a big fight and ended up in prayer. We've even had meetings where people were being so noisy, so disrespectful that we've said, "Okay, we've had it! You come and get us when you're ready to meet!" and walked out. Usually they asked us to stay. When we did leave, we always came back later and apologized.

The point I'm trying to make is this: It's not always easy. And it's usually not convenient. Sometimes you even wonder whether your children are getting anything out of it. In fact, you may not be able to see the real results for years.

But it's like the story of the man in the railroad station in St. Louis who accidentally moved a small piece of railroad track a mere three inches. As a result the train that was supposed to arrive in Newark, New Jersey, ended up in a station in New Orleans, Louisiana, some thirteen hundred miles away. Any change—even a tiny one—in your direction today will make a significant difference hundreds of miles down the road.

Maria (*daughter*):

I remember times when we'd have our weekly family meetings and Sean and David were lying on the couches sound asleep. Catherine would be saying, "My boyfriend's trying to call, and we've got the phone off the hook!" I'm sure at the time our parents wondered, "Are they getting anything at all out of these meetings?"

Catherine (*daughter*):

I remember being difficult in those meetings sometimes. But as I grew up and left home, I often thought about specific things I learned then. They made a real difference in my life. And that's very encouraging to me because now I look at my own children and think, "Are they getting anything from this?" And I realize that even though it sometimes seems as if they're not, they really are. Foundations are being laid that will make a huge difference down the road. Just the fact that we're doing it, that we're trying, is tremendously important.

We've held weekly meetings in our family for over thirty years now, and as I look back and as I talk with our grown children about this experience, I am absolutely convinced that it has been one of the most powerful, one of the most significant forces in keeping our family on track.

One-on-One Bonding Times

Perhaps you've seen the compelling mountain scene poster with the invitation at the bottom: "Let the mountain have you for a day." Magnificent nature draws us into itself. We feel more relaxed, more at peace, more tranquil, more at home.

The same thing takes place in a human relationship when you spend time with another person. Perhaps we should change that slogan to: "Let your spouse have you for a day" or "Let your child have you for an afternoon" or "Let your teenager have you for an evening." In this mode—in a relaxed state of mind—you are, in a sense, letting the other have his or her way with you. Now I'm not talking about compromising principles or becoming soft and permissive and indulging someone else's lower nature whims. What I am talking about is being "completely present" with another person, about transcending your own personal interests and concerns and fears and needs and ego, about being fully with your husband, wife, son, or daughter, and allowing that person to have his or her interests and goals expressed or worked on, subordinating your agenda to the other's.

Times such as these have been so meaningful and so pivotal in our family life that I would say, without doubt, that *the second most absolutely foundational family structure to create is these one-on-one bonding times*. These one-on-ones are where most of the real work of the family is done. This is where there is the deepest nurturing of heart and soul. This is where the most significant sharing, the most profound teaching, the deepest bonding takes place.

> *One-on-ones are where most of the real work of the family is done. This is where there is the deepest nurturing of heart and soul.*

As the late Dag Hammarskjöld, past secretary general of the United Nations, has said, "It is more noble to give yourself completely to one individual than to labor diligently for the salvation of the masses." One-on-one bonding times provide the opportunity for you to give yourself to the one.

One-on-Ones in a Marriage

There is no way I can describe the value of private time with Sandra. For many years the two of us have shared some time together each day. When we're both in town, we go for a ride on our Honda Scooter. We spend time away from children, away from phones, away from office and home and other people and everything else that might divert us or distract us. We ride up into the foothills and just talk.

We share what's going on in our lives. We discuss any issues or concerns. We role-play situations in the family that we need to address and resolve. And when we can't be together, we talk on the telephone—often several times a day. That rich communication, that bonding, builds our marriage and strengthens it so that we go into the family arena with deep love and respect for each other and with a tremendous sense of unity that helps us pull together instead of apart.

We have some married friends who enjoy one-on-one time together in a different way. Every Friday night they arrange for their children to be cared for while they spend several hours together just focused on building their relationship. They go out to dinner, to a movie, or to a play, or just take a hike in the mountains and photograph wildflowers. And they have done this for nearly thirty years. They also go on a "retreat" together once or twice or year. They often use frequent-flyer miles and go to California, where they walk barefoot on the beach, watch the waves, review their marriage mission statement, and work on their goals for the coming year. And then they go back into their family life renewed and refocused. They feel so strongly about the value of this one-on-one time in their marriage that they sometimes tend their grandchildren so that their married children and their spouses can also have this special renewing time together.

This kind of "retreat" time is vital to a marriage and a family. There is a tremendous need for husbands and wives to sit down together and carefully plan or, in a sense, mentally or spiritually create their own future. Planning isn't easy. It requires thinking, and many of us are so busy following hectic schedules, being tyrannized by the telephone, and meeting small crises that we go for long periods without any deep, meaningful communication with our husband or wife. Yet planning is of overwhelming significance in any endeavor of life, and certainly it must be in the most important endeavor: successfully raising a family. It must play a vital, central role because it brings enormous benefits. When a couple comes together to work through matters in their shared stewardship—particularly in dealing with children—it opens the floodgates to synergy, insight, and strengthened resolve. The insights are more profound and the solutions more practical and workable—and the entire process is enormously bonding and unifying to the relationship.

> *There is a tremendous need for husbands and wives to sit down together and carefully plan or, in a sense, mentally or spiritually create their own future.*

In doing the research for this book, I've found that many couples find different ways to have regular, meaningful one-on-one time together. A mother with older children shared this:

Three to four nights a week our kids tuck us in. We go to our room an hour before the kids go to bed. That's when we unwind. We talk together. Sometimes we listen to music or watch TV. We share our experiences at work. We talk through issues in the family. We help balance each other out.

This together time makes a huge difference in our family life. When we get home from work, we no longer let our needs supersede the children's needs. We just kind of let ourselves go, because we know that when 10:30 comes, we'll have our time together. So we just focus on the family and the kids and getting the house picked up and the laundry done and the dog fed, because we know that at the end of the day, we're going to have some quality time together.

And the kids understand and do not interfere with that time. Unless it's something really important, they never knock. They don't call. They don't try to get in. And they never complain because they know what this time means to us as a couple. And they know that if we're a strong couple, we're going to have a stronger family.

For us, this works better than going out on a date where there are things that interfere with your private time—a waiter, people you run into, and so on. This is more than a date, it's a commitment to a true reuniting on a daily basis—a reaffirming of why we are together, why we fell in love, why we chose each other.

I think to remind yourself of that daily is probably the greatest gift any couple can give each other. You get into a routine. You get so busy and focused on other things that as time goes by you don't even realize what you're missing. But time together like this reunites you and reminds you of what you are missing.

And you don't let it die. You just don't.

In my own family I've noticed that my one-on-one time with Sandra strengthens the entire family tremendously. As someone said, "The greatest thing you can do for your children is love your spouse." The strength of this bonding in the marriage creates a sense of security in the entire family. This is because the most significant relationship in the family by far is that of husband and wife. The quality of that relationship truly governs the quality of family life. And even when there have been problems and a breaking of that relationship, it is very important that the parents are civil toward each other and that one never attacks the other in front of the children or even behind the children's backs. The "vibes" get out, and children will take it personally. They will identify—particularly if they are young and impressionable.

> "*The greatest thing you can do for your children is love your spouse.*"

I remember one time revealing my dislike for a particular person, and my six-year-old son Joshua immediately said to me, "Dad, do you like me?" In other words, he was saying, "If you are capable of that attitude or sentiment toward that person, you are also capable of it toward me. And I want the reassurance that you don't feel that way."

Children get much of their sense of security from the way their mother and father treat each other. So building the marriage relationship will have a powerful effect on the entire family culture.

One-on-Ones with Children

It's also vital to spend one-on-one time with each child for which the child usually writes the agenda. This means time between one parent and one child. Remember, as soon as a third person is introduced, the dynamic changes. And it may be appropriate at times to have that dynamic change. Both mother and father may spend time with one child, or two children may spend time with one parent. Generally, however, the basic relationship-building time is one-on-one. Doing this well and often strikes at the root of sibling rivalry.

One-on-ones with children include private visits, private dates, private teaching moments, and private times together in which the full emotional and social dynamic is deepened and there develops a sense of unconditional love, of positive regard and respect that does not change, is never altered. These special bonding times build the assurance that when troubles and problems come along, the relationship can be depended on, relied on. They help to create a changeless core that—along with changeless principles—enables people to live with constant external change.

Catherine (daughter):

I remember when I was ten years old and loved Star Wars. *It was everything to me. So when my turn came for a one-on-one date with my dad, I wanted to see* Star Wars, *even though I'd already seen it four times.*

The thought crossed my mind that this might be a problem because my dad might prefer getting his teeth pulled than having to watch science fiction. But when he asked me what I wanted to do with him that night, it was my agenda he had in mind—not his. "We'll do anything you want to do, Catherine," he said. "It's your night."

To a ten-year-old, this sounded like a dream come true: a night alone with my father and seeing my favorite movie, too. So I told him about the plan. I could sense a slight hesitation before he said with a smile, "Star Wars! Sounds great! You can explain it to me." And away we went.

As we settled down in our theater seats, popcorn and candy in hand, I remember feeling so important to my father. When the music began and the lights dimmed, I began my soft explanation. I told him about "the force" and how it was good. I told him about the empire and how it was evil. I told him that this was the saga of the never-ending battle between these amazing powers. Throughout the movie I explained the planets, the creatures, the droids, the spaceships—anything that seemed foreign or strange to my dad. He sat in silence, nodding his head and listening.

After the show, we went for ice cream, and I continued my explanation of the movie with all the emotion of my heart, all the while answering the many questions my dad threw at me.

At the end of the evening he thanked me for going on a private date with him and for opening up his mind to the world of science fiction. As I was falling asleep that night in my bed, I openly thanked God for giving me a father who cared, who listened, and who made me feel important to him. I never knew whether or not he liked Star Wars the way I did, but I did know that he loved me. And that's all that mattered.

Nothing communicates the value you place on a child or your relationship with that child more than giving your time to the child.

One woman told us her greatest childhood memory was her father taking her out to a McDonald's breakfast every other week for almost ten years. He would then drop her off at school before going to work.

A mother of five sons shared her insights about the deep bonding that resulted from consistent one-on-ones with a son:

The other day I took my twenty-two-year-old son Brandon out to lunch. As we ate together, we started talking about a number of things in his life, including his classes at school, his and his wife's plans for the future, and so on. Through the process he jokingly said, "Mom, I really don't know what I want to be when I grow up!"

I said, "Well, I don't know what I want to be when I grow up, either! Life changes as you go along, but sometimes you just have to focus on one thing and remain open to the possibility of change."

We had a great discussion brainstorming possibilities for his future and ended up with ideas he had never considered before: getting a degree in international business and a minor in Portuguese and doing business in Brazil.

We had a wonderful time just being together and sharing, and as I thought about it later, I realized that this was something that didn't just happen. As a result of writing my personal mission statement years ago, I decided to set a goal of having special one-on-one time with each of my sons during the month. I started this tradition when they were in elementary school, and I certainly wasn't perfect in doing it. But it has really made a difference in our relationships. I don't think there is any way I could have had this kind of one-on-one time with my son when he was twenty-two if we hadn't started doing it when he was younger. This is something we've developed together and feel comfortable with as we go through life with each other.

I have come to realize that as kids get older, parents need to make the transition from being "the parent" to being a best friend. My one-on-ones with my children through the years have made that transition much, much easier because we have a friendship already.

Many one-on-ones can be scheduled on your family calendar. But this woman also observed that you can't always plan ahead for quality one-on-one time.

In addition to our planned one-on-ones, there were times when my husband or I could tell that one of our sons was a little on edge. As parents, we'd try to pick up on that and arrange time to talk. Usually Dave would take him fishing or I would take him to lunch. Dave and I tried to take turns. We didn't both go because we didn't want our boys to feel that their parents were ganging up on them.

When our boys felt comfortable, they would usually share what was on their minds. Sometimes it was something that was happening with the other boys that they didn't like. Sometimes it was a problem at school—they felt a particular teacher didn't like them or they were behind in their homework and didn't know how to make it up.

We'd say, "Would you like to go back home and discuss it? Would you like us to help you with this?" It was always their decision. We recognized that they needed to learn how to make decisions and fix things for themselves. But we also realized that everyone needs someone to talk to, to give additional perspective, to help with exploring options.

This is not something you can always plan. It has to be in you. It has to be part of your heart. It has to come naturally out of being a kind, caring parent who can look at your children and realize that things are not okay and that you need to spend some one-on-one time. Your child needs you.

The most important thing is that family comes first, no matter what. We are convinced that if we put family first, we won't have the crises in our family that take months, even years of trying to fix. We'll nip it in the bud, right at the beginning.

Notice that even more than a matter of scheduling, prioritizing the family is a way of thinking. It's constantly reconnecting with the importance of family, and acting based on that value rather than reacting to whatever is happening at the moment.

"I Don't Care How Much You Know Until I Know How Much You Care"

I will never forget an experience I had with one of our daughters during one of our one-on-one times. She seemed very cross, very irritable, and had been acting that way toward everyone in the house. When I asked her what was wrong, she'd say, "Oh, nothing."

One of the ground rules Sandra and I have in our one-on-ones with the children is that we always let them talk about whatever they want to talk about for as long as they want to talk. They can beef about something, they can complain or moan to their heart's content, and we can't give any advice unless they ask for it. In other words, as parents we simply seek to understand.

So I just listened. As a young adult, this daughter looked back on that experience and wrote the following:

Cynthia (*daughter*):

When I was five years old, my parents moved to Belfast, Ireland, for three years. I picked up on my playmates' Irish accent, and when I returned to third grade, I had a strong Irish brogue.

Because I had lived in Ireland, I hadn't learned to play American games such as kick the can, baseball, capture the flag, or jump rope rhymes, and I felt very out of it. I could sense the kids in my class thought I was different because they couldn't understand me, and I didn't know how to play any of the games they had been playing for years.

My teacher stuck me in speech therapy to get rid of my accent and tried to help me catch up academically because I lagged far behind. I was having trouble especially in math but was afraid to admit that I didn't know some of the basics. I didn't want to stand out any more, and I longed to be accepted and have friends.

Instead of asking for help in math, I discovered that all the answers to our worksheets were on cards in the back of the room. I began sneaking those cards out and then copying the answers without being caught. It seemed for a time all my problems were solved. In my heart I knew it was wrong, but it seemed to me the end justified the means. I began getting attention from the teacher and other students for doing so well. In fact, I was presented as the model student who worked hard, finished my work quickly, and consistently scored the highest in the class.

It was wonderful for a while because I was popular and a lot of kids liked me. But my conscience kept after me because I knew I had betrayed myself and what my parents had always taught me about honesty. I wanted to stop. I was so ashamed of cheating. But now I was in a trap and didn't know how to get out of it without totally humiliating myself. I had to keep cheating because the teacher expected me to do well every time now. I was miserable, and the problem seemed insurmountable to an eight-year-old with no way out.

I knew I should tell my parents what was happening, but I was too embarrassed because I was the oldest. I began acting out at home, losing my temper easily because of the pressure of dealing with this problem alone. My parents told me later that they could sense something was very wrong in my life, but they didn't know what it was.

In Ireland, we had started the practice of having "private interviews" with a parent once a month. This was a time when we could talk about anything we wanted, complain about home duties or unfairness shown, talk about our friends or anything that interested us, give ideas for activities, share problems, or whatever. The rule was that Mom or Dad could only listen—not talk or criticize, or give advice or suggestions without being invited to. We all looked forward to our private interviews.

During one of these interviews, my dad let me go off about some injustice I felt my parents dealt me without defending himself or getting angry. He could sense that wasn't the real problem, and he just let me talk. Finally, when I felt accepted and not condemned, I cautiously started to open up a little to sense his reaction. He asked if things were going well in school and if I was happy there. Defensively, I blurted out, "If you only knew, you'd think I was terrible! I can't tell you about it."

For a few minutes he affirmed his unconditional love and acceptance of me, and I felt his sincerity. I had opened up on other occasions about things without rebuke, and so I felt I could trust him with the awful truth.

Suddenly it just blurted from me, and I found myself crying and yelling, "I'M CHEATING IN MATH!" Then I fell into his arms. It was such a relief to get it out, even though I couldn't see a solution and feared the consequences. I had shared my terrible secret with my father, and I still felt his love and support of me in spite of it.

I remember him saying, "Oh, how awful for you to have had this inside you for so long! I wish you had told me so I could have helped you." He asked if he could call my mother into the room, and then I told them the whole story. I saw no way out, but amazingly enough they helped me work out a solution that would not totally humiliate me. We would go together to the teacher. I would get a sixth grader to help me with my math.

They affirmed me and understood what happened, and to this day I can still feel the relief of that moment. Who knows what pattern I would have established in my life and what road I would have taken if I had continued in my dishonesty. But I was able to share my problem with parents who had already established a relationship of trust and a track record of consistent love and encouragement. They had made such huge deposits over the years that my large withdrawal did not leave me totally bankrupt. Instead, that day I collected interest.

I often think back to that experience, and I wonder what would have happened if I had been so busy, so rushed, so anxious to get to an appointment or to get on to something "more important" that I didn't take the time to really listen. What more would that daughter have gone through? What different choices might she have made?

I'm so grateful, at least in that circumstance, that we had set aside the time to be together, to focus on the relationship. That one hour together made a profound difference in both our lives.

One of the greatest opportunities of being a parent is to teach children the principles that will ultimately bring them the greatest happiness and success in life. But you can't do that without the relationship. "I don't care how much you know until I know how much you care."

Jenny (daughter):

One of my favorite memories of one-on-one time with my dad was during the summer of 1996. Every morning Dad would wake me up at 6:00 and we would go biking on an upper mountain road together. We would spend a full hour riding alongside each other, talking things over and telling stories. He would teach me so many things, and I could tell him anything. We would end the morning by watching the sun rise and drinking water from a fresh spring. I often reflect on those rides and remember how wonderful it was.

One-on-one bonding times give you the opportunity to build that relationship, that Emotional Bank Account, so that you can teach. Sandra and I have found that when we take one child aside from the others, go where there is some privacy, and give full attention—when we are completely present—we are amazed how effective our teaching, discipline, or communication can be. But when out of a sense of time pressure and practical necessity we attempt to teach, discipline, or correct when others are present, we are amazed at how ineffective we usually are.

I am convinced that many children know what they should do, but their minds are not made up to do it. People don't act on what they know; they act on how they feel about what they know and about themselves. If they can come to feel good about themselves and about the relationship, they are encouraged to act on what they know.

Put the Big Rocks in First

These weekly family times and one-on-ones are vital—even foundational—in dealing with fundamental family needs, in building Emotional Bank Accounts, and in creating the entire culture in the family.

So how do you do it? How do you manage your time to have a weekly family time and regular, meaningful one-on-one bonding times with the members of your family?

I'd like to ask you to use your imagination for a moment. Imagine that you're standing behind a table, and on this table is a large openmouthed jar that is almost completely filled with small pebbles. On the table beside the jar are several large-fist-sized rocks.

Now suppose that this jar represents the next week of your life. Let the pebbles in the jar represent all the things you'd normally do. Let the big rocks represent family time and one-on-ones and other things that are really important to you—maybe things such as exercising or working on a family mission statement or just having fun together. Make the rocks represent things that in your heart of hearts you know you really should do but at this point haven't been able to "fit into" your schedule.

As you stand behind this table, imagine that your task is to fit in as many of the big rocks as you possibly can. You begin to work at it. You try to force the big rocks into the jar. But you're able to get only one or two in. So you take them out again. You look at all the big rocks. You study their size. You look at their shape. You realize that maybe if you choose different rocks, you could get more of them in. So you try again. You work at it and rearrange things until you're finally able to fit three big rocks into the jar. But that's it. As hard as you try, that's all you can fit in.

How do you feel? You look at the jar. It's full to the brim, and you have all these really important things—including these family things—that aren't getting done. And it's the same thing every week. Maybe it's time to consider a different approach.

Suppose you take out those three big rocks. Suppose you get another container, and you pour all the pebbles into it. And then you *put the big rocks in first!*

Now how many of those rocks are you going to fit in? A lot more, for sure. And when you have the jar full of big

rocks, *then* you can pour the pebbles in over them. And look how many of them will still fit in!

The point is this: If you don't put the big rocks in first, they hardly ever get in at all! The key is to put the big rocks in first.

Cynthia (*daughter*):

Dad was out of town quite a bit while I was growing up, but we did more together as a family than most. I had more one-on-one time with him than any of my friends whose fathers had nine-to-five jobs.

I think there were two reasons. One was that he always planned ahead. He really believed in being proactive, in making it happen, in beginning with the end in mind. At the first of every school year he always wanted to know, "When are the boys' football games? When are the girls' scheduled activities?" And he hardly ever missed anything important. He was rarely out of town on family night. He was always home on the weekends so that we could do activities and go to church together.

There were times when people would say, "Oh, your dad's out of town again!" But a lot of my friends whose parents worked nine to five would sit in front of the TV at night and not even communicate.

I realize now the work it took for us to have family time together—to have family devotionals, family prayers, family activities. With a hectic job and nine kids in five different schools, my parents really had to fight for it. But they did. The bottom line is that it was important to them, and so they wrestled with it and figured out how to do it.

I think the second reason for our time together was the rules. You don't go anywhere on Sunday—that's a family day and a church day. You never miss Monday night—that's family night. We'd usually do something as a family on one weekend night. It was just kind of required. And sometimes as teenagers we'd resent it a little bit. But it was kind of accepted as part of the culture, and after a while we didn't fight it.

My early experiences of feeling the pain and frustration of not prioritizing some of our children's plays and ball games and other important activities led me to get into the habit of always trying to put the big rocks in first. At the beginning of each school year, Sandra and I have pressed the schools for calendars of events that may involve our children and grandchildren. We've placed high priority on scheduling and being at our children's events. We've also encouraged our children to attend each other's events. With almost fifty people (children, spouses, and grandchildren) in the family now, we can't go to every activity. But we do what we can and always try to communicate to all family members how important they and their activities are to us. We also plan major family vacations two, three, or even four years in advance. And family nights and one-on-one time continue to be held sacred in our home.

We have found that there is nothing to compare with the happiness that has come from making family a priority. With many pressures in our lives to do otherwise, it's not always easy to do these things. *But it is much, much harder not to!* When you don't put the advance prevention time in building relationships and investing in unifying and organizing the family, you spend much more time later trying to repair broken relationships, save marriages, or influence children who are being powerfully pulled by social forces outside the family.

To those who would say, "We don't have time to do these kinds of things!" I would say, "You don't have time not to!" The key is to *plan ahead and be strong.* "Where there's a will, there's a way."

And when you really do put those big family rocks in first, you begin to feel this deep sense of inner peace. You're not constantly feeling torn between family and work. In fact, you will find there's actually more of you to contribute in other places because of it.

Commitment to these family structures brings life to the principles of effective family living. It creates a beautiful family culture that enables you not to be seduced by the popular culture's system of extrinsic rewards. When you're on the periphery and don't actually experience this beautiful family culture, it's easy to become distracted, to be pulled in other directions. But when you're in the middle of it, your only question is "How could there possibly be anything better?"

> *To those who would say, "We don't have time to do these things!" I would say, "You don't have time not to!" The key is to plan ahead and be strong.*

Organizing Around Roles

Instead of just selecting activities, Sandra and I have found that one of the best ways to put the big rocks in first in our lives is to organize around our most important roles—including our family roles—and to set goals in each of these roles each week. Some weeks, one or two goals will be so consuming that we make the decision not to set goals in other roles. For example, when Sandra spends a week helping one of our daughters with a new baby, that means she chooses not to do any public speaking, community service, or extra projects around the home that week. But it's a consciously made decision, and she feels peaceful knowing that the following week she will look at each of her roles and set goals again. We've found that by using "roles and goals," our lives are much more balanced. Each role is attended to, and we're less likely to get overwhelmed by the urgency of all the day-to-day pressures.*

A Quick Look Back and Ahead

Now before we move on, let's take a moment to look back and think in a larger sense about Habits 1, 2, and 3.

Habit 1—Be proactive—is the most fundamental decision of all. It determines whether you're going to be responsible or a victim.

*For complimentary samples of the roles and goals worksheet from the 7 Habits Organizer, call (44) 0121-604-6999 or visit www.franklincovey.com on the Internet.

If you make the decision to be responsible—to take initiative, to be the creative force of your life—then the most primary decision facing you is what is your life about. This is Habit 2—Begin with the end in mind—which is creating your family mission statement. This is what is called a strategic decision because every other decision will be governed by it.

Habit 3, then—Put first things first—becomes secondary or tactical. It deals with how to make those first things happen. We have primarily focused on two main structural interventions in a world where "outside in" fails: the weekly family time and one-on-one bonding experiences between members of the family. When outside-in worked, such structures weren't as necessary because they were happening naturally all the time. But the more society is extracted from nature, the more we see the globalization of technology and markets that change the whole economic picture, the more we see the secularization of the culture away from principles, the more we see the erosion of laws and the social will driving the political will to where elections become more and more popularity contests based on sound bites and camera opportunities—the more we must be strong and decisive in creating and using new structures to keep us on track.

As you think about implementing these habits in your family, I want to remind you again that *you are the expert on your family*, and you alone know your situation.

During a recent visit to Argentina, I talked with parents who had gathered from all over Latin America to attend a conference. I asked them for feedback on the ideas in this book. The feedback was very positive and supportive, but these parents didn't relate to the formalizing of a weekly family time and one-on-ones. They live in a very family-oriented culture, and for them almost every night is "family time" and one-on-ones are a natural part of daily life.

But with other families, the idea of developing a family mission statement and creating new structures of a weekly family time and planned one-on-one bonding experiences is totally off their screen. They don't want any form or structure in their lives. Perhaps they are angry and rebelling against the structures they already have in their lives—structures that they feel have suppressed the full sense of freedom and individuality they value. Those structures may be so filled with negative energy and judgments that any other structure is guilty by association. There's just too much social and psychic baggage.

If this is your situation, you may still want to prioritize your family. You may recognize some value in a family mission statement and some of these structures but feel that doing some of these things is just going too far for now. That's okay. Start where you are. Don't lay a big guilt trip on yourself about the necessity of all this interdependence if you're not ready to move in this direction.

You may want to start by simply applying some of these ideas in your own life. Perhaps all you feel you can do is make some promise and keep it, or select some simple goal and go for it. This may be sufficient structure for you at this time. Later, you may come to feel that you can take on another, little larger task or goal and then go for that. Eventually, by making and keeping promises, your sense of honor will become greater than your moods or any baggage you may carry with you. Then you will find you can move out into entirely new arenas—including working toward these interdependent activities such as creating a family mission statement, holding weekly home evenings, and having special one-on-one bonding experiences.

> *Eventually, by making and keeping promises, your sense of honor will become greater than your moods or any baggage you may carry with you.*

The key is to recognize where you are and to start where you are. You can't do calculus until you understand algebra. You can't run before you can walk. Some things of necessity come ahead of other things. Be patient with yourself. Even be patient with your own impatience.

Now, you may be saying, "But my situation is different! It's just too difficult, too challenging. There is no way I can do these things!" If so, I encourage you to think about the experience of Admiral James B. Stockdale as related in his book *A Vietnam Experience*. A prisoner in Vietnam for several years, Admiral Stockdale tells of how American POWs living in solitary confinement and completely isolated from one another for long periods were able to develop a social will that was powerful enough to enable them to create their own culture with their own rules and norms and communication process. Without interacting verbally, they were able to establish communication with one another by tapping on walls and using wires. They were even able to teach this communication to new prisoners who were brought in and didn't know the code.

Admiral Stockdale wrote:

The Communist Regime put each of us in solitary confinement in an attempt to sever our ties with one another and with our cultural heritage. This hits hard after a few months— particularly a few months of intermittent torture and extortion. In fits of depression, a man starts seeing the bottom of the barrel and realizes that unless he gets some structure, some ritual, some poetry into his life he is going to become an animal.

In these conditions, clandestine encrypted tap and flash codes get improvised and start linking lives and dreams together. Then comes the need for common practice and united resistance, and in due course if things are working right, codified law commences to emanate from the senior prisoner's cell. The communication network strengthens the bonds of comradeship as over the months and years a body politic of common customs, common loyalties, common values take shape.[26]

Just think about it: They hardly even saw one another. Yet through the brilliant use of their four gifts, these prisoners built a civilization—a powerful culture of unbelievable social will. They created a sense of social responsibility and account-ability so that they were able to encourage and help one another through incredi-bly difficult times.

There is so much truth to the expression, "Where there's a will, there's a way!"

Though less dramatic, consider how you could use family times and one-on-one times to create the same kind of powerful bonding and social will in the family.

Catherine (daughter):

My mother loved the arts, and she enjoyed planning trips to the ballet, the symphony, the opera, or any other play or performance in town. Tickets for these events were usually top priority, and came well before money was spent on movies, junk food, or just plain goofing off. At times, I remember complaining that all this culture wasn't doing any good. But as I look back on those experiences, I realize how wrong I was.

I'll never forget one experience I had with my mother that changed my life forever. We had a Shakespearean festival near our community, and one day my mother announced that she had bought us all tickets to see Macbeth. At the time, this meant nothing to me, because I was only eleven and completely unacquainted with Shakespeare.

On the night of the play, we all piled into our car and headed toward the theater. I dis-tinctly remember the snide remarks that were made that night about how we were all too tired to pay attention. We asked, "Couldn't we just go to a movie?"

But my mother only smiled as she patiently drove on, knowing secretly that the incred-ible talent of "the Bard" would do her full justice. And it did! I can't ever remember a time when the emotions of the universe all seemed so vividly clear to me as they did that night. The dark secrets of Macbeth and his wife haunted me throughout the play as the innocence of my youth slipped away. Yet in its place, an understanding and an epiphany that only Shakespeare could have penned opened my heart and spoke to me. I immediately knew that my life would never be the same, for I had discovered something that touched me so deeply that I knew I could not reverse its effects even if I had wanted to.

As we drove home from the theater that night, we were all silently bonded in a way I can never explain. My mother's love for the beautiful things of the world has been passed on to me and my children, and I can never thank her enough for this beautiful gift.

Just think of the power of this bonding, this creation of the social will, this spirit of "we" in the family! How to further develop that spirit of "we" in the family will be our focus as we move into Habits 4, 5, and 6.

SHARING THIS CHAPTER WITH ADULTS AND TEENS

Prioritize the Family

- Ask family members: How important is family to us? How much time did we spend last week doing family activities? How do we feel about it? Are we making family a priority in our lives?

- Review the material on pages 120–135. Discuss together: What are the forces in society that tend to destroy the family? How can we overcome these forces?

- Discuss the idea of family time and one-on-ones. Ask: How could a weekly family time be helpful to our family? How could it promote planning? Teaching? Problem-solving? Having fun together? Discuss making the commitment to hold a weekly family time. Work together to generate a variety of ideas for family time activities.

- Talk about one-on-one bonding times. Encourage individuals to share special one-on-one times they've had with other family members. Consider: What bonding time would you like to plan for in your marriage? With your children?

- Review the "big rocks" demonstration on pages 160–161 and try this experiment with your family. Discuss what the "big rocks" are for each individual and for the family as a whole.

For Further Thought

- Discuss this idea: "This is perhaps the greatest role of parenting: helping children connect with their own gifts—particularly conscience." How can you help your child connect with his or her four unique human gifts?

Sharing This Chapter with Children

Some Fun Activities

- Sit down with your family and schedule family activities for the next month or two. Plan things such as visits to family members, holiday activities, one-on-ones with family members, sports events or performances you want to watch together, and trips to the park. Make sure the children contribute their ideas.

- Visit a relative and point out the importance of valuing each member of your extended family. On the way to this relative's house, share stories of fun and interesting moments you enjoyed with your family as you grew up.

- Have the children help you make a visual chart to remind them of their chores and also the fun things you will do each week.

- Conduct the big rock demonstration on pages 160–161 and ask each child to identify his or her big rocks—the most important things he or she has to do this week. This might include activities such as soccer practice, piano lessons, swimming, attending a friend's birthday party, and doing homework. You can use walnuts or marshmallows for big rocks and jelly beans for small pebbles, or the children can bring real rocks they have found, painted, or decorated.

- Make a collection of family pictures.

- Make the commitment to hold family times, planning meetings, or activity days. Children will feel greater joy and pride in their family as you review weekly the accomplishments and activities that have taken place and plan for the next week.

- Teach children who can write how to keep track of their activities in a planner of some kind. Also have them schedule times to do special kinds of activities and services to strengthen relationships. Remind them to always bring their planner to family meetings.

- Identify what type of one-on-one activities each family member would enjoy. Schedule one-on-one time with one of your children each week. You could call it "Susan's special day" or whatever you feel would make it unique.

- Share the story of the "Phantom family" on page 141 and decide how you could serve your neighbors and friends in a clever and original way.

Habit 4
Think "Win-Win"

As we begin this chapter, I'd like to give you an overview of Habits 4, 5, and 6. You may ask yourself, "Why are we getting into Habits 5 and 6 when we're just beginning Habit 4?" It's because these three habits are highly interwoven, and together they create a process that will be immensely helpful to you in accomplishing all the things we've talked about so far. In fact, I often teach these habits first because once you grasp the essence of this process, you have the key to working together effectively to solve any problem or accomplish any goal.

To illustrate how helpful this process is, let me share with you a demonstration I often use in teaching these habits. I typically select a man from the audience who is young, tall, strong, and obviously fit. I invite him to the stage and then challenge him to an arm wrestling contest. As he's coming up, I tell him that I have never lost and don't intend to start now. I tell him he's going to lose and to get ready to lose. When he gets up to the stage, I stick my face right in his face and tell him the same things all over again. I get rather pushy, aggressive, and obnoxious. Obviously exaggerating a little, I let him know that in a few seconds he's going to be lying flat out on the ground. I look at his belt and tell him that I have a black one and that his brown one is an entire order of magnitude different. I tell him that even though he's twice my size, I will put him down. Almost inevitably this type of confrontation stirs the man up and steels his resolve to best me.

Then I ask the people in the front row if they will fund this operation so that if I put him down, I get a dime, and if he puts me down, he gets a dime. They always agree. I ask another audience member to keep track throughout the contest, because each time one of us puts the other down, that person gets another dime. I ask them to time us for thirty seconds and tell us when to start. Then I grab the man's right hand, stand up right next to him, and give a grimacing, intimidating stare as we clasp hands and wait for the signal to go.

By this time the other person almost always is steeled to the task. The signal is given, and I immediately make my arm go limp. He puts me down. He usually tries to hold me there. Sometimes, feeling confused, he lets me up a little and then starts pushing to get me down again, which I quickly let him do. Then I struggle to get back up, and again the resistance starts. When we get to the top, he pushes me back down again.

This usually goes on for a few seconds, and then I say to the person, "Look, why don't we both win?" Usually the other person gets the message and allows me to put him down once. But there is still tension and strain. Then I go limp and let him put me down again. It takes only a few more seconds before the two of us are working together—almost effortlessly—moving back and forth rapidly, putting each other's arms down.

Then I look over to the front row and say, "Okay, how much do you owe us?" Everyone sees the point and begins to laugh.

Can you see the tremendous difference in what is happening at the beginning and the end of this demonstration? At first the feeling is completely adversarial. It's "win-lose": "I win; you lose." There's no effort to understand, to cooperate. There's no seeking of a solution that's good for both of us. There's just a feeling of competition and the desire to win, to put the other down. Can you see how the tension of this "win-lose" approach translates into typical family squabbles—into arguments between marriage partners, between parents and children, between extended family members?

But by the end of the demonstration there's been a significant shift in thinking. It's no longer "I win; you lose." It's "Hey, we can both win—and win big! By understanding and cooperating creatively together, we can do something totally different that benefits us both far more than if either of us had 'won' in the other sense." Can you sense something of the freedom, the creativity, the feeling of unity and shared accomplishment that comes when this is the typical approach to solving family problems?

To some extent we all have family interaction that resembles the beginning, but the more we can move toward the kind of creative and synergistic interaction where everyone wins, the more "beautiful," the more effective, our family culture will be.

I often like to think of these three habits in terms of the *root*, the *route*, and the *fruit*.

- Habit 4—Think "win-win"—is the *root*. It's the fundamental paradigm of seeking mutual benefit, or the "Golden Rule." It's the underlying motive, the nurturing attitude out of which understanding and synergy grow.
- Habit 5—Seek first to understand . . . then to be understood—is the *route*. It's the method, the pathway that leads to rich interdependent interaction. It's the ability to step out of your own autobiography and really get into the head and heart of someone else.
- Habit 6—Synergize—is the *fruit*. It's the result, the end product, the rich reward of the effort. It's creating transcendent third-alternative solutions. It's not "your way" or "my way"; it's a better, a higher way.

Together, these three habits create the process that leads to the most phenomenal magic in family life—the ability to work together to create new ideas, new solutions that are better than any individual family member could ever come up with alone. In addition, they build moral authority into the culture by integrating the principles of mutual respect, mutual understanding, and creative cooperation into the very structures, systems, and processes of the family. This goes way beyond the goodness of the people and the quality of their relationships. It causes perpetuation and internalization and institutionalization of these principles into the norms and mores and traditions of the culture itself.

The question is this: "Would you be willing to search for a solution that is better than what either of us is now proposing?"

And what a difference this makes! Going back to the airplane metaphor, we could say that while it may be challenging to reach your destination when there's turbulent weather *outside* the plane, it's even more difficult when the turbulence is in the social weather *inside* the plane—when there's contention, bickering, fighting, complaining, and criticizing between pilots or between the pilots and the crew or control tower.

Creating great social weather inside the cockpit is the focus of Habits 4, 5, and 6. And what it essentially involves is helping family members learn to ask one question and make one commitment.

The question is this: "Would you be willing to search for a solution that is better than what either of us is now proposing?"

The commitment is this: "Let me listen to you first" or "Help me understand."

The commitment is this: "Let me listen to you first" or "Help me understand."

If you have the personal security and the skill and will to do these two things sincerely and consistently, you will be able to live Habits 4, 5, and 6.

Now most of this process is completely within your Circle of Influence. Going back to the arm wrestling demonstration, notice that all it takes to change the situation is for one person to think win-win—not two, only one. This is an extremely important point because most people are willing to think win-win if others will, but all it takes is one proactive person to think it deep inside and to genuinely want a solution that is ultimately win-win. *You* think win-win—not win-lose or lose-win— even when and even *because* others do not.

It also takes only one person to seek first to understand. In the arm wrestling example, this is manifested by immediately going limp and seeking first the interest of the other person. In life it means to seek first the interest of the other, to understand the other person's needs, wants, and concerns.

So both Habits 4 and 5 can be done by one proactive person.

But Habit 6—Synergize—takes two. This is the exciting adventure of creating something new with someone, and it grows out of the win-win thinking and understanding created by Habits 4 and 5. The magical thing about synergy is that not only does it create new alternatives but it is also tremendously bonding to the relationship because you create something new together. It's like what happens between parents who have created a child together. That child becomes a powerful bonding force in the relationship. It brings them together. It gives them a common bond, a common vision, a common interest, a common stewardship that transcends and subordinates other interests. Can you see how this builds the relationship, how it builds the Emotional Bank Account?

These three habits represent the essence of "family"—the deep inner movement from "me" to "we." So let's take a closer look now at these habits, beginning with Habit 4—Think "win-win."

No One Likes to Lose

One father shared this experience in coming to understand why his son was so unhappy:

Our two boys were very competitive in their relationship with each other. This resulted in frequent squabbles between the two. When the oldest was twelve and the youngest was ten, we went on a long-awaited vacation. But just when we should have been enjoying ourselves the most, the conflict between these two heated up to the point that it was affecting us all in a negative manner. I felt that the older boy was more to blame than the younger one, so I went for a walk with him so that we could talk. When confronted with my criticism of his behavior, he abruptly announced, "The thing you don't understand is that I can't stand my brother."

When I asked him why, he said, "He's always saying things to me that really bug me. On this vacation we're always around each other in the car or wherever we go, and I get so I can't stand to be near him. I wish you would buy me a bus ticket and just let me go home so I wouldn't have to see him anymore."

I was shocked by the intensity of his negative feelings toward his brother. Nothing I could say had any effect in making him see things differently.

We returned to the tent where we were camped. I asked my younger son to come for a walk with us. He didn't want to go when he found out his older brother was going to go along. The older one didn't want to go, either, but I encouraged both boys to give it a chance. They finally agreed, so we hiked to the top of a nearby ridge where the three of us sat down and began to talk.

I addressed the older boy, "You said some things about your brother. Now he is here, and I'd like you to tell him personally what you told me."

He spoke right up and said, "I hate this vacation, and I want to go home just to get away from you."

The younger boy was hurt by these cutting words. Blinking at the sudden tears that came to his eyes, he looked down and quietly said, "Why?"

His older brother was quick and certain with his answer, "Because you're always saying things that make me mad. I just don't want to be around you."

The younger brother sighed. "I just do that because every time we play a game you always win."

"Well, sure I always win," the older boy quickly replied. "I'm better than you."

With that the little boy could hardly speak. But then from the depths of his heart he said, "Yeah, but every time you win, I lose. And I just can't stand to lose all the time. So I say things to bug you. . . . I don't want you to go home. I like being with you. But I just can't stand to lose all the time."

These tearful words reached the heart of the older brother. The tone of his words softened as he said, "Okay, I won't go home. But will you please just stop saying and doing the stupid things that make me so mad at you?"

"Okay," the younger boy replied. "And will you stop feeling that you always have to win?"

That little talk saved our vacation. It didn't make things perfect, but it made them tolerable. I don't think the older boy ever forgot his little brother's words: "I just can't stand to lose all the time."

I know I'll never forget my young son's words. Losing all the time or even most of the time can make any of us say and do stupid things that bug others and even bug ourselves.

No one likes to lose—especially in close family relationships. But we typically go into situations with a win-lose mind-set. And most of the time we don't even realize it.

Many of us came out of homes where we were always being compared to a brother or sister. In school we were graded "on the curve," which means that if one person got an A, it was usually because someone else got a C. Our society is literally saturated with win-lose—forced ranking systems, normal distribution schools, competitive athletics, job openings, political contests, beauty contests, television games, and lawsuits.

And all of this also gets scripted into our family life. So when we have preschool children struggling for autonomy, or teenagers struggling for identity, or siblings competing for attention, or parents trying to maintain order and discipline, or marriage partners arguing for their own way, we naturally fall into win-lose patterns of behavior.

The Consequence of Win-Lose

I remember one day when I returned home to my little girl's third-year birthday party and found her in the corner of the front room, defiantly clutching all of her presents, unwilling to let the other children play with them. The first thing I noticed was several parents in the room witnessing this selfish display. I was embarrassed, and doubly so because at the time I was teaching university classes in human relations. And I knew, or at least felt, the expectation of these parents.

The atmosphere in the room was really charged. The children were crowding around my little daughter with their hands out, asking to play with the presents they had just given, and my daughter was adamantly refusing. I said to myself, "Certainly I should teach my daughter to share. The value of sharing is one of the most basic things we believe in."

I first tried a simple request: "Honey, would you please share with your friends the toys they've given you?"

"No!" she replied flatly.

My second method was to use a little reasoning: "Honey, if you learn to share your toys with them when they are at your home, then when you go to their homes, they will share their toys with you."

Again the immediate reply was "No!"

I was becoming a little more embarrassed, for it was evident I was having no influence. The third method was bribery. Very softly I said, "Honey, if you share, I have a special surprise for you. I'll give you a piece of gum."

"I don't want gum!" she exploded.

Now I was becoming exasperated. For my fourth attempt I resorted to fear and threat: "Unless you share, you will be in real trouble!"

"I don't care!" she cried. "These are mine! I don't have to share!"

Finally, I resorted to force. I simply grabbed some of the toys and tossed them to the other kids. I said, "Here, kids! Play with these."

Since our daughter's birthday party, both Sandra and I have come a long way as parents in understanding that children go through developmental stages. We now understand that expecting that kind of sharing for a child younger than five or six is not realistic. And even then, tiredness, confusion, or special issues of ownership may make it difficult.

But when you're caught up in a moment like that—with all that emotion, with all that pressure—*it is hard!* You feel you're right. In fact, you know you're right. You're bigger. You're stronger. And it seems *so much easier* to go for "win-lose," to have your own way.

But what's the result of that choice in terms of the relationship, in terms of the Emotional Bank Account? And what's going to happen if you keep thinking win-lose down the road? And what about a marriage? What happens when win-lose is the typical interaction?

You're right. You're bigger. You're stronger. And it seems so much easier to go for "win-lose," to have your own way.

I know of one man who worked in a profession that was not interesting to his wife. She didn't like what he did or the people he worked with. They weren't "her kind of people." When his work group planned a Christmas party, he hopefully but skeptically asked her to go. She flatly refused, saying that there was no way she would be at a party with people who engaged in activities that were repulsive to her. He attended the party alone. She won. He lost.

Two months later her social group sponsored a lecture. A noted author was coming to speak. There would be a reception prior to the lecture. She was to be the hostess. She assumed that he would go with her. She was shocked when he told her that morning that he wasn't going to go. In an annoyed tone she asked, "Why not?" He curtly replied, "I don't want to be around your friends any more than you wanted to be around my friends at my Christmas party." He won. She lost.

She didn't speak to him that afternoon when he came home from work. She left for the reception without saying good-bye, and he went to the family room and turned on the TV to watch a football game.

Now what is the impact on the relationship and on the family when a marriage is filled with ego battles, when partners are more concerned about having their own way than in building the relationship? Does anyone ever really "win"?

The Consequence of Lose-win

On the other hand, what happens if the typical interaction is lose-win?

One woman shared this experience:

I was very successful in school—captain of the debate team, editor of the yearbook, first chair clarinet player. I always seemed to excel at whatever I decided I wanted to do. But as I went away to college, I knew that I really didn't want a career. I felt that being a wife and mother was the most important thing I could do with my life.

After my freshman year of college I married Steve, a young man I had been dating from the time I was fourteen. Being Miss Overachiever, I had several children in a very short period of time. I can remember feeling overwhelmed by all the tasks related to having that many young children.

The most difficult part was that I had virtually no help at all from my husband. His job kept him on the road quite a bit, but even when he was home, he basically felt that it was his job to provide, and all the responsibilities for the care and upkeep of the home and children were mine.

My idea had been very different. I thought we were functioning together as a unit, and while I understood that I was at home to nurture these children and to help take care of their physical needs and all that, I had thought that we would be working together as husband and wife in deciding what the course of our lives would be. But that wasn't the case at all.

I can remember getting through days when I would look at the clock and think, "Okay, it's 9:00. I can do this for the next fifteen minutes, and I can do it with a good attitude." I almost had to manage myself in those fifteen-minute increments because if I tried to look at the whole day, it just seemed overwhelming to me.

My husband's expectations of me were extremely high. I was expected to be the perfect housekeeper, the perfect cook, the perfect mother. He would come home after being gone for a week, and the whole house would be immaculate, the children would be asleep, and I would offer him a piece of a cherry pie I had baked. It was his favorite kind of pie. He would sit down at the table, look at it, and say, "You know, the crust is burned a little bit." I felt worthless. I thought I had failed. Regardless of what accomplishment I made, it seemed it was never good enough. There was never a pat on the back or praise—always just continual criticism and, ultimately, abuse.

He became more and more violent. He also became involved in extramarital sex. On his business trips he would go to places for the purpose of meeting people with whom he could have sex. I even discovered later that he had membership cards for such clubs in eight different cities across the country.

At one point I begged him to go to counseling with me. He finally agreed, but there wasn't any real interest on his part at all. One evening when we went in, he was particularly angry. As we walked into his office and sat down, the counselor turned to my husband and said, "You seem really agitated tonight. Do you have something on your mind?"

My husband said, "Yes. I am sick and tired of having to constantly clean up after everybody."

I was dying inside, thinking that I had put all that work and all that energy and years *of effort into creating the perfect home. I had made all my own curtains and toss pillows and all the children's clothes. I had baked bread, kept the house very, very clean, and was always caught up with the laundry, and so forth. What had I missed?*

The counselor said to Steve, "Could you help me understand exactly what it is that you are picking up after other people?" There was a long silence, and we could feel Steve thinking. He was thinking and thinking, and finally, with a lot of passion, he blurted out, "This morning when I took a shower, someone had left the cap off the shampoo bottle!"

I can remember feeling as though I was growing smaller and smaller as I sat there in my chair and thought, Something doesn't feel right here. It just doesn't feel right.

Then the counselor asked another question: "Steve, what else did you have to clean up today?" Again, the long pause. You could feel Steve thinking and thinking, and his response was "Well, that was enough!"

It was right at that point, when I was feeling about one inch high, that I realized for the first time that no matter what I did, he would continue to criticize and see things wrong. For the first time I began to realize that the problem was his—not mine.

I went through a lot of internal struggle during those years. I spent a lot of time trying to please him and to fix me. I even went to the hospital emergency room to ask them to admit me. When they asked why I felt I needed to be admitted to the hospital, I said, "I have created an answer to my problem, and the answer frightens me."

They said, "What do you mean?"

And I said, "I have made a decision and purchased the equipment to shoot each of my children as they come in the door from school and then to turn the gun on myself because life is unbearable." At that time I was thinking that the world was a big and wicked place anyway, and the best thing to do for them would be to take them with me. It scared the heck out of me when I realized that that was my decision. Luckily, I was lucid enough to be able to go to the hospital and say, "I have decided to do it, I have the stuff to do it, and I plan to do it. But I know it's not right. Please help me."

I look back now and realize how interesting it is that I wasn't going to shoot him. It was me. It was always me.

Ultimately, this woman showed tremendous proactive courage in realizing that this was her husband's problem. She ended up getting a college degree, moving her family to a new location, and building a new life—without "Steve." But just look at what happened as a result of all those years when her attitude was essentially lose-win and she was codependent on a husband who was filled with the spirit of chauvinism and irresponsibility.

For most people the lose-win attitude is "I'm a martyr. Go ahead, step on me. Have your way with me. Everyone else does." But what is the consequence of this type of attitude in a relationship? Is there any way that this pattern is going to build a rich, long-term relationship of trust and love?

Win-Win—the Only Long-term Viable Alternative

Really, the only long-term viable alternative is win-win. In fact, it is the essence of a beautiful family culture. Both win-lose and lose-win will ultimately result in lose-lose.

If you're a parent, habitual win-lose will absolutely bankrupt the Emotional Bank Account. You may get your way in the short run, particularly when children are little. You're bigger, you're stronger, you can get your way. But what happens when those children become teenagers? Will they be clear-thinking adolescents, empowered to make good choices on their own? Or will they be so engaged in a reactive struggle for identity, so focused on "winning" in the relationship, that they have no real chance to connect with their own unique gifts or with you as a genuine source of help?

On the other hand, with lose-win you may be popular in the short run because you essentially take the course of least resistance and continuously let others have their way with you. But there's no vision, no standard, no respect. And children end up reaping the consequences of myopic decisions made without the perspective of a parent's guidance and experience and decisive strength. There's no doubt that it's a long-term loss for a child who grows up without principle-based values and a relationship of respect with parents. And it's a loss for both child and parent when the relationship is based on manipulation and popularity rather than trust.

> *There's no doubt that it's a long-term loss for a child who grows up without principle-based values and a relationship of respect with parents.*

And what about a marriage? What kind of impact does it have on the relationship and on the culture when marriage partners are constantly engaged in ego battles, when they're more concerned about *who* is right than *what* is right? Or what is the impact when one spouse becomes a doormat, a martyr? There's no win in it. It's a lose for everyone in the family.

I've been working with this win-win habit in the context of the 7 Habits now for over twenty years, and many have asked, particularly when it comes to the family, whether or not it's always applicable. It's my experience that the concept of trying to develop a win-win relationship is always applicable, but all decisions and agreements won't necessarily be win-win.

Sometimes you may make an unpopular or a win-lose decision with a child because you know it's wise. You know it's not a win, for example, for a child to stay out of school, to avoid being inoculated, or to play in the street instead of the playground—even though the child may really want to. But you can explain unpopular decisions in a way that does not show disrespect to that child and that keeps your decisions from becoming withdrawals. If it's on an issue that is terribly important to the child, you may need to spend more time understanding and explaining so that that child will eventually feel the spirit of win-win even though he or she may not like the decision—and sometimes even you—for a short season.

At other times you may choose to go for what appears to be lose-win because of time pressure and because the issue is peripheral or secondary and the person is central or primary. The principle is this: What is important to another person must be as important to you as the other person is to you. In other words, in your heart you essentially say, "My love for you is so great and our happiness is so entwined that I would not feel good if I got my way and you were unhappy— particularly when you feel so strongly about it."

> The principle is this: What is important to another person must be as important to you as the other person is to you.

Now some might say that by doing this you have given in, capitulated, or compromised. But this is not so. You have merely shifted your emotional focus from the particular issue or decision to the value of the person you love and the quality of your relationship with that person. And in doing so, what might seem to be lose-win is really a win-win.

In other situations it may be that the issue that is important to someone else is also really important to you, and so you'll need to move toward synergy—to find some transcendent purpose or value that unites you, enabling the release of creative juices to find a better way in actualizing that value or achieving that goal or purpose. But as you can see, in all of these instances the spirit and the eventual outcome is always win-win.

Win-win is really the only solid foundation for effective family interaction. It's the only pattern of thinking and interacting that builds long term relationships of trust and unconditional love.

From "Me" to "We"

One man shared this experience:

One day several years ago my wife and I learned that my mother and stepfather had died in a plane crash. We were devastated. Family gathered from all over the country to attend the funeral, and afterward we sadly turned to the task of packing up all their possessions.

During the packing it became evident that some of my siblings had strong feelings about having certain things, and they did not hesitate to make them known.

"Who are you to assume that you get that chest?"

"I can't believe that he thinks he is going to get that antique painting!"

"Just look at how 'grabby' she is—and she's an in-law."

I found myself being sucked into the same spirit of criticism, and I soon realized that dividing these possessions could deeply divide the family and leave a wake of hurt and isolation. To keep that from happening, I decided to focus on things I could influence in a positive way.

First, I suggested to the others that we allow ourselves some time—weeks or even months if necessary—before we attempted to decide who got what. Meanwhile, everything could be placed in storage.

Second, I suggested that we all work on developing a process for dividing the things that would help draw us together as a family and strengthen our relationships, and would also enable us to have items that we either needed or would really enjoy and that would help us remember Mother and John. Everyone seemed to like the ideas and agreed.

But it wasn't that simple. In the months that followed, it was easy to get sucked into thinking, Hey, wait a minute! I wanted that, too. But I kept coming back to the end in mind. I said, "Okay, what's most important here? It's the relationships. It's the outcome. So how can we do this?" I just kept trying to affirm that we needed to work so that everyone would be happy.

We finally put together a list of all the possessions so that everyone knew what was available. We gave a copy of the list to everyone with a little note reminding them of our end goal as a family. We said, "Would you please go through this list and number in order the top five things that you would like? As you do that, consider the other members of the family, because we want everyone to be happy."

We asked all to come prepared so that if another family member was bashful about expressing a desire, they could be sensitive and plead for that family member's getting a certain thing.

When the day for dividing the possessions came, I realized that, despite all our good intentions, there was a high potential for quite a volatile situation. Feeling the need to reconnect with our purpose, I said, "Remember, we are here because we love these two people and we love one another. We want to come out of this experience happy. We want these next few hours to be something that would bring Mom and John happiness if they were here."

And so we all agreed: "We are not going to leave this place until we all feel good about what each person has." We tapped into everyone's love for both of these people and into a sense of responsibility to maintain a spirit of love and kindness and consideration toward other family members. We tapped into people's highest qualities. And the results were amazing.

Each of us took a turn expressing what we had put on our list and why it was important to us. As we shared memories around these things, we found ourselves reminiscing about our experiences with Mom and John. We found ourselves laughing and joking and really enjoying sharing and being together.

When we'd all had our turns, we realized that there was really very little overlap. And when two people expressed a desire for the same thing, one would say, "Gosh, that was on my list, but I can totally see why that would mean so much to you. I'd really like for you to have it."

And toward the end we felt much love for one another and love and gratitude for Mom and John and their lives. It was like an experience dedicated to their honor.

Notice how this man was able to become a transition person in his family. Notice how he made the proactive choice that the welfare of this entire family was his highest priority. This man was truly thinking win-win.

Most of the people in this situation had what we could call a *scarcity mentality*: "There's only one pie, so if you get a bigger piece, then I get less." So everything has to be win-lose.

But this man was able to develop an *abundance mentality*, the idea that there's plenty for everyone and that there is an infinite number of third-alternative solutions, better ways to work things out that make a win for everyone.

This abundance mentality is the spirit of "family." It's the spirit of "we." And this is what marriage and family are all about.

There are some who would say, "The hardest thing about getting married or having children is that it changes your entire lifestyle. You can no longer just focus on your own schedule, your own priorities. You have to sacrifice. You have to think about others, about meeting their needs, about what makes them happy."

And this is true. A good marriage and a good family require service and sacrifice. But when you truly love another and share a transcendent sense of purpose in creating the "we"—such as raising a child—then sacrifice is nothing more than giving up something small for something big. True fulfillment comes from sacrifice. It is this very shift from "me" to "we" that makes family, family!

As J. S. Kirtley and Edward Bok said:

He who carries a wrong heart into the married life and cherishes it in selfishness or finds there a selfish heart that persists in remaining wrong, will make or find married life irritating, galling, unbearable. . . . One who expects to be ministered to in the married state is acting on a principle that will pervert the whole life. He who marries for the purpose of receiving, rather than bestowing, makes a false start. . . . "Married life can never be what it ought to be while the husband or wife makes personal happiness the main object."[1]

> *This abundance mentality is the spirit of "family." It's the spirit of "we." And this is what marriage and family are all about.*

The spirit of wanting the best for everyone and being willing to love and sacrifice to make that happen is the true spirit of win-win.

The reality is that—not in spite of but *because* of their challenges—marriage and family life are the character-building crucible out of which true joy and fulfillment come. As Michael Novak has observed:

Marriage is an assault upon the lonely, atomic ego. Marriage is a threat to the solitary individual. Marriage does impose grueling, humbling, baffling, and frustrating responsibilities. Yet if one supposes that precisely such things are the preconditions for all true liberation, marriage is not the enemy of moral development in adults. Quite the opposite. . . .

Being married and having children has impressed on my mind certain lessons, for whose learning I cannot help being grateful. Most are lessons of difficulty and duress. Most of what I am forced to learn about myself is not pleasant. . . . My dignity as a human being depends perhaps more on what sort of husband and parent I am, than on any professional work I am called upon to do. My bonds to [my family] hold me back (and my wife even more) from many sorts of opportunities. And yet these do not feel like bonds. They are, I know, my liberation. They force me to be a different sort of human being, in a way in which I want and need to be forced.[2]

It is totally and sadly amazing to see beautiful marriage ceremonies take place with all the excitement, social support, beauty, and romance and then see those marriages turn sour and end up in bitterness, in vindictiveness, in the polarization of even families and friends who were once so warm to one another, so knitted together.

When you think about it, the two people haven't changed that much. What has changed is the movement from independence to interdependence—which ultimately changes all circumstances. With the coming forth of children and responsibilities, the rigors and demands of emotional, intellectual, social, and spiritual interdependence far exceed any understanding or vision the original "honeymooners" had. If there is continual growth on both their parts—and growth together—the increasing responsibilities and obligations will unite and bond them in profound ways. If not, it will eventually tear them apart.

It's also interesting to see how there are always two sides to every breakup and how both sides are usually convinced they are right and the other is wrong. And again, both sides generally represent individuals who are basically good, and haven't really changed that much. But independent mind-sets simply will not work in an interdependent relationship and environment. Marriage and family life is truly the "graduate school" of mortality.

One man who married at the age of thirty said this:

When I first got married, I thought I was the most giving, kind, generous, outgoing, unselfish person. But I came to realize I am one of the most selfish, egotistical, self-absorbed people around. And I'm brought up against it constantly because the challenge is always there: doing what I know I should do versus doing what I want to do short term.

I get home from work. It's been a long day and I'm tired, and what I want to do is crawl into my own little cave. I want to escape. I don't want to worry about a relationship or anyone or anything else. I just want to immerse myself in a hobby or a project or anything where I don't have to think.

And yet I know I ought to focus on that relationship and spend some quality time with my wife. I need to realize that she has needs and wants, and I need to listen to her.

For thirty years my life was about me. It wasn't about anyone else. And now that I'm married, I realize my life can't be about me anymore. It's about us. If I'm serious about making my marriage work, then I've got to make that commitment. "My life is not about me; it's about us." Sure there's personal development and I still need personal time. But there's also that relationship, and if it's important to me, I must put the time and effort into it—even when I don't feel like it, even when I'm tired or cranky or ornery.

In her book *Lucky in Love: The Secrets of Happy Couples and How Their Marriages Thrive*, Catherine Johnson shares her research regarding factors that make marriages happy and long-lasting. Among those factors, she highlights two beautiful ideas:

1. Both partners stop being single at heart and become married at heart. Their two souls become one, and each sees the other as his or her best friend.

2. They care more about the health of the relationship than they do about winning arguments. They are self-aware and can hear and evaluate themselves from their partner's perspective.[3]

The kind of sacrifice and service required to achieve a beautiful family culture creates the ultimate "win" in terms of character and fulfillment for those who love as well as for those who are loved. And that is the true spirit of win-win. In fact, it's really win-win-win—a win for the individual, a win for the marriage and family, and a huge win for the society that's benefited by fulfilled individuals and strong families.

How to Cultivate the Spirit of Win-Win

To think win-win means that you try to have this spirit of win-win in all family interactions. You always want what's best for everyone involved.

As a parent, you know that there will be times when your children want to do things that aren't going to create a win for them. Most young, inexperienced people tend to act on their wants, not their needs. Those who care for them are usually more mature, more experienced, and wiser, and are willing to focus on needs rather than wants. Therefore, they often make decisions that are unpopular and that appear to be win-lose.

But parenting is not about being popular and giving in to every child's whim and desire. It's about making decisions that truly are win-win—however they may appear to the child at the time.

Always keep in mind that parenting is basically a "dissatisfaction" business, and it takes a high level of maturity and commitment for parents to realize that and adjust their expectations accordingly. Remember, what makes kids happy is not the opposite of what makes them unhappy or what dissatisfies them. The lack of air, for example, is a dissatisfier. Air doesn't really satisfy you—but if you don't have it, you are extremely dissatisfied. "Air" in the home is what you as a parent provide in terms of understanding, support, encouragement, love, and consistency. To not have these things is a dissatisfier. Without them, the kids would be unhappy. But having them won't make the kids happy. So parents need to adjust their expectations accordingly.

> *Parenting is not about being popular and giving in to every child's whim and desire. It's about making decisions that truly are win-win—however they may appear to the child at the time.*

Frederick Herzberg first introduced this satisfaction/dissatisfaction idea in his "hygiene motivation theory," which has staggering implications for parents.

1. Don't expect a lot of praise and appreciation from your children. If it comes, it's icing on the cake. But don't expect it.
2. Be happy and eliminate as many dissatisfiers as possible.
3. Don't define satisfactions for your kids. You simply can't force natural processes.[4]

As a parent, you're going to deal with all kinds of expressions of dissatisfaction from your children. But remember that all the things you do to provide the basic underpinnings of happiness and security for your child usually aren't talked about. So don't make the mistake of thinking that your children's expressions of dissatisfaction represent the quality of the job you're doing as a parent.

The key is the relationship. People will basically allow you to deal with their needs rather than with their wants when they trust you and know that you sincerely care. So if you cultivate the spirit of win-win whenever you possibly can, children will have the context to understand and accept those decisions that seem to them to be win-lose. And there are several ways that you can do this.

You can let them win in the little things. When children are little, 90 percent of the things are small. In our own family, if our children wanted to set up a swing in the family room, go outside, get dirty, or leave a fort in the house for weeks, we'd generally let them do it. It was a win for them; it was a win for us. It strengthened the relationship. In general we try to distinguish between matters of principle and matters of preference, and take a stand only on the things that really count.

You can interact with them around the big things. In this way they will know you have their welfare in mind, that you're not out to build your own ego or focus on your own selfish concerns. You can be open to their influence. As much as you can, involve them in the problem and work out the solution together. They may have an idea that's genuinely better than yours. Or maybe by interacting you can synergize and create a new alternative that's better than either yours or theirs.

You can take steps to offset the competition focus. One time I went to watch my granddaughter play in a soccer match. She's a good player, and we all felt excited because this was the key game between two top teams from two different cities. The parents on both sides of the field got really involved as the players battled back and forth in a very close game. Finally, the game ended in a tie—which to our coach was not as bad as a loss, but almost.

After the game was over, players from both teams went through the mechanical process of saying, "Good game, good game," as they shook hands. But our team was demoralized. You could see it in their faces. And the coach was out there trying to assuage them a little, but they knew that he was also deeply disappointed. And so they were walking across the field with their heads down.

As they approached the group of parents where I was standing, I spoke up enthusiastically, "All right, kids! That was a great game! You had five goals: to try your best, to have fun, to work together as a team, to learn, and to win. And you accomplished four and a half of those goals. That's ninety percent! That's tremendous! Congratulations!"

You could just see their eyes brighten up, and it wasn't long before both players and parents were celebrating over the four and a half goals these kids had achieved.

A teenage girl shared this experience:

As a sophomore I played on the girls high school basketball team. I was pretty good for my age and tall enough to be a starter on the varsity team although I was just a sophomore. My friend Pam, a sophomore as well, was also moved up to be a starter on the varsity squad.

I had a sweet little shot I could hit quite regularly from ten feet out. I began making four or five of those shots a game and getting recognized for it. It soon became apparent that Pam didn't like all the attention I was getting and decided, consciously or not, to keep the ball from me. It didn't matter how open I was for the shot, Pam stopped passing the ball to me.

One night after playing a terrible game in which Pam kept the ball from me most of the game, I was as mad as I had ever been. I spent many hours talking with my dad, going over everything, and expressing my anger toward my friend-turned-enemy, Pam the jerk.

After a long discussion, my dad told me that the best thing he could think of was to give Pam the ball every time I got it. Every time. I thought it was the stupidest suggestion he had ever given me. He told me it would work and left me at the kitchen table to think about it. But I didn't. I knew it wouldn't work and put it aside as silly fatherly advice.

For the next game I planned and plotted and went out with a mission to ruin Pam's game. On my first possession of the ball, I heard my dad above the crowd. He had a booming voice, and though I shut out everything around me while playing basketball, I could always hear Dad's deep voice. At the moment I caught the ball, he yelled out, "Give her the ball!" I hesitated for one second and then did what I knew was right. Although I was open for a shot, I found Pam and passed her the ball. She was shocked for a moment, then turned and shot, sinking the ball for two points.

As I ran down the court to play defense, I felt something I had never felt before: true joy for the success of another human being. And, even more, I realized that it put us ahead in the game. It felt good to be winning. I continued to give her the ball every time I got it in the first half. Every time. In the second half I did the same, shooting only if it was a designated play or if I was wide open for a shot.

We won that game, and in the games that followed, Pam began to pass me the ball as much as I passed it to her. Our teamwork was getting stronger and stronger, and so was our friendship. We won the majority of our games that year and became a legendary small town duo. The local newspaper even did an article on our ability to pass to each other and sense each other's presence. It was as if we could read each other's mind. Overall, I scored more points than ever before. When I scored, I could feel her genuine happiness for me. And when she scored more than I did, I felt especially good inside.*

Even in a win-lose situation such as in athletics, there are things you can do to help create a win-win spirit and to emphasize the overall context of win-win. In our family we've discovered we often have a more enjoyable time together if we go for a "team" score.

Sandra:

When our family included infants to teenagers, it was hard to find an activity that everyone could enjoy. Sometimes we would go bowling. All could participate at the level they were at, but the winners were always the same people—the larger, stronger, and more skilled.

We tried to figure out a way that it could become a win for everyone and finally found a system that worked. Instead of adding up individual scores and having the person with the most points win, we added up the total of everyone's score. We set an arbitrary goal of so many points we had to reach in order to win as a family. If we met the goal, we would

*For additional information on how teenagers can apply the 7 Habits, look for Sean Covey's forthcoming book, The 7 Habits of Highly Effective Teens.

be able to have ice cream sundaes or root beer floats or banana splits as a reward for meeting our goal. So instead of getting upset when someone else had a strike or did much better, we were cheering all of us to do our best so our points would add up to our goal.

This became a win-win for the entire family and a very synergistic solution. Instead of having winners and losers, we hoped each person would do his or her best. We cheered each other on. We had a common goal. One extra point would make the difference in going out for pizza or ice cream instead of going home.

We've also found that involving one child in training another child diminishes the rivalry between those children. Both children honor and respect the one child's achievement because they were both involved.

Sandra:

Sean and David were only eighteen months apart in age. Sometimes there was competition and rivalry. When David was learning to read, for example, Sean would often mimic him and make him cry. Slowly and haltingly, David would stumble on the words, "Mary . . . went . . . to . . . the . . . store." Sean would crawl out from his hiding place and repeat in the same slow manner, "Mary . . . went . . . to . . . the . . . store," teasing and laughing and making fun of David until he started crying.

We would interact with him: "Sean, David is trying to learn to read. You had to learn to read. It's hard at first. Stop teasing him. He's your little brother, for heaven sakes! Don't make him cry—just leave him alone."

This went on for some time until we finally came up with a better solution. Taking Sean aside, we visited with him. "Sean, how would you like to take an assignment? You are older than David, and you already know how to read. Do you think that you could teach David to read? That would be so nice. Sit down with him every day for one half-hour and see if you can help him better than we were able to."

Sean thought about this and decided to do it. After a few days he brought David by the hand and presented him to us with this exclamation: "Listen to David read. I've been teaching him every day, and he sounds really good." David would open his book and proceed to read, "Mary . . . went . . . to . . . the . . . store," sounding slow and unsteady, just as he had a few days earlier.

We said, "Congratulations, Sean! You've taught David how to read." Sean was beaming, full of pride for being the master teacher. David was happy, too, knowing that his brother thought he sounded great. It was a win for both of them. Sean had become the teacher, bringing his student to us for approval. David had become the learner, proud of his accomplishments.

There are many ways to create win-win situations—even for the youngest of children. As became clear at our daughter's birthday party, young children go through many developmental stages, including the need to own or possess their toys before they're willing to share. Once we as parents understand these types of concepts, we can help our children move toward win-win:

"What's all the crying about? Oh, look, Johnnie feels bad. Why do you think he feels bad? Do you think it's because you took that toy away from him? These are your toys. They belong to you. What do you think we can do to make Johnnie feel happy and make you feel good inside, too? You want to share? What a good idea! Now both of you will be happy."

Sandra:

I remember our two-year-old being mildly resentful and anxious about the time I spent nursing her younger brother. Finally, I said, "Why don't you run and choose your favorite book for me to read to you while I'm nursing the baby? The baby is so little, he just eats and falls asleep, and you and I have all this time to spend together by ourselves." It became our story reading time and solved the problem.

Creating Win-Win Agreements

Some of the biggest deposits and withdrawals in the family come from how you handle expectations. Sometimes people just assume certain things about relationships. These things are never talked about, but the assumptions, the expectations, are there. And when these expectations are not fulfilled, it becomes a major withdrawal.

The key is in creating clear expectations up front, and family "win-win agreements" can help you do this. One woman shared this experience of developing a win-win agreement with a daughter who was taking the lower road:

We have a daughter who is very social. She enjoys all forms of activities and always has been involved in every form of dancing, cheerleading, sports, drama, and music.

When she entered high school, it seemed like heaven to her with so many opportunities for fun and socializing—and especially getting to know all the new boys she was meeting. But it wasn't long before her grades started to drop and home became more of a hotel. It seemed as if she had lost her good sense and was just bouncing of the wall in her attempt to be part of the "real world" and fit in.

We were deeply concerned because we could see a smart girl starting to go down a very unhealthy and unproductive path. So one night we sat down with her and explained in detail what a win-win agreement was and how it worked. We asked her to think about it, and we set a time to meet with her the following night to draw up an agreement that all of us could live with.

The next night we all met in the living room and got out our notepads. We first asked her to tell us about her needs. There were many: She needed more freedom, more involvement in high school activities, later curfews, permission to drive with boys, money to attend the dances, extracurricular lessons so she could improve in an area she wanted to try out for, nicer clothes, parents who were more understanding and not so "outdated," and so on. As we listened, we could tell that these concerns were very important to her at this stage in her life.

We then asked if we could state our concerns—which we did. And we had just as many. We listed things such as acceptable grades, planning for the future, helping out at home, obeying curfews, reading on a regular basis, being nice to her brothers and sisters, and hanging out with kids who had good values and habits.

Naturally, she had objections to many things we brought up. But the fact that we made it a meeting, that we wrote everything down and seemed to be so organized, and that we had the attitude of really wanting to reach a solution that everyone could be happy with, made a deep positive impression on her. We were able to draw up a win-win agreement very quickly, one that involved every aspect of her life. There were gives and takes on both sides. She insisted on signing it and having us sign it, and she has kept it in her room as her contract with us.

Since that evening she has totally relaxed. It's as though she doesn't have to prove to anyone anymore that she is getting older and needs new boundaries. There's no longer a reason to challenge situations and prove her point.

She has referred to the agreement many times since—always because we forgot something we had agreed to. It has given her peace. She knows where she stands. And it impressed her that we were so willing to negotiate, to change, and to try to understand where she's coming from right now in her life.

A divorced mother shared this experience in developing a win-win agreement with a son on drugs:

My husband and I divorced when our son was sixteen, and this was very hard for him to deal with. He experienced great pain that got him into drugs and other problems.

When I had the opportunity to attend a 7 Habits course, I invited this struggling son to come with me, which he did. This laid the foundation for a major transformation in his life.

At first he actually went further downhill. But he was finally able to use these habits to pull himself up again. Together we developed a win-win agreement. Part of the agreement was that I would help him purchase a car, which he desperately needed, and that he would make the remaining payments. He was in financial difficulties so he couldn't get a loan, but I would get it. He would also go through drug therapy. We were very specific about five or six issues that needed to be taken care of, and he agreed. He wrote up the *agreement, and we signed it. We were both very clear on what needed to happen.*

He had been in great despair and facing very difficult challenges, but he became entirely responsible for his past and courageously began to travel down a different road. He honored every single commitment he made. In a three-month period he was able to totally and completely turn his life around.

He is now well employed and is going to the university. He's the top student in his class. He wants to be a doctor and is back on track, while it had looked before as if he would never reach this goal.

Can you see how, in each of these situations, the agreements nurtured a spirit of win-win in the culture?

Can you also see how these agreements helped build the Emotional Bank Account? They were based on shared understanding. They helped create shared vision. They clarified expectations. They involved commitment. They built trust. And they were a win for everyone involved.

Let the Agreement Govern

One mother shared how a win-win agreement helped her get off her children's backs and let them learn responsibility:

When our children were small, I had always made sure their clothes were clean, neatly folded, and put away. As they got older, I taught them to sort the laundry and put away their own clothes. But when they reached their early teens, we felt the time had come to give them the stewardship of really being responsible for their own clothes. So at one of our family times just before school started, we talked about it. We decided together what would be a win for them and a win for us. And we set up a win-win clothing agreement.

We agreed that we would provide them with a certain amount of money for a "clothing allowance" each week, transportation for them to buy clothes, and help with clothing repair. In turn they agreed that they would wash, fold, and put away their laundry each week, keep their clothes drawers and closets neat and orderly, and not leave clothes lying around. We set up an "unwanted box" for anything left lying around. Each item put in the box cost twenty-five cents of their clothing allowance to redeem.

We also agreed that every week we would have an accountability session. They would turn in a sheet of paper that listed the allowance they had earned that week by doing chores. Also on the paper was a place for them to check off whether or not they had done their laundry.

The year started out great. We taught them how to use the laundry machines. They were excited about having money to buy their own clothes, and they went through several weeks with clean, folded clothes. But as they became more involved in school activities, they began to miss a week here and there. At one point they were missing more than they were making it happen.

It was a big temptation to nag them about it, and sometimes I did. They were always sorry and always had plans to do better. But after a while I began to realize that I had given them a responsibility and then had taken it back. As long as I was reminding them, it was my problem, not theirs.

So I bit my tongue and let the agreement play itself out. Every week I cheerfully sat down with them and accepted their paper. I paid them the allowance they earned. If they had done their clothes, I gave them their clothing allowance. If not, I didn't. Week after week they were brought face-to-face with their own performance.

Before long, clothes began to wear out. Shoes got too small. They began to say, "I really need some new clothes!"

"Great!" I said. "You have your clothing allowance. When would you like me to take you shopping?"

The reality suddenly seemed to get through. They realized that some of their choices about the way they were spending their time may not have been the best. But they couldn't complain. They had helped create the agreement in the first place. It wasn't long before they began to take a much greater interest in getting their laundry done.

The best thing about this whole experience is that the agreement helped me be calm and let them learn. They chose; they got the consequence. I was loving, I was supportive, but I didn't get in the way. I wasn't being pulled apart by "Mom, please get me a new shirt!" or "Can't we please go to the mall and get some new pants?" The agreement governed. They knew they couldn't come to me and beg for money for clothes.

Notice how this woman let the win-win agreement govern in the relationship. Can you see how doing that enabled her to be less reactive when problems came up? The agreement gave her a sense of security. It freed her to be more loving and kind when the children had problems because she wasn't subject to their whims and persuasions.

Can you see how this approach would build the Emotional Bank Account? The relationship didn't turn into a power struggle because the agreement was in place. This woman was doing what she had agreed to do. She let them learn from the consequences of their choice. And she was free to be loving and sympathetic when they didn't get the result they wanted.

Notice, too, how this woman was able to teach her children several important principles through this win-win agreement. She had given them the example: They had lived with clean, folded clothes for many years. She gave them the education and training they needed to succeed: She taught them how to sort their laundry and how to use the laundry machines. Then she fixed the responsibility through the agreement and didn't take it back. She patiently, lovingly let them learn.

The Five Elements of a Win-Win Agreement

> *You cannot hold people responsible for results if you supervise their methods.*

Some years ago Sandra and I had an interesting experience that taught us a lot about creating win-win agreements with our children. Probably the most significant thing it taught us is this: You cannot hold people responsible for results if you supervise their methods.

This story is the most popular story I've ever told. In fact, entire conferences put on by different groups have been based on it. As you read this story, notice how the five elements of a win-win agreement—desired results, guidelines, resources, accountability, and consequences—come into play.

Green and Clean

Our little son Stephen had volunteered to take care of the yard. Before I actually gave him the job, I began a thorough training process.

[Notice through the next several paragraphs how we identify the desired results.]

I wanted him to have a clear picture in his mind of what a well-cared-for yard was like, so I took him next door to our neighbor's. "Look, son," I said. "See how our neighbor's yard is green and clean? That's what we're after: green and clean. Now come look at our yard. See the mixed colors? That's not it; that's not green. Green and clean is what we want. [Notice how we set up the guidelines.] *Now how you get it green is up to you. You're free to do it any way you want except paint it. But I'll tell you how I'd do it if it were up to me."*

"How would you do it, Dad?"

"I'd turn on the sprinklers. But you may want to use a bucket or a hose, or you can spit all day. It makes no difference to me. All we care about is that the color is green. Okay?"

"Okay."

"Now let's talk about 'clean,' son. Clean means no messes around—no paper, strings, bones, sticks, or anything that messes up the place. I'll tell you what let's do. Let's just clean up half the yard right now and look at the difference."

So we got out two paper sacks and picked up one side of the yard. "Now let's look at this side. Look at the other side. See the difference? That's called clean."

"Wait!" he called. "I see some paper behind that bush!"

"Oh, good! I didn't notice that newspaper back there. Good eye, son!

"Now before you decide whether or not you're going to take the job, let me tell you a few more things—because when you take the job, I don't do it anymore. It's your job. It's called a stewardship. Stewardship means 'a job with trust.' I trust you to do the job, to get it done.

"Now who's going to be your boss?"

"You, Dad?"

"No, not me. You're the boss. You boss yourself. How do you like Mom and Dad nagging you all the time?"

"I don't."

"We don't like doing it, either. It sometimes causes a bad feeling, doesn't it? So you boss yourself. [Notice how we make clear what his resources are.] Now guess who your helper is."

"Who?"

"I am," I said. "You boss me."

"I do?"

"That's right. But my time to help is limited. Sometimes I'm away. But when I'm here, you tell me how I can help. I'll do anything you want me to do."

"Okay!"

"Guess who judges you."

"Who?"

"You judge yourself."

"I do?"

"That's right. [Notice the setting up of accountability.] Twice a week the two of us will walk around the yard, and you can show me how it's coming. How are you going to judge?"

"Green and clean."

"Right!"

I trained him with those two words for two weeks before I felt he was ready to take the job. Finally, the big day came.

"Is it a deal, son?"

"It's a deal."

"What's the job?"

"Green and clean."

"What's green?"

He looked at our yard, which was beginning to look better. Then he pointed next door. "That's the color of his yard."

"What's clean?"

"No messes."

"Who's the boss?"

"I am."

"Who's your helper?"

"You are, when you have time."

"Who's the judge?"

"I am. We'll walk around two times a week, and I can show you how it's coming."

"And what will we look for?"

"Green and clean."

At that time, I didn't set up an extrinsic consequence such as an allowance, but focused on helping him understand the intrinsic satisfaction and natural consequences of a job well done. [Notice the recognition and explanation of consequences.]

Two weeks and two words. I thought he was ready.

It was Saturday, and he did nothing. Sunday, nothing. Monday, nothing. As I pulled out of the driveway on my way to work Tuesday, I looked at the yellow, cluttered yard and the hot July sun on its way up. "Surely he'll do it today," I thought. I could rationalize Saturday because that was the day we made the agreement. I could rationalize Sunday; Sunday was for other things. But I couldn't rationalize Monday. And now it was Tuesday. Certainly he'd do it today. It was summertime. What else did he have to do?

All day I could hardly wait to return home to see what happened. As I rounded the corner, I was met with the same picture I had left that morning. And there was my son at the park across the street playing.

This was not acceptable. I was upset and disillusioned by his performance after two weeks of training and all those commitments. We had a lot of effort, pride, and money invested in the yard, and I could see it going down the drain. Besides, my neighbor's yard was manicured and beautiful, and the situation was beginning to get embarrassing.

I was ready to go back to being the boss. "Son, you get over here and pick up this garbage right now or else!" I knew I could get the golden egg that way. But what about the goose? What would happen to his internal commitment?

So I faked a smile and yelled across the street, "Hi, son. How's it going?"

"Fine!" he returned.

"How's the yard coming?" I knew the minute I said it I had broken our agreement. That's not the way we had set up an accounting. That's not what we had agreed.

So he felt justified in breaking it, too. "Fine, Dad."

I bit my tongue and waited until after dinner. Then I said, "Son, let's do as we agreed. Let's walk around the yard together, and you can show me how it's going in your stewardship."

As we started out the door, his chin began to quiver. Tears welled up in his eyes, and by the time we got out to the middle of the yard, he was whimpering.

"It's so hard, Dad!"

What's so hard? I thought to myself. You haven't done a single thing! But I knew what was hard—self-management, self-supervision. So I said, "Is there anything I can do to help?"

"Would you, Dad?" he sniffed.

"What was our agreement?"

"You said you'd help me if you had time."

"I have time."

So he ran into the house and came back with two sacks. He handed me one. "Will you *pick that stuff up?"* He pointed to the garbage from Saturday night's barbecue. *"It makes me sick!"*

So I did. I did exactly what he asked me to do. And that was when he signed the agreement in his heart. It became his yard, his stewardship.

He only asked for help two or three more times that entire summer. He took care of that yard. He kept it greener and cleaner than it had ever been under my stewardship. He even reprimanded his brothers and sisters if they left so much as a gum wrapper on the lawn.

It was hard to live by the agreement we had created! But I learned the power of doing it—and the power of a win-win agreement that has the five elements in it. The fact is, you're going to deal with these five elements sooner or later. If you don't choose do it in leadership time up front, you do it in crisis management time down the road:

"Oh, was that what I was supposed to do? I didn't understand."

"Well, why didn't you tell me I wasn't supposed to do it that way?"

"I didn't know where the instructions were."

"You never said I had to have it done by today."

"What do you mean I can't go out tonight? You never said anything about not being able to go out if I didn't get it done. Sharon didn't get her work done, and you let her go out!"

At the beginning it will probably seem as if the five elements take a lot of time to set up. And they usually do. But it is far more effective to invest the time early on rather than deal with the consequences of not doing it later on.

The "Big Picture"—the Key to Thinking Win-Win

Obviously, to think win-win is at the heart of what "family" is all about. But as I said at the beginning of this chapter, when you're caught up in the emotion and the behavior of the moment, it can be incredibly hard to do. And so that pause between what happens to us and our response becomes vitally important.

In our own family life Sandra and I have found that the greatest single key to living Habit 4 is to use that pause to connect with the "big picture."

Several years ago Sandra covered the walls in our family room from floor to ceiling with pictures of the family at all stages of their lives. There are family pictures of our fathers, mothers, grandparents, and great-grandparents: black-and-white pictures taken just after our wedding, baby and school pictures of our nine children taken through the years, pictures of them with no teeth, with freckles, with zits and braces, high school pictures, college pictures, mission pictures, and wedding pictures. There are family group photos and a grandchildren's wall. There are even pictures of me from years ago when I had hair!

Sandra wanted to create this family wall covering because she wanted all the family members to see one another as she saw them. When she looked at our thirty-three-year-old married son with four children, for example, in her mind she would also see this same son as a four-year-old boy coming inside to get comfort and a Band-Aid for a scraped knee. She would see him as a twelve-year-old facing his fears on the first day of junior high. She would see him as a seventeen-year-old quarterback fighting to rally his courage after a first-half championship game defeat, as a nineteen-year-old leaving home to spend two years in a foreign country, as a twenty-three-year old embracing his new bride, as a twenty-four-year-old holding his first child.

You see, to Sandra there is so much more to everyone in the family than what anyone can see at any given moment in time. And she wanted to communicate that, to involve others so that they could appreciate this vision she had of the people she loves.

Sandra:

It's been wonderful seeing how everyone who comes to our house is immediately drawn to the picture wall. They notice family resemblances and point out how one of the grandchildren looks exactly like his mother or father used to look. Our children and grandchildren always flock to it.

"Oh, I remember that pink dress—it was my favorite!"

"Wasn't your mother pretty?"

"See, I had to wear braces, too."

"This picture was taken of our team when we won the state football championship."

"That's the formal I wore when I was Boys' Day Queen."

Our sons were thrilled when I snapped a picture of them on the boat dock after they had had their muscles pumped up by water skiing. I made it into a large poster and gave it to them for Christmas. They come in and point it out proudly to their sons.

"See how muscular I was?"

And there they are with tan, bronzed bodies—muscles rippling in the sun.

"That's your dad there," they tell their children. "I lifted weights for three years to look like that!"

Whenever I think of my children, I don't think of how they look and act today. I'm flooded with memories of familiar expressions they used, favorite outfits they wore. Baby, toddler, preschool, teen, young adult—all these images flash before my mind as I see the finished product before me. I remember the ages and stages, the looks, laughter, tears, failures, and triumphs.

A glance at this picture wall is like having your whole life flash before you in a few seconds. I'm flooded with memories, nostalgia, pride, joy, and renewal. Life goes on, and it's so wonderful. We have lots of scrapbooks, and I enjoy those, too. But this is our family—our life—all around me. And I love it.

I have often wished we could expand that wall to include pictures of the future as well—to see ourselves, our spouses, and our children ten, twenty, even fifty years down the road. How mind and heart expanding it would be if we could see the challenges they will face, the character strength they will develop, the contributions they will make! And what a difference it would make in our interactions with each other if we could see beyond the behavior of the moment—if we could treat everyone in the family from the perspective of all they have been and all that we can help them become, as well as whatever they may happen to be doing at any given moment.

To act on that kind of vision—instead of on the emotion or the behavior of the moment—makes all the difference in parenting. Take a jugular issue such as disciplining a child, for example. One of the most valuable things Sandra and I have learned as a result of "big picture" thinking is the difference between *punishment* and *discipline*. Perhaps I can illustrate with the common practice of sending a child to a "time-out" room.

Many people use a "time-out" room as a place to send a misbehaving child until he or she settles down. How this time-out room is used clearly represents the distinction between punishment and discipline. Punishment would be saying to the child, "Okay, you've got to go into the time-out room for thirty minutes." Discipline would be saying, "Okay, you need to go into the time-out room until you decide to live by what we agreed." Whether the child stays in the room for one minute or one hour doesn't matter, as long as the child has exercised the necessary proactivity to make the right choice.

For example, if a son clearly misbehaves, then he needs to go into the time-out room until he makes up his mind to do otherwise. If he comes out and continually misbehaves, then that means he hasn't made up his mind, so that issue would have to be discussed. But the point is that you're showing respect and affirming that he has the power to choose the behavior that is consistent with the principles in the agreement. Discipline is not emotional. It's handled in a very direct and matter-of-fact way, carrying out the consequences agreed to beforehand.

Whenever a child misbehaves, it's important to remember Habit 2 (Begin with the end in mind) and to be clear about exactly what it is you're trying to do. Your end in mind as a parent is to help the child learn and grow, to nurture a responsible person. The objective of discipline is to help the child develop internal discipline—the capacity to make right choices even when there are influences to do otherwise.

In light of that, one of the most important things you can do is involve Habit 1 (Be proactive) on the child's level and affirm his or her capacity to be "response-able." Make it clear that the issue is the behavior, not the child. Affirm, rather than deny, the child's ability to make choices. You can also help children improve their ability to make good choices by encouraging them to keep a personal journal. In that way they strengthen their own unique human gifts by observing their own involvement and educating their conscience. You can also use Habit 4 to come up with win-win agreements regarding rules and consequences in advance.

Sandra and I find that when our children experience this kind of discipline, they have a whole different spirit about them. Their energy is focused on dealing with their own conscience instead of with us. They become more open and teachable. And often, discipline actually builds the Emotional Bank Account. There's good will in the relationship rather than rejection and harshness. Children may still make bad choices, but they come to trust the sense of dependability and stability in principles and in a principle-centered home environment.

The ability to see the "big picture" makes an enormous difference in every family interaction. Perhaps when all of us look at the members of our family (including ourselves), we ought to envision everyone wearing a T-shirt that says, "Be patient; I'm not finished yet." And we ought always to assume good faith. By acting on the assumption that others are trying to do their best as they see it, we can exert a powerful influence in bringing out the best in them.

If we can always see each other as constantly changing and growing and acting in good faith—and if we can keep our destination, the end, in mind—we'll have the motivation and the commitment it takes to always go for win-win.

SHARING THIS CHAPTER WITH ADULTS AND TEENS

Learning to Think "Win-Win"
- Discuss the arm wrestling demonstration on pages 169–170. Why is the win-win way of arm wrestling and thinking so much better for family relationships?
- Discuss how one person with a win-win attitude can change a situation.
- Ask family members: Why is internal contention more destructive to the family than the turbulent pressures from outside?

Interdependence Is the Goal
- Ask family members: What needs to happen for family members to be able to work together to come up with solutions that are better than any one family member could come up with alone? How would the "one question, one commitment" idea be helpful?
- Discuss the consequences of win-lose and lose-win thinking. Ask: Can you think of any situation in which either of these alternatives would work better than win-win?

Moving from "Me" to "We"
- Review the funeral story on pages 179–181 as an example of how a very sensitive situation was turned into a win-win for everybody by one man with a vision and a plan. Discuss how you can develop and model a win-win attitude and behavior in some situation in your life.
- Talk about the difference between a "scarcity" and an "abundance" mentality as described on page 181. Identify a situation in which an abundance mentality would benefit your family. Try to use abundance thinking for a week. Talk over the difference it makes in your family culture.

Developing Win-Win Agreements with Family Members
- Discuss the stories in this chapter that deal with the development of family win-win agreements (pages 185–195). Talk about the difference these agreements make for children and for parents. Try creating a win-win agreement with another family member. Live with it for a week. Discuss the benefits and challenges.
- Discuss the difference between discipline and punishment. Ask: How can we discipline without punishing?
- Discuss what it means to see the big picture. When a family member is being disagreeable, how can seeing beyond the behavior of the moment help you think win-win?

SHARING THIS CHAPTER WITH CHILDREN

Enough for Everyone

- Enjoy an afternoon in the sun with your children. Go to a place such as the beach, the park, or the mountains and talk with them about how wonderful the sun is and how there is enough for everyone. Point out that it doesn't take anything away from the sun whether one or one million people are enjoying it. There is an abundance of sunshine, just as there is an abundance of love. Loving one person doesn't mean you cannot love other people as well.

- Play a game. Tell the children that this time, "winning" means it's got to be a win for everyone. Decide on some new rules which say that being kind and considerate to the other players is more important than getting the most points. See what happens. Children might decide to give up a turn now and then, share the game money or candy, go for a team score, or offer advice on how to make a better move. After the game, have them discuss how helping everyone win made them feel. Help them to understand that the world has room for lots of winners.

- Invite the family to a ball game and explain on the way that the plan is for everyone to take note of the "best" they see on the playing field—best play, best teamwork, best sportsmanship, best coordination—not only from the team they're rooting for, but also from the opposing team. After the game, compare notes and have them point out all the good things they observed. Ask family members to share their insights and feelings.

- Share the story about the two young brothers who had such a competitive relationship that they couldn't enjoy being together. Discuss how the win-win approach they developed could help in solving any similar problems you might have between your children.

- Select an issue that has created a struggle between you and your children. It could be something such as getting a swingset they want badly, visiting an amusement park, or doing something you're not sure you want them to do. Sit down and discuss it. Lay all cards on the table. Determine what would constitute a win for each person involved and try to come up with a true win-win solution. Discuss together how you feel when the solution is reached.

- Choose areas in your family life that need additional cooperation, teamwork and better attitudes. Write each one on a note and put them all in a hat. Have the children draw the notes out of the hat one at a time, and explain what they would do to make that situation a win for everyone.

HABIT 5
SEEK FIRST TO
UNDERSTAND...
THEN TO BE
UNDERSTOOD

To learn to seek first to understand and then to be understood opens the floodgates to heart-to-heart family living. As the fox said in the classic *The Little Prince*, "And now here is my secret, a very simple secret: It is only with the heart that one can see rightly; what is essential is invisible to the eye."

As we begin this chapter, I'd like to ask you to try an experiment. Please take a few seconds and just look at the picture on this page.

Now look at this picture and carefully describe what you see.

Do you see an Indian? What does he look like? How is he dressed? Which way is he facing?

You would probably say that the Indian has a prominent nose, that he's wearing a feathered warbonnet, and that he is looking to the left of the page.

But what if I were to tell you that you're wrong? What if I said that you were not looking at an Indian but at an Eskimo, and that he is wearing a coat with a hood that covers his head, that he has a spear in his hand, and that he is facing away from you and toward the right side of the page?

Who would be right? Look at the picture again. Can you see the Eskimo? If you can't, keep trying. Can you see his spear and hooded coat?

If we were talking face-to-face, we could discuss the picture. You could describe what you see to me, and I could describe what I see to you. We could continue to communicate until you showed me what you see in the picture and I showed you what I see.

Because we can't do that, turn to page 244 and study the picture there. Then look at this picture again. Can you see the Eskimo now? It is important that you see him clearly before you continue reading.

For many years I have used these kinds of perception pictures to bring people to the realization that the way they see the world is not necessarily the way other people see the world. In fact, people do not see the world as *it* is; they see it as *they are*— or as they have been conditioned to be.

Almost always this kind of perception experience causes people to be humbled and to be much more respectful, more reverent, more open to understanding.

Often when I teach Habit 5, I will go out into the audience and take a pair of glasses from one person and try to talk another person into wearing them. I usually tell the audience that I'm going to use several methods of human influence to try to get this person to wear these glasses.

People do not see the world as it is; they see it as they are—or as they have been conditioned to be.

When I put these glasses on the person—let's say a woman— she will usually quickly recoil in some way, particularly if they are strong prescription glasses. And so I appeal to her motivation. I say, "Try harder." And there's even more recoiling. Or if she feels intimidated by me, she'll outwardly tend to go along, but there's no real buy-in inside. So I say, "Well, I sense you're kind of rebelling. You've got an 'attitude.' You've got to be positive. Think more positively. You can make this work." So she'll kind of smile, but that doesn't work at all and she knows it. So she'll usually say, "That doesn't help at all."

So then I try to create a little pressure or to intimidate her in some way. I step into the role of a parent and say, "Look, do you have any idea of the sacrifices your mother and I have made for you—the things we've done for you, the things we've denied ourselves to help you? And you're going to take this kind of an attitude! Now wear these!" And sometimes that stirs up even more feelings of rebellion. I step into the role of a boss and try to exert some economic pressure: "How current is your résumé anyway?" I appeal to social pressure: "Aren't you going to be part of this team?" I appeal to her vanity: "Oh, but they look so good on you! Look, everyone. Don't they complement her features?"

I tap into motivation, attitude, vanity, economic and social pressure. I intimidate. I guilt-trip. I tell her to think positively, to try harder. But none of these methods of influence works. Why? Because they all come from me—not from her and her unique eye situation.

This brings us to the importance of seeking to understand before you seek to influence—of diagnosing before prescribing, as an optometrist does. Without understanding, you might as well be yelling into the wind. No one will hear you. Your effort may satisfy your ego for a moment, but there's really no influence taking place.

We each look at the world through our own pair of glasses—glasses that come out of our own unique background and conditioning experiences, glasses that cre-

ate our value system, our expectations, our implicit assumptions about the way the world is and the way it should be. Just think about the Indian/Eskimo experience at the beginning of this chapter. The first picture conditioned your mind to "see" or interpret the second picture similarly. But there was another way to see it that was just as accurate.

One of the main reasons behind communication breakdowns is that the people involved interpret the same event differently. Their different natures and background experiences condition them to do so. If they then interact without taking into account why they see things differently, they begin to judge each other. For instance, take a small thing such as a difference in room temperature. The thermostat on the wall registers 75 degrees. One person complains, "It's too hot," and opens the window; the other complains, "It's too cold," and closes it. Who is right? Is it too hot or too cold? The fact is they are both right. Logic would say that if two disagree and one is right, the other is wrong. But it isn't logic; it's psycho-logic. Both are right—each from his or her own point of view.

As we project our conditioning experiences onto the outside world, we assume we're seeing the world the way it is. But we're not. We're seeing the world as *we* are—or as we have been conditioned to be. And until we gain the capacity to step out of our own autobiography—to set aside our own glasses and really see the world through the eyes of others—we will never be able to build deep, authentic relationships and have the capacity to influence in positive ways.

And that's what Habit 5 is all about.

At the Heart of Family Pain Is Misunderstanding

Years ago I had a profound, almost shattering experience that taught me the essence of Habit 5 in a forcible and humbling way.

Our family was on a sabbatical for about fifteen months in Hawaii, and Sandra and I had begun what was to become one of the great traditions of our lives. I would pick her up a little before noon on an old red trail cycle. We would take our two preschool children with us—one between us and the other on my left knee—and ride out in the cane fields by my office. We would ride slowly along for about an hour, just talking. We usually ended up on an isolated beach; we parked the trail cycle and walked about two hundred yards to a secluded spot where we ate a picnic lunch. The children would play in the surf, and we would have great in-depth visits about all kinds of things. We would talk about almost everything.

One day we began to talk about a subject that was very sensitive for us both. I had always been bugged about what I considered Sandra's inordinate attachment to buying Frigidaire appliances. She seemed to have an obsession about Frigidaire that I was at an absolute loss to understand. She would not even consider buying another brand. Even when we were just starting out and on a very tight budget, she insisted that we drive the fifty miles to the "big city" where Frigidaire appliances were sold, because no dealer in our small university town carried them at that time.

What bothered me the most was not that she liked Frigidaire but that she persisted in making what I considered illogical and indefensible statements that had no basis in fact whatsoever. If she had only agreed that her response was irrational and purely emotional, I think I could have handled it. But her justification was really upsetting. In fact it was such a tender issue that on this particular occasion we kept riding and postponed going to the beach. I think we were afraid to look each other in the eye.

But the spirit was such that we were very open. We started talking about our appliances in Hawaii, and I said, "I know you would probably prefer Frigidaire."

"I would," she agreed, "but these seem to be working out fine." Then she began to open up. She said that as a young girl, she realized that her father worked very hard to support his family. He worked as a high school history teacher and coach for years, and to help make ends meet, he went into the appliance business. One of the main brands he carried in the store was Frigidaire. When he returned home after a full day of teaching and working late into the evening at the appliance store, he would lie on the couch and she would rub his feet and sing to him. It was a beautiful time they enjoyed together almost daily for years. Often during this time he would talk through his worries and concerns about the business, and he shared with Sandra his deep appreciation for Frigidaire. During an economic downturn, he had experienced serious financial difficulties, and the only thing that had enabled him to stay in business was that Frigidaire financed his inventory.

As Sandra shared these things, there were long pauses. I knew that she was tearing up. This was a deeply emotional thing for her. The communication between father and daughter had taken place spontaneously and naturally, when the most powerful kind of scripting takes place. And perhaps Sandra had forgotten about all this until the safety of our year of communication, when it could also come out in very natural and spontaneous ways.

My eyes began to tear as well. I finally started to understand. I had never made it safe for her to talk about it. I had never empathized. I had simply judged. I had just moved in with my logic and my counsel and my condemnation and never even made an effort to really understand. But as Blaise Pascal has said, "The heart has its reasons which reason knows not of."

We spent a long time in the cane fields that day. And when we finally did arrive at the beach, we felt so renewed, so bonded to each other, so reaffirmed in the preciousness of our relationship, that we just held each other. We didn't even need to talk.

> *There's no way to have rich, rewarding family relationships without real understanding.*

There's no way to have rich, rewarding family relationships without real understanding. Relationships can be superficial. They can be functional. They can be transactional. But they can't be transformational—and deeply satisfying—unless they're built on a foundation of genuine understanding.

In fact, at the heart of most of the real pain in families is *mis*-understanding.

A short time ago a father shared with me the experience of punishing his young son who kept disobeying him by constantly going around the corner. Each time he did so, the father would punish him and tell him not to go around the corner again. But the little boy kept doing it. Finally, after one such punishment, this boy looked at his father with tear-filled eyes and said, "What does 'corner' mean, Daddy?"

Catherine (daughter):

For quite a while I couldn't figure out why our three-year-old son would not go over to his friend's house to play. The friend would come over several times a week and play at our house, and they got along well. Then this friend would invite our son to play in his yard, which had a big sand pile, swing sets, trees, and a large green lawn. Each time he said he would go, but after walking halfway there, he would always come running back with tears in his eyes.

After I listened to him and tried to discover what his fears were, he finally opened up and told me that he was afraid to go to the bathroom at his friend's house. He didn't know where it was. He was afraid he might accidentally wet his pants.

I took him by the hand, and we walked together over to the friend's house. We talked to his mother, and she showed our son where the bathroom was and how to open the door. She offered to help him find it if he was in need. Feeling greatly relieved, he decided to stay and play, and hasn't had a problem since.

One of our neighbors related an experience he had had with one of his daughters who was in grade school. All of their other children were very bright, and school was easy for them. He was surprised when this daughter started doing poorly in math. The class was studying subtraction, and she just didn't seem to get it. She would come home frustrated and in tears.

This father decided to spend an evening with his daughter and get to the bottom of the problem. He carefully explained the concept of subtraction and let her try a few problems. She still wasn't making the connection. She just didn't understand.

He patiently lined up five shiny red apples in a row. He took away two apples. All of a sudden her face lit up. It was as if a light had gone on inside her. She blurted out, "Oh, nobody told me we were doing take away." No one had realized that she had no idea that "subtraction" meant "take away."

From that moment on, she understood. With young children we have to understand where they are coming from, what they are thinking, because they usually don't have the words to explain it.

Most mistakes with our children, with our spouses, with all family members are not the result of bad intent. It's just that we really don't understand. We don't see clearly into one another's hearts.

If we did—if an entire family could develop the kind of openness we're talking about—over 90 percent of the difficulties and problems could be resolved.

> *Most mistakes with family members are not the result of bad intent. It's just that we really don't understand. We don't see clearly into one another's hearts.*

A Flood of Witnesses

People have begun to realize that much of the pain in families is caused by lack of understanding. And if you take a look at the best-selling family books on the market today, you can get an idea of how significant this pain and this growing awareness are.

Books such as Deborah Tannen's *You Just Don't Understand* and John Gray's *Men Are from Mars, Women Are from Venus* have become tremendously popular because they touch on this pain. And these books come on the crest of a wave of recognition of the problem. In the recent past there have been many other writers on the family, including Carl Rogers, Thomas Gordon, and Haim Ginott, who have recognized and attempted to deal with this issue. They provide a flood of witnesses who affirm the vital importance of seeking to understand.[1]

The fact that these books, programs, and movements have had enduring value illustrates how much people hunger to feel understood.

Satisfactions and Judgments Surround Expectations

Perhaps the greatest contribution of these materials is in helping us realize that by understanding the differences between people, we can learn to take them into account and adjust our expectations accordingly. Much of the material focuses on gender differences, but there are also other powerful dimensions that create differences, such as past and present experiences in the family and on the job. By understanding these differences we can adjust our expectations.

Basically, our satisfactions come from our expectations. So if we're aware of our expectations, we can adjust them accordingly and—in a very real sense—adjust our satisfactions as well. To illustrate: I knew of one couple who came into marriage with totally different expectations. She expected everything to be sunshine, daffodils, and "happily ever after." When the realities of marriage and family life hit, she spent much of her time feeling disappointed, frustrated, and dissatisfied. He, on the other hand, anticipated having to deal with the challenges of marriage and family life. And every moment of joy was a wonderful, happy surprise to him, for which he was deeply grateful.

As Gordon B. Hinckley, a wise leader, commented:

Of course all of marriage is not bliss. Stormy weather occasionally hits every household. Connected inevitably with the whole process is much of pain—physical, mental, and emotional. There is much of stress and struggle, of fear and worry. For most there is the ever haunting battle of economics. There seems never to be enough money to cover the needs of the family. Sickness strikes periodically. Accidents happen. The hand of death may reach in and with dread stealth to take a precious one. But all of this seems to be part of the processes of family life. Few indeed are those who get along without experiencing some of it. [2]

To understand that reality—and to adjust expectations accordingly—is, to a great extent, to control our own satisfaction.

Our expectations are also the basis for our judgments. If you knew, for example, that children in a growth stage of around six or seven had a very strong tendency to exaggerate, you wouldn't overreact to that behavior because you would understand. That's why it is so important to understand growth stages and unmet emotional needs, as well as what changes are taking place in the environment that stir up emotional needs and lead to particular behavior. Most child experts agree that almost all "acting out" can be explained in terms of growth stages, unmet emotional needs, environmental changes, just plain ignorance, or a combination.

> When you understand, you don't judge.

Isn't it interesting: When you understand, you don't judge. We even say to each other, "Oh, if you only understood, you wouldn't judge." You can see why the wise, ancient king Solomon prayed for an understanding heart, why he wrote, "In all thy getting, get understanding." Wisdom comes from such understanding. Without it, people act unwisely. Yet from their own frame of reference, what they are doing makes perfect sense.

The reason we judge is that it protects us. We don't have to deal with the person; we can just deal with the label. In addition, when you expect nothing, you're never disappointed.

But the problem with judging or labeling is that you begin to interpret all data in a way that confirms your judgment. This is what is meant by "prejudice" or "prejudgment." If you have judged a child as being ungrateful, for example, then you will subconsciously look for evidence in his behavior to support that judgment. Another person looking at the exact same behavior may see it as evidence of gratitude and appreciation. And the problem is compounded when you act on the basis of what you consider reconfirmed judgment—and it produces more of the same behavior. It becomes a self-fulfilling prophecy.

If you label your child as lazy, for example, and you act based on that label, your child will probably see you as bossy, domineering, and critical. Your behavior itself will invoke a resisting response in your child that you interpret as further evidence of his laziness—which gives you justification for being even more bossy, domineering, and critical. It creates a downward spiral, a form of codependency and collusion that feeds on itself until both parties are convinced they are right and actually need the bad behavior of the other to confirm their rightness.

This is the reason that the tendency to judge is such a major obstacle to healthy relationships. It causes you to interpret all data to support your judgment. And whatever misunderstanding existed before is compounded tenfold by the emotional energy surrounding this collusion.

Two major problems in communication are perception, or how people interpret the same data, and semantics, or how people define the same word. Through empathic understanding, both of these problems can be overcome.

Seeking to Understand: The Fundamental Deposit

Consider the following account of a father's journey in seeking to understand his daughter and how it profoundly influenced them both:

Around the time our daughter Karen turned sixteen, she began to treat us very disrespectfully. She would make a lot of sarcastic comments, a lot of put-downs. And this began carrying over to her younger brothers and sisters.

I didn't do much about it until it finally came to a head one night. My wife and I and our daughter were in our bedroom, and Karen let fly some very inappropriate comments. I decided that I had had enough, so I said, "Karen, listen. Let me tell you how life works in this household." And I went through this long, authoritative argument that I was sure would convince her that she should treat her parents with respect. I mentioned all the things we had done for her recent birthday. I talked about the dress we had bought her. I reminded her how we had helped her get her driver's license and how we were now letting her drive the car. I went on and on, and the list was quite impressive. By the time I finished, I was expecting Karen to almost drop on her knees and worship her parents. Instead, somewhat belligerently she said, "So?"

I was furious. I said angrily, "Karen, you go to your room. Your mother and I are going to talk about consequences, and we'll let you know what's going to happen." She went storming off and slammed her bedroom door. I was so angry, I was literally pacing back and forth, seething with anger. And then suddenly it hit me. I had done nothing to try to understand Karen. I certainly wasn't thinking win-win. I was totally on my own agenda. This realization caused a profound shift in my thinking and in the way I felt toward Karen.

When I went to her room a few minutes later, the first thing I did was apologize for my behavior. I didn't excuse any of her behavior, but I apologized for my own. I had been pretty abrupt. I said, "Look, I can tell that something's going on here, and I don't know what it is." I let her know that I really wanted to understand her, and I was finally able to create an atmosphere where she was willing to talk.

Somewhat hesitantly she began to share her feelings about being brand-new in high school: the struggle she was having trying to make good grades and make new friends. She said she was concerned about driving the car. It was such a new experience for her, and she worried whether she was going to be safe. She had just started a new part-time job and was wondering how her boss felt she was doing. She was taking piano lessons. She was teaching piano students. Her schedule was extremely busy.

Finally, I said, "Karen, you're feeling totally overwhelmed." And that was it. Bingo! She felt understood. She had been feeling overwhelmed by all these challenges, and her sarcastic comments and disrespect to her family were basically a cry for attention. She was saying, "Please, somebody, just listen to me!"

So I said to her, "Then when I asked you to treat us with a little more respect, that just sounded like one more thing for you to do."

"That's right!" she said. "Another thing for me to do—and I can't handle what's on my plate now."

I got my wife involved, and the three of us sat down and brainstormed ways in which Karen might simplify her life. Ultimately, she decided to stop taking piano lessons and stop teaching her piano students—and she felt wonderful about it. In the weeks that followed, she was like a totally changed person.

From that experience she gained more confidence in her ability to make choices in her life. She knew her parents understood her and would support her. And soon after that, she decided to leave her job because it wasn't as good a job as she wanted. She *found a very good job elsewhere and reached manager status.*

In looking back, I think much of that confidence came because we didn't say, "Okay, there's no excuse for behaving like that. You're grounded!" Instead, we were willing to take the time to sit down and understand.

Notice how Karen's father was able to rise above his concern about Karen's outward behavior and seek to understand what was going on in her mind and heart. Only after doing this was he able to get at the real issue involved.

The argument between Karen and her parents was superficial. Karen's behavior camouflaged the real concern. And as long as her parents focused only on her behavior, they never got to that concern. But then her father stepped out of the role of judge and became a genuinely concerned and affirming listener and friend. When Karen felt that her father really wanted to understand her, she began to feel safe in opening up and sharing on a deeper level. She herself may not even have realized what her own real concern was until she had someone who was willing to listen and give her the chance to get it out. Once the problem was clear and she really felt understood, Karen then *wanted* the guidance and direction her parents were able to give.

As long as we're in the role of judge and jury, we rarely have the kind of influence we want. Perhaps you remember the story from the first chapter of this book of the man who "found his son again." Do you remember how "overdrawn" that relationship was, how strained it was, how totally void of any authentic communication? (You may want to review that story on page 13 because it's a wonderful example of the power of Habit 5.) That was another situation in which there were difficult, painful problems between parent and child, but there was no real communication. Only when the father stopped judging and really tried to understand his son was he able to begin to make a difference.

> *As long as we're in the role of judge and jury, we rarely have the kind of influence we want.*

In both these cases, parents were able to turn the situation around because they made the most significant deposit you can ever make into anyone's Emotional Bank Account: They sought to understand.

Giving "Psychological Air"

One of the primary reasons seeking to understand is the first and most important deposit you can make is that it gives other people "psychological air."

Try to remember a time when you had the wind knocked out of you and were gasping for air. At that moment, did anything else matter? Was anything as important as getting air?

That experience demonstrates why seeking to understand is so important. Being understood is the emotional and psychological equivalent of getting air, and when people are gasping for air—or for understanding—until they get it, nothing else matters. Nothing.

Sandra:

I remember one Saturday morning when Stephen was working at the office. I called him and said, "Stephen, come home fast. I'm going to be late for my appointment downtown, and I need help."

"Why don't you get Cynthia to help you?" he suggested. "She can take over, and you can be on your way."

I replied, "She won't help me at all. She's totally uncooperative. I need you to come home."

"Something must have happened in your relationship with Cynthia," Stephen said. "Cure that relationship, and everything will work out."

"Look, Stephen," I said impatiently, "I don't have time. I've got to go. I'm going to be late. Will you please just come home?"

"Sandra, it will take me fifteen minutes to get home," he replied. "You can solve this thing in a matter of five or ten minutes if you'll just sit down with her. Try to identify anything you've done that has in any way offended her. Then apologize. If you don't find anything you've done, just say, 'Honey, I've been rushing around so fast that I haven't really paid attention to your concern. I can tell something is bothering you. What is it?' "

"I can't think of a thing I've done to offend her," I said.

"Well," Stephen replied, "then just sit there and listen."

So I went to Cynthia. At first she refused to cooperate. She was just kind of numb and stolid. She wouldn't respond. So I said, "Honey, I've been rushing around and haven't listened to you, and I sense something really important is bothering you. Would you like to talk about it?"

For a couple of minutes Cynthia refused to open up, but finally she blurted out, "It's not fair! It's not fair!" Then she talked about how she had been told she could have a sleepover with her friends like her sister had had, and it never happened.

I just sat and listened. At that point I didn't even attempt to solve the problem. But as she got out all her feelings, the air began to clear.

Suddenly she said, "Go on, Mom. Take off. I'll take over." She knew the challenge I had been going through—trying to handle all kinds of issues with the children when no one was being cooperative. But until she got that emotional air, nothing else mattered. Once she got that air, she was able to focus on the problem at hand and do what she knew she needed to do to help out.

Remember the phrase "I don't care how much you know until I know how much you care." People do not care about anything you have to say when they're gasping for psychological air—to be understood, the first evidence of caring.

Think about it: Why do people shout and yell at each other? They want to be understood. They're basically yelling, "Understand me! Listen to me! Respect me!" The problem is that the yelling is so emotionally charged and so disrespectful toward the other person that it creates defensiveness and more anger—even vindictiveness—and the cycle feeds on itself. As the interaction continues, the anger deepens and increases, and people end up not getting their point across at all. The relationship is wounded, and it takes far more time and effort to deal with the problems created by yelling at each other than simply practicing Habit 5 in the first place: exercising enough patience and self-control to listen first.

Next to physical survival, our strongest need is psychological survival. The deepest hunger of the human heart is to be understood, for understanding implicitly affirms, validates, recognizes, and appreciates the intrinsic worth of another. When you really listen to another person, you acknowledge and respond to that most insistent need.

> The deepest hunger of the human heart is to be understood.

Knowing What Constitutes a "Deposit" in Someone's Account

I have a friend who is happily married. For years her husband constantly said, "I love you," and every so often he would bring her a single beautiful rose. She was delighted with this special communication of affection. It was a deposit in her Emotional Bank Account.

But she sometimes felt frustrated when he didn't get to projects that she felt needed to be done around the home: hanging curtains, painting a room, building a cupboard. When he finally did get to these things, she responded as though he had suddenly made a hundred-dollar deposit into the account, compared to the ten-dollar deposits he was making whenever he gave her a rose.

This went on for years. Neither one of them really understood what was happening. And then one night as they were talking, she began to reminisce about her father, about how he was always working on projects around the house, repairing things that were broken, painting, or building something that would add to the value of their home. As she shared these things, she suddenly realized that to her, the things her father did represented a deep communication of his love for her mother. He was always doing things for her, helping her, making their home more beautiful to please her. Instead of bringing her roses, he planted rosebushes. Service was his language of love.

Without realizing it, our friend had transferred the importance of this form of communication to her own marriage. When her husband didn't respond immediately to household needs, it became a huge but unrecognized withdrawal. And the "I love you's" and the roses—though they were important to her—didn't balance the account.

When they made this discovery, she was able to use her gift of self-awareness to understand the impact the culture in her own home had had on her. She used her conscience and creative imagination to look at her current situation with a new perspective. She used her independent will to begin to place greater value on her husband's expressions.

In turn, her husband also engaged his four human gifts. He realized that what he had thought would be great deposits over the years were not as important to her as these little acts of service. He began communicating to her more often in this different language of love.

This story demonstrates another reason that seeking to understand is the first and foremost deposit you can make: *Until you understand another person, you are never going to know what constitutes a deposit in his or her account.*

Maria (*daughter*):

One time I planned an elaborate surprise birthday party for my husband, expecting him to be thrilled about it. He wasn't! In fact, he hated it. He didn't like a surprise party. He didn't like a fuss being made over him. What he really would have liked was a nice, quiet dinner with me and a movie after. I have learned the hard way that it's best to find out what's really important to someone before trying to make a deposit.

> Each person needs to be loved in his or her own special way. The key to making deposits, therefore, is to understand—and to speak—that person's language of love.

It's a common tendency to project our own feelings and motives on other people's behavior. "If this means something to me, it must mean something to them." But you never know what constitutes a deposit to others until you understand what is important to them. People live in their own private worlds. Your mission may be their minutia. It may not matter to them at all.

Because everyone is unique, each person needs to be loved in his or her own special way. The key to making deposits, therefore, is to understand—and to speak—that person's language of love.

One father shared this experience of how understanding—rather than trying to "fix" things—worked in his family:

I have a ten-year-old daughter, Amber, who loves horses more than anything else in the world. Recently, her grandfather invited her to go on a daylong cattle drive. She was so excited. She was thrilled about the cattle drive and also about the fact that she would get to be with her grandfather, who also loves horses, all day long.

The night before the drive I came home from a trip to find Amber in bed with the flu. I said, "How are you doing, Amber?"

She looked at me and said, "I'm so sick!" And she started crying.

I said, "Boy, you must really feel bad."

"It's not that," she said, sniffling. "I won't be able to go on the cattle drive." And she started crying again.

Through my mind went all of those things I thought a dad should say: "Oh, it will be fine. You can do it again. We'll do something else instead." But instead I just sat there and held her and didn't say anything. I thought of times when I'd been bitterly disappointed. I just hugged her and felt her pain.

Well, the dam broke loose. She just bawled. She was shaking all over as I held her for a couple of minutes. And then it passed. She gave me a kiss on the cheek and said, "Thanks, Dad." And that was it.

I thought again of all those wonderful things I could have said, all that advice I could have given. But she didn't need that. She just needed someone to say, "It's okay to be hurt, to cry when you're disappointed."

Notice how in both these situations people were able to make significant deposits into Emotional Bank Accounts. Because they sought to understand, they were able to speak their loved one's language of love.

People Are Very Tender, Very Vulnerable Inside

Some years ago someone shared a beautiful expression with me anonymously through the mail. Reading this out loud slowly has moved audiences in incredible ways. It captures the essence of why Habit 5 is so powerful. I suggest you read it slowly and carefully, and attempt to visualize a safe setting where another person you care a lot about is really opening up.

Don't be fooled by me. Don't be fooled by the mask I wear. For I wear a mask. I wear a thousand masks—masks that I'm afraid to take off—and none of them is me. Pretending is an art that is second nature with me, but don't be fooled.

I give the impression that I'm secure, that all is sunny and unruffled with me, within as well as without; that confidence is my name, and coolness is my game; that the waters are calm, and I'm in command and I need no one. But don't believe it. Please don't.

My surface may seem smooth, but my surface is my mask—my ever-varying and ever-concealing mask. Beneath lies no smugness, no coolness, no complacence. Beneath dwells the real me—in confusion, in fear, in loneliness. But I hide this; I don't want anybody to know it. I panic at the thought of my weakness being exposed. That's why I frantically create a mask to hide behind, a nonchalant sophisticated facade to help me pretend, to shield me from the glance that knows. But such a glance is precisely my salvation—my only salvation. And I know it. It's the only thing that can liberate me from myself, from my own self-built prison walls, from the barriers I so painstakingly erect. But I don't tell you this. I don't dare. I'm afraid to.

I'm afraid your glance will not be followed by love and acceptance. I'm afraid that you'll think less of me, that you'll laugh, and that your laugh will kill me. I'm afraid that deep down inside I'm nothing, that I'm just no good, and that you'll see and reject me. So I play my games—my desperate pretending games—with the facade of assurance on the outside and a trembling child within. And so begins the parade of masks, the glittering but empty parade of masks. And my life becomes a front.

I idly chatter with you in the suave tones of surface talk. I tell you everything that's really nothing—nothing of what's crying within me. So when I'm going through my routine, don't be fooled by what I'm saying. Please listen carefully and try to hear what I'm NOT saying . . . what I would like to be able to say . . . what for survival I need to say, but I can't say. I dislike the hiding. Honestly I do. I dislike the superficial phony games I'm playing. I'd really like to be genuine.

I'd really like to be genuine, spontaneous, and me; but you have to help me. You have to help me by holding out your hand, even when that's the last thing I seem to want or need. Each time you are kind and gentle and encouraging, each time you try to understand because you really care, my heart begins to grow wings—very small wings, very feeble wings, but wings. With your sensitivity and sympathy, and your power of understanding, I can make it. You can breathe life into me. It will not be easy for you. A long conviction of worthlessness builds strong walls. But love is stronger than strong walls, and therein lies my hope. Please try to beat down those walls with firm hands, but with gentle hands, for a child is very sensitive, and I AM a child.

Who am I? you may wonder. I am someone you know very well. For I am every man, every woman, every child . . . every human you meet.

> *Creating a warm, caring, supportive, encouraging environment is probably the most important thing you can do for your family.*

All people are very, very tender and sensitive. Some have learned to protect themselves from this level of vulnerability—to cover up, to pose and posture, to wear a safe "mask." But unconditional love, kindness, and courtesy often penetrate these exteriors. They find a home in others' hearts, and others begin to respond.

This is why it is so important to create a loving, nurturing environment in the home—an environment where it is safe to be vulnerable, to be open. In fact, the consensus of almost all experts in the field of marriage and family relations and child development is that creating such a warm, caring, supportive, encouraging environment is probably the most important thing you can do for your family.

And this does not mean just for little children. It also means for your spouse, your grandchildren, your aunts, uncles, nieces, nephews, cousins—everyone. The creation of such a culture—such an unconditionally loving and nurturing feeling— is more important than almost everything else put together. In a very real sense, to create such a nurturing culture is tantamount to having everything else put together.

Dealing with Negative Baggage

Creating such a culture is sometimes very difficult to do—especially if you're dealing with negative baggage from the past and negative emotions in the present.

One man shared this experience:

When I met my future wife, Jane, she had a six-month-old boy named Jared. Jane had married Tom when they were both quite young, and neither of them had been ready for marriage by any stretch of the imagination. The realities and stresses of married life hit them hard. There was some physical violence involved, and he left her when she was about five months pregnant.

When I met Jane, Tom had filed for divorce and joint custody of the child he had never seen. It was a difficult, complicated situation. There were many bitter feelings. There was no communication between Jane and Tom whatever. The judge swayed heavily in favor of Jane.

After Jane and I married, I took a job that required us to move to another state. Every other month Tom would come and visit with Jared, and in alternating months we would make Jared available in California.

Things began to settle down in a way that seemed superficially okay. But I ended up doing most of the communicating between Jane and Tom. About one out of every three times that Tom would phone, Jane would hang up on him. Often Jane would leave before Tom got there for visitations, and I would be the one to see Jared off. Tom would frequently call me and say, "Should I talk to you about this, or should I talk to Jane?" It was very uncomfortable for me.

This spring, Tom called me and said, "Hey, Jared turns five in August, and then he will be legally able to fly by himself. Rather than my coming to visit out there where I sit in a hotel room with no car or friends, why don't I pay for Jared to fly here?" I told him I would bring it up with Jane.

"No way!" she said emphatically. "Absolutely not! He's just a little boy. He can't even go to the bathroom on a plane by himself." She wouldn't even discuss it with me—and especially not with Tom. At one point she said, "Just leave it to me. I'll handle it." But as the months passed, nothing happened. Finally, Tom phoned me and said, "What's happening? Is Jared going to fly down? What's the deal?"

I was convinced that there was a lot of good potential in both Jane and Tom. I knew that if they could just be focused on doing the best thing for Jared, they could communicate and understand each other and work something out. But there were so many personal animosities and bitter feelings that they couldn't see beyond them.

I tried to encourage them to have a discussion. I told them there would have to be strict guidelines to prevent verbal attacks and things of that nature. They both trusted me and agreed to do it. But I became increasingly nervous that I would not be able to facilitate that discussion because I was too close to it. I felt that one or both of them would end up hating me for one reason or another. In the past when Jane and I were having a discussion and I tried to look at an issue objectively, she would accuse me of taking "his" side. On the other hand, Tom felt that Jane and I had an agenda. I didn't know what to do.

I finally decided to call Adam, a friend and coworker who facilitates the 7 Habits, and he agreed to talk with both of them. Adam taught them the principle of empathic listening. He taught them how to set aside their own autobiography and really listen to the words and feelings that were being expressed. After Jane shared some of her feelings, Adam said to Tom, "Now Tom, what did Jane just tell you?" He said, "She's afraid of me. She's afraid one day if I lose my temper I might slap Jared." Jane was wide-eyed. She realized that Tom had been able to hear more than just her words. She said, "That's exactly how I feel deep down in my heart. I'm worried that one day this man could easily lose it and hurt Jared."

And after Tom expressed himself, Adam asked Jane, "What did Tom just say?" She replied, "He said, 'I'm afraid of rejection. I'm afraid of being alone. I'm afraid no one cares at all.'" Even though she'd known him for fifteen years, Jane had no idea that Tom had been abandoned by his father when he was small and that he was determined not to do that to Jared. She didn't realize how alienated he felt from her family after the divorce. For Tom it had been like being abandoned all over again. She began to realize how lonely Tom had been during the past five years. She began to understand how his declaration of bankruptcy a few years earlier made it impossible for him to get a credit card, so that when he came to visit Jared, he had no car. He was alone in a hotel room, with no friends and no transportation. And, she realized, we had just dropped Jared off.

Once Jane and Tom felt really understood and got down to the issues, they discovered that there was not a single thing on either of their lists that the other did not also want. They talked for three and a half hours, and the issue of visitation never even came up. Independently, they both told me later, "You know, this isn't about Jared. It's about trust between the two of us. Once we have this solved, the problem with Jared is a no-brainer."

After this meeting with Adam, the atmosphere was much more relaxed and congenial.

We all went to a restaurant together, and Jane said to Tom, "You know, it's kind of tough with the kids here to talk about things, but when I come down next month for visitation, let's take some time to talk."

I thought, This is Jane talking? I had never heard her say anything like this before.

When we dropped Tom off at his hotel with Jared, Jane said, "What time are we picking Jared up tomorrow?"

He said, "Well, my shuttle to the airport leaves at 4:00 P.M."

"Let us take you to the airport," she said.

"That would be great, if you want to."

"No problem," she replied.

Again I was thinking, Wow! This is a major turnaround!

Two weeks later, Jane went down for visitation. One of her bones of contention had been that he never acknowledged what he had done to her. But when they had their talk, for the first time Tom apologized to her in great detail for everything. "I'm sorry for pulling your hair. I'm sorry for taking drugs. I'm sorry for walking out on you." And this led her to say, "Well, I'm sorry, too."

Following his visit with us, Tom began saying "thank you." Tom had never said "thank you" for much of anything before. His conversations were now filled with thank-yous. And the week after his visit here, Jane received this brief letter from him:

Dear Jane,

I find it necessary to put in written word my thanks to you. We have shared so many ill feelings toward each other in the past, but the initial steps we took together last Saturday toward their resolution should be documented. And so . . . thank you.

Thank you for agreeing to meet with Adam. Thank you for sharing the things you shared. Thank you for listening to me. Thank you for the love from which we created our boy. Thank you for being his mother.

I mean it as sincerely as can be,

Tom

At the same time he sent me a letter.

Dear Mike,

I wanted to take a formal moment to thank you for putting Jane and me together with Adam. It has done more for my outlook toward my relationship with Jared and Jane than I can find the words for. . . .

Your desire to do what's right both now and in past years is quite commendable. Without your good offices, there is no telling how ugly things would have gotten between Jane and me. . . .

My deepest appreciation,
Tom

When we received these letters, we were stunned. And in the phone conversations that followed, Jane said, "We talked almost like giddy school kids." The understanding, the letting go, the forgiving, was so unleashing.

So many good things are happening now. Jane even went so far as to say to me, "Maybe when Tom comes up here, we could let him use one of our cars." I had thought about that many times, but I didn't dare mention it for fear of being accused of taking his side. I thought her attitude would be, "How dare you! You're trying to accommodate the enemy." But now she is recommending it. She even said, "What would you think about letting Tom stay in our spare room to help with his costs?" And I thought, Is this really Jane? It was a 180-degree turnaround.

I'm sure there will be challenges ahead, but I believe the groundwork has been laid. The tools for appropriate communication are there. There's almost a feeling of deep respect now for one another and a genuine concern that I see in Jane and Tom for each other and for our kids.

It's been a real challenge at times, but through it all it's been crystal clear to me that anything less than this would make life worse for everyone.

Notice how Tom and Jane were able to rise above the hate, the blaming and accusing. They were able to diffuse the conflict and act based on principles instead of reacting to each other. How did they do that?

In seeking to understand each other, they both got psychological air. It freed them to stop fighting each other and to connect with their own inner gifts, particularly conscience and awareness. They became open, vulnerable. They were each able to acknowledge their part in the situation, to apologize, to forgive. And this healing, this cleansing, opened the door to more authentic relationships, to creating a synergy in which they were able to establish a better situation for their child, for themselves, and for everyone involved.

As you can see in this story—and in every other story in this chapter—*not* seeking to understand leads to judgment (usually misjudgment), rejection, and manipulation. Seeking to understand leads to understanding, acceptance, and participation. Obviously, only one of these paths is built on the principles that create quality family life.

Overcoming Anger and Offense

Probably more than any other single factor, what gets families off track and gets in the way of synergy is negative emotions, including anger and taking offense. Temper gets us into problems, and pride keeps us there. As C. S. Lewis said, "Pride is competitive in nature. Pride gets no pleasure out of having something, only out of having more of it than the next man. . . . It is the comparison that makes you proud: the pleasure of being above the rest. Once the element of competition has gone, pride has gone."[3] One of the most common and debilitating forms of pride is the need to be "right," to have it your way.

Again, remember: Even if anger surfaces only one-tenth of 1 percent of the time, that will affect the quality of all the rest of the time because people are never sure when that raw nerve might be touched again.

> *Temper gets us into problems, and pride keeps us there.*

I know of one father who was pleasant and agreeable most of the time, but on occasion his vicious temper was aroused. And this affected the quality of all the rest of the time because family members had to brace themselves for the possibility that it might happen again. They would avoid social situations for fear of embarrassment. They would walk around minefields throughout the day to avoid stepping on a raw nerve. They never became authentic or real or opened up. They never dared to give him feedback for fear that it would stir up the anger more than ever. And without feedback, this man lost all contact with what was really happening in his family.

When someone in the family becomes angry and loses control, the effects are so wounding, so intimidating, so threatening, so overpowering that others lose their bearings. They tend to either fight back, which only exacerbates the problem, or capitulate and give in to this win-lose spirit. And then even compromise is not likely. The more likely scenario is that people will separate and go their own ways, refusing to communicate at all about anything meaningful. They try to live with the satisfactions of independence, since interdependence seems too hard, too far off, and too unrealistic. And no one has the mind-set or the skill-set to go for it.

This is why it is so important when this kind of culture has developed for people to go deep within themselves. Then they can do the necessary work within to acknowledge their negative tendencies, to overcome them, to apologize to others, and to process their experiences so that gradually those labels are unfrozen and people can come to trust the basic structure, the basic relationship, again.

> *Taking offense is a choice. We may be hurt, but there is a big difference between being hurt and taking offense.*

Of course, some of the most important inner work is prevention work. It includes making up our minds not to say or do those things we know will offend and learning to overcome our anger or to express it at better times and in more productive ways. We need to be deeply honest with ourselves and realize that most anger is merely guilt overflowing when provoked by the weakness of another. We can also make up our minds not to be offended by others. Taking offense is a choice. We may be hurt, but there is a big difference between being hurt and taking offense. Being hurt is having our feelings wounded—

and it does smart for a time—but taking offense is choosing to act on that hurt by getting back, getting even, walking out, complaining to others, or judging the "offender."

Most of the time offenses are unintentional. Even when they are intentional, we can remember that *forgive*—like *love*—is a verb. It's the choice to move from reactivity to proactivity, to take the initiative—whether you've offended someone or been offended yourself—to go and make reconciliation. It's the choice to cultivate and depend on an internal source of personal security so that we are not so vulnerable to external offenses.

And above all it's the choice to prioritize the family, to realize that family is too important to let offenses keep family members from talking to one another, prevent grown brothers and sisters from going to family events, or weaken or break the intergenerational and extended family ties that provide such strength and support.

Interdependency is hard. It takes tremendous effort, constant effort, and courage. It's much easier in the short run to live independently inside a family—to do your own thing, to come and go as you wish, to take care of your own needs, and to interact as little as possible with others. But the real joys of family life are lost. When children grow up with this kind of modeling, they think that is the way family is, and the cycle continues. The devastating effect of these cyclical cold wars is almost as bad as the destruction of the hot wars.

It's often important to process negative experiences—to talk them through, resolve them, empathize with each other, and seek forgiveness. Whenever ugly experiences take place, you can unfreeze them by acknowledging your part in them and by listening empathically to understand how other people saw them and how they felt about them. In other words, by modeling vulnerability yourself, you can help others become vulnerable. The deepest bonding arises out of such mutual vulnerability. You minimize the psychic and social scarring, and clear the path to the creation of rich synergy.

Becoming a "Faithful Translator"

Really listening to get inside another person's mind and heart is called "empathic" listening. It's listening with empathy. It's trying to see the world through someone else's eyes. Of five different kinds of listening, it is the only one that really gets inside another person's frame of reference.

You can ignore people. You can pretend to listen. You can listen selectively or even attentively. But until you listen empathically, you're still inside your own frame of reference. You don't know what constitutes a "win" for others. You don't really know how they see the world, how they see themselves, and how they see you.

5 Empathic Listening

WITHIN THE OTHER'S FRAME OF REFERENCE

4 Attentive Listening

3 Selective Listening

2 Pretend Listening

1 Ignoring

WITHIN ONE'S OWN FRAME OF REFERENCE

At one time I was in Jakarta, Indonesia, teaching the principle of empathic listening. As I looked out over the audience and saw many people wearing earphones, a thought came to me. I said, "If you want a good illustration of empathic listening, just think about what the interpreter or translator is doing right now through your earphones." These translators were doing instantaneous translation, which meant that they had to be listening to what I was saying at the moment as well as restating what I had just said. It took incredible mental effort and concentration, and it required two translators to work in tandem, based on their level of fatigue. Both of those translators came up to me afterward and told me that what I had said was the finest compliment they had ever been given.

Even though you may be emotionally involved in a particular exchange with somebody, you can push your pause button and step outside of that emotion if you simply change the way you see your role—if you think of yourself as a "faithful translator." Your job, then, is to translate and communicate back to the other person in new words the essential meaning (both verbal and nonverbal) of what that person communicated to you. In doing this you're not taking a position yourself on what the person is talking about. You're simply feeding back the essence of what he or she said to you.

One of the most effective ways to learn how to listen empathically is to simply change the way you see your role—to see yourself as a "faithful translator."

Psychologist and author John Powell has said:

Listening in dialogue is listening more to meanings than to words. . . . In true listening, we reach behind the words, see through them, to find the person who is being revealed. Listening is a search to find the treasure of the true person as revealed verbally and nonverbally. There is the semantic problem, of course. The words bear a different connotation for you than they do for me.

Consequently, I can never tell you what you said, but only what I heard. I will have to rephrase what you have said, and check it out with you to make sure that what left your mind and heart arrived in my mind and heart intact and without distortion.

How to Do It: Principles of Empathic Listening

Now let's go through a scenario together that will help us get at the heart of the understanding—or "faithful translator"—response.

Suppose for several days you've sensed that your teenage daughter is unhappy. When you've asked her what's wrong, she's replied, "Nothing. Everything's okay." But one night while you're washing dishes together, she begins to open up.

"Our family rule that I can't date until I'm older is embarrassing me to death. All my friends are dating, and that's all they can talk about. I feel like I'm out of it. John keeps asking me out, and I have to keep telling him I'm not old enough. I just know he's going to ask me to go to the party on Friday night, and if I have to tell him no again, he'll give up on me. So will Carol and Mary. Everyone's talking about it."

How would you respond?

"Don't worry about it, honey. No one is going to give up on you."

"Just stick to your guns. Don't worry about what others say and think."

"Tell me what they're saying about you."

"When they talk about you like that, they're really admiring you for your stand. What you're feeling is normal insecurity."

Any one of these might be a typical response, but not an understanding one.

"Don't worry about it, honey. No one is going to give up on you." This is an **evaluating** or judging response based on *your* values and *your* needs.

"Just stick to your guns. Don't worry about what others say and think." This is **advising** from *your* point of view or in terms of *your* needs.

"Tell me what they're saying about you." This response is **probing** for information *you* feel is important.

"When they talk about you like that, they're really admiring you for your stand. What you're feeling is normal insecurity." This is **interpreting** what's happening with your daughter's friends and inside her as *you* see it.

Most of us either seek first to be understood, or if we do seek to understand, we are often preparing our response as we "listen." So we *evaluate, advise, probe,* or *interpret* from our own point of view. And none of these is an understanding response. They all come out of our autobiography, our world, our values.

So what would an understanding response be?

First, it would attempt to reflect back what your daughter feels and says so that she feels you really understand. For example, you might say, "You feel kind of torn up inside. You understand the family rule about dating, but you also feel embarrassed when everyone else can date and you have to say no. Is that it?"

Then she might respond, "Yes, that's what I mean." And she might continue, "But the thing I'm really afraid of is that I won't know how to act around boys when I do start dating. Everyone else is learning, and I'm not."

Again, an understanding response would reflect back: "You feel somewhat scared that when the time comes, you won't know what to do."

She might say yes and go on further and deeper into her feelings, or she might say, "Well, not exactly. What I really mean is . . ." and she would go on to try to give you a clearer picture of what she's feeling and facing.

If you look back at the other responses, you'll see that none of them accomplishes the same results as the understanding response. When you give an understanding response, both of you gain a greater understanding of what she's really thinking and feeling. You make it safe for her to open up and share. You make it comfortable for her to engage her own inner gifts to help deal with the concern. And you build the relationship, which will prove immensely helpful further down the road.

Let's look at another experience that shows the difference between the typical and the empathic response. Consider the contrast in these two conversations between Cindy, a varsity cheerleader, and her mother. In the first, Cindy's mother seeks first to be understood:

CINDY: *Oh, Mom, I have some bad news. Meggie got dropped from the cheer squad today.*

MOTHER: *Why?*

CINDY: *She was caught in her boyfriend's car on the school grounds, and he was drinking. If you get caught drinking on the school grounds, you get in big trouble. Actually, it's not fair because Meggie wasn't drinking. Just her boyfriend was drunk.*

MOTHER: *Well, Cindy, I think it serves Meggie right for keeping bad company. I've warned you that people will judge you by your friends. I've told you that a hundred times. I don't see why you and your friends can't understand. I hope that you learn a lesson from this. Life is tough enough without hanging around with someone like that guy. Why wasn't she in class? I hope you were in class when all this was going on. You were, weren't you?*

CINDY: *Mom, it's okay! Mellow out. Don't get so mad. It wasn't me, it was Meggie. Gosh, all I wanted to do was tell you something about somebody else, and I get the ten-minute lecture on my bad friends. I'm going to bed.*

Now look at the difference when Cindy's mother seeks first to understand:

CINDY: *Oh, Mom, I have some bad news. Meggie got dropped from the cheer squad today.*

MOTHER: *Oh, honey, you really seem upset.*

CINDY: *I feel so bad about it, Mom. It wasn't her fault. It was her boyfriend's. He's a jerk.*

MOTHER: *Hmm. You don't like him.*

CINDY: *I sure don't, Mom. He's always in trouble. She's a good girl, and he drags her down. It makes me sad.*

MOTHER: *You feel he's a bad influence on her, and that hurts you because she's your good friend.*

CINDY: *I wish she'd drop this guy and go with someone nice. Bad friends get you in trouble.*

Notice how this mother's desire to understand was reflected in the way she responded to her daughter the second time. At that point she didn't attempt to share her own experience or ideas—even though she may have had real value to add. She didn't evaluate, probe, advise, or interpret. And she didn't take Cindy on, although she may have disagreed with what her daughter seemed to be saying.

What she did was respond in a way that helped clarify her own understanding of what Cindy was saying and communicate that understanding back to Cindy. And because Cindy didn't have to engage in a win-lose conversation with her mother, she was able to connect with her four gifts and come to a sense of the real problem on her own.

The Tip and the Mass of the Iceberg

Now, it's not always necessary to reflect back in words what someone is saying and feeling in order to empathize. The heart of empathy is understanding how people see the situation and how they feel about it, and the essence of what they are trying to say. It's not mimicking. It's not necessarily summarizing. It's not even attempting to reflect back in all cases. You may not need to say anything at all. Or perhaps a facial expression will communicate that you understand. The point is that you don't get hung up on the technique of reflecting back but instead focus on truly empathizing and then allow that genuine, sincere emotion to drive your technique.

The problem comes when people think the technique *is* empathy. They mimic, use the same phrases repeatedly, and rephrase what others say in ways that seem manipulative or insulting. It's like the story about the serviceman who was complaining to the chaplain about how much he hated army life.

The chaplain responded, "Oh, you don't like army life."

"Yeah," said the serviceman. "And that C.O.! I couldn't trust him as far as I could throw him."

"You just feel that you couldn't trust a C.O. as far as you could throw him."

"Yeah. And the food—it's so plain!"

"You feel that the food is really plain."

"And the people—they're so low-caliber."

"You feel that the people are low-caliber."

"Yeah . . . and what in the heck is wrong with the way I'm saying it anyway?"

It may be good to practice the skill. It may even increase the desire. But always remember that the technique is just the tip of the iceberg. The great mass of the iceberg is a deep and sincere desire to truly understand.

That desire is ultimately based on respect. This is what keeps empathic listening from becoming just a technique.

If this sincere desire to understand isn't there, efforts to empathize will be sensed as manipulative and insincere. Manipulation means that the real motive is hidden even though good techniques are being used. When people feel manipulated, they are not committed. They may say "yes," but they mean "no"—and it will be evidenced in their behavior later on. Pseudodemocracy eventually shows its true colors. And when people feel manipulated, a major withdrawal takes place, and your next efforts—even though sincere—will be perceived as another form of manipulation.

When you're willing to acknowledge the true motive behind your methods, then truthfulness and sincerity replace manipulation. Others may not agree or go

> *The technique of empathic listening is just the tip of the iceberg. The great mass of the iceberg is a deep and sincere desire to truly understand.*

along, but at least you have been forthright. And nothing baffles a person who is full of tricks and duplicity more than simple, straightforward honesty on the part of another.

Based on respect and a sincere desire to understand, responses other than "reflective responses" can also become empathic. If someone were to ask you, "Where's the rest room?" you wouldn't just respond, "You're really hurting."

There are also times when, if you really understand, you can sense that someone wants you to probe. They want the additional perspective and insight your questions are based on. This might be compared to visiting a doctor. You want the doctor to probe, to ask about your symptoms. You know that the questions are based on expert knowledge and are necessary in order to give a proper diagnosis. So in this case probing becomes empathic rather than controlling and autobiographical.

When you sense that someone really wants you to ask questions to draw them out, you might consider questions such as these:

What are your concerns?
What is truly important to you?
What values do you want to preserve the most?
What are your most pressing needs?
What are your highest priorities in this situation?
What are the possible unintended consequences of such an action plan?

These kinds of questions can be combined with reflective statements such as:

I sense your underlying concern is . . .
Correct me if I'm wrong, but I sense that . . .
I'm trying to see it from your point of view, and what I sense is . . .
What I hear you saying is . . .
You feel that . . .
I sense you mean . . .

In the right situation any of these questions and phrases could show an attempt to achieve understanding or empathy. The point is that the attitude or desire is what must be cultivated first and foremost. The technique is secondary and flows out of the desire.

Empathy: Some Questions and Guidelines

As you work on Habit 5, you may be interested in the answers to some of the questions other people have asked over the years.

Is empathy always appropriate? The answer is "yes!" Without exception, empathy is always appropriate. But reflecting back, summarizing, and mirroring are sometimes extremely inappropriate and insulting. They may even be perceived as manipulation. So remember the heart of the matter is a sincere desire to understand.

What can you do if the other person doesn't open up? Remember that 70 to 80 percent of all communication is nonverbal. In this sense you cannot *not* communicate. If you truly have an empathic heart, a heart that desires to understand, you will always be reading the nonverbal cues. You'll be noticing body and face language, tone of voice, and context. Voice inflection and tone are the keys to discerning the heart on the phone. You'll be attempting to discern the spirit and heart of another, so don't force it. Be patient. You may even sense that you need to apologize or make restitution for some wrongdoing. Act on that understanding and do it. In other words, if you sense that the Emotional Bank Account is overdrawn, act on that understanding and make the appropriate deposits.

> *R*emember that 70 to 80 percent of all communication is nonverbal. If you truly have an empathic heart, you will always be reading the nonverbal cues.

What are other expressions of empathy besides mirroring, summarizing, and reflecting techniques? Again, the answer is to do what the mass of the iceberg tells you—what your understanding of the person, the need, and the situation direct you toward. Sometimes total silence is empathic. Sometimes asking questions or using expert knowledge showing conceptual awareness is empathic. Sometimes a nod or a single word is empathic. Empathy is a very sincere, nonmanipulative, flexible, and humble process. You realize you're on sacred ground and that the other person is perhaps even a little more vulnerable than you.

You may also find these guidelines helpful:

- The higher the trust level, the more you can easily move in and out of empathic and autobiographical responses—particularly between reflecting and probing. Negative and positive energy is often, though not always, a key indicator of the level of trust.
- If the trust is very high, you can be extremely candid and efficient with each other. But if you are attempting to rebuild trust or if it is somewhat shaky and the person won't risk vulnerability, then you need to stay longer and with more patience in the empathic mode.
- If you're not sure that you understand or if you're not sure the other feels understood, then say that and try again.
- Just as you come from the depth of the iceberg under the water, learn to listen to the depth of the iceberg inside the other person. In other words, focus primarily on the underlying meaning, which is usually found more in feeling and emotion than in content or the words the person is using. Listen with the eyes and with the "third ear"—the heart.
- The quality in a relationship is perhaps the factor that most determines what is appropriate. Remember that relationships in the family require constant atten-

tion because the expectation of being emotionally nurtured and supported is constant. This is where people get into trouble—when they take others, particularly their loved ones, for granted and treat a stranger at the door better than the dearest people in their lives. There must be constant effort in the family to apologize, to ask for forgiveness, to express love, appreciation, and the valuing of others.

• Read the context, the environment, the culture so that the technique you use is not interpreted differently from what you intended. Sometimes you have to be very explicit by saying, "I'm going to try to understand what you mean. I am not going to evaluate, agree, or disagree at all. I am not going to try to 'figure you out.' I want to understand only what you want me to understand." And that understanding often comes only when you also understand the "bigger picture."

When you are truly empathizing, you are also understanding what's going on in the relationship and in the nature of the communication taking place between you—not just in the words the other person is attempting to communicate. You are empathic about the whole context as well as the meaning that is being communicated. And then you act based on that larger empathic understanding.

For instance, if the entire history of the relationship is one of judging and evaluation, the very effort to empathize will probably be seen in that context. To change the relationship will probably require apologizing and deep interior work to make sure one's attitude and behavior are congruent with that apology, and then being open and sensitive to opportunities to show understanding.

I remember one time when Sandra and I had been on our son's case for several weeks regarding his schoolwork. One evening we asked him if he wanted to go to dinner with us as a kind of special date. He said he wanted to go and asked who else was going. We said, "No one else. This is just a special time with you."

He then said that he didn't want to go. We talked him into it, but there was very little openness in spite of our best efforts to show understanding. Near the end of the dinner we began talking about another issue that was indirectly related to schoolwork, and the emotional energy was such that it drove us into the sensitive subject and caused bad feelings and further defensiveness on everyone's part. Later, when we apologized, this son told us, "This is why I didn't want to go to dinner." He knew it would be another judgment experience. It took us some time to make enough deposits so that he trusted the relationship and became open again.

One of the greatest things we've learned in this area is that mealtimes should always be happy, pleasant occasions for eating, sharing pleasant talk, and learning—sometimes even serious discussions about various intellectual or spiritual topics—but never a place for disciplining, correcting, or judging. When people are extremely busy, they may be with their family only at mealtimes, and they therefore try to take care of all important family matters then. But there are other, better times to handle these things. When mealtimes are pleasant and devoid of judgment or instruction, people look forward to them and to being together. It is well worth the careful planning and considerable discipline it takes to preserve the happiness and pleasantness of mealtimes and to make dinner a time when family members enjoy one another and feel relaxed and emotionally safe.

When relationships are good—and both parties are genuinely understanding—people can often rapidly communicate with unusual candor. Sometimes just a few nods or an "uh-huh" is sufficient. In these situations people can cover great territory rapidly with each other. An outsider, watching this without understanding the quality of the relationship and the larger context, might observe that there was no reflective listening or understanding or empathy taking place at all, when in fact it was deeply empathic and very efficient.

Sandra and I were able to achieve this level of communication in our own marriage on that sabbatical in Hawaii. Through the years, we have fallen back into old ways from time to time. But we find that by working at it, we are able to regain it fairly rapidly. So much depends on the amount of emotion being generated, the nature of the subject, the time of the day, the level of our personal fatigue, and the nature of our mental focus.

Many people struggle with this iceberg approach to empathy because it's not as easy as skill development. It requires a great deal more internal work, and it takes more of an inside-out approach. With skill development you can get better just by practicing.

The Second Half of the Habit

"Seek first to understand" does not mean seek *only* to understand. It doesn't mean that you bag your role to teach and influence others. It simply means that you listen and understand *first*. And as you can see in the examples given, this is actually the key to influencing others. When you are open to their influence, you'll find you almost always have greater influence with them.

Now we come to the second half of the habit —"seek to be understood." This has to do with sharing the way you see the world, with giving feedback, with teaching your children, with having the courage to confront with love. And when you attempt to do any of these things, you can readily see another very practical reason for seeking first to understand: When you really understand someone, it's much easier to share, to teach, to confront with love. You know how to speak to others in the language they understand.

One woman shared this experience:

For a long time in our marriage, my husband and I did not see eye to eye on spending. He would want to buy things I felt were unnecessary and expensive. I couldn't seem to explain to him the pain I felt as the debt kept mounting and we had to spend more and more of our income on interest and credit card bills.

Finally, I decided I needed to find a different way of expressing my point of view and to influence the situation. I tried to listen more, to understand how he was thinking. I came to realize that he was more of a "big picture" thinker, but sometimes he just didn't see the connection between his spending decisions and the consequences they brought.

So when he would say, "You know, it would really be nice to have [something]," instead of arguing with him, I began to say, "You know, it really would. Let's see what would happen if we bought that. Let's look at the big picture." And I would take out the budget and say, "Now, if we spend this here, we won't have money to do that." I found that when he saw the consequences of spending decisions, he often came to the conclusion himself that we were better off not buying the item in question.

In doing this I also discovered that with some of the purchases he wanted to make, the benefits actually outweighed the drawbacks. He wanted to buy a computer, for example. I was not in favor of this at first, but when I calculated the difference it would make in our earning capacity, I could see that my response came out of the baggage of the past instead of the logic of the present.

I also found that having a financial mission statement helped keep us both on track. When we had a shared purpose in front of us, it became much easier for us to work together to accomplish it.

Notice how understanding helped this couple work together to make better decisions. But notice, too, how understanding the way her husband thought made it possible for this woman to "seek to be understood" much more effectively. She was able to communicate better because she knew how to express her ideas in the language he understood.

Giving Feedback

I know of one man whom people generally consider to be easygoing and accepting of others. One day his wife said, "Our married children have told me that they feel you are too controlling in your relationship with them. They adore you in many ways, but they resent the way you try to channel their activities and their energy."

This man was devastated. His first response was "There's no way the children would ever say such a thing! You know that isn't true. I never interfere in any way with their desires. Such talk is ridiculous, and you know it as well as I do!"

"Nevertheless, that's the way they feel," she replied. "And I have to tell you that

I've noticed it, too. You have a way of pressuring them to do what you think is best."

"When? When? When did I ever do that? Just tell me one time when I did that."

"Do you really want to hear?"

"No, I don't want to hear, because it isn't true!"

There are times when "being understood" means giving feedback to other family members. And this can be very hard to do. People often don't want to hear feedback. It doesn't match the image they have of themselves, and they don't want to hear anything that reflects an image that is any less than the one they have in their minds.

Everyone has "blind spots"—areas in their lives that they don't even see but that need to be changed or improved. So when you really love someone, you need to care enough to confront—but in ways that are filled with positive energy and respect. You need to be able to give feedback in a way that actually builds the Emotional Bank Account instead of making withdrawals.

> *When you really love someone, you need to care enough to confront—but in ways that have positive energy and show respect.*

When you need to give feedback, you may find these five keys helpful:

1. Always ask yourself, "Will this feedback really be helpful to this person, or does it just fulfill my own need to set this person straight?" If there's any anger inside you, it's probably not the time or the place to give feedback.

2. Seek first to understand. Know what's important to the person and how your feedback will help that person accomplish his or her goals. Always try to speak that person's language of love.

3. Separate the person from the behavior. We must continually strive to do this and never judge the person. We might judge the behavior against standards and principles. We might describe our feelings and observe the consequences of this behavior. But we must absolutely refuse to put a label on another person. It is so damning to the person and to the relationship. Instead of describing a person as "lazy" or "stupid" or "selfish" or "dominating" or "chauvinistic," it is always better to describe instead our observation of the consequences of these behaviors and/or our own feelings, concerns, and perceptions that flow from these behaviors.

4. Be especially sensitive and patient regarding blind spots. They are "blind" spots because they're too sensitive to be admitted into conscious awareness. Unless people are prepared to improve things they already know should be improved, giving them information on blind spots is threatening and counterproductive. Also, don't give feedback on something they can't realistically do anything about.

5. Use "I" messages. When you give feedback, it's important to remember that

you're sharing your own perception—the way you see the world. So give "I" messages: "This is my perception." "My concern is . . ." "This is how I see it." "This is the way I feel." "This is what I observed." The moment you start sending "you" messages—"You are so self-centered!" "You are causing so much trouble!"—you're playing God. You're making yourself the ultimate judge of that person. It's as if that's the way the person is. And this becomes a huge withdrawal. What offends people the most—particularly when their heart is right but their behavior is wrong—is the idea that they're fixed, labeled, categorized, judged. That they can't change. "I" messages are more horizontal—between human equals. "You" messages are more vertical, indicating that one is better or of greater worth than another.

> "I" messages are more horizontal—between human equals. "You" messages are more vertical, indicating that one person is better or of greater worth than another.

I remember one time when Sandra and I were concerned about what we felt was a selfish pattern developing in one of our sons. It had been going on for a relatively long period of time, and it was becoming offensive to everyone in the family. We could easily have given quick feedback—just fed it to him really fast and hoped the pattern would change. We've done that sometimes. But in this case I said to myself, I've really got to pay the price on this one. This is a deeply embedded tendency, but this is not his nature. This is not like him. He has so much graciousness and selflessness and goodness. He needs to know how we feel about his actions.

At the time, we were on a family vacation at a lake. I asked him if he wanted to go for a ride around the lake on our trail cycle. We went for a long, long ride. We took our time. We stopped for drinks at a fresh stream. We were gone probably two and a half to three hours and had a great time. The depth of our interaction, the laughter, the fun, really enhanced our relationship.

Toward the end of our time together, I finally said to him, "Son, one of the reasons I wanted to have this private time with you is that your mother and I have a concern. Would you mind if I shared it with you?"

He said, "Not at all, Dad."

So I shared with him what we were feeling. He wasn't offended because I was describing us, not him. "This is what's concerning us. This is what we feel. This is our perception." I wasn't saying, "You are so selfish. You are offending the entire family."

As well as sharing our concerns, I also shared our perception of his true nature. And the immediate response was so positive! He said, "Oh, yeah, Dad, I can see that. I guess I've just really been into myself, and that's not right." And he acknowledged this to his mother and to other family members, and he began a process of what you might call "going the second mile."

Carl Rogers—one of the truly great and insightful researchers and writers on the subject of communication—created a "congruency" model that teaches the importance of both self-awareness and courage to express that awareness in communicating with others. He taught that when people are not aware of what they are feeling inside, they are "incongruent" within. They then have a tendency to intellectualize, compartmentalize, or unknowingly project their own motives on another. This internal incongruency is sensed by others and contributes to an inauthentic communication that is superficial and boring—like small talk at parties.

But he also taught that when people are internally congruent—that is, they're aware of what they're feeling—but they deny it and try to act or express themselves otherwise, this external incongruency is usually called insincerity, posturing, or even hypocrisy.

Both forms of incongruency undermine the ability to listen fully to another, and that's why a great deal of interior work must be done—both to grow in self-awareness and to have the courage to authentically express what you are feeling and thinking inside through authentic "I" messages rather than judgment messages.

We simply must care enough to confront other people. Often the key to developing strong and deep relationships with people is to level with them, to speak the truth in love—to not give in to them but to not give up on them, either. This takes time and patience, but it also takes tremendous courage and the skill of knowing when and how to give "I" messages with respect and tact—sometimes even with forcefulness and sharpness. There are times when really loving people means giving them a shock treatment—shocking them into an awareness of what they're doing—and then showing more love than ever afterward so they know you really care.

As I think about students I've taught over the years, the ones with whom I've had the deepest continuing relationships and who have expressed the deepest appreciation to me are usually those with whom I really "leveled" at an appropriate time and place. I was even able to help them understand their blind spots and the ultimate consequences of those blind spots, and to help them work through the process of getting on a growth track.

Joshua (son):

One nice thing about having older brothers or sisters is the feedback they give you.

When I come home from a high school basketball or football game, Mom and Dad will meet me at the door and go over all the key plays that I made. Mom will rave about the talent I have, and Dad will say it was my leadership skills that directed the team to victory.

When Jenny comes in the kitchen to join us, I'll ask her how I did. She'll tell me how ordinary I played, and I'd better get my act together if I want to keep my starting posi-

tion, and she hopes I'll play better the next game and not embarrass her.
Now that's feedback!

Whenever you give feedback, always remember that the relationship—the level of trust in the Emotional Bank Account—determines the level of communication you will have. Remember, too, that "I" messages build that account. They are affirming, especially when you couch constructive feedback in the best "I" message of all: "I love you. I believe you are a person of infinite worth. I know this behavior is just a tiny part of all that you are. And all that you are, I love!"

Without question, those three magic words, "I love you," are the most sought-after message of all. I remember arriving home one evening after a full day of travel that included covering hundreds of miles on an airplane, navigating through crowded airports, and driving home through the traffic. I was literally exhausted.

When I went into the house, I was met by my son who had spent almost all day cleaning up a workroom. The project had involved tremendous effort—carrying things, cleaning out things, throwing away the "junk." He was only a little boy but old enough to have judgment on which things to keep and which to throw out based on the guidelines I had given him.

As soon as I came into the room to look at it, my first observation was negative: "Why didn't you do this? Why didn't you do that?" I even forget now what it was he didn't do. But what I do remember—and will never forget—was watching the light go out of his eyes. He had been so excited, so thrilled with what he had done—and so anxious for my favorable approval. He had lived on the energy of that positive expectation for hours as he did this work. And now my first observation was negative.

When I saw the light go out of his eyes, I knew immediately that I had made a mistake. I tried to apologize. I tried to explain. I tried to focus on the good things he had done and to express my love and appreciation for it all, but the light never came back that entire evening.

It wasn't until several days later in talking more fully about the experience and processing it that his feelings came out. This taught me forcibly that when people have done their best, whether it meets your standards or not is irrelevant. That is the time to give them appreciation and praise. When someone has completed a major task or project, or has accomplished something that required supreme effort, always express admiration, appreciation, and praise. Never give negative feedback—even though it may be deserved and even though you do it in a constructive way and with good motives in order to help the person do better. Give the constructive feedback at a later time when the person is ready for it.

But at the time, praise the effort. Praise the heart that went into it. Praise the worth of the person, the personal identity that was transmitted into the project or work. You're not compromising your integrity when you take such an encouraging, appreciating, affirming approach. You're simply focusing on that which is more important than some nervous definition of excellence.

Nurturing a Habit 5 Culture

As in every other habit, the real fruits of Habit 5 are not just in the momentary "aha!" that comes when you have a one-time glimpse of real understanding of another person. They're in the *habit*—in the cumulative effect of constantly seeking to understand and to be understood in the day-to-day interactions of family life. And there are several ways you can develop this kind of Habit 5 culture in the home.

One woman shared this experience:

Several years ago we had two teenage boys who often got into squabbles. When we learned about Habit 5, we decided that this might be the key to greater peace in our home.

During one of our weekly family times, we introduced the idea to the boys. We taught them the process of empathic listening. We role-played situations where two people disagreed, and we showed them how one person could let go of judgment or trying to make a point and simply seek to understand. Then when that person felt totally understood, the other person could do the same. We told the boys that if they got into any squabble during the week, we were going to put them in a room together and they couldn't come out until they were both convinced that they were understood.

When the first squabble came up, I put them in a room where they could be alone. I sat them down on two chairs and said, "Okay, Andrew, you tell David exactly how you feel." He started to talk, but before he could get out two sentences, David interrupted by saying, "Hey, that's not how it happened!"

I said, "Wait a minute! It's not your turn yet. Your job is simply to understand what Andrew is saying and be able to explain his position to his satisfaction."

David rolled his eyes. We tried again.

About five sentences later, David jumped out of his chair. "That's not right!" he yelled. "You were the one who—"

"David!" I said. "Sit down. Your turn will come. But not before you can explain to me what Andrew is saying and he is satisfied that you really understand. You might as well sit down and try to listen. You don't have to agree with Andrew; you just have to explain his view of this to his satisfaction. You can't tell your side of this issue until you can completely explain his."

David sat down. For a few more minutes he made noises of disgust at some of the things Andrew said. But when he realized that he really wasn't going anywhere until he could do this, he settled down and tried to understand.

Each time he thought he understood, I asked him to repeat back to Andrew what Andrew had just said. "Is that right, Andrew? Is that what you said?"

And each time Andrew said either "That's right!" or "No. David doesn't understand what I was trying to say," and we'd try again. Finally we reached the point where David was able to explain how Andrew felt to Andrew's satisfaction.

Then it was David's turn. It was almost funny to see how, when he tried to return to his own point of view, his feelings had actually changed. He did see some things differently, but much of the wind had been taken out of his sails when he realized how Andrew saw the situation. And feeling genuinely understood, Andrew was much more willing to listen to David's point of view. So the boys were able to talk without getting into blaming and accusing. And once all the feelings were out, they found it relatively easy to come up with a solution they both felt good about.

That first experience took about forty-five minutes of their time and mine. But it was worth it! The next time it happened, they knew what we were going to do. As we kept working at it over the years, we found it often wasn't easy. Sometimes there were intense feelings and deep issues involved. There were even times when they would start to get into an argument and suddenly stop, realizing they would rather be free to be with their friends than spend half an hour in a room together working things out. But the more they did it, the better they got.

One of my best moments as a parent came several years after they had both left home. One had been in another state and one in another country, and they hadn't seen each other in several years. They came to our home to go through some things that had been left to them by their great-grandfather. Their camaraderie was wonderful. They laughed and joked together, and enjoyed each other immensely. And when the time came to decide who got what, they were extremely solicitous of each other. "You could use this—you take it." "I know you would like to have this. You take it."

It was easy to see they had a win-win attitude, and it grew out of a deep understanding of each other. I am convinced that seeking to understand each other as they were growing up made a big difference.

Notice how this woman patiently used family time to teach the principles of empathic listening in her home. Notice how she followed through in helping them integrate the principles into their daily lives, and notice the fruits of such efforts years later.

In our own family we have found this one simple ground rule to be very powerful in creating legitimacy for empathic listening in the culture: *Whenever there is a difference or disagreement, people can't make their own point until they restate the other person's point to that person's satisfaction.* This is amazingly powerful. It might be prefaced with words to this effect, particularly if you sense that people have already made up their minds and are basically just going to fight each other: "We are going to be talking about important things that people have strong feelings about. To help us in this communication, why don't we agree to this simple little ground rule"— and then state the rule. Initially, this approach may seem to slow things down, but in the long run it saves tenfold on time, nerves, and relationships.

We've also tried to organize so that all family members know they will get "their day in court" in one-on-ones or in family meetings. Regarding family meetings, we developed a process of problem-solving in which the person who had the concern or the problem would take the responsibility to lead the family through that meeting on the problem itself. We posted a sheet of paper on the refrigerator, and anyone who wanted to talk about any issue, problem, hope, or plan would simply write the issue and his or her name on the paper. This paper helped us develop the content for the family council discussion. And each person who put an item on the agenda was responsible to take us all through the process of solving the problem or doing whatever it involved.

We found that when the culture basically rewards those who speak up first and those who take action first, then other people feel their day in court never comes. Feelings gradually begin to go inside, where they remain bottled up and unexpressed. And those unexpressed feelings never die. They are buried alive and come forth later in uglier ways—in overreactive comments, in anger, in violent verbal or physical expressions, in psychosomatic illnesses, in giving people the silent treatment, in extreme statements or judgments, or in simply acting out in other dysfunctional and hurtful ways.

> *When people know they will have their day in court, they can relax. They know that their time to be heard and understood will come.*

But when people know they will have their day in court—that is, they will have an opportunity to be fully heard and to process others' reactions to what they say—they can relax. They don't have to become impatient and overreactive because they know that their time to be heard and understood will come. This dissipates negative energy and helps people develop internal patience and self-control.

This is one of the great strengths of Habit 5. And if you can cultivate a family culture where Habit 5 is central to the whole way of dealing with things, then everyone will feel that his or her day in court will come. And this eliminates many of the foolish, impulsive reactions people get into when they feel they will not be heard.

We have to admit, though, that even with all our effort to ensure that everyone in the family is heard, some have had to be really proactive to make it happen.

Jenny (*daughter*):
Growing up in a family of nine kids sometimes made it difficult for me to get the atten-

*tion I wanted. There was always so much going on at our home, and everyone was con-
stantly talking or doing something. So in order for me to get attention, I would motion to
Dad or Mom to come over, and I would whisper whatever I had to say. I made sure that
I whispered soft enough that they would have to give me their full attention and make
everyone else be quiet. It worked.*

Making sure you are heard—and understood—is what the second half of Habit
5 is all about.

Understanding Developmental Stages

Another way you can practice Habit 5 in the home is to seek to understand the way
your children see the world by becoming aware of their "ages and stages."

Growth is based on universal principles. A child learns to turn over, to sit, to
crawl, then to walk and run. Each step is important. No step can be skipped. Of
necessity, some things must come ahead of other things.

As surely as this is true in the area of physical things, it is also true in the areas
of emotions and human relations. But while things in the physical area are seen and
constant evidence is supplied, things in the other areas are largely unseen and evidence is not as direct or as plain. It is tremendously important, therefore, that we
understand not only the physical but also the mental, emotional, and spiritual
stages of development, and that we never attempt to shortcut, violate, or bypass the
process.

If we do not make a sincere effort to understand our children's development and
to communicate with them on their level of awareness, we often find ourselves
making unreasonable expectations of them and being frustrated when we can't seem
to get through.

I remember one afternoon I found myself criticizing our young son for throwing
all his clothes in a heap on the floor of his room. I said, "Don't you realize you
shouldn't do this? Don't you understand what will happen, how your clothes will get
dirty and wrinkled like this?"

This son didn't resist me. He didn't rebel. He agreed. I even sensed he wanted
to do as I asked. But still, day in and day out, he threw his clothes on the floor.

Finally, one day I thought, Maybe he simply doesn't know how to hang up his
clothes. He's just a little kid. So I took half an hour to train him in hanging up his
clothes. We practiced how to take his Sunday suit pants by the cuffs, hang them over
the bottom wire of the hanger, and then put the hanger on the lower bar of the closet.
We practiced how to button up the front of his shirt, turn it over, fold one third of
each side toward the center, fold the sleeves in, and lay the shirt in his drawer.

He really enjoyed the training. In fact, when we were through, we even took all his clothes out of his closet and hung them back up again, we were having so much fun. There was a good feeling between us, and he learned. He was able to do the job well.

As I discovered with this son, the problem was not that he didn't recognize the importance of hanging up his clothes. It wasn't even that he didn't want to hang up his clothes. It was simply that he didn't have the competency; he didn't know how to do it.

Years later, as a teenager, this son had the same problem again. But the nature of the problem at that point wasn't competence, it was motivation. And it took a motivational solution to solve it.

The first key in solving any training problem is to diagnose it correctly. You wouldn't bring in a cardiologist if you had a foot problem. You wouldn't bring in a plumber if the roof leaked. Neither can you solve a competency problem with a value or motivational solution—or vice versa.

When we want a child to perform a task in our family, I've found it helpful to always ask three questions:

Should the child do it? (a value question)
Can the child do it? (a competency question)
Does the child *want* to do it? (a motivation question)

Based on the response, we know where to direct our effort effectively. If it's a value question, the solution usually lies in building the Emotional Bank Account and educating. If it's a competency question, the answer generally lies in training. There's a difference between education and training. Education means "to draw forth"—in this case, to provide a deep and proper explanation that tends to draw forth the sense of "this is what I should do." Training means "to put in"—in this case, to put into the child the knowledge of how to do the task. Both educating and training are important, and which you would use depends on the nature of the problem. If the value question is one of competing "shoulds"—"Should I do my chores or party with my friends?"—then the key is in the quality of the relationship and the character and culture of the family.

If it's a question of motivation, the answer generally lies in reinforcing the desired behavior either extrinsically or intrinsically, or in combination. You could provide extrinsic rewards (such as an allowance or recognition or some privilege or "perk") or you could stress the intrinsic rewards (the inner peace and satisfaction that comes when people do things because they're the right thing to do, when they listen to and obey their conscience). Or you could do both. To determine the nature of the problem is a Habit 5 (Seek first to understand, then to be understood) issue.

Over the years Sandra has brought unbelievable enlightenment and intuitive wisdom to our family in the area of understanding the developmental stages of our children. She graduated from college with a degree in child development and has both studied and practiced it all her adult life. As a result, she has gained tremendous insights into the importance of listening to your heart and to the natural developmental stages children go through.[4]

Sandra:

I was in a grocery store the other day and saw a young mother struggling with her two-year-old. She quietly tried to comfort, console, and reason with him, but he was completely out of control—shaking, screaming, sobbing, and holding his breath until he broke into a temper tantrum, to the distress of his embarrassed, desperate mother.

As a mother, my heart reached out to her as she tried to come to grips with the situation. I wanted to tell her all the rational thoughts that raced through my mind in rapid succession: Don't take it personally. Act in a matter-of-fact way. Don't reward this kind of behavior. Don't let this child get any mileage out of this episode. Remind yourself that two-year-olds aren't yet emotionally able to handle complex emotions (exhaustion, temper, stress), and so they blow a fuse and break the circuit with a tantrum.

After you've gone through it a few times, you start to recognize that a child behaves the way he does partly because he's at a certain stage of growth. Development occurs one step at a time, in a kind of predictable sequence. We often hear phrases such as "the terrible twos," "the trusting threes," "the frustrating fours," and "the fascinating fives" used to describe phases of behavior—often predicting hard times during the even years and hoping for smoother sailing during the odd years.

Each child is an individual and different from all others, yet all seem to follow a similar path. Solitary play will gradually evolve into parallel play. These little people, side by side with separate toys and different dialogues, will eventually be able to interact with one another in cooperative play as they grow and mature. Similarly, a child needs to feel ownership and must possess before he can share, crawl before he can walk, understand before he can talk. It's important for us to be aware of this process—to notice, read about, and learn to recognize growth patterns and stages of development in our own children and their peers.

In so doing you don't take it personally when your two-year-old breaks away, defies you with a "no!" and tries to establish himself as an independent person. You don't over-react when your four-year-old uses toilet words and shocking language to get your attention and vacillates between being a self-confident, capable child and a regressive, whiny baby. You don't call up your mother in tears, confessing that your six-year-old cheats, lies, and steals in order to be first or best, and that your nine-year-old thinks you are dishonest and have no character because you often drive over the speed limit and were caught telling a white lie. Neither do you excuse irresponsible behavior in the name of growth and development or label your child because of birth order, socioeconomic position, or IQ.

Each family learns to understand and solve its own problems by applying the best knowledge, insight, and intuition it has. This might include repeating to yourself phrases such as "This too will pass," "Steady as she goes," "Roll with the punches," "Someday we'll laugh at this"—or holding your breath and counting to ten before you respond.

The Sequence Is the Key

As you teach Habit 5 to your family and as you begin to operate in your Circle of Influence to live Habit 5 yourself, you will be amazed at the impact it will have on your family culture—even on small children. One father shared this:

I realized the impact of seeking first to understand in the family the other day when I was watching our three sons interact.

Jason, who is one and a half, had just knocked over Matt's toys, and Matt, who is four years old and not too articulate, was just about to slug his baby brother.

Just at that time Todd, our six-year-old, walked over to Matt and said, "You're feeling really angry now, aren't you, Matt! Baby Jason just knocked down all your toys, and you are so angry you want to hit him." Matt looked at Todd for a moment, mumbled a few words, raised his hands, and walked out of the room.

I thought to myself, Wow, this really works!

Remember, the key to Habit 5 is in the sequence. It's not just what to do, it's also why and when. Habit 5 helps us listen—and speak—from the heart. It also opens the door to the incredible family synergy we'll talk about as we move into Habit 6.

Sharing This Chapter with Adults and Teens

Seek First to Understand

- Review the Indian/Eskimo perception experience. Explore the value of realizing that people do not see the world as it is but as they are, or as they have been conditioned to see it.

- Discuss together: How important is it to truly understand and empathize with each family member? How well do we really know the members of our family? Do we know their stresses? Their vulnerabilities? Their needs? Their views about life and about themselves? Their hopes and expectations? How can we get to know them better?

- Ask family members: Do we see some of the fruits of *not* understanding in our home, such as frustration over unclear expectations, judgment, slamming doors, blaming and accusing, rudeness, poor relationships, sadness, loneliness, or crying? Discuss what family members could do to ensure that everyone has the opportunity to be heard.

- Give some thought to the way you deal with family communication. Discuss the four major autobiographical responses—evaluating, advising, probing, and interpreting (page 225). Practice together learning how to give an understanding response.

- Review the guidelines on pages 228–231 and the story on pages 224–226. Discuss how this information can help you practice Habit 5 in your family.

Then Seek to Be Understood

- Review the material on pages 201–232. Discuss why seeking first to understand is fundamental to being understood. How can it help you better communicate in the language of the listener?

- Consider together how you can nurture a Habit 5 "understanding culture" in your home.

SHARING THIS CHAPTER WITH CHILDREN

- Take the children through the Indian/Eskimo perception experience. When they are able to see both pictures, talk about how there are usually two or more ways of looking at things, and how we really don't always see or experience things in the same way others do. Encourage them to share any experiences when they felt misunderstood.

- Get several pairs of glasses—some prescription, some sunglasses. Let each child look at the same object through a different set of glasses. One might say it's blurry, dark, blue-tinted, or clear, all depending on what glasses he or she is wearing. Explain that the differences in what they see represent the different ways people see things in life. Let them trade glasses to get an idea of seeing something the way someone else sees it.

- Prepare a "taste" platter with a number of different items of food on it. Let everyone taste each item. Compare responses, and talk about how some people may really love a particular food, such as sour pickles, that others find distasteful or bitter. Point out how this is symbolic of how differently people experience life, and explain how important it is for all of us to really understand how other people may experience things differently than we do.

- Visit an older family member or friend and ask him or her to share an experience from the past with your children. After the visit, share any information you have that would increase your children's understanding of what things were like when that person was younger. "Did you know that Mr. Jacobs used to be a tall, good-looking policeman?" "Mrs. Smith was once a schoolteacher and all the kids loved her." "Grandmother was known as the best pie-maker in town." Talk about how knowledge and understanding of people help you see them more clearly.

- Invite to your house people who have something to share—a musical talent, a recent trip, or an interesting experience. Talk about how much we can learn from listening to and understanding others.

- Commit to be a more understanding family by listening better and being more observant. Teach your children to listen—not just with their ears, but also with their eyes, mind, and heart.

- Play "mood charades." Ask children to demonstrate a mood such as anger, sadness, happiness, or disappointment, and let the rest of the family guess what they're feeling. Point out that you can learn a lot about others by simply watching their faces and body movements.

HABIT 6
SYNERGIZE

A friend of mine shared an insightful experience he had with his son. As you read it, think about what you might have done in his situation.

After one week of practice, my son told me that he wanted to quit the high school bas-ketball team. I told him that if he quit basketball, he would just keep quitting things all of his life. I told him how I had wanted to quit things when I was young, but I didn't, and that made a dramatic difference in my life. I also told him that all our other sons had been basketball players and that the hard work and cooperation involved in being on the team helped them all. I was confident it would help him, too.

My son didn't seem to want to understand me at all. With choked emotion he replied, "Dad, I'm not my brothers. I'm not a good player. I'm tired of being harassed by the coach. I have other interests besides basketball."

I was so upset that I walked away.

For the next two days I felt frustrated each time I thought of this son's foolish and irre-sponsible decision. I had a fairly good relationship with him, but it upset me to think that he cared so little about my feelings in this matter. Several times I tried to talk to him, but he simply would not listen.

Finally, I began to wonder just what had led him to make the decision to quit. I deter-

mined to find out. At first he didn't even want to talk about it, so I asked him about other things. He would answer "yes" or "no" to my small talk, but he wouldn't say any more than that. After some time he began to get teary-eyed, and he said, "Dad, I know you think you understand me, but you don't. No one knows how rotten I feel."

I replied, "Pretty tough, huh?"

"I'll say it's tough! Sometimes I don't even know if it's all worth it."

He then poured his heart out. He told me many things I had not known before. He expressed his pain at constantly being compared to his brothers. He said his coach expected him to play ball as well as his brothers. He felt that if he went down a different path and blazed a new trail, the comparisons might end. He said he felt I favored his brothers because they brought me more glory than he could. He also told me about the insecurities he felt—not only in basketball but in all areas of his life. And he said he felt that he and I had somehow lost touch with each other.

I have to admit that his words humbled me. I had the feeling that what he said about the comparisons with his brothers was true and that I was guilty. I acknowledged my sorrow to him and—with much emotion—apologized. But I also told him that I still thought he would benefit greatly from playing ball. I told him that the family and I could work together to make things better for him if he wanted to play. He listened with patience and understanding, but he would not budge from his decision to quit the team.

Finally, I asked him if he liked basketball. He said he loved basketball but disliked all the pressure associated with playing for the high school team. As we talked, he said that what he would really like to do was play for the church team. He explained that he just wanted to have fun playing, not try to conquer the world. As he talked, I found myself feeling good about what he was saying. I admit I still felt a little disappointed that he wouldn't be on the school team, but I was glad that at least he still wanted to play.

He started telling me the names of the guys on the church team, and as he talked, I could sense his excitement and interest. I asked him when the church team played games so that I could attend. He told me he wasn't sure, and then he added, "But we need to get a coach or they won't even let us play at all."

At that point, almost by magic, something shot between us. A new idea came into both of our minds at the same time. Almost in unison we said, "I/You could coach the church team!"

All of a sudden my heart felt light as I thought about how much fun it would be to coach the team and have my son as one of the players.

The weeks that followed were among the happiest of my athletic experiences. And they provided some of my most memorable experiences as a father. Our team played for the sheer joy of playing. Oh, sure, we wanted to win and we did get a few victories, but no one was under pressure. And my son—who had hated to have the high school coach shout at him—would beam each time I would shout, "Way to go, son! Way to go! Good shot, son! Nice pass!"

That basketball season transformed the relationship between my son and me.

This story captures the essence of Habit 6—synergy—and of the Habits 4, 5, and 6 process that creates it.

Notice how this father and son at first seemed to be locked in a win-lose situation. The father wanted his son to play ball. His motives were good. He thought that playing ball would be a long-term win for his son. But the son felt differently. Playing high school ball wasn't a win for him; it was a lose. He was always being compared to his brothers. He didn't like dealing with the pressure. It seemed to be "your way" or "my way." Whatever decision was made, someone was going to lose.

But then this father made an important shift in his thinking. He sought to understand why this wasn't a win for his son. As they talked, they were able to get past the positioning and into the real issues. Together they came up with a *better* way, an entirely new solution that was a win for both. And that's what synergy is all about.

Synergy—the *Summum Bonum* of All the Habits

Synergy is the *summum bonum*—the supreme or highest fruit—of all the habits. It's the magic that happens when one plus one equals three—or more. And it happens because the relationship between the parts is a part itself. It has such catalytic, dynamic power that it affects how the parts interact with one another. It comes out of the spirit of mutual respect (win-win) and mutual understanding in producing something new—not in compromising or meeting halfway.

A great way to understand synergy is through the metaphor of the body. The body is more than just hands and arms and legs and feet and brain and stomach and heart all thrown together. It's a miraculous, synergistic whole that can do many wonderful things because of the way the individual parts work together. Two hands, for example, can do far more together than both hands can do separately. Two eyes working together can see more clearly, with greater depth perception, than two eyes working separately. Two ears working together can tell sound direction, which is not the case with two unconnected ears. The whole body can do far more than all the individual parts could do on their own, added up but unconnected.

So synergy deals with the part between the parts. In the family, this part is the quality and nature of the relationship between people. As a husband and wife interact, or as parents interact with children, synergy lies in the relationship between them. That's where the creative mind is—the new mind that produces the new option, the third alternative.

You might even think of this part as a third person. The feeling of "we" in a marriage becomes more than two people; it's the relationship between the two people that creates this third "person." And the same is true with parents and children.

The other "person" created by the relationship is the essence of the family culture with its deeply established purpose and principle-centered value system.

In synergy, then, you have not only mutual vulnerability and the creation of shared vision and values, new solutions, and better alternatives, but you also have a sense of mutual accountability to the norms and values built into those creations. Again, this is what puts moral or ethical authority into the culture. It encourages people to be more honest, to speak with more candor, and to have the courage to deal with the tougher issues rather than trying to escape or ignore them or avoid being with people so as to minimize the likelihood of having to deal with such issues.

This "third person" becomes something of a higher authority, something that embodies the collective conscience, the shared vision and values, the social mores and norms of the culture. It keeps people from being unethical or power hungry, or from borrowing strength from position or credentials or educational attainment or gender. And as long as people live with regard to this higher authority, they see things such as position, power, prestige, money, and status as part of their "steward-ship"—something they are entrusted with, responsible for, accountable for. But when people do not live in accordance with this higher authority and become a law unto themselves, this sense of a "third person" disintegrates. People become alienated, wrapped up in ownership and self-focus. The culture becomes independent rather than interdependent, and the magic of synergy is gone.

The key ultimately lies in the moral authority of the culture—to which everyone is accountable.

Synergy Is Risky Business

Because it's stepping out into the unknown, the process of creating synergy can sometimes be near chaos. The "end in mind" you begin with is not *your* end, *your* solution. It's moving from the known to the unknown and creating something entirely new. And it's building relationships and capacity in the process. So you don't go into the situation seeking your own way. You go in not knowing what's going to come out of it, but knowing that it's going to be a lot better than anything you brought into it.

And this is risky business—an adventure. This is the magic moment of mutual vulnerability. You don't know what's going to happen. You're at risk.

This is why the first three habits are so foundational. They enable you to develop the internal security that gives you the

Synergy is the magic moment of mutual vulnerability. You don't know what's going to happen. You're at risk.

courage to live with this kind of risk. As paradoxical as it sounds, it takes a great deal of confidence to be humble. It takes a great deal of internal security to afford the risk of being vulnerable. But when people have the confidence and the kind of principle-based internal security that gives birth to humility and vulnerability, they then cease being a law unto themselves. Instead, they become conduits of exchanging insights. And in that very exchange is the dynamic that unleashes creative powers.

Truly, nothing is more exciting and bonding in relationships than creating together. And Habits 4 and 5 give you the mind-set and the skill-set to do it. You have to think win-win. You have to seek first to understand and then to be understood. In a sense you have to learn to listen with the third ear to create the third mind and the third alternative; in other words, you have to listen heart to heart in genuine respect and empathy. You have to reach the point where both parties are open to influence, teachable, humble, and vulnerable before the third mind that is the part between the two minds can become creative and produce alternatives and options that neither had considered initially. This level of interdependence requires two independent persons who recognize the interdependent nature of the circumstance, issue, problem, or need so that they can choose to exercise those interdependent muscles that enable synergy to happen.

Truly, Habit 6 is the *summum bonum* of all the habits. It's not transactional cooperation where one plus one equals two. It's not compromise cooperation where one plus one equals one and a half. And it's not adversarial communication or negative synergy where more than half the energy is spent in fighting and defending so that one plus one equals less than one.

Synergy is a situation in which one plus one equals at least three. It is the highest, most productive and satisfying level of human interdependence. It represents the ultimate fruit on the tree. And there is no way to get that fruit unless the tree has been planted and nurtured and becomes mature enough to produce it.

The Key to Synergy: Celebrate the Difference

The key to creating synergy is in learning to value—even celebrate—the difference. Going back to the metaphor of the body, if the body were all hands or all heart or all feet, it could never work the way it does. The very differences enable it to accomplish so much.

A member of our extended family shared this powerful story of how she came to value the difference between her and her daughter:

When I turned eleven, my parents gave me a beautiful edition of a great classic. I read those pages lovingly, and when I turned the last one, I wept. I had lived through them.

Carefully, I kept the book for years, waiting to give it to my own daughter. When Cathy was eleven, I presented the book to her. Very pleased by her gift, she struggled through the first two chapters, then deposited it on her shelf where it remained unopened for months. I was deeply disappointed.

For some reason I had always supposed that my daughter would be like me, that she would like to read the same books I read as a girl, that she would have a temperament somewhat similar to mine, and that she would like what I liked.

"Cathy is a charming, bubbly, quick-to-laugh, slightly mischievous girl," her teachers told me. "She's fun to be around," said her friends. "She's excited about life, quick to seek humor everywhere, a sensitive soul," said her father.

"This is really hard for me," I said to my husband one day. "Her interminable zest for activities, her insatiable desire to 'play,' her ever-bubbling laughing and joking, are overwhelming to me. I've never been like that."

Reading had been the singular joy of my preteen years. In my mind I knew I was wrong to be disappointed in the difference between us, but in the recesses of my heart I was. Cathy was something of an enigma to me, and I resented it.

Those unspoken feelings pass quickly to a child. I knew she would sense them and they would hurt her, if they hadn't already. I agonized that I could be so uncharitable. I knew my disappointment was senseless, but as dearly as I loved this child, it did not change my heart.

Night after night when all were sleeping and the house was dark and quiet, I prayed for understanding. Then as I lay in bed one morning, very early, something happened. Quickly passing through my mind, in just seconds, I saw a picture of Cathy as an adult. We were two adult women, arms linked, smiling at each other. I thought of my own sister and how different we were. Yet I would never have wished that she be like me. I realized that Cathy and I would both be adults someday, just like my sister and me. And dearest friends do not have to be alike.

The words came to mind, "How dare you try to impose your personality on her. Rejoice in your differences!" Although it lasted but seconds, this flash, this reawakening, changed my heart when nothing else could.

My thankfulness, my gratitude, was renewed. And my relationship with my daughter took on a whole new dimension of richness and joy.

Notice how initially this woman assumed that her daughter would be like her. Notice how this assumption caused her frustration and blinded her to her daughter's precious uniqueness. Only when she learned how to accept her daughter as she was and to rejoice in their differences was she able to create the rich, full relationship she wanted to have.

And this is the case in every relationship in the family.

One day I was presenting a seminar dealing with right and left brain differences to a company in Orlando, Florida. I called the seminar "Manage from the Left, Lead from the Right." During the break, the president of the company came up to me and said, "Stephen, this is intriguing, but I have been thinking about this material more in terms of its application to my marriage than to my business. My wife and I have a real communication problem. I wonder if you would have lunch with the two of us and just kind of watch how we talk to each other."

"Let's do it," I replied.

As the three of us sat down together, we exchanged a few pleasantries. Then this man turned to his wife and said, "Now, honey, I've invited Stephen to have lunch with us to see if he can help us in our communication with each other. I know you feel I should be a more sensitive, considerate husband. Can you give me something specific you think I ought to do?" His dominant left brain wanted facts, figures, specifics, parts.

"Well, as I've told you before, it's nothing specific. It's more of a general sense I have about priorities." Her dominant right brain was dealing with sensing and with the gestalt, the whole, the relationship between the parts.

"What do you mean, 'a general sense about priorities'? What is it you want me to do? Give me something specific that I can get a handle on."

"Well, it's just a feeling." Her right brain was dealing in images, intuitive feelings. "I just don't think our marriage is as important to you as you tell me it is."

"What can I do to make it more important? Give me something concrete and specific to go on."

"It's hard to put into words."

At that point, he just rolled his eyes and looked at me as if to say, Stephen, could you endure this kind of dumbness in your marriage?

"It's just a feeling," she said, "a very strong feeling."

"Honey," he said to her, "that's your problem. And that's the problem with your mother. In fact, it's the problem with every woman I know."

Then he began to interrogate her as though it were some kind of legal deposition.

"Do you live where you want to live?"

"That's not it," she said with a sigh. "That's not it at all."

"I know," he replied with forced patience. "But since you won't tell me exactly what it is, I figure the best way to find out what it is, is to find out what it is not. Do you live where you want to live?"

"I guess."

"Honey, Stephen's here for just a few minutes to try to help us. Just give me a quick 'yes' or 'no' answer. Do you live where you want to live?"

"Yes."

"Okay, that's settled. Do you have the things you want to have?"

"Yes."

"All right. Do you do the things you want to do?"

This went on for a little while, and I could see I wasn't helping at all, so I intervened and said, "Is this kind of how it goes in your relationship?"

"Every day, Stephen," he replied.

"It's the story of our marriage," she said.

I looked at the two of them, and the thought crossed my mind that they were two half-brained people living together. "Do you have any children?" I asked.

"Yes, two."

"Really?" I asked incredulously. "How did you do it?"

"What do you mean, how did we do it?"

"You were synergistic!" I said. "One plus one usually equals two. But you made one plus one equal four. Now that's synergy. The whole is greater than the sum of the parts. So how did you do it?"

"You know how we did it!" he replied.

"You must have valued the differences!" I exclaimed.

Now contrast that experience with that of some friends of ours who were in the same situation—except their roles were reversed. The wife said:

My husband and I have very different thinking styles. I tend to be more logical and sequential—more "left brained." He tends to be more "right brained," to look at things more holistically.

When we were first married, this difference created something of a problem in our communication. It seemed that he was always scanning the horizon, looking at new alternatives, new possibilities. It was easy for him to change course midstream if he thought he saw a better way. On the other hand, I tended to be diligent and precise. Once we had a clear direction, I would work out the details, burrow in, and stay the course, no matter what.

This gave rise to a number of challenges when it came to making decisions together on everything from setting goals to buying things to disciplining the children. Our commitment to each other was very solid, but we were both caught up in our own ways of thinking and it seemed like a lot of work to try to make decisions together.

For a time we tried to separate areas of responsibility. In doing the budget, for example, he would do much of the long-range planning, and I would keep the records. And this proved to be helpful. We were both contributing to the marriage and family in our own areas of strength.

But when we discovered how to use our differences to create synergy, we came to a new level of richness in our relationship. We discovered that we could take turns listening to each other and have our eyes opened to a whole new way of seeing things. Instead of approaching problems from "opposite" sides, we were able to come together and approach problems with shared and much greater understanding.

This opened the door to all kinds of new solutions to our problems. It also gave us something wonderful to do together. When we finally realized that our differences were parts of a greater whole, we began exploring the possibilities of putting those parts together in new ways.

We discovered that we love to write together. He goes for the big concepts, the holistic ideas and the right brain ways of teaching. I challenge and interact with him on the ideas, arrange the content, and do the wordsmithing. And we love it! This has brought us together in a whole new level of contribution. We've found that our togetherness is much better because of our differences rather than in spite of them.

Notice how both couples were dealing with right and left brain differences in thinking. In the first situation, these differences led to frustration, misunderstanding, and alienation. In the second, they led to a new level of unity and richness in the relationship.

How was the second couple able to get such positive results?

They learned how to value the difference and use it to create something new. As a result, *they're better together than they are alone.*

As we said in Habit 5, everyone is unique. And that uniqueness, that difference, is the basis of synergy. In fact, the whole foundation of the biological creation of a family hinges on the physical differences between a man and a woman that produce children. And that physical creative power serves as a metaphor for other kinds of good things that can come as a result of differences.

> *You must be able to say sincerely, "The fact that we see things differently is a strength—not a weakness—in our relationship."*

It's not enough to simply tolerate differences in the family. You can't just accept differences. You can't just diversify family functions to accommodate differences. To have the kind of creative magic we're talking about, you must actually *celebrate* differences. You must be able to say sincerely, "The fact that we see things differently is a strength—not a weakness—in our relationship."

From Admiration to Irritation

Ironically, often the very things that attract people to each other in the beginning of a relationship are the differences, the ways in which someone is delightfully, pleasantly, excitingly different. Yet as they get into the relationship, somehow admiration changes to irritation, and some of those differences are the very things that cause the greatest distress.

I remember coming home one night after having been away from meaningful communication with our young children for two or three days. I was feeling somewhat guilty about this lack of communication, and when I feel guilty, I tend to become a bit indulgent.

Because I was often away, Sandra had to compensate for my indulgence by coming on a bit too strong. Her toughness caused me to become a little softer. My increased softness caused her to become a little harder. Thus, the discipline system in our home was sometimes driven more by politics than by the consistent application of principles that create a beautiful family culture.

When I came home that night, I went to the top of the stairs and yelled, "Boys, are you there? How's it going?"

One of the younger boys ran down the hall, looked up at me, and then shouted back to his brother, "Hey, Sean, he's nice." (In other words, "He's in a good mood!")

What I didn't know was that these boys were in bed under threat of their lives. They had used every conceivable excuse to get up and keep playing and goofing off. That had gone on until my wife's patience had come to an end. She had sent them to bed with a final command: "Now you boys stay in bed or else!"

So when they saw Dad's car lights shine through the window, a new ray of hope was born. They thought, Let's see what kind of mood Dad is in. If he's in a good mood, we can get up and play some more. When I came into the house, they were waiting. The words, "Hey, Sean, he's nice," were their cue. We started wrestling around in the front room and having all kinds of fun.

Then out came Mom. With a mixture of frustration and anger in her voice, she shouted, "Are those kids still up?"

I quickly replied, "Hey, I haven't seen much of them lately. I want to play with them for a little while." Needless to say, she didn't like my response, nor did I like hers. And there were the boys, watching Mom and Dad arguing right in front of them.

The problem was that we had not synergized on this issue and come up with agreements we were both willing to live with. I was too much a product of my moods and feelings, and I wasn't consistent. I didn't show respect for the fact that these boys were in bed and should have stayed in bed. But I also hadn't seen them for some time. And a pertinent question was "How important is the bedtime rule anyway?"

The solution to this problem was not worked out immediately, but eventually we concluded that the bedtime rule wasn't that important *for our family*—particularly as the children became teenagers. We felt that what were normal bedtimes for many families were important and fun family times for us. The kids would sit around and talk, eat, and laugh—particularly with Sandra, since I typically went to bed earlier. The thing that enabled that synergistic solution for our family was acknowledging the differences and allowing all of us to do what we individually and collectively felt strongly about.

Sometimes living with differences and appreciating other people's uniqueness is hard. We tend to want to mold people in our own image. When we get our security from our opinions, to hear a different opinion—particularly from someone as close as our spouse or children—threatens that security. We want them to agree with us, to think the way we think, to go along with our ideas. But as someone once said, "When everybody thinks alike, nobody thinks very much." Another said, "When two agree, one is unnecessary." Without difference, there's no basis for synergy, no option to create new solutions and opportunities.

The key is to learn to blend the best of them together in a way that creates something entirely new. You can't have a delicious stew without diversity. You can't have a fruit salad without diversity. It's the diversity that creates the interest, the flavor, the new combination that puts together the best of all different things.

Over the years Sandra and I have come to recognize that one of the very best things about our marriage is our differences. We share an overarching commitment and value system and destination, but within that, we have great diversity. And we love it! Most of the time, that is. We count on each other's different perspectives to increase our judgment, to help us make better decisions. We count on each other's strengths to help compensate for our individual weaknesses. We count on each other's uniqueness to give spice and flavor to our relationship.

We *know* we're better together than we are alone. And we know that one of the primary reasons is that we are different.

Cynthia (daughter):

If you wanted advice about something, you'd go to Dad, and he'd give it to you. He'd say, "I'd do this." And he'd outline everything.

But sometimes you didn't want advice. You just wanted someone to say, "You're the best. You're the greatest. They should have chosen you as cheerleader [or class president or whatever] instead of that other girl." You just wanted someone to be really supportive and loyal to you, no matter what. And that was Mom. In fact, she was so loyal, I was always afraid she was going to call whoever I was mad at and bawl them out and say, "Why are you being so rude to my daughter? Why don't you ask her out?" or "Why didn't you choose her to be the lead in the play?"

She thought we were the greatest. It wasn't so much that she thought we were better than other kids, but she thought a lot of us. And we could feel that even though we knew she was prejudiced about us and usually exaggerated what we did. But it felt good to know that someone believed in you that much. And that's what she instilled in us: "You can do anything. You will rise and accomplish your goals if you just stick with it. I believe in you, and you can do it."

Somehow each of them taught us the best of what they were.

The Process in Action

Synergy is not just teamwork or cooperation. Synergy is *creative* teamwork, *creative* cooperation. Something new is created that was not there before and could not have been created without celebrating differences. Through deep empathic listening and courageous expressing and producing new insights, the third alternative is born.

> *Synergy is not just teamwork or cooperation. Synergy is creative teamwork, creative cooperation. Something new is created that was not there before.*

Now you can apply Habits 4, 5, and 6 to create new third-alternative solutions in any family situation. In fact, I'd like to suggest that you try to do just that.

I'm going to share with you a real-life situation and ask you to engage your four human gifts to see how you would resolve it. I'll interrupt this experience at points along the way and ask questions so that you can use your pause button and think through specifically how you could use your gifts and just what you would do. I suggest you take the time to think deeply about and answer each question before you continue reading.

My husband didn't earn much money, but we were finally able to buy a small house. We were thrilled to have a home of our own even though the payments were such that we would just barely be able to stay financially solvent.

After living in the home for a month we became convinced that our front room looked shabby because of the threadbare couch that my husband's mother had given us. We decided that although we couldn't afford it, we had to have a new couch. We drove to a nearby furniture store and looked at the couches. We saw a beautiful Early American couch that was just what we wanted, but we were astonished at the high price. Even the least expensive couch was twice the price we had thought it would be.

The salesman asked us about our house. We told him, with some degree of pride, how much we loved it. Then he said, "How would that Early American couch look in your front room?"

We told him it would look grand. He suggested that it be delivered the following Wednesday. When we asked him how we could get it without any money, he assured us that would be no problem because they could defer the payments for two months.

My husband said, "Okay. We'll take it."

[Pause: Use your self-awareness and your conscience. Assuming you were the woman, what would you do?]

I told the salesman that we needed more time to think. [Notice how this woman used her Habit 1 proactivity to create a pause.]

"My husband replied, "What is there to think about? We need it now, and we can

pay for it later." But I told the salesman that we would look around and then maybe come back. I could tell my husband was upset as I took hold of his hand and began to walk away.

We walked to a little park and sat on a bench. He was still upset and hadn't said a word since we left the store.

[Pause: Use your self-awareness and your conscience again. How would you handle this situation?]

I decided to let him tell me how he felt and to listen so that I could understand his feeling and thinking. [Notice the Habit 4 win-win thinking and the use of Habit 5.]

Finally, he told me that he felt embarrassed anytime anyone came to our home and saw that old couch. He told me that he worked hard and couldn't see why we made so little money. He didn't think it was fair that his brother and others got paid so much more than he did. He said that sometimes he felt he was a failure. A new couch would be a sign that he was okay.

His words sank into my heart. He almost convinced me that we should go back and get the couch. But then I asked him if he would listen while I told him my feelings. [Notice the use of the second half of Habit 5.] *He said that he would.*

I told him how proud I was of him and that to me he was the world's greatest success. I told him how I could barely sleep at night sometimes because I was worried that we didn't have enough money to pay the bills. I told him that if we bought that couch, in two months we'd have to pay for it—and we wouldn't be able to do it.

He said that he knew that what I was saying was true, but he still felt bad that he could not live as well as all those around him.

[Pause: Use your creative imagination. Can you think of a third alternative solution?]

Somehow we got to talking about how we could make our front room more attractive without spending a lot of money. [Notice the beginning of Habit 6 synergy.] *I mentioned that the local thrift store might have a couch that we could afford. He laughed and said, "They could have an Early American couch there that's far more Early American than the one we've just seen." I reached out and took his hand, and we sat there for a long moment just looking into each other's eyes.*

Finally, we decided to go over to the thrift store. We found a couch there that was mostly wood. The cushions were all detachable. They were terribly worn, but I didn't think it would be too much trouble to re-cover them in some fabric that would match the colors of the room. We bought the couch for thirteen dollars and fifty cents and headed home. [Notice the use of conscience and independent will.]

The next week I enrolled in a furniture upholstery class. My husband refinished the wooden parts. Three weeks later we had a lovely Early American couch.

As time went by, we'd sit on those golden cushions and hold hands and smile. That couch was the symbol of our financial recovery. [Finally, notice the results.]

What kind of solutions did you come up with as you went through this experience? As you connected with your own gifts, you may even have come up with answers that would work for you better than the one this couple discovered.

Whatever solution you came up with, think about the difference it would make in your life. Think about the difference this couple's synergy made in their lives. Can you see how they used their four gifts, how they created the pause that enabled them to act instead of react? Can you see how they engaged in the Habits 4, 5, and 6 process to come to a synergistic third-alternative solution? Can you see the value that was added to their lives as they developed their talents and created something beautiful together? Can you imagine the difference it will make each time they look at their couch and see something they bought with cash and worked together to beautify rather than something they bought on credit and are paying interest on every month?

One wife described living these habits in these words:

With Habits 4, 5, and 6, my husband and I are constantly seeking each other's exploration. It's like a ballet or dance of two dolphins—a very natural moving together. It has to do with mutual respect and trust, and the way these habits play out in day-to-day decisions—whether it's huge decisions, like whose house we lived in after we were married, or what we should have for dinner. These habits themselves have become a habit between us.

The Family Immune System

This kind of synergy is the ultimate expression of a beautiful family culture—one that's creative and fun, one that's filled with variety and humor, one that has deep respect for every person and every person's varied interests and approaches.

Synergy unleashes tremendous capacity. It gives birth to new ideas. It brings you together in new multidimensional ways, making huge deposits in the Emotional Bank Account because creating something new with someone else is enormously bonding.

It also helps you create a culture in which you can successfully deal with any family challenge you might face. In fact, you could compare the culture created by Habits 4, 5, and 6 to a healthy immune system in the body. It determines the family's ability to handle whatever challenges are thrown at it. It protects family members so that when mistakes are made or when you get blindsided by some totally unexpected physical, financial, or social challenge, the family doesn't get overcome by it. The family has the capacity to accommodate it and rise above it, to adapt—to deal with whatever life throws at it and to use it, learn from it, run with it, optimize it, and make the family stronger.

With this kind of immune system, you actually see "problems" differently. A problem becomes something of a vaccination. It triggers the immune system to produce antibodies so that you never get the full-blown disease. So you can take any problem in your family life—a problem in your marriage, a struggle with one of your teenage children, a layoff, an estranged relationship with an older brother or sister—and look at it as a potential vaccination. Undoubtedly it will cause some pain and perhaps a little scarring, but it can also trigger an immune response, the development of the capacity to fight.

Then, no matter what difficulties come along, the immune system can wrap its arms around that difficulty—that setback, that disappointment, that deep fatigue or whatever it may be that threatens family health—and turn it into a growth experience that makes the family more creative, more synergistic, more capable of solving problems and of dealing with any kind of challenge you may confront. So problems don't *discourage* you; they *encourage* you to develop new levels of effectiveness and immunity.

Seeing problems as vaccinations gives new perspective to the way you see even the challenge of dealing with your most difficult child. It will build strength in you and in the entire culture as well. In fact, the key to your family culture is how you treat the child that tests you the most. When you can show unconditional love to your most difficult child, others know that your love for them is also unconditional. And that knowledge builds trust. So strive to be grateful for the most difficult child, knowing that the very challenge can build strength in you and in the culture as well.

> *The key to your family culture is how you treat the child that tests you the most.*

When we come to understand the family immune system, we come to look upon small problems as reinoculations of the family body. They cause the immune system to kick in, and by properly communicating and synergizing around them, the family builds greater immunity so that other small problems are not blown out of proportion.

The reason AIDS is such a horrific disease is that it destroys the immune system. People don't die of AIDS; they die of the other diseases that take over because they have a compromised immune system. Families do not die from a particular setback; they die because they have a compromised immune system. They have overdrawn Emotional Bank Accounts and no organizing processes to institutionalize—or build into the day-to-day processes and patterns of family life—the principles or the natural laws on which family is based.

A healthy immune system fortifies you against four "cancers" that are deadly to family life: criticizing, complaining, comparing, and competing. These cancers are the opposite of a beautiful family culture, and without a healthy family immune system, they can metastasize and spread their negative consuming energy throughout the family.

"You See It Differently. Good! Help Me Understand."

Another way to look at this Habits 4, 5, and 6 culture is through the airplane metaphor. We said at the outset that we're going to be off track 90 percent of the time, but we can read the feedback and get back on course.

"Family" is about learning the lessons of life, and feedback is a natural part of that learning. Problems and challenges give you feedback. Once you realize that each problem is asking for a response instead of just triggering a reaction, you start to learn. You become a learning family. You welcome challenges that test your capacity to synergize and to respond with higher levels of character and competence. You have differences, and you say, "You see it differently. Good! Help me understand." You also draw upon the collective conscience, the moral or ethical nature of everyone in the family.

> *Once you realize that each problem is asking for a response instead of just triggering a reaction, you start to learn. You become a learning family.*

But in order to do this, you have to get beyond the blaming and accusing. You have to get beyond the criticizing, complaining, comparing, and competing. You have to think win-win, seek to understand and be understood, and synergize. If you don't, at best you'll end up satisfying, not optimizing; cooperating, not creating; compromising, not synergizing; and, at worst, fighting or flighting.

You also have to live Habit 1. As one man said, "This process is magic! All it takes is character." And so it does. It takes character to think win-win when you and your spouse feel differently about buying a car, when your two-year-old wants to wear pink pants and an orange shirt to the grocery store, when your teenager wants to come home at 3 A.M., when your mother-in-law wants to rearrange your house. It takes character to seek first to understand when you think you really know what someone's thinking (you usually don't), when you're sure you have the perfect answer to the problem (you usually don't), and when you have an important appointment you have to be at in five minutes. It takes character to celebrate differences, to look for third-alternative solutions, to work with the members of your family to create this sense of synergy in the culture.

That's why proactivity is foundational. Only as you develop the capacity to act based on principles instead of reacting to emotion or circumstance and only as you recognize the priority of family and organize around it will you be able to pay the price that's necessary to create this powerful synergy.

One father shared this experience:

As I thought about Habits 4, 5, and 6 and worked to develop them in our family, I came to feel that I needed to work on my relationship with my seven-year-old daughter,

Debbie. She often reacted very emotionally, and when things didn't go her way, she tended to run to her room and cry. It seemed that no matter what my wife and I did, it put her in a tailspin.

And her frustration led to our frustration. We found ourselves reacting to her and constantly getting on her. "Settle down! Stop crying! Go into your room until you're under control!" And this negative feedback caused her to act up even more.

But one day as I was thinking about her, an insight came. My heart was touched as I realized that her emotional nature was a very special gift that would be a great source of strength to her in life. I had often seen her show unusual compassion for her young friends. She was always one to make sure that everyone's needs were met, that no one was left out. She had a great heart and a wonderful ability to express love. And when she wasn't in one of her emotional tailspins, her cheeriness was like tangible sunshine in our home.

I realized that her "gift" was a vital competency that could bless her whole life. And if I kept up this negative, critical approach, I was likely to snuff out what could become her greatest strength. The problem was that she didn't know how to deal with all her emotions. What she needed was someone to hang in there with her, to believe in her, to help her work it out.

So the next time she lost it, I didn't react. And when her inner storm had spent itself, we sat down together and talked about what it really takes to solve problems, to find alternatives that everyone feels good about. I realized that in order for her to be willing to remain in the process, she needed a few victories, so I consciously helped provide her with experiences where synergy really worked. And this enabled her to develop the courage and belief that if she pushed her own pause button and hung in there with us, it would pay off.

We still have our moments, but we have found that she is much more cooperative, much more willing to work things out. And I have found that when she does have her struggles, things work out much better if I hang in there with her and don't let her run away. I don't say, "You don't run away." I say, "Come over here. Let's work through this and solve it together."

Notice how this father's insight and vision of his daughter's true nature helped him to value her unique difference and to be proactive in working with her. And notice, too, how even young children can learn and practice Habits 4, 5, and 6.

Based on a number of variables, you may find yourself at different levels of proactivity at different times. The circumstances you're in, the nature of the crisis, the strength of your resolve around a particular purpose or vision, the level of your physical, mental, and emotional fatigue, and the amount of sheer willpower you have all affect the level of proactivity you bring to a potentially synergistic experience. But when you can get all these things in line and you can value the difference, it's amazing how much resourcefulness and energy and intuitive wisdom you can access.

You also have to live Habit 2. This is the leadership work. This is creating the unity that makes diversity meaningful. You have to have a destination because destination defines feedback. Some say that feedback is the "breakfast of champions." But it isn't. Vision is the breakfast. Feedback is the lunch. Self-correction is the dinner. When you have your destination in mind, then you know what feedback means because it lets you know whether you're headed toward your destination or you're off track. And even when you have to go to other places because of the weather, you can keep coming back so that eventually you will reach it.

You also need to live Habit 3. One-on-one bonding times give you the Emotional Bank Account to interact authentically and in synergistic ways with the members of your family. And weekly family times provide the forum for synergistic interaction.

> *Some say that feedback is the "breakfast of champions." But it isn't. Vision is the breakfast. Feedback is the lunch. Self-correction is the dinner.*

You can see how interwoven these habits are, how they come together and reinforce one another to create this beautiful family culture we've been talking about.

Involve People in the Problem and Work Out the Solution Together

Another way of expressing Habits 4, 5, and 6 can be found in one simple idea: *Involve people in the problem and work out the solution together.*

We had an interesting experience with this in our own family some years ago. Sandra and I had read a great deal about the impact of television on the minds of children, and we had begun to feel that in many ways it was like an open sewage pipe right into our home. We had set up rules and guidelines to limit the amount of TV watching, but it seemed that there were always exceptions. The rules kept changing. We were constantly in the position of dispensing privileges and judgments, and we had grown weary of negotiating with the children. It had become a power struggle that occasionally caused feelings to flare in negative ways.

Although we agreed on the problem, we didn't agree on the solution. I wanted to take an authoritarian approach inspired by an article I'd read about a man who actually threw the family TV set into the garbage! In some ways that kind of dramatic action seemed to demonstrate the message we wanted to send. But Sandra favored a more principle-based approach. She didn't want the children to resent the decision, to feel it was not a win for them.

As we synergized together, we realized we were trying to decide how we could solve this problem for the children when what we needed to do was help them solve it for themselves. We decided to engage Habits 4, 5, and 6 on a family-wide basis. At our next family night we introduced the subject "TV—how much is enough?" Everyone's interest was immediately focused because this was an important matter for all involved.

One son said, "What's so bad about watching TV? There's a lot of good stuff on. I still get my homework done. I can actually study while the TV is on. My grades are good, and so are everyone else's. So what's the problem?"

A daughter added, "If you're afraid we're going to be corrupted by TV, you're wrong. We don't usually watch bad shows. And if one is bad, we usually turn to another station. Besides, what's shocking to you is not all that shocking to us."

Another said, "If we don't watch certain shows, we're socially out of it. All the kids watch these shows. We even talk about them every day at school. These shows help us see how things really are in the world so that we don't get caught up in all the dumb things that are going on."

We didn't interrupt the kids. They all had something to say about why they didn't think we should make any drastic changes in our TV habits. As we listened to their concerns, we could see how deeply they were into their feelings about TV.

Finally, when their energy seemed spent, we said, "Now let us see if we really understand what you've just said." And we proceeded to restate all we had heard and felt them say. Then we asked, "Do you feel that we truly understand your point of view?" They agreed that we did.

"Now we would like you to understand where we're coming from."

The response was not very favorable.

"You just want to tell us all the negative things people are saying about watching TV."

"You want to pull the plug and take away our only escape from all the pressure we feel at school."

We listened empathically and then assured them that this was not our intent at all. "In fact," we said, "when we've gone over these articles together, we're going to leave the room and let you kids decide what you feel we should do about watching TV."

"You're kidding!" they exclaimed. "What if our decision is different from what you want?"

"We'll honor your decision," we said. "All we ask is that you be in total agreement about what you recommend that we do." We could see by the expressions on their faces that they liked the idea.

So, all together, we went over the information in the two articles we had brought to the meeting. The children sensed this material would be important in their upcoming decision, so they listened very attentively. We began by reading some shocking facts. One article said that the average television diet for a person between the ages of one and eighteen is six hours a day. If there is cable in the home, that increases to eight hours per day. By the time young Americans have graduated from school, they will have spent thirteen thousand hours in school and sixteen thousand hours in front of a television set. During that time they will have witnessed twenty-four thousand killings.[1]

We told the children that, as parents, those facts were scary to us and that when we watched as much TV as we did, it became by far the most powerful socializing force in our lives—more than education, more than time spent with the family.

We pointed out the discrepancy concerning TV program directors who claim there is no scientific evidence to link TV viewing to behavior and then quote evidence showing the powerful impact a twenty-second commercial has on behavior. Then we said, "Just think about how different you feel when you watch a television show and when you watch a commercial. When a thirty- to sixty-second commercial comes on, you know it's an advertisement. You don't believe a lot of what you see and hear. Your defenses are up because it's advertising, it's just hype, and we've all been burned by it again and again. But when you're watching a show, your defenses are down. You become emotionally invested, vulnerable. You're letting images come into your head, and you're not even thinking about it. You're just absorbing it. Of course, the commercials impact us in spite of our defensiveness. Can you imagine the impact the regular programs are having on us when we're in a much more receptive posture?"

We continued these discussions as we read more. One author pointed out what happens when television becomes the baby-sitter for parents who are not cautious about what their children watch. He said that unsupervised TV watching is like inviting a stranger into your home for two or three hours every day to tell the children all about a perverse world where violence solves problems and all anyone needs to be happy is the right beer, a fast car, good looks, and lots of sex. Of course, the parents are not there while all this is happening because they trust this television character to keep the children as quiet, interested, and entertained as possible. This teacher could do a lot of damage during that long daily visit, planting misperceptions no one could ever change and causing problems no one could solve.

One U.S. government study linked watching television with being obese, hostile, and depressed. In this study the researchers found that those who watched TV four or more hours a day were more than twice as likely to smoke cigarettes and be physically inactive as those who viewed the tube one hour or less a day.[2]

After discussing the negative impact of watching too much television, we turned to some of the positive things that might happen if we changed our habit. In one of the articles a study was quoted which showed that families who cut back on TV watching found more time for conversation at home. One person said, "Before it was, like, mostly we'd see Dad before he left for work. When he came home he'd watch TV with us, and then it was like, 'Good night Dad.' Now we talk all the time, we're really close."[3]

Another author pointed out that research data indicate that families that limit television viewing to a maximum of two hours a day of carefully selected programs may see the following significant changes in family relationships:

- Value setting will be taught and reinforced by the family. Families will learn how to establish values and how to reason together.
- Relationships between parents and youth will improve in families.
- Homework will be completed with less time pressure.
- Personal conversations will increase substantially.
- Children's imaginations will come back to life.
- Each family member will become a discriminating selector and evaluator of programs.
- Parents can become family leaders again.
- Good reading habits may be substituted for television viewing.[4]

After we shared this information, we got up and left the room. About an hour later we were invited to return for the verdict. One of our daughters later gave us the full report of what happened in that vitally important hour.

She said that after we had left the room, her brothers and sisters quickly appointed her the discussion leader. They knew she was an advocate of watching TV, and they anticipated a quick resolution.

At first the meeting was chaotic. They all wanted to speak up and get their views known in a hurry so they'd be able to get a liberal decision—perhaps to cut down just a little on the amount of TV they were watching. In order to satisfy us as parents, someone suggested that they all promise to do their household chores cheerfully and get their homework done without being reminded.

But then our oldest son spoke up. Everyone turned to listen as he told how the articles had impressed him. He said TV had put some ideas into his mind that were not what he wanted to be there, and he felt he would be better off if he watched a lot less TV. He also said he felt the younger children in the family were starting to see things far worse than what he had seen as a young boy.

Then one of the younger children spoke up. He told everyone about a show he had seen that made him feel scared when he went to bed. At that point the spirit of the meeting became very serious. As the children continued to discuss the issue, a new feeling gradually began to emerge. They started to think differently.

One said, "I think we're watching too much TV, but I don't want to give it up altogether. There are some shows I feel good about and I really want to watch." Then others talked about shows they enjoyed and wanted to continue to watch.

Another said, "I don't think we should talk about how much time to watch each day because some days I don't want to watch at all, but on other days I want to watch more." So they decided to determine how many hours each week—rather than each day—would be appropriate. Some thought twenty hours would not be too much; some thought five hours would be better. Finally, they all agreed that seven hours a week was about right, and they appointed this daughter the monitor to ensure that the decision was carried out.

This decision proved to be a turning point in our family life. We began to interact more, to read more. We eventually reached the point where television was not an issue. And today—aside from news and an occasional movie or sports event—we hardly ever have it on.

By involving our children in the problem, we made them participators with us in finding a solution. And because the solution was their decision, they were invested in its success. We didn't have to worry about "snoopervising" and keeping them on track.

Also, by sharing information about the consequences of excessive television watching, we were able to move beyond "our way" or "their way." We were able to get into the principles involved in the issue and tap into the collective conscience of everyone involved. We were able to help them realize that a commitment to win-win is more than a commitment to having everyone temporarily pleased with the outcome. It's a commitment to principles because a solution that is not based on principles is never a win for anyone in the long run.

An Exercise in Synergy

If you'd like to see how this Habits 4, 5, and 6 process can work in your own family, you might try the following experiment:

Take some issue that needs to be resolved, an issue where people have different opinions and different points of view. Try working together to answer the following four questions:

1. *What is the problem from everyone's point of view?* Really listen to one another with the intent to understand, not to reply. Work at it until other people can express each person's point of view to that person's satisfaction. Focus on interests, not positions.
2. *What are the key issues involved?* Once the viewpoints are expressed and everyone feels thoroughly understood, then look at the problem together and identify the issues that need to be resolved.
3. *What would constitute a fully acceptable solution?* Determine the net results that

would be a win for each person. Put the criteria on the table and refine and prioritize them so that everyone is satisfied they represent all involved.

4. *What new options would meet those criteria?* Synergize around creative new approaches and solutions.

As you go through this process, you'll be amazed at the new options that open up and the shared excitement that develops when people focus on the problem and desired results instead of personalities and positions.

A Different Kind of Synergy

Up to this point we have primarily focused on the synergy that takes place when people interact, understand one another's needs, purposes, and common objectives, and then produce insights and options that are truly better than those originally proposed. We could say that an integration has taken place in the thought processes, and the third mind has produced the synergistic result. This approach could be called *transformational*. In the language of nuclear change, you could compare this kind of synergy to the formation of an entirely new substance resulting from changes on the molecular level.

But there is another kind of synergy. This is the synergy that comes through a complementary approach—an approach in which one person's strength is utilized and his or her weaknesses are made irrelevant by the strength of another. In other words, people work together like a team, but there's no effort to integrate their thought processes to produce better solutions. This kind of synergy could be called *transactional plus*. Again, in nuclear language, the identifying properties of the substance would remain unchanged, and it would be synergistic in a different sense. In *transactional plus* synergy, the cooperation between the people involved—rather than the creation of something new—is the essence of the relationship.

> *In transactional plus synergy, the cooperation between the people involved—rather than the creation of something new—is the essence of the relationship.*

This approach requires significant self-awareness. When a person is aware of a weakness, it instills humility sufficient to seek another's strength to compensate for it. Then that weakness becomes a strength because it enabled complementariness to take place. But when people are unaware of their weaknesses and act as if their strengths are sufficient, their strengths become their weaknesses—and their very undoing for lack of complementariness.

For instance, if a husband's strength lies in his courage and drive but the situation requires empathy and patience, then his strength can become a weakness. If a wife's strength is sensitivity and patience, and the situation requires forceful decisions and actions, her strength can become a weakness. But if both husband and wife were aware of their strengths and weaknesses and had the humility to work as a complementary team, then their strengths would be well used and their weaknesses made irrelevant—and a synergistic result would occur.

I worked with an executive one time who was absolutely full of positive energy, but the executive to whom he reported was full of negative energy. When I asked him about this, he said, "I see my responsibility as finding out what's lacking in my boss and supplying it. My role is not to criticize him but to complement him." This man's choice to be interdependent required great personal security and emotional independence. Husbands and wives, parents and children, can do similarly with one another. In short, complementariness means that we decide to be a light, not a judge; a model, not a critic.

When people are open to feedback regarding strengths and weaknesses—and when they have sufficient internal security so that the feedback will not destroy them emotionally and also sufficient humility to see the other's strengths and work as a team—marvelous things begin to happen. Going back to the body metaphor: The hand cannot take the place of the foot, or the head the place of the heart. It works in a complementary way.

This is exactly what happens on a great athletic team or in a great family. And it requires much less intellectual interdependence than the other form of synergy. Perhaps it also requires a little less emotional interdependence, but it also requires great self-awareness and social awareness, internal security and humility. In fact, you might say that humility is the "plus" part between the two parts that enables this kind of complementariness. Transactional plus synergy is probably the most common form of creative cooperation, and it's something even little children can learn.

Not All Situations Require Synergy

Now, not all decisions in the family require synergy. Sandra and I have synergistically arrived at what we've found to be a very effective way of making many decisions without synergy. One of us will simply say to the other, "Where are you?" That means, "On a scale of one to ten, how strongly do you feel about your point?" If one says, "I'm at a nine," and the other says, "I'm at about a three," then we go with the approach of the person who feels the strongest. If we both say five, we may go for a quick compromise. To make this work, both of us have agreed that we will always be totally honest with each other about where on the scale we are.

> "On a scale of one to ten, how strongly do you feel about your point?"

We also have the same kind of agreement with our children. If we get into the car and people want to go different places, we sometimes say, "How important is this to you? Where are you on a scale of one to ten?" Then we all try to show respect for those who feel the strongest. In other words, we've tried to develop a kind of democracy that shows respect for the depth of feeling behind a person's opinion or desire so that his or her vote counts more.

The Fruit of Synergy Is Priceless

This Habits 4, 5, and 6 process is a powerful problem-solving tool. It's also a powerful tool that is tremendously helpful in creating family mission statements and enjoyable family times. I often teach Habits 4, 5, and 6 *before* teaching Habits 2 and 3 for this very reason. Habits 4, 5, and 6 cover a whole range of needs for synergy in the family—from the everyday decisions to the deepest, most potentially divisive, and most emotionally charged issues imaginable.

At one time, I was training two hundred MBA students at an eastern university, and many faculty and invited guests were there as well. We took the toughest, most sensitive, most vulnerable issue they could come up with: abortion. Two people came to the front of the classroom—a pro-life person and a pro-choice person who felt deeply about their positions. They had to interact with each other in front of these two hundred students. I was there to insist that they practice the habits of effective interdependence: think win-win, seek first to understand, and synergize. The following dialogue summarizes the essence of the interchange.

"Are you two willing to search for a win-win solution?"

"I don't know what it could be. I don't feel she—"

"Wait a minute. You won't lose. You will both win."

"But how can that possibly be? One of us wins, the other loses."

"Are you willing to find a solution that you both feel good about, that is even better than what each of you is thinking now? Remember not to capitulate. Don't give in and don't compromise. It has to be better."

"I don't know what it could be."

"I understand. No one does. We'll have to create it."

"I won't compromise!"

"Of course. It has to be better. Remember now, seek first to understand. You can't make your point until you restate his point to his satisfaction."

As they began to dialogue, they kept interrupting each other.

"Yeah. But don't you realize that—"

I said, "Wait a minute! I don't know if the other person feels understood. Do you feel understood?"

"Absolutely not."

"Okay. You can't make your point."

You cannot believe the sweat those people were in. They couldn't listen. They had judged each other right from the beginning because they took different positions.

After about forty-five minutes, they started to really listen, and this had a great effect on them—personally and emotionally—and on the audience. As they listened openly and empathically to the underlying needs, fears, and feelings of people on this tender issue, the entire spirit of the interaction changed. People on both sides began to feel ashamed of how they had judged one another, labeled one another, and condemned all who thought differently. The two people in front had tears in their eyes, and so did many in the audience. After two hours each side said of the other, "We had no idea that's what it meant to listen! Now we understand why they feel the way they do."

Bottom line: No one really wanted abortion except in very exceptional situations, but everyone was passionately concerned about the acute needs and profound pain of people involved in these situations. And they were all trying to solve the problem in the best way they could—the way they thought would really meet the need.

As the two speakers let go of their positions, as they really listened to each other and understood each other's concerns and intent, they were able to start working together to figure out what could be done. Out of their different points of view came an unbelievable synergy, and they were astonished at the synergistic ideas that resulted from the interaction. They came up with a number of creative alternatives, including new insights into prevention, adoption, and education.

There isn't any subject that isn't amenable to synergistic communication as long as you can use Habits 4, 5, and 6. You can see how interwoven mutual respect, understanding, and creative cooperation are. And you'll find there are different levels in each of these habits. Deep understanding leads to mutual respect, and that takes you to an even deeper level of understanding. If you persist, opening each new door as it comes, more and more creativity is released and even greater bonding takes place.

One of the reasons this process worked with the MBA students was that everyone in the audience became involved, which brought a whole new level of responsibility to the two in front. The same is true in a family when parents realize that they are providing the most fundamental model of problem-solving for their children. The awareness of that stewardship tends to enable us to rise above our less effective inclinations or feelings and to take the higher road—to seek to truly understand and creatively seek the third alternative.

The process of creating synergy is both challenging and thrilling, and it works. But don't be discouraged if you aren't able to solve your deepest challenges overnight. Remember how vulnerable we all are. If you get hung up on the toughest, most emotional issues between you, perhaps you can put them aside a little while and go back to them later. Work on the easier issues. Small victories lead to larger ones. Don't bag the process and don't bag each other. If necessary, go back to the smaller issues.

And don't become frustrated if you're now in a relationship where synergy seems like the "impossible dream." I've found that sometimes when people get a taste of how wonderful a truly synergistic relationship can be, they conclude that there is no way they will ever have this kind of relationship with their spouse. They may think their only hope of having this kind of relationship is with someone else. But once again remember the Chinese bamboo tree. Work in your Circle of Influence. Practice these habits in your own life. Be a light, not a judge; a model, not a critic. Share your learning experience. It may take weeks, months, or even years of patience and long-suffering. But with rare exception it will eventually come.

> *Small victories lead to larger ones. Don't bag the process and don't bag each other. If necessary, go back to the smaller issues.*

Never fall into the trap of allowing money or possessions or personal hobbies to take the place of a rich, synergistic relationship. Just as gangs can become a substitute family for young people, these things can become a substitute for synergy. But they are a poor substitute. While these things may temporarily soothe, they will never deeply satisfy. Always be aware that happiness does not come from money, possessions, or fame; it comes from the quality of relationships with the people you love and respect.

As you begin to establish the pattern of creative cooperation in your family, your capacity will increase. Your "immune system" will become stronger. The bonding between you will deepen. Your positive experiences will put you in a whole new place to deal with your challenges and opportunities. Interestingly, your use of this process will increase your power and capacity to convey the most precious message that could ever be given, particularly to a child: "There is no circumstance or condition in which I would give up on you. I will be there for you and hang in there with you regardless of the challenge." In ways unlike any other, it will affirm this message: "I love and value you unconditionally. You are of infinite worth, never to be compared."

The fruit and bonding of true synergy are priceless.

SHARING THIS CHAPTER WITH ADULTS AND TEENS

Learning About Synergy

- Discuss the meaning of "synergy." Ask family members: What examples of synergy do you see in the world around you? Responses might include: two hands working together; two pieces of wood holding more weight than both could support separately; living things functioning together synergistically in the environment.
- Discuss together the stories on pages 251–255 and 258–260. Ask: Does our family operate synergistically? Do we celebrate differences? How could we improve?
- Consider your marriage. What differences initially attracted you to each other? Have those differences turned into irritations, or have they become the springboard for synergy? Together, explore this question: In what ways are we better together than we are alone?
- Discuss the idea of the family immune system. Ask family members: Do we look at problems as negative obstacles to be overcome or as opportunities to grow? Discuss the idea that challenges build your immune system.
- Ask family members: In what ways are we fulfilling our four basic needs—to live, to love, to learn, to leave a legacy? In what areas do we need to improve?

Family Learning Experiences

- Review the section entitled "Not All Situations Require Synergy." Develop an approach to making cooperative family decisions without synergy. As a family, go through the "Exercise in Synergy" on page 268.
- Conduct some fun experiments that show how much easier it is to do a job with the help of another person rather than alone. For example, try to make a bed, carry a heavy box, or lift a large table by the edge with one hand. Then invite others to participate and help. Use you imagination and come up with your own experiments to demonstrate the need for synergy.

SHARING THIS CHAPTER WITH CHILDREN

- Pretend that you are stranded in your home for an entire month with just your family. Ask: What kind of family synergy is available for us to draw on to make it through—and perhaps even enjoy—the challenge? Create a list of contributions each family member could make:

MOM	DAD	SPENCER	LORI	GRANDMA
Great cook	Can fix anything	Fun to play with	Plays the piano	Great storyteller
Can sew	Loves to read to us	Loves sports	Good with kids	Plays violin
Loves crafts	Plays games	Is artistic	Loves to bake	Bakes pies
Loves to hike	Can fish	Hunts	Good organizer	Was a nurse

- Perform some experiments that teach the strength of synergy, such as the following: *Experiment #1:* Ask your children to tie their shoes with one hand. It cannot be done! Then ask another family member to help with one hand. It works! Point out how two working together can do more than one—or even two—working separately. *Experiment #2:* Give your children a Popsicle stick. Ask them to break it. They probably will be able to do so. Now give them four or five sticks stacked together and ask them to do the same. They probably won't be able to do it. Use this as an illustration to teach that the family together is stronger than any one person alone.
- Share the experience about deciding on TV guidelines (pages 264–268). Synergistically decide what the guidelines should be in your home.
- Ask your children to work together to create a poster for the family.
- Let your children plan a meal together. If they are old enough, let them prepare it together also. Encourage them to come up with dishes such as soup, fruit salad, or a casserole where the blending of a number of different ingredients creates something entirely new.
- Teach your children the system on page 270: "On a scale of one to ten, how strongly do you feel about your point?" Practice it with your children in different situations. It's fun to use and solves lots of problems!
- Plan a family talent night. Invite all family members to share their musical or dancing talent, a sports performance, scrapbooks, writings, drawings, woodwork, or collections. Point out how wonderful it is that we all have different things to offer, and that an important part of creating synergy is learning to appreciate others' strengths and talents.

HABIT 7
SHARPEN THE SAW

One divorced man shared this experience:

During our first year of marriage, my wife and I spent a lot of time together. We went for walks in the park. We went on bike rides. We went to the lake. We had our own special time, just the two of us, and it was really great.

The turning point came when we moved to a different location and became heavily involved in separate careers. She was working the graveyard shift, and I was working the day shift. Sometimes it would be days before we even saw each other. Slowly, our relationship started disintegrating. She started building her circle of friends, and I started building my circle of friends. We gradually drifted apart because we didn't build on the friendship we had together.

Entropy

In physics, "entropy" means that anything left to itself will eventually disintegrate until it reaches its most elemental form. The dictionary defines entropy as "the steady degradation of a system or society."

This happens in all of life, and we all know it. Neglect your body, and it will deteriorate. Neglect your car, and it will deteriorate. Watch TV every available hour, and your mind will deteriorate. Anything that is not consciously attended to and renewed will break down, become disordered, and deteriorate. "Use it or lose it" is the maxim.

Richard L. Evans put it this way:

All things need watching, working at, caring for, and marriage is no exception. Marriage is not something to be treated indifferently or abused, or something that simply takes care of itself. Nothing neglected will remain as it was or is, or will fail to deteriorate. All things need attention, care, and concern, and especially so in this most sensitive of all relationships of life. [1]

So also with regard to the family culture: It requires constant deposits into the Emotional Bank Account to *just keep it where it is now*, because you're dealing with continuing relationships and continuing expectations. And unless those expectations are met, entropy will set in. The old deposits will evaporate. The relationship will become more stilted, more formal, colder. And *to improve it* requires new creative deposits.

Imagine how the entropic effect is multiplied by the pressing environmental forces of the turbulent physical and social weather we're trying to navigate in. That is why it's so necessary for every family to take the time to renew itself in the four key areas of life: physical, social, mental, and spiritual.

> *Every family must take time to renew itself in the four key areas of life: physical, social, mental, and spiritual.*

Imagine for a moment that you're trying to fell a tree. You're sawing through this huge, thick tree trunk. Back and forth, back and forth you pull the heavy saw. You've been laboring at it all day long. You've hardly stopped for a minute. You've been working and sweating, and now you're about halfway through. But you're feeling so tired that you don't see how you're going to last another five minutes. You pause for a minute to catch your breath.

You look up and see another person a few yards away who has also been sawing a tree. You can't believe your eyes! This person has sawed almost completely through his tree trunk! He started about the same time you did and his tree is about the same size as yours, but he stopped to rest every hour or so while you kept working away. Now he's almost through, and you're only halfway there.

"What's going on?" you ask incredulously. "How in the world have you gotten so much more done than I have? You didn't even stay with it all the time. You stopped to rest every hour! How come?"

The man turns and smiles. "Yes," he replies. "You saw me stop every hour to rest, but what you didn't see was that every time I rested, I also sharpened the saw!"

Sharpening the saw means attending regularly and consistently to renewal in all four dimensions of life. If sharpening the saw is done properly, consistently, and in a balanced way, it will cultivate all the other habits by using them in the renewing activities themselves.

Going back to the airplane metaphor, this habit fulfills the need for constant refueling and maintenance of the plane and for continual upgrading of the training and skill level of the pilots and crew.

I recently had two very instructive experiences—a flight on an F-15 and a visit to the nuclear submarine *Alabama*. I was amazed by the degree and amount of training those involved were required to have. Even the most veteran professional pilots and seamen constantly practiced the elemental and beginning steps and kept constantly updated on new technology in order to be current and prepared.

The evening before the F-15 flight, I was taken through a complete dressing procedure. I put on the flight suit and was instructed in all aspects of the flight and of emergency procedures should anything go wrong. Everyone went through the procedure regardless of their level of experience. When we landed, those involved put on a twenty-minute drill in arming the plane. This drill demonstrated an amazing level of skill, speed, interdependence, and innovation.

On the nuclear submarine it was evident that training was constant—both in the basics and also in all the new technology and procedures. Those on the sub were constantly upgrading their training and constantly doing maintenance drills.

This level of investment in renewal reaffirmed to me how constant practicing allows for quick reaction in the moment of need. It also seemed to affirm the importance of having a shared end in mind, and it created a strength of purpose that transcended the monotony of the repetition.

Once again I was reminded of the importance and the impact of Habit 7, sharpening the saw, in all aspects of life.

The Power of Interdependent Renewal

There are many ways you and your family can be involved in "sharpening the saw" renewal, both independently and interdependently.

Independently, you can exercise, eat healthy foods, and work on stress management (physical). You can become regularly involved in building friendships, giving service, being empathic, and creating synergy (social). You can read, visualize, plan, write, develop talents, and learn new skills (mental). You can pray, meditate, read inspirational or sacred literature, and renew your connection and commitment to principles (spiritual). Doing something independently every day in each of these four areas will help you build your individual capacity and regenerate your ability to practice Habits 1, 2, and 3 (Be proactive, Begin with the end in mind, Put first things first) in your own life.

PERSONAL RENEWAL

PHYSICAL
Exercise, Eat healthy
foods, Manage stress

SOCIAL/EMOTIONAL
Build friendships, Give
service, Listen empathically,
Create synergy

SPIRITUAL
Meditate, Pray, Read
inspirational or
sacred literature, Recommit
to principles

MENTAL
Read, Visualize, Plan,
Write, Develop talents,
Learn new skills

Notice that these activities are all intrinsic, not extrinsic; in other words, none of them is based on any form of comparison with other people. All of them develop an intrinsic sense of personal and family worth that is independent of others and of the environment—even though it manifests itself in relationships and in the environment. Also notice how each lies within a personal or family Circle of Influence.

In addition, in a family, any renewal activity done together builds relationships as well. For example, family members who exercise together not only build their individual physical strength and endurance but they also increase bonding through such physical activity. Family members who read together multiply both learning and bonding through discussing, synergizing, and "piggybacking" ideas. Family members who worship and serve together strengthen one another's faith as well as their own. They become more unified and connected as they join together in a sacred expression of things that are important to them all.

Consider the way in which consistent one-on-one dates with your spouse or child renew the relationship. Precisely because these dates take such commitment and proactive energy—particularly in the face of a dozen other activities you have to juggle—they say how important that person is to you.

Consider the intimate relationship between a husband and wife. When intimacy is more than physical—when it is emotional, social, mental, and spiritual—it can reach dimensions of the human personality and fulfill some of the deepest hungers that lie in both husband and wife in ways that nothing else can. In addition to procreation, that is one of its central purposes. It requires time and patience, respect and careful thought, honest communication and even prayer. But people who neglect the full approach and deal only with the physical side never know the unfathomable level of unity and satisfaction that can be achieved when all four dimensions are involved.

Consider the weekly family time. When it is planned and prepared for, and when everyone is sincerely involved in the teaching of values, in fun activities, sharing talents, prayer, making refreshments, and so forth, then all four dimensions are integrated, expressed, and renewed.

When these kinds of renewing, relationship-building, saw-sharpening activities take place, the whole dynamic of the family culture is upgraded.

The Essence of Family Renewal: Traditions

In a way you could say that in addition to renewing interpersonal family relationships, the family itself must constantly nurture its collective conscience, social will, social awareness, and common vision. Essentially, that's what Habit 7 in the family is. These repeating patterns of family renewal are called traditions.

Family traditions include rituals and celebrations and meaningful events that you do in your family. They help you understand who you are: that you are part of a family that's a strong unit, that you love one another, that you respect and honor one another, that you celebrate one another's birthdays and special events, and make positive memories for everybody.

Through traditions you reinforce the connection of the family. You give a feeling of belonging, of being supported, of being understood. You are committed to one another. You are a part of something that's greater than yourself. You express and show loyalty to one another. You need to be needed, you need to be wanted, and you're glad to be part of a family. When parents and children cultivate traditions that are meaningful to them, every time they go back to that tradition it renews the emotional energy and bonding of the past.

In fact, if I were to put into one word the essence of building this account and sharpening the saw in all four dimensions in the family, that word would be "traditions." Just think about how traditions such as weekly family times and one-on-ones regenerate your family in all four areas on an ongoing basis.

FAMILY RENEWAL

Family Times & One-on-Ones

PHYSICAL
Exercise together
Do physical activities together
Reclarify expectations and goals
around financial and physical assets

SOCIAL/EMOTIONAL
Love and affirm one another
Laugh at "inside jokes"
and relax together
Build relationships of trust
and unconditional love

SPIRITUAL
Renew commitments
Clarify directions and goals
Pray and worship together
Read inspirational or
sacred literature together

MENTAL
Learn new things together
Share and discuss ideas

In our own family the traditions of family nights and one-on-one dates—particularly when the children write the agenda—have probably been the most enriching, renewing, and powerfully bonding parts of our family life over the years. They've sharpened our family's saw. They've kept the culture focused on having fun, on constantly renewing our commitments to our central values, and on listening deeply and expressing fully.

In this chapter we're going to look at a number of other kinds of sharpening-the-saw traditions. I want to acknowledge at the outset that the traditions we share from our family are those that have been meaningful to us. I realize that you may have other traditions in your family and may not relate to these at all. That's fine. I'm not trying to teach our way of doing it or suggest that our way is best. I'm simply trying to point out the importance of having some renewing traditions in the family culture, and I'm using some of our own experiences to illustrate this.

You will need to decide what traditions truly represent the spirit of your family culture. The main point is that renewing family traditions will help you create and nurture a beautiful family culture that encourages you to keep on track and keeps family members coming back to the flight plan time and time again. These ideas are shared in the hope that they will stimulate thinking and discussion in your family as to what traditions you want to create or strengthen in your own family culture.

Family Dinners

We all have to eat. The way to the heart, mind, and soul is often through the stomach. It takes careful thought and determination, but it's possible to organize meaningful mealtimes—times without television, without just gulping something down on the run. And it doesn't have to take forever, either, particularly if everyone does some part in the preparation and in the cleanup.

Family meals are important—even if you have only one family meal each week and that family meal is essentially the "family time" for the week. If the mealtime is meaningful and fun and well prepared, the family table becomes more of an altar than an eating counter.

Marianne Jennings, professor of legal and ethical studies at Arizona State University, wrote an article in which she observed from her own experience just how vital the kitchen table is to family life. Notice how all four dimensions—physical, social, mental, and spiritual—are involved.

I cut out my wedding dress at the same place where I memorized my spelling words. It was in that same place that I ate Archway cookies each day after school. And it was there that I prepared for my SAT. My husband-to-be was grilled mercilessly in that same spot. Much of what I have learned and hold dear is inextricably intertwined with the kitchen table. This 4-by-6 scratched and worn piece of furniture was a small physical part of my home. Yet as I look back on what we did there, I realize that it was a key to the life I now have.

Each night during my youth it was the kitchen table where I was held accountable for the day's events. "When is the next report card?" "Did you clean up the mess in the basement?" "Did you practice your piano today?"

If you wanted dinner, you had to accept the accompanying interrogation that would have violated my Miranda rights if I had done something more than attempt to bathe the neighbor's parakeet. There was no escaping the nightly confrontation with accountability.

But that kitchen table was not just a source of fear, it was my security blanket. No matter how rough the day's tauntings had been and no matter how discouraged I was over long division, the kitchen table and its adult caretakers were there every night to comfort and support.

The fear generated by the Cuban missile crisis and my fourth air-raid drill in a week disappeared in the daily certainty of a family gathered around that table graced with Del Monte canned peas, cloverleaf rolls, and oleo (margarine). Regardless of the day's schedule or demands, the kitchen table brought us back together for roll call at 6:00 P.M. every night.

And following my dismal task of doing dishes at a time when automatic dishwashers were country club novelties, I returned to the kitchen table to sweat bullets over home-work. I read "Dick, Jane, and Spot" stories aloud to my father, who then did his "home-work" while I wrote and rewrote the math tables I carry in my mind even today.

Each morning that table sent me off fed and duly inspected for clean fingernails and pressed Bobbie Brooks. No one left that table without a review of the day's events and assigned chores. That kitchen table nurtured. It was my constancy amid the insecurities of crooked teeth, more freckles than skin, and geography bees on state capitals.

Years have gone by since my days of Black Watch plaid and white anklets. Life has given me more challenges, joy, and love than I could have fathomed as my legs shook beneath that kitchen table when faced with parental inquiries. When I return to my par-ents' home to visit, I find myself lingering after breakfast to enjoy their company around the kitchen table. After dinner, the dishes wait as my father and I discuss everything from the Jackie Onassis estate auction to potty-training.

And then shortly after we restore the kitchen to its spotless pre-dinner state, my chil-dren return. We sit together, three generations, as Breyer's ice cream and Hershey's syrup melt, drip, and stick to new tiny faces at that old table.

They tell Grandpa of their spelling tests and which word they missed. And Grandpa explains, "Your mother missed the same word. We sat right here and reviewed it. She still got it wrong."

Perhaps it's in the genes. Or perhaps it is that kitchen table. That magical simple place where I learned responsibility and felt love and security.

As I struggle each night to get dinner on my kitchen table and round up my children from the four corners of our neighborhood, I wonder why I just don't send them to their rooms with a chicken pot pie and Wheel of Fortune. I don't because I am giving them the gift of the kitchen table.

In all the treatises on parenting, in all the psychological studies on child development, and in all the data on self-esteem, this humble key to rearing children is overlooked.

A recent survey revealed that only half of our teenagers eat dinner on a regular basis with their parents. Ninety-eight percent of female high school students who live with their birth parents go on to college. Teenagers who don't have dinner with their families are four times as likely to have premarital sex.

Last year my daughter said she could only find one other student in her homeroom who had dinner each night at the kitchen table with her family.

They are both honor students. The other kids, my daughter explained, "make some-thing in the microwave and then head to their rooms to watch TV." They have no com-pany, no questions—just Wheel of Fortune, and the grades to show for it. How sad that not all children's lives are touched by the miracle of childhood. There's something about a kitchen table.[2]

Notice how the traditions around this table are renewing to this woman and her family. They're physically renewing—but they are mentally, spiritually, and socially renewing as well.

I know one family that builds spiritual renewal into their family dinner by having their mission statement on the wall near their dining table. They often will talk about some aspect of it as they discuss the challenges of the day. A good percentage of families build in spiritual renewal by having prayer before they eat.

Many families also build mental renewal into the family dinner by using it as a time to share the learnings of the day. I know of one family that has "one-minute speeches" during dinner. They give a family member a topic—anything from honesty to the funniest thing that happened that day—and the person speaks for one minute on it. This not only provides interesting conversation and keeps everyone entertained and often "cracking up," but it also builds mental and verbal skills.

Another family keeps a set of encyclopedias by the dinner table. When anyone asks a question, they look up the answer on the spot. They once had a visitor from Delaware who mentioned that his state was very small.

"How small is it?" someone wondered. So they went to the encyclopedia and discovered that Delaware is two thousand square miles.

"Is that really small?" someone else asked. They looked up some other states. Alabama, they discovered, was about fifty-two thousand square miles—26 times as big as Delaware. Texas was over 131 times as big as Delaware. And, of course, Delaware was a giant compared to Rhode Island, which was only twelve hundred square miles!

There is so much to know! Which state is the Peach State? Does it produce the most peaches? How much can a bird eat in a day compared to its body weight? How big is a whale compared to an elephant?

While it may not be very important for children to know just how big each state is, it is extremely important for them to love learning. And when they find that learning is exciting and that the adults in their life love to learn, they become enthusiastic learners.

There are many things you can do to make dinnertime a time of mental renewal. You can occasionally invite interesting guests to share your meal and conversation. You can play a classical music selection and talk about the work and the life of the composer as you eat. You can borrow a different work of art from the library each week, hang it on the wall by your dining table, and talk about the work and the artist. The very food itself gives you the opportunity to talk about manners, nutrition, or different countries and their cuisines and customs.

Cynthia (*daughter*):
Mom always felt the dinner hour was really important. We always had dinner together, and everyone was always there. Mom was also really big on educating us during dinner.

Two or three nights a week we'd have a theme. She would have some centerpiece, and we would have a discussion, usually correlating with the current holiday or event. On the Fourth of July, for example, she'd read two or three things about Patrick Henry or about the Declaration of Independence. Whatever holiday or special thing was coming up, she would share something educational about it, and then we'd have a family discussion. Sometimes we'd sit there talking for an hour and a half, eating and talking. This got to be really fun when we were in high school and college and could really talk about issues and other things. Those dinner table conversations got us interested in education and in the world.

David (son):

I remember a time when I was going through a difficult time in a relationship with a girl who was not good for me. One night when we were at the dinner table, everyone started talking about people who had not been good for them and how they got out of difficult situations. They shared their feelings about how good it was to get out of those situations.

It was all geared toward me, but I had no idea at the time. I didn't even know what was going on until later. I just thought it was a family dinner. The comments were good, and they seemed very applicable to my situation. Later I realized what a great thing it was to have this support system of people who genuinely cared about me and my welfare and my success.

Sometimes a family dinner can be expanded to include an additional purpose, such as showing appreciation and giving service.

Colleen (daughter):

One of the things I really enjoyed was our "favorite teacher" dinners. Mom and Dad were very involved in the education process. They knew all our teachers and how we were doing in each class, and they wanted our teachers to know that we appreciated them. So every couple of years Mom would ask each of the children who their favorite teacher was that year. Then she made a list and sent them an invitation to dinner at our house. It was a dress-up dinner. She used her best china and made it really special. Each of us would sit by our teacher and have dinner with him or her. It got to be funny after a while because the teachers knew about this dinner and each year would hope to be the favorite teacher.

Maria (daughter):

I remember one year inviting Joyce Nelson, an English teacher from Provo High. I was twenty-one at the time. Several of us had had her as our teacher, and we all celebrated her. We each told what she had done for us. When my turn came, I said, "I am an English major today because of you. You influenced me to go into English because of the literature *we read and what you said and did." The teachers who were invited were thrilled because teachers usually don't get that kind of appreciation.*

The dinner table gives you the perfect opportunity to create such a renewing tradition because of the food. As one of our daughters said, "It seems as though many important traditions are surrounded by food, food, food. Food is the key. Everyone loves to have good food." With good food, good company, and good discussion, the family dinner tradition is hard to beat.

Family Vacations

Relaxation and fun are part of our family mission statement, and I know of no more renewing force in a family than a family vacation. Planning for it, anticipating it, and thinking about it—as well as discussing what happened on our last vacation and laughing about the fun times and the dumb times we had—are enormously renewing to our family. Every few years we plan a very special kind of vacation.

Sandra:

In building traditions I have always felt that it's important to teach children patriotism. Most children learn the Pledge of Allegiance at an early age. They hold their hands over their hearts when the flag goes by. At parades they hear the bands playing the anthems of the Navy, Air Force, and Army. They learn patriotic songs and perform in programs at school celebrating the Fourth of July. I believe they need to know about the men who died in the wars and fought for the principles they believed in. They need to understand how our country began, how the Constitution was written, and the price that was paid by the men who signed the Declaration of Independence.

For many years we talked about the possibility of going to some of the famous historic sites in Massachusetts, Pennsylvania, and New York, where many of the events of the American Revolution happened: the Old Church in Boston (where the lantern was held in the window telling of the arrival of the British—"One if by land, two if by sea"), the Freedom Trail, the Liberty Bell, the homes of the famous patriots, the hovels and remaining barracks where George Washington mobilized and trained his hungry, frozen army, and Independence Hall (where the Declaration of Independence was signed).

We talked about and planned this trip for many years. Finally, during America's bicentennial in 1976, we decided to do it. We rented a motor home, and, armed with books, tapes, music, and information, we set forth. I had recently read the book Those Who Love *by Irving Stone. It was the love story of John and Abigail Adams and their great sacrifices and contributions during this period of unrest and revolution. I was uplifted and inspired by their patriotism and devotion to this country. I had the teenagers and older children read it also, knowing that they would feel likewise.*

We had only a day and a half in Philadelphia, but we planned accordingly. We saw the

Liberty Bell and visited the chambers of the Continental Congress. On the lawns outside the building was an outdoor summer theater presenting 1776, the prize-winning musical reenacting the signing of the Declaration of Independence and making us familiar with the roles of the famous men and women involved—including John and Abigail Adams, Benjamin Franklin, Thomas Jefferson and his wife, Martha, Richard Henry Lee, John Hancock, and George Washington.

The program included these inspiring words: "These were not wild-eyed, rabble-rousing ruffians. They were soft-spoken men of means and education—lawyers and jurists, merchants, farmers, and large plantation owners, men of means, well educated. They had security, but they valued liberty more. Standing tall, straight, and unwavering, they pledged: 'For the support of this declaration with a firm reliance on the protection of the Divine Providence we mutually pledge to each other our lives, our fortunes, and our sacred honor.' They gave us an independent America, and they did sacrifice their lives, their fortunes, and their families."

The location, the music, and the theater all combined to make this an evening we will never forget. Patriotism burned in our hearts. One son said he wanted to be an architect and build a monument to John and Abigail Adams so that no one would ever forget what they did for us. Another wanted to be a musician and write songs in their honor. We were all changed: inspired, uplifted, patriots forever!

There were moments that made our family vacation wonderful! But I have to say that there were also other moments which were . . . well, less inspiring, to say the least.

We had planned that every morning one of us would drive while the other sat at the table in the motor home with the children, discussing what we would see that day and presenting lessons on important subjects associated with those sights. Our planning was extensive and our spirits high. We were truly psyched for a magnificent four-to-five-week trip around the country.

But in one sense our trip turned out to be the most miserable time we'd ever spent together. Everything that could go wrong did go wrong. Things were constantly breaking down, and we were all mechanical klutzes and could fix nothing. We probably had only one or two of the discussions we'd planned; instead we spent most of our time repairing things that were broken or trying to get other people to fix them during holiday periods when no one wanted to get involved in repairs.

It was July. The weather was hot and humid. The air conditioner and the generator that drove it were constantly breaking down. We were frequently lost, either searching for campgrounds or finding them filled. We often ended up in the back of a service station or in a church parking lot rather than in the trailer court or beautifully appointed campground we had envisioned.

On the Fourth of July, the air conditioner quit entirely. We pulled into a service station to get some help, but the mechanic said, "We don't work on anything like that, and particularly on a holiday. In fact, I don't think you'll find anyplace in town where you can get any help." The temperature was 100 degrees and the humidity about 98 percent. We were dripping in sweat. Everyone was close to tears.

Then all of a sudden somebody started to laugh. Then everyone started to laugh. And we laughed so hard we couldn't stop laughing. We have never laughed that much before or since. We asked the man (who undoubtedly thought we were crazy) for directions to the nearest amusement park. He told us which way to go, and we headed out to have some fun.

During the remainder of the trip we saw some interesting historical sites, but in each area we also sought out the local amusement parks. When we headed home, we were better authorities on the amusement parks of America than on the historical sites. In fact, only one morning on the entire trip did we have the kind of family meeting we had dreamed we would have each day. But we had a glorious time—one we will never forget. We came back renewed—physically, socially, and at least somewhat mentally.

It has always amazed Sandra and me that, despite broken air conditioners, flat tires, mosquitoes, forgotten articles of clothing, arguments over who sat where and what we were going to do, hours-late departures, and myriad other complications, those times together are what our family members remember and talk about.

"Boy, didn't we have fun that year at Six Flags!"

"Remember the time you thought we were lost?"

"I can't stop laughing when I think about you falling in the creek that year."

"Do you remember the look on her face when you dropped that hamburger?"

The added social dimension of "family" makes doing everything more exciting and more fun because you have someone special to share it with. In fact, those family bonds are often even more important than the event itself.

Jenny (daughter):

I remember one time when Dad decided he would take me and my little brother camping. Our family has never been big on camping; in fact, we didn't know anything about it. But he was determined to make it a good experience.

Absolutely everything went wrong. We burned our tinfoil dinners, and it poured rain throughout the night until our tent collapsed and our sleeping bags were soaked clear through. My dad woke us up around 2:00 A.M., and we gathered up our stuff and headed home.

The next day we laughed—and we continue to laugh—about that "miserable" experience. Despite the disasters, it created a sense of bonding. We went through it together, and we had a common experience we could look back on and talk about.

I know one family who had planned for years to go to Disneyland. They had saved the money and scheduled the time to go. But three weeks before the departure date, a feeling of gloom seemed to settle in their home.

Finally, at dinner one evening, the seventeen-year-old son blurted out, "Why do we have to go to Disneyland?"

This question took the father by surprise. "What do you mean by that?" he replied. Then his eyes narrowed. "Have you and your friends planned something? It seems that nothing we plan in the family is as important to you as being with your friends."

"It isn't that," the son replied, looking down at his plate.

After a moment his sister said softly, "I know what Jed means, and I don't want to go to Disneyland, either."

The father sat in stunned silence. Then his wife put her hand on his arm. "Your brother phoned today and told us his children are really sad that we're going to miss Kenley Creek this year to go to Disneyland. I think that is what's bothering the children."

Then everyone started talking. "We want to see our cousins!" they all cried. "That's more important than going to Disneyland!"

The father replied, "Hey, I want to see the family, too. I'd really like to spend some time with my brothers and sisters, but I thought you all wanted to go to Disneyland. Since we go to Kenley Creek every year, I decided this time we'd do what you wanted to do."

The seventeen-year-old replied, "So can we change our plans, Dad?"

They did. And everyone was happy.

This father later told me the story of Kenley Creek.

When my father and mother were young, we didn't have much money. We couldn't go on vacation to any place that cost a lot. So every year Mom and Dad would pack the wooden grub box with all kinds of food. We'd tie the old canvas tent to the top of the 1947 Ford. All the children would pile in like sardines in a can, and off we would go to the mountains and to Kenley Creek. We did that every year.

After my older brother got married—his wife was sort of a fancy rich girl who had been all over the country on vacations—we didn't think they would go with us to Kenley Creek. But they did, and she had the time of her life.

One by one we all got married, and every summer at a certain time we would all drive up to Kenley Creek.

The year after Dad died, we wondered if we should go. Mom said that Dad would want us to go and he'd be there with us, so we all went.

The years passed, and each of us had children. Still we all gathered each year at Kenley Creek. Each night under the moonlight of the Kenley Creek sky, my brother would play polkas on his accordion and all the kids would dance with their cousins.

After Mom died, it seemed as if she and Dad came back and sat by the campfire with all of us every year at Kenley Creek, in the quiet of the mountain evenings. With the eyes of our hearts we could see them smile as they watched the grandkids dance and eat the watermelon that had been cooled in the cold waters of the stream.

Our time at Kenley Creek always renewed us as a family. We loved one another more and more as the years went by.

Any family vacation can be a great renewing experience, but many families—including our own—have found an added dimension of renewal in going back to the same place year after year.

In our family the place is a cabin at Hebgen Lake in Montana, about twenty miles outside West Yellowstone. Spending part of the summer there is a tradition started by my grandfather some forty-five years ago. He had a heart attack, and in order to recuperate, he went to Snake River and then to Hebgen Lake. That area was the best medicine for him. He started with a cabin on the river, and then he put a trailer and later a cabin by the lake. Every summer after that he went there, and he always invited his family to go with him. There are several cabins up there now, and at least five hundred descendants go there regularly.

The word "Hebgen" has become something of an intergenerational family mission statement. It means family love, unity, service, and joy to each of us in the family. At Hebgen the children and grandchildren learned to run on the scalding sand, catch frogs under the dock, build sand castles on the shores of the lake, swim in the ice-cold glacier waters, catch rainbow trout, spot moose drinking at the shore of the meadow, play volleyball on the beach, and follow bear tracks. It's been the scene for many late-night bonfires, singing around the fire, summer romances, the Playmill Theater, shopping in West Yellowstone, and enjoying the beautiful green forests and starry nights. Up until ten years ago, there was no telephone or television there. I'm even wondering now whether we ought to go back to those "good old days."

Stephen (son):

When I was younger, we used to spend three weeks every summer at Hebgen. It was so enjoyable, I used to wish I could be there all summer. I especially remember the opportunities it gave me to spend time with one or both of my parents or one of my brothers or sisters. We'd do anything from fishing to riding motorcycles, from water-skiing to canoeing. It was just natural to pair up and do things together. And everybody loved it. You'd miss anything but Hebgen.

Sean (son):

I remember going to Hebgen one year when I was in college. The football season was starting in just a couple of weeks. There was a lot of pressure coming. So one morning I went up to a place our family named Prayer Rock. It's a big rock on the hill that overlooks the entire lake. The sun was just coming up, and there was a cool breeze. The lake was beautiful. I spent several hours up there just gathering myself, bracing myself for the season coming up. I felt that this was kind of my last moment of peace before the onslaught of war. Many times during the season—when it was wild and hectic and there was so much pressure—I would visualize that scene of being on top of the mountain, being calm and peaceful. It steadied me. It was, in a sense, kind of like returning home.

Joshua (son):

Since I'm the youngest at home, Mom always uses me to help carry out her family schemes, projects, and traditions.

Among other things I get drafted to help out with the traditional Pirate Treasure Hunt that takes place at our family vacation every summer in Hebgen Lake. We sneak into West Yellowstone and "raid" the dollar stores, buying all kinds of small dollar items to fill our pirate's chest. We get balls, Slinkies, magic ink, bear bells, Indian canoes, plastic handcuffs, rabbit foot chains, rubber knives, bow-and-arrow sets, coin purses, Yo-yo's, slingshots, Indian bead jewelry—something for everyone. Then the chest is loaded, wrapped in huge black garbage bags, and piled into the boat—along with shovels, a pirate flag, and handwritten clues burned at the edges to look old and authentic (another one of my jobs).

After beaching the boat on what we call Goat Island, we search for a place on the beach to bury the treasure. We cover the hiding place with clean sand and throw brush on it so that it looks untouched. Finally, we run all over the island leaving clues in trees and shrubs and under rocks. Then we scatter coins—pennies, nickels, dimes, and even silver dollars—for the little kids to find.

Half dead, we return to the mobs of kids at the beach, waving an old battered pirate flag with its black skull and bones logo and hysterically screaming (that's Mom's job) that we scared off some pirates who left their buried treasure behind.

Everyone—kids, grownups, and dogs—piles into boats, canoes, dinghies, inner tubes, and Ski-Doos and invades the island. We scramble and run from clue to clue until the treasure is discovered, the loot is distributed, and the tradition is complete.

These kinds of traditional vacations seem to give an added sense of stability and connection. And it's great if you can return to one place year after year.

But, again, it isn't so much where you go as that you're together and doing things that create strong family ties. The tradition of family vacations builds renewing memories that, as someone put it, "bloom forever in the garden of the heart."

Birthdays

One year when our son Stephen had started a new job, his wife, Jeri, gave him a very unusual birthday gift. She said:

Because of moving, buying a house, paying off school debts, starting a new and challenging job, and other pressures of life, my husband was under tremendous stress. I knew the best way to reduce this stress was for him to be around his brother David. No one made him relax more. They were crazy together! They always had so much fun.

So for Stephen's birthday I bought an airplane ticket for David to come and be with him for the weekend. I kept this gift as a surprise, telling my husband we would attend a professional basketball game that was scheduled on his birthday, and sometime during the game I would give him a very special gift.

About halftime, his beloved brother arrived, announcing, "Surprise, I'm your birthday present," to the amazement of my husband.

For the next twenty-four hours these two had the most wonderful celebration—laughing, playing, and talking nonstop. I just stayed out of their way. I have never seen such pure fun as they generated together.

When David left, it was as if he took all the stress with him, and my husband was completely renewed.

Birthdays can be a wonderful time to express love and affirm family members—to celebrate the fact that they're here and part of your family. And traditions around birthdays can be very renewing.

In our own family, birthdays are tremendously important. Over the years we haven't really had birth*days*, we've had birth *weeks*. For the entire week we would try to focus on letting our children know how special they are to us. We would have rooms decorated with signs and balloons, presents at breakfast, a "friend" party, a special dinner out with Mom and Dad, and dinner with the extended family, complete with the person's favorite meal, favorite cake, and compliments:

"I love Cynthia because she is so spontaneous. She'll go to a movie with you at the drop of a hat."

"Maria is so well read that whenever you need a quote, you just have to call her up and ask her, and she'll come up with four or five excellent things to choose from."

"One of the things I like about Stephen is that he's not only a good athlete but he's happy when he helps other people become good athletes. He's always willing to spend the time to show you how to improve or teach you some fundamental."

Colleen *(daughter):*

To tell you the truth, that was one bummer about getting married. I woke up on my first birthday after I was married, and there were no balloons. The house wasn't even decorated! There were no birthday posters. I told my husband I missed my mom's decorations, so the next year—and every year since—he's gone all out to make my birthday nice.

I've even known of extended family members who have gone out of their way to make sure that birthdays are recognized and celebrated.

Two single sisters shared this experience:

*Our nieces and nephews (three, five, eleven, and fourteen) all love our birthday tra-
ditions. On the Saturday morning of their birthday week, we pick them up to go shopping.
No parents, no siblings—just the birthday child and us. They receive the same amount of
money to spend and get to choose where to shop. They can take as short or as long an
amount of time as they like. Then we go out to lunch to a grown-up restaurant—not
McDonald's or fast food but a real restaurant! They order whatever they want, and they
even get a dessert.*

*We've often been surprised at the careful way they make their decisions concerning
what to buy and what to order. They show amazing maturity and take it all very seriously—even the three-year-old. Last year she picked out four outfits, then said, "Only
two. Only need two." We hadn't said a word to her about limiting herself. And it was hard
for her to decide, but she did it.*

*We've been doing this for thirteen years now. Our nieces and nephews start talking
about it weeks before their birthday. They call it their "Aunt Toni and Aunt Barbie Day."
And they love it almost as much as we do!*

To celebrate a birthday is to celebrate the person. It's a wonderful opportunity
to express love and affirmation and make huge deposits into the Emotional Bank
Account.

Holidays

A single woman in her thirties shared this experience:

*I recently bought my own home with the idea of having my entire family come over for
Thanksgiving. I bought a ten-seat table and ten chairs to go around it. Now everyone who
comes over says, "You're single. Why do you need this table?" And I tell them, "You don't
know what this table represents. It represents our whole family being together. My mom
can't cook anymore. My brother is divorced. My sister can't do it at her house. But being
together like this is so important to me. I want to do it here."*

Probably more than almost anything else, people remember and love family traditions around important holidays. They often come together from long distances
and long separations. There's food. There's fun. There's laughter. There's sharing.
And often there's a unifying theme or purpose.

There are many different traditions around each of the holidays. There are
Thanksgiving turkeys, New Year's Day football games, and Easter egg hunts. There's
Christmas caroling, talent sharing, and going to parades. There are traditions

around the kind of food that's served, traditions that come from particular countries or cultures, traditions that have been passed down through the generations, and new traditions that are developed when people marry. And all of these things give a sense of stability and identity to the family.

The point is that holidays provide an ideal time to build traditions. They happen every year. It's easy to create a sense of anticipation and fun as well as meaning and camaraderie around them.

In our own family we've developed some fairly unique traditions around holidays.

Catherine (*daughter*):

I remember doing a special Valentine's Day tradition with my dad every year. We would make valentines and attach long strings to them. Then we'd go and put them on people's porches, ring the doorbell, and run and hide behind the bushes or around the corner of the house.

When people opened the door, they would be thrilled to receive a valentine. But when they bent down to pick it up, we would jerk it a few inches away. They would stumble a little. They would look at it in astonishment and try again. We'd pull the string a little farther. Finally, they would grab it, and we would come out laughing.

After a while the people in our neighborhood caught on. The first time the valentine moved, they'd say, "Oh, that's Steve Covey. What's he up to now?" But they looked forward to it. And I always loved it. We had so much fun!

Dad also has the tradition of sending flowers and chocolates to all his daughters on Valentine's Day—even now that we're married. And it's the greatest because we get these beautiful roses on Valentine's Day. We sometimes think they're from our husbands, but they're from Dad. It makes us feel special because we have two expressions of love. We get two bunches of flowers, and it's really fun to try to guess who they're from and what Dad will send this year.

This tradition started when I was very young. I remember getting chocolates from Dad on Valentine's Day when I was about ten years old and how special it made me feel. It was my own box of chocolates that no one else could touch.

Dad also sends us flowers on Mother's Day.

David (*son*):

Mom was well known among my friends for her involvement in Saint Patrick's Day each March. She would dress up in her green leprechaun outfit and appear uninvited in each of her children's classrooms. She would engage the whole class in singing Irish songs and telling stories with an Irish lilt in her voice. Then each child was given a shamrock cookie, and she would pinch the boys and girls who weren't wearing green. This tradition has continued into the next generation, and the grandchildren have increased self-esteem because they know that their Mère Mère knows who they are and makes an effort to be part of their lives.

Jenny *(daughter):*

The Covey house was a "must do" on everyone's list at Halloween. Mom and Dad would invite the trick-or-treaters into the house to sit down, visit, get warm, and have hot cider and doughnuts. But first they would have to perform some sort of talent—sing, dance, rap, recite a poem. Even college students at the local university heard about it and came for a warm drink.

One particular year a bunch of junior high school boys whom my mom described as "hoodlums" came trick-or-treating. They almost died when they learned they would have to perform a talent. Wanting the cider and doughnuts, though, they forced themselves to do something. The next year the same group of "hoodlums" came—this time prepared and excited about performing a song they had memorized and rehearsed in advance, with hand gestures included.

In the fall of 1996, after living in our home for thirty years, we moved to a new house. Our new neighbors all told us we would get only about 30 trick-or-treaters because we were too far off the beaten track. But we knew better. Mom served about 175—most of them former neighborhood kids, new high school friends, families, newly-married, and lots of university students. They all came to perform, visit, drink hot cider, and eat doughnuts. By this time all the older kids' friends were married, but they still came with their little children to trick-or-treat at our house. It was tradition.

Because holidays come every year, they continually bring opportunity to enjoy traditions and renew the sense of fun, camaraderie, and meaning we feel around them. Holidays seem to provide the ideal natural and ongoing opportunity for being together and renewing family ties.

Extended and Intergenerational Family Activities

As you've probably noticed from the stories throughout this book, aunts, uncles, grandparents, cousins, and other extended family members can have a tremendous positive influence on the family. Many activities lend themselves to larger family involvement, especially major holiday celebrations such as Thanksgiving, Christmas, or Hanukkah. But almost any family activity can be broadened to include extended family members.

Sense the excitement of these grandparents in organizing special family times:

One of our favorite traditions is our monthly "family time" with the extended family. Once a month we invite our married children and grandchildren to join us and our children still at home for a potluck dinner and evening together. Everyone brings a part of the meal, and we enjoy eating and catching up on what's happening in everyone's life. Then we clean up and sit together in the family room. We arrange the chairs in a circle and bring out a big basket of toys for the little ones to play with in the middle while we talk. Someone usually shares a talent. Often we'll discuss some aspect of our family mission statement or something else that's important. When the little ones get tired, everyone goes home. It's a great time to be together and renew relationships.

A couple in their seventies shared this:

We have a tradition of having Sunday dinners at which our daughter (our only child), her husband, and their children still living at home are always guests. Each week we also invite one of the four married grandchildren and their family—the first week of the month, the oldest; the second week, the next; and so on. In this way we are able to talk with each family—to find out how their lives are changing, what their plans and goals are, and how we might be able to help with those plans.

The desire to create this tradition came about thirty years ago when our daughter married and moved thirteen hundred miles away. For a long time our communication was limited to phone conversations and visits a couple of times a year. We often thought how nice it would be if we could have her and her family over to dinner and be of help, particularly when there was illness in the family.

So in our retirement years we moved closer so that we could do just that. Our Sunday dinners have been a tradition for thirteen years now. It brings us enjoyment to be able to serve, to learn about our grandchildren, to see their growth, and to be part of an extended family.

Notice how these families have taken normal family activities—family times and Sunday dinners—and expanded them to include members of their extended and intergenerational families. And think of the memories and the relationships this is building!

Extended and intergenerational family members can be involved in almost everything you do. Over the years, Sandra and I have made it a point to go to our children's programs, recitals, and sporting events—or whatever individual family members were involved in. We've tried to provide a support system from the family to show that we care and that each person in the family is appreciated and loved. We always have an open invitation for anyone in the extended and intergenerational family who can to come to such activities. And Sandra and I often attend the activities that involve our brothers and sisters and their families as well.

Colleen (*daughter*):
I remember one time in high school, I was in a play—Joseph and the Amazing

Technicolor Dreamcoat. *I had a small part—"proud-to-be-crowd," I'd call it. But on opening night my brothers, sisters, in-laws, nieces, nephews, aunts, and uncles as well as my parents were in the audience. They filled up three rows! The girl who played the lead looked out and said, "I can't believe this! I'm the lead, and the only one here to see me is my mom. But you have this dinky little part, and your family takes up half the audience!" That extended family support made me feel very important.*

We find that with these kinds of intergenerational activities, siblings and cousins usually end up the best of friends. We feel a great sense of strength in and appreciation for the members of our extended and intergenerational families. We firmly believe they go a long way toward reweaving the safety net that's become unraveled in society.

Sean (son):

One of the things I appreciate most about our family is this huge intergenerational support network. My kids are growing up very close to their cousins. A lot of them are the same age, and they're close. They're the best of friends. And I think this is going to make a tremendous difference when they're teenagers. They'll have this huge network of support. And if someone starts having problems, there will probably be too much support to ever let anyone go off the deep end.

Learning Together

There are so many opportunities to learn and do things together as a family! And this can be tremendously renewing in all dimensions.

One tradition that developed when our family went on trips together was singing in the car. That's the way most of the kids learned the folk songs of America, the campfire songs, patriotic songs (even the verses to *The Star-Spangled Banner*), Christmas carols, and hit tunes from Broadway musicals. When you think about it, the younger children really need someone to take the time to teach them the words and music to the old familiar songs we all seem to know. Otherwise, how can they join in?

Another way to learn together is to share in a family member's particular hobby or interest. Get involved in it. Learn about it. Read books. Join associations. Subscribe to magazines. Soak it up. Make it a focus. Talk about it together.

Learning together is socially and mentally renewing. It gives you a shared interest, something fun to talk about. There's joy in discovering and learning together. It can also be physically renewing when you learn a new sport or a new physical skill, and it can be spiritually renewing when you learn more about the principles that govern in all of life.

Learning together can be a wonderful tradition and one of the greatest joys of family life. It also affirms that when you raise your children you are also raising your grandchildren.

Sean (son):

Our parents took us everywhere. We went with them on trips. Dad took us with him on speaking engagements. We were always exposed to a lot of good things. And I feel this was a real advantage for me. My comfort zone in situations is really high because I've experienced a lot. I've been camping. I've been in the outdoors. I've been on survival treks. I've been in the water—swimming and waterskiing. I've tried every sport at least a few times.

And I consciously try to do that with my kids. If I'm going to a baseball game, I take them. If I'm going to the mall to pick up something, I take them. If I'm going outside to try to build something in the yard, I take them. I'm trying to expose them to a lot of different things in life.

Another vitally important learning tradition is reading. Families can read together. In addition, children need to read on their own—and to see their parents read as well.

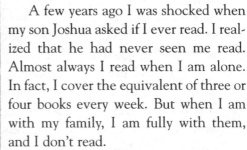

A few years ago I was shocked when my son Joshua asked if I ever read. I realized that he had never seen me read. Almost always I read when I am alone. In fact, I cover the equivalent of three or four books every week. But when I am with my family, I am fully with them, and I don't read.

I have recently read some research which indicates that the number one reason children don't read is that they don't see their fathers read.[3] I think this is one of the mistakes I have made over the years. I wish that I'd kept my study more open so that my children would have seen me reading more often. And I wish I'd been more conscientious about sharing what I was learning and what excited me.

Sandra:

One learning tradition we developed in our family was that every two weeks I would pile all the kids into the car and we'd go to the public library. Each person was able to get twelve books that could be taken out for two weeks. Each got to choose the books he or she wanted and was interested in.

My main task was to make sure that the books didn't get mutilated, destroyed, or dis-

appear during this two-week period. I remember my fear as we tried to gather them all up for the day of deliverance.

Learning together as a family is more than a tradition, it's a vital need. It is true in today's world that "unless you run faster, you will get farther behind" because the pace of life and the growth of technology are incredible. Many products are obsolete the day they appear on the market. The half-life of many professions is only three to four years. That's startling. It's scary. That's why it's so important for there to be a family tradition and culture that focuses on continual learning.

Worshiping Together

One father shared this:

When I was growing up, it was very important to my parents that we all worship together. At the time I didn't think it was important. I didn't understand why they thought it was important. But they did, so we all went to church together and sat together. And I have to admit as young boys we were bored together most of the time.

But as I got older, I began to notice that we were more aligned as a family than was the case with a lot of my friends. We had common values and goals. We relied on one another to solve problems and find answers. We knew what we believed, what we all believed. We were together. And "worship" wasn't just a matter of once a week in our home. Religion and worship were treated almost as an educational process. We had lessons—formal and informal—where our parents would teach us about what was right and wrong. They would listen as we disagreed, then help us figure things out and find our own answers. But they taught us about values and faith.

In addition, we had little family traditions. For example, we prayed together every evening. It was sometimes grueling to listen to my brothers go on and on. But as I got older I realized how much I learned as I listened to them. I learned what was important to them, what they needed and wanted, what they were afraid of or concerned about. Now that I think about it, I realize that it really drew us all together.

We also prayed and fasted in times of emergency. I remember when my grandma was in the hospital with cancer. A call went out to our entire family—aunts, uncles, and cousins. We all gathered in family prayer and fasted together for her. It gave us strength to be together. And when she passed away, it was wonderful to have everyone near. The unity was overwhelming. And although there were tears and sadness, it was a lovely, strengthening, bonding funeral. I came away from it with a special understanding and appreciation for the full circle of life, from birth to death. And I think the fact that we all share common beliefs made things much more meaningful to us.

Notice how worshiping brought this family together spiritually, mentally, and socially.

George Gallup reports that 95 percent of Americans believe in some form of supreme being or higher power, and that more than ever before, people are feeling the need to reach beyond self-help to find spiritual help.[4] Research also clearly shows that worshiping together is one of the major characteristics of healthy, happy families. It can create context, unity, and shared understanding—much in the same way that a family mission statement does.

In addition, studies have shown that religious involvement is a significant factor in mental and emotional health and stability, particularly when individuals are internally motivated. When they are extrinsically motivated—by public approval or conformity, for example—the religious context is not always benevolent. In fact, it sometimes nurtures a culture that is extremely strict and sets unrealistically high expectations, causing people who are emotionally vulnerable to experience even more emotional problems.[5]

But when the environment is focused on growth based on moral principles rather than on an outward perfectionism that reinforces rule-bound rigidity, people experience greater health. The culture allows for honest recognition of moral imperfections and acceptance of self, even as it encourages acceptance of and living in harmony with the principles that govern in all of life.

C. S. Lewis related his own convictions in squaring his private and public selves in this way:

When I come to my evening prayers and try to reckon up the sins of the day, nine times out of ten the most obvious one is some sin against charity; I have sulked or snapped or sneered or snubbed or stormed. And the excuse that immediately springs to mind is that the provocation was so sudden or unexpected; I was caught off my guard, I had not time to collect myself. . . . Surely what a man does when he is taken off his guard is the best evidence for what sort of man he is. Surely what pops out before the man has time to put on a disguise is the truth. If there are rats in the cellar you are most likely to see them if you go in very suddenly. But the suddenness does not create the rats: it only prevents them from hiding. In the same way the suddenness of the provocation does not make me an ill-tempered man: it only shows me what an ill-tempered man I am. . . . Now that cellar is out of reach of my conscious will. . . . I cannot, by direct moral effort, give myself new motives. After the first few steps . . . we realize that everything which really needs to be done in our souls can be done only by God.[6]

In our own family, we have found great strength in worshiping together. Through the years we've placed a high priority on attending our church services together and supporting one another in working and serving in the church and community. We've found that this unites us as a family and also gives us opportunities to work together for something higher than self.

We've also tried to hold our own daily devotionals in our home. We try to have some time together for a few minutes each morning to begin our day with a feeling of togetherness and inspiration.

Stephen (*son*):

As I was growing up, we always had family devotionals in the morning. It was a pattern. Whether we were little kids or high school students, we always got up at 6:00. We'd read together, talk about needs and plans for the day, and have a family prayer. We'd have our blankets and lie down on the couches. There were times that some of us would sleep right through it—until it was our turn to read. It may not have been as effective as it could have been, but we made the effort. And a lot of it sunk in. I think we all learned a lot more than we thought we did.

This tradition, including the daily reading of scriptures and other "wisdom literature," has been a tremendously renewing tradition for our family. This is something any family can do. Depending on your belief, "wisdom literature" could be anything that connects you with timeless principles. It could be the Bible, the Koran, the Talmud, *Native American Wisdom*, or the Bhagavad-Gita. It could be James Allen's *As a Man Thinketh*, Thoreau's *Walden*, or modern collections such as William Bennett's *Book of Virtues* or Jack Canfield and Mark Victor Hansen's *Chicken Soup for the Soul*. It could be inspiring autobiographies or anthologies, insightful essays, or uplifting stories—whatever addresses the principles and values you believe in.[7]

The point is that if you organize your family life to spend even ten or fifteen minutes a morning reading something that connects you with these timeless principles, it's almost guaranteed that you will make better choices during the day—in the family, on the job, in every dimension of life. Your thoughts will be higher. Your interactions will be more satisfying. You will have a greater perspective. You will increase that space between what happens to you and your response to it. You will be more connected to what really matters most.

You will also be more connected to your family. This can be a great time to get in touch with the needs of each person for that day—whether someone is taking a test or has an important assignment to get or a presentation to give. It enables you to start your day renewing the relationships that matter most.

Daily devotionals can provide tremendous spiritual, social, and mental renewal. And if you want to add the physical dimension, you can always do a few sit-ups, go

> *If you organize your family life to spend even ten or fifteen minutes a morning reading something that connects you with timeless principles, you will make better choices during the day—in the family, on the job, in every dimension of life.*

for a walk, or take up tai chi. Whatever you choose to include, you'll find that mornings are a great time for family renewal. It's an incredibly wonderful way to start your day.

Working Together

One man shared this:

One of my most vivid memories of growing up was working beside my father in our garden. When he first suggested the idea, my brother and I were excited. At that time we didn't realize that it would translate into spending hours in the backyard in the hot sun, shovel in hand, digging and getting blisters and doing a lot of other things you don't necessarily associate with fun.

And the work was hard. But my dad worked right alongside us. He took the time to teach and educate us so that we could see the vision of what an ideal garden would look like. And this provided a great learning experience—from the first time we dug those holes and wondered what in the world we were doing, to four or five years later when I was able to walk out there as a teenager and find great joy and satisfaction in the fruits of our labors.

I remember the buy-in that came when I was twelve or thirteen. Suddenly it became a source of great joy to pick bushels of beautiful fruit—peaches and apples and pears—and to have corn growing in the backyard that rivaled the best corn you've ever tasted and tomato plants that grew to look like trees because of the holes we carefully dug and prepared for them. I remember how after that—even when I was extremely busy as a teenager—I always wanted to find time to make sure our garden was in order, that our trees were pruned and sprayed and taken care of.

I think that one of the greatest learning experiences I had during those years was in seeing what our family could accomplish together. Walking down those garden rows and knowing that we had done this was a source of incredible satisfaction.

And now I find that that experience helps me in almost every task I have before me. Whenever I become involved in a project where I need to have someone buy into the end result and the vision, I think back on that experience and how my father helped me realize what it would do to our family and our relationships as a family. I can translate that now to a project here in the office and say, "Okay, we have this task at hand. We need to accomplish this. What's the end in mind?"

When I need to create order in my life, I think back to that row of beautiful green pepper plants. I remember how I thought it was a joke when we bought them in the little plastic canisters. I said, "How are we going to get them to grow?" But weeks later I saw those full plants with leaves that looked like silk because they were so healthy. And I know I can do it.

I think often, too, about my dad's example in all of this. He got such joy out of doing it. I think he also got joy from seeing me have joy in doing it and in seeing the results of our hard work and God's help and the wonders of nature and natural law.

Notice how this tradition of working together in the garden renewed this boy and his family. It renewed them socially by giving them the opportunity to work together. Can you imagine the wonderful teaching moments this would create? Look at how it renewed them physically as they worked together out in the hot sun. Think about the mental renewal involved as this boy learned about nurturing grow-ing things. Think about the way this knowledge helped him even in his business career as an adult. This is because he learned in that garden some of the natural laws that govern in every dimension in life, and he was able to apply those laws or prin-ciples years later in a completely different situation. So it was spiritual renewal as well. He was close to nature and close to natural law.

Notice, too, what you can read between the lines about this father's attitude about working with his children. Another father has said:

I think it's very easy for anyone who works for a living to become task oriented. I know it is for me. So when I'm working with my children, I tend to become very directive and demanding.

I've come to realize, though, that the objectives are different when you work with children. The work you're doing is the work of nurturing character and future capacity. And when you keep that end in mind, you don't get frustrated. You have peace and joy in doing it.

It's like the story one man told of a time when he decided to buy some cows to help his boys learn responsibility. A neighbor—a farmer of many years—came up to him one day and began criticizing some of the things the boys were doing. The man smiled and said, "Thank you for your concern. But you don't understand. I'm not raising cows; I'm rais-ing boys."

That thought has helped me through many teaching moments in working with my children.

It used to be that families had to work together in order to survive, so work was something that kept families close. But in today's society "work" often pulls families apart. You have parents going "off to work" in different directions—all of them away from home. You have children who don't really need to work economically but are growing up in a social environment that views work as a curse rather than as a blessing.

So creating the tradition of working together today is really a matter of inside out. But there are many ways to do it and many benefits of doing it. As we've already observed, having a family garden is a great "working together" tradition—

one in which you can really enjoy the fruits of your labors. Many families do their regular household chores together on Saturdays. Some parents involve older children in summer work in their profession.

Catherine (*daughter*):

One tradition we had in our family was the "ten-minute program." Whenever we'd have a big party and there was a total mess—even sometimes when we'd just have the normal mess we created during the hours after school—Dad would stand up and say, "Okay, let's have the ten-minute program before we go to bed." That meant that every person in the family would work really hard for ten minutes to clean up the place. We all knew that if we had eighteen hands working in the kitchen, it would go a lot faster than two. So we knew it wasn't going to be an hourlong process, and that made it nice.

We also had what we called "work parties." That may seem like a contradiction in terms, but that's what they were. We'd work really hard for three or four hours to get something done, but we'd have food and we'd laugh and talk as we worked. We'd also do something fun afterward—like go to a movie—and we'd look forward to that. Everyone expected they'd have to work. It was just part of life. But it made it so much better by adding these little treats at the end or doing something that made it seem like fun.

Serving Together

A mother shared this experience:

My husband, Mark, grew up in a Polynesian village where people had to work together to survive. And my own mom was always helping people—whether it was in the church or in the neighborhood or just someone she heard about that had a need. So Mark and I both grew up with a sense of working and serving together. And when we married and began to have our own children, we decided that one of the values we wanted to instill in them was a sense of service to others.

We've never had much in the way of financial resources, so we felt a little limited about making charitable contributions. But as we talked together, we realized that there was one thing we could do: We could make quilts. Piece goods are fairly inexpensive. And tying a quilt is quite simple—something we could do as a family, something that requires physical effort and skill. And a quilt is something people can use and appreciate.

So every year we piece together about twelve quilts for different families. This year we made some for my aunt's family, who have had some hard times. We've just started one for a neighbor who's going through a divorce.

The kids have been a big part of identifying people in need because young children are more open with one another and are not so embarrassed by the need. And they really enjoy helping. We sit around the quilting frames and talk about a lot of things—so it helps with communication, too. And they love to deliver the finished quilts, whether we do it secretly or not (although I think they enjoy the secret drop-offs the best).

We have a lot of good times doing this together as a family. Even the little girls (three and five) have things they can do, such as cutting out pieces of fabric and clipping the yarn. Sometimes they make the little cards to go with the quilt. But everyone is involved. We feel that's important.

A father shared this:

Some time ago my wife and I decided that we have been given a lot in life and need to give back more than we take. So we started a youth group—a kind of outreach group—in our home. We also have teenage children, and we thought what better way could there be to understand and be part of their lives than to offer something like this to them and their friends.

So we had twelve or thirteen kids come over to our home on a weekly basis. It was an interdenominational, interracial group. The only thing they had in common was that they were in the same school district. They understood up front that this was on a trial basis to see if they liked getting together once a week. We set up a contract so that everyone would understand and agree on what was to happen. We came up with some guidelines for behavior, such as "when one person is talking, everyone else listens." And we tried to plan the meetings around the things they wanted to talk about.

In the beginning we talked about things like honesty, respect, apologizing for mistakes, having a sense of contribution. The group evolved to the point where they started asking questions like "What is trust?" and "What is peer pressure?" My wife and I did research on whatever they asked about and presented it at the following week's meeting. We didn't do a lot of teaching through words. We spent maybe fifteen minutes doing that, but from there it went to physical activities. Some activities were outdoors; some were indoors. All of them highlighted the concepts they told us they wanted to hear about.

After we completed that first contract, the kids were very eager to continue with the second. They liked having a place where they could talk and ask questions about things that were important to them. And the parents appreciated it, too. One of the mothers called us up to say, "I don't know what you do at your house for that hour and a half to two hours, but it must be something remarkable. The other day I made a negative comment to my daughter about someone else, and she said, 'You know, Mom, we really don't know that girl. We shouldn't be saying that. That's just what we're hearing from someone else.' I'm so glad she brought that to my attention. I wish adults could do this, too."

Can you see how tremendously renewing this tradition of serving together can be? It's spiritually renewing because it's focused on something higher than self. It can also be part of fulfilling and renewing your family mission statement.

Depending on the nature of the service, it can be mentally or physically renewing as well. It can involve developing talents, learning new concepts or skills, or being involved in physical activity. And there's tremendous social renewal in it: Can you imagine anything more bonding, more unifying, more energizing to the relationship than working together to accomplish something that is really meaningful and worthwhile?

Having Fun Together

Probably the most important dimension of all these traditions is having fun together—genuinely enjoying one another, enjoying the home environment, making home and family the happiest, biggest "warm fuzzy" in people's lives. Having fun together is so vital and so important that it could even be listed as a tradition in and of itself. And it can be nurtured and expressed in many ways.

In our family we've built a lot of social camaraderie around humor. For example, we have a number of what we call "Covey cult films." These movies are hilarious, and we frequently watch them together and have the funniest times. Everyone enjoys them immensely. We've learned the dialogue so well that many times we get into situations and the whole family reenacts an entire scene from the movie, word for word. Everyone cracks up and outsiders wonder.

As we observed in Habit 1, humor puts things in perspective so you don't take yourself too seriously. You don't get hung up on small issues or other little irritating things that can be divisive and create polarization in the family. Sometimes it takes only one person to inject a little humor into the situation and change the entire course of an event or turn an otherwise mundane task into an adventure.

Maria (daughter):

I remember when we lived in Hawaii, Dad used to give Mom Saturdays sometimes to recover from all of us. He'd say, "Okay, kids, today I'm taking you all on adventures." We'd never know what the adventures were going to be. We were so excited. We didn't know this until later, but he'd make them up as he went along.

The first adventure might be to go swimming in the ocean. Then we'd go to Goo's Store, and everyone would get an ice cream cone. Then we'd hike a little trail. There might be seven adventures in all, and each of them would be a big event.

I also remember Dad taking us to the swimming pool and playing with us for hours— just throwing us around. He was crazy. He had no inhibitions, no embarrassment at all. A lot of parents won't play with their kids, but Mom and Dad were both very fun-loving and would always play with us and do things with us.

David (son):

I remember when it would be Dad's turn to drive the car pool. We'd have this whole car full of kids, and Dad would do the funniest, the craziest things. He'd tell jokes. He'd get people to recite a poem or sing a song. He always had everyone in stitches.

As we got older, we would sometimes feel embarrassed by his behavior. But he'd always say, "Okay. Crazy or boring—take your choice."

"Boring!" we'd say. "Don't embarrass us, Dad." So he would just sit there stiff and silent. But then the other kids would yell, "Crazy! We want crazy!" And off he'd go again. The kids in the car pool just loved it.

Sandra:

I think there are some traditions that should have never gotten started—and they are very hard to stop! For instance, one time during dinner Stephen was called to the phone for a long-distance conversation with some business associates. The boys were anxious for him to get off the phone, and they kept pleading with him in pantomime to hang up. But he just waved them off and put his finger to his lips in a hushing motion.

Finally realizing that their father couldn't possibly keep up his end of the business conversation and negotiation and keep them occupied and quiet at the same time, they recognized his vulnerability and immediately acted upon it. One boy got a jar of peanut butter out of the cupboard and started spreading it on his shiny bald head. Another put a layer of red raspberry jam on top of the peanut butter, and a third boy topped it with a slice of Wonder bread. They built a perfectly marvelous sandwich on the top of his head, and there was nothing he could do about it.

After that they looked forward to this opportunity every time he was caught on a long-distance phone call. They especially enjoyed it if their friends were there to witness it. Stephen wasn't too excited about this tradition, but the final blow to his ego came on a hot summer evening when we were sitting on the lawn with some neighbors and friends watching a performance by some of our younger children, who were using the front porch as their stage.

A car full of teenagers pulled up, coming to a screeching stop. Five or six of them jumped out of the car and ran toward my husband. They were on a video-recording scavenger hunt. "Mr. Covey! Mr. Covey!" they cried. "We need you! We have to win this game. Please help us out." They surrounded him with jars of peanut butter and jam and a loaf of bread and made a glorious sandwich atop the crown of his head, videotaping the entire production. They finally left and Stephen went into the house to wash off his head. He then returned to watch the rest of the plays.

Just as he (and our astonished neighbors) had settled down, a second car full of enthusiastic and eager teenagers pulled into the driveway. They ran to him with the same request. They assured him that they knew how to make the sandwich since they had been well taught by Sean, David, and Stephen.

Before the night was over, three cars managed to win their points by following suit. Our neighbor, whose children hosted the party, said the highlight of the evening was the playback of the peanut butter sandwich episode. They assured us that Stephen was the star of the video scavenger hunt.

What an honor—and what a tradition!

Nurturing the Spirit of Renewal

Whatever traditions you decide to create in your family culture, you'll find there's a lot you can do that will nurture the "spirit" or feeling of renewal in your everyday interactions.

Sandra:

One simple tradition that we've developed through the years is that of making a fuss over comings and goings. When the children come home from school, it takes only a few minutes to greet them warmly and ask about their day. As they put their books away, take their coats off, and start to unwind, I have found it's nice to take time out from whatever I am doing and concentrate on them—to ask how their day went, to sense their attitude, spirit, or mood, and to help them prepare some fruit, a drink, or a snack as we talk it over. It's so easy to keep being involved in the things that you were doing before they came, but it really enriches the relationship when you stop completely and focus on them—even follow them into their bedroom, asking questions and getting involved in their life and day's activities.

Everyone likes to feel as if they were missed. It's nice to be greeted and have a fuss made over you so that you feel assured that you're an important part of the family. It's very rewarding to have someone listen to you, ask about your concerns, sense your mood, and seem to love being with you. It takes a little practice and effort, but it's well worth it.

I remember at a small dinner party at a friend's house one night, one of the guests arrived alone, stating that her husband had been delayed and would come within the hour. He came in about forty-five minutes later, apologizing for the delay. When he arrived, our friend Sabra's eyes and face lit up. Her smile and sense of excitement in seeing him conveyed to everyone their love for each other. It was obvious that they missed each other during the time they had been separated.

I thought to myself, What a warm welcome! He's a lucky man. About a year later Woody, the husband, had a sudden illness. Within weeks he died unexpectedly. Everyone was shocked. I think Sabra was glad she had always made so much of their comings and goings by taking a moment to express her love for him.

We've also tried to "adopt" our children's friends.

Sean (son):

In high school I had a few friends on the football team who were kind of wild. What Mom and Dad did, basically, was adopt my friends. They videotaped every game, and afterward invited everyone to our house for pizza. About half the team would show up, and we'd watch the game together. So all my friends got to like my parents. They thought my parents were cool, and so did I. The really neat thing about that was that many of my friends ended up being influenced by our family instead of the other way around. And some of those kids turned their lives around.

David (son):

Our house was always the neighborhood hangout because my mother welcomed all our friends and was willing to put up with the chaos that often accompanied our get-togethers. There were times when I would show up from high school with four or five ravenous football friends, and upon entering the kitchen, I would pound the table and jokingly bellow to my mother, "Feed my face! Feed my friends' faces!" She would laugh and win my friends' loyalty with a fine meal, regardless of the hour. Her sense of humor and willingness to put up with such inconveniences made our home a welcome environment that I felt confident bringing friends into.

These traditions—big and small—are the things that bond us, renew us, and give us identity as a family. And each family is unique. Each family must discover and create its own. Our children have grown up with a lot of traditions, but they have discovered—as everyone does—that when you marry, you may well enter into a relationship with someone who has an entirely different set of traditions. And this is why it's important to practice Habits 4, 5, and 6 and decide together which traditions reflect the kind of family you want to be.

Traditions Bring Family Healing

Over time, these renewing traditions become one of the most powerful forces in the family culture. And no matter what your past or current situation, they are something you can become aware of, create in your own family, and possibly even extend to others who may never have had the benefit of such renewal in their lives.

I know of one man who grew up in a very cynical home environment. He eventually married a wonderful woman who began to help him find out who he really was and discover his great untapped potential. As his confidence grew, he became increasingly aware of the toxic nature of his past environment and began to identify more and more with his wife's family and parents. Her family had its normal challenges, but their culture was fundamentally nurturing, caring, and empowering.

For this man, to return "home" was to go to his wife's home—to laugh with her family and to talk late at night with her parents who loved him, believed in him, and encouraged him. In fact, recently, this man—who is now forty years old—called his in-laws to ask if he could spend a weekend with them—visiting with the family, staying in the guest bedroom, and joining in their meals. They quickly replied, "Of course you can come!" It was like returning to his childhood and being healed by "the family." After the visit, this man remarked, "It's like being bathed and renewed again—and overcoming my youth and finding hope." With new strength, this man is becoming a model and mentor to his own mother and family and helping to rebuild stability and hope there.

In any distress or disease, true healing involves all four dimensions: the physical (including the best art and science available in the medical or alternative medical field, as well as keeping the body vital and strong), the social/emotional (including generating positive energy and avoiding negative energy such as criticism, envy, and hatred, as well as being connected to the support base created by family and friends who are all adding their faith, prayers, and support), the mental (including learning about illness and visualizing the immune system of the body fighting it), and the spiritual (including exercising faith and tapping into those spiritual powers higher than our own). Family renewal helps make this four-dimensional healing available to everyone in the family. It helps create the powerful immune system we talked about in Habit 6 that enables people to handle difficulties and setbacks, and promotes physical, social, mental, and spiritual health.

> *Sharpening the saw is the single highest leverage activity in life because it affects everything else so powerfully.*

Recognizing the power of renewal and renewing traditions in the family opens the door to all kinds of interaction and creativity in developing a beautiful family culture. In fact, sharpening the saw is the single highest leverage activity in life because it affects everything else so powerfully. It renews all the other habits and helps create a powerful magnetlike force in the family culture that consistently draws people toward the flight path and helps them stay on track.

As important as traditions are, it's good to remember that the best of them don't always work out perfectly. In our own family, for example, we get ready to go into the family room on Christmas morning. We line everyone up—youngest to oldest—on the stairs. We turn on Christmas music and set up the video camera. We say, "Is everyone excited? Okay, let's go!" And inevitably, in the stampede, the youngest one falls down and starts crying. When we all get together, there are a lot of people in one place. It's very crowded. And we occasionally have our arguments.

But, amazingly, through it all these traditions are the things people remember. These are the things that bond and unify and renew us as a family. They renew us socially and mentally and physically and spiritually. And with this renewal we are able to return refreshed to the everyday challenges of life.

SHARING THIS CHAPTER WITH ADULTS AND TEENS

Can Family Relationships Drift Apart?

- Review the material on pages 276–278. Ask family members: What is entropy? Discuss the idea that "all things need watching, working at, caring for, and marriage is no exception." Ask: In what ways might entropy become evident in a relationship?

What Are Some Ways to Bond the Family Together?

- Discuss: What traditions work best for our family? Responses might include family dinners, birthday celebrations, family vacations, holidays, or other occasions.

- Ask family members what traditions they have noticed in other families. Ask what they have seen these families do to effectively nurture their traditions.

- Review the material on pages 295–297. Ask family members what extended and intergenerational family traditions they enjoy or would like to establish.

- Discuss how renewing activities—such as having fun together, learning together, worshiping together, working together, and serving together—meet the basic needs to live, to love, to learn, to leave a legacy, and to laugh.

How Do You Nurture the Spirit of Family Renewal?

- Discuss the stories on pages 297–309. Ask family members: Are we taking the time to "sharpen the saw"? What can we do as a family to better practice the spirit of renewal?

SHARING THIS CHAPTER WITH CHILDREN

- Give each child paper and a pencil with a broken lead. Ask him or her to draw a picture of the family. It won't work. Ask the child to press a little harder. It still won't work. Ask: What needs to happen? The child will respond that the pencil needs to be sharpened. Now share the story of the woodcutter on page 277 and see what other things he or she can think of that need to be constantly maintained and renewed in order to work. Ask: What would happen if we forgot to buy gas? To have the brakes checked on the car? To buy groceries? To celebrate Mother's Day, someone's birthday, or some other event important to a family member? What can we do to ensure that we always sharpen the family saw?
- Exercise with your children. Play sports with them. Go for regular walks together. Sign up with them for swimming, golf, or some other lesson or activity. Continually remind one another of the importance of exercise and good health.
- Teach your children what you want them to know! Teach them the importance of working, reading, studying, completing homework. Don't assume that someone else will teach them life's most important lessons.
- Attend age-appropriate cultural events together, such as plays, dance recitals, concerts, and choir performances. Encourage your children to participate in activities that will help them develop their talents.
- Sign up to learn some new skill together with your child, such as sewing, woodworking, pie-making, or word processing.
- Involve your children in planning your family vacations.
- Together, decide on ways to make family birthdays extra special.
- Talk about what makes holidays special for your children.
- Involve your children in your spiritual life. Let them accompany you to your place of worship. Share any special feelings you have about a higher power. Worship together. Read together. Pray together, if that is part of your belief.
- Become involved with your children in weekly family service projects.
- Schedule on your calendar fun times together such as going to ball games, hiking in the mountains, playing on the swings in the park, playing miniature golf, or going to the ice cream store.
- Involve the children in making dinnertime more special. Have them take turns setting and decorating the table, choosing the dessert, and maybe even selecting a conversation topic. Be consistent in gathering your family around the dinner table to enjoy a meal together.

FROM SURVIVAL...
TO STABILITY...
TO SUCCESS...
TO SIGNIFICANCE

I don't know what your destiny will be, but one thing I know: The only ones among you who will really be happy are those who have sought and found how to serve.

—Albert Schweitzer

Now that we've been through each of the 7 Habits, I'd like to share with you the "bigger picture" of the power of this inside-out approach and how these habits work together to make it happen.

To begin with, I'd like to ask you to read a fascinating account of one woman's inside-out odyssey. Notice how this experience reveals a proactive, courageous soul becoming a force of nature in her own right. Notice the impact her approach has on her, on her family, and on society:

By the time I was nineteen, I was divorced with a two-year-old child. We were in difficult circumstances, but I wanted to make the best possible life for my son. We had very little food. In fact, I reached the point where I would give food to my son but I wouldn't eat. I lost so much weight that a coworker asked me if I was sick, and I finally broke down and told her what had happened. She put me in touch with Aid to Families with Dependent Children, which made it possible for me to attend community college.

At that point I still had this vision in my mind that I'd had when I was seventeen and pregnant with my son—a vision that I would go to college. I had no idea how I was going to do it. At seventeen I didn't even have a high school diploma. But I just knew I was going to make a difference in the lives of others and be a light to others who faced the darkness I was facing. That vision was so strong that it got me through everything—including doing what was necessary to graduate from high school.

As I entered community college at nineteen, I still didn't see how my vision was going to be fulfilled. How was I going to help anybody when I was still pretty traumatized from going through it all myself? But I felt driven because of the vision and because of my son. I wanted him to have a good life. I wanted him to have food and clothes and a yard to play in and an education. And I couldn't provide those things for him without getting an education myself. So I kept rationalizing, "If I can just get a degree and make money, we will have a good life." And I went to school and worked really hard.

When I was twenty-two I got married for the second time—this time to a wonderful man. We had a beautiful little daughter. I quit school to be with my children while they were small. We managed to make it okay financially, but I was still obsessed with fighting that monster called hunger. I just could not let that go. So when my children were a little older, it was "get the degree or bust." My husband was basically "Mom" to the kids while I went to school.

I finally completed my degree—two, in fact: a four-year degree and a master's degree in business administration. And this turned out to be very helpful. Later, when my husband lost his job as a factory worker, I was able to help him through school. My education saved us financially. He got his bachelor's and master's degrees and has been a counselor for several years now. He said he doesn't think he would have done it without my support.

For some time I was very busy working and raising my family, and I thought: I've done it. I got my degree. I have a successful family. I should be happy. But then I realized that my vision had included helping others, and that still wasn't part of my life. So when one of the alumni directors at school asked me to speak at an honors night for graduating seniors, I agreed. When I asked her what she wanted me to talk about, she said, "Just tell them how you got your education."

To be quite honest, standing up in front of a group of at least two hundred highly educated women who were going to be honored for their expertise in science and math was a bit overwhelming. The thought of telling them where I had come from was not very thrilling to me. But by this time I'd learned about mission statements and I'd written one. It basically said that my mission in life was to help others to see the best in themselves. And I think it was the mission statement that gave me the courage to share my story.

I went into that speech making deals with God: "Okay, I'm going to do this. But if it fails, I'm never going to tell my story again." It turned out to be a success because of what occurred afterward. After listening to my story, several of the faculty women got together and decided to do something to help welfare mothers, and the school started a scholarship fund. It was named after a woman who believed that if you educate a woman, you make a great impact not only on her life but on the lives of her children.

I was happy about what had happened and figured I'd done my part to help others, but then a little later I went through a developmental course for women where I had the opportunity to share my story again. One of the women there got the idea that we should fund a scholarship for one low-income woman, and we all agreed that we would each contribute $125 a year to do this.

From those beginnings my efforts have grown so that now I act as an advisor on a scholarship board for welfare women at a local women's liberal arts college. I'm also involved in fund-raising for a scholarship for low-income women with high potential. These things may not seem like much to some, but I know what a big difference they can make. I had a lot of help along the way from people who felt they were doing "small things," and I hope the small things I do for others now show my thanks.

All of this has had a positive impact on my family as well. My son, who is now working on his master's degree, has a job where he helps people who have disabilities. He is very committed to these people and to their welfare. And my daughter—a first-year college student—is a volunteer teacher of English as a second language. She is also very committed to the underprivileged. They both seem to have a sense of responsibility to others. They have a deep awareness of the importance of contribution and actively seek it. And my husband's work as a counselor provides a constant opportunity for him to serve people in a very personal way as well.

I guess I hadn't really thought about it before, but as I look at it now, I see that in one way or another our entire family is serving and contributing to society as a whole. That makes me feel as though my vision is coming to pass—in a more expanded and complete way than I had originally understood it.

I believe that helping others is the most significant contribution anyone can make in life. I'm grateful that we've developed to the point where we're able to do it.

Just think about the difference this woman's proactivity has made in her own life, in the lives of the members of her family, and in the lives of all those who have benefited from her contribution. What a tribute to the resiliency of the human spirit! Instead of allowing her circumstances to overpower the vision she had inside, she held on to it and nurtured it so that it eventually became the driving force that empowered her to rise above those circumstances.

Notice how, in the process, she and her family moved through each of the four levels mentioned in the title of this chapter.

Survival

At first this woman's consuming concern was for the basic need for food. She was hungry. Her child was hungry. The one focus of her life was to make enough to feed her son and herself so that they wouldn't starve. This need to survive was so basic, so fundamental, so vital that even when her circumstances changed, she was still "obsessed with fighting that monster called hunger" and "could not let that go."

This represents the first level: *survival*. And many families, many marriages, are literally fighting for it—not only economically but also mentally, spiritually, and socially as well. These people's lives are filled with uncertainty and fear. They're scrambling to make it through the day. They live in a world of chaos with no predictable principles to operate from, no structures or schedules to depend on, no sense of what tomorrow is going to hold. They often feel that they are victims of circumstances or of other people's injustice. They're like a person who has been rushed into the emergency room and then put into the intensive care unit: Their vital signs may be present but are unstable and unpredictable.

Eventually these families may hone their survival skills. They may even have brief breathing spaces between their efforts to survive. But their day-in, day-out objective is simply to survive.

Stability

Going back to the story, you'll notice that through her efforts and help from others, this woman eventually moved from survival to *stability*. She had food and the basic necessities of life. She even had a stable marriage relationship. Although she was still struggling with scars from the "survival" days, she and her family were functional.

This represents the second level, which is what many families and marriages are trying to achieve. They're surviving, but different work schedules and different habit patterns result in their hardly ever getting together to talk about what would bring more stability to the marriage or family. They live in a state of disorganization. They don't know what to do; they have a sense of futility and feel trapped.

But the more knowledge these individuals acquire, the more hope they get. And as they act on this knowledge and begin to organize some schedules and some structures for communication and problem-solving, even more hope emerges. The hope overcomes ignorance and futility. And the family, the marriage, becomes stable, dependable, and predictable.

So they're stable—but they're not yet "successful." There's a degree of organization so that food is provided and bills are paid. But the problem-solving strategy is usually limited to "flight or fight." People's lives touch from time to time in order to deal with the most pressing issues, but there's no real depth in the communication. People generally find their satisfactions away from the family. "Home" is just a place that has to take you in. There's boredom. Interdependence is exhausting. There's no sense of shared accomplishment. There's no real happiness, love, joy, or peace.

Success

The third level, *success*, involves accomplishing worthy goals. These goals can be economic, such as having more income, managing existing income better, or agreeing to cut expenses in order to save or have money for education or a planned vacation. They can be mental, such as learning some new skill or getting a degree. You'll notice that most of the goals reflected in this woman's story were in these two areas. They involved economic well-being and education. But goals can also be social, such as having more time together as a family with good communication or establishing traditions. Or they can be spiritual, such as creating a sense of shared vision and values and renewing their faith and common beliefs.

In successful families, people set and achieve meaningful goals. "Family" matters to people. There's genuine happiness in being together. There's a sense of excitement and confidence. Successful families plan and carry out family activities and organize to accomplish different tasks. The focus is on better living, better loving, and better learning, and on renewing the family through fun family activities and traditions.

But even in many "successful" families, a dimension is missing. Look back once again at this woman's account. She said, "For some time I was very busy working and raising my family, and I thought: I've done it. I got my degree. I have a successful family. I should be happy. But then I realized that my vision had included helping others, and that still wasn't part of my life."

Significance

The fourth level, *significance*, is where the family is involved in something meaningful outside itself. Rather than being content to be a successful family, the family has a sense of stewardship or responsibility to the greater family of mankind, as well as a sense of accountability around that stewardship. The family mission includes the leaving of some kind of legacy—of reaching out to other families who may be at risk, of participating together to make a real difference in the community or in the larger society, possibly through their church or other service organizations. This contribution brings a deeper and higher fulfillment—not just to individual family members but to the family as a whole.

The woman in this story felt a sense of responsibility and began to contribute in her own life. And because of her example, her children developed it in their lives. Families ideally would reach the point where this sense of stewardship or responsibility would be an integral part of their family mission statement—something the entire family would be involved in.

At times that might mean that one family member would contribute in a particular way and the rest of the family would work together to support that effort. In our own family, for example, it meant that we all rallied around Sandra to support her when she spent hours working as president of a women's service organization. We tried to provide support and encouragement for some of our children when they chose to devote a couple of years to church service in foreign lands. We've all felt a sense of unity and contribution over the years as the family supported me in my work—and later some of our children's work—in the Covey Leadership Center (now Franklin Covey). All of these things have been family efforts, though not all family members were involved directly in making the contribution.

There are other times when the entire family is directly involved in something such as a community project. I know of one family that works together to provide visits and entertaining videos for elderly people in rest homes. This began when their own grandmother had a stroke that forced them to put her in a rest home, and it seemed the only thing she really enjoyed was videos. The family decided that they would visit her at least once a week and bring her different old movies from the video store. It became such a success with the grandmother and with other patients that they started getting videos for others as well. Through all the years the five children in this family were teenagers, they continued serving in this manner. And it helped these kids not only to stay close to their grandmother but also to serve many other older people.

Another family spends each New Year's Eve cooking for and feeding the homeless. They hold several planning meetings beforehand, deciding what they want to serve, how to decorate the tables, and who's going to take care of what responsibility. It's become a joyous tradition for them to work together to provide a wonderful evening in the county soup kitchen for the poor.

I'm aware of many other families in which contribution has meant, at least for a time, rallying around an extended or intergenerational family member in need. One husband and father shared how his family did this:

Near the end of 1989 my father was diagnosed with a brain tumor. For sixteen months we fought it with chemotherapy and radiation. Finally, near the end of 1990, he was no longer able to take care of himself, and my mother—who was in her 70s—was unable to provide the help he needed.

My wife and I were therefore confronted with some very serious decisions. After discussing it together, we decided to move my mother and father into our home. We put my father in a hospital bed in the middle of our family room, and that's where he stayed for the next three months until he died.

I realize now that had I not had the grounding of principles and a clear understanding of what "first things" meant in my life, I might not have made that decision. But although this was one of the most difficult times in my life, it was also one of the most rewarding. I feel I can look back and know that we did what was the right thing to do in our circumstances. We did everything we possibly could to make him comfortable. We gave him the best it is humanly possibly to give—our selves. And we feel good about that.

The intimacy we were able to develop with my father in those last months was profound. Not only did my wife and I learn from this experience, but my mother did also. She knows she can look forward to the future and trust how we would handle the situation should she get into a similar position. And our children learned invaluable lessons in service as they watched what my wife and I did, and helped in the ways they could.

For those few months the significant contribution of this family was to help a father and grandfather die with dignity, surrounded by love. What a powerful message this sent to his wife and to everyone else in the family! And how enabling this experience will be for these children as they grow up with a sense of genuine service and love.

Often, even those who suffer in these difficult situations can leave a legacy of inspiration for their families. My own life has been profoundly affected by my sister Marilyn's example of contribution and significance as she lay dying of cancer. Two nights before she passed away, she told me, "My only desire during this time has been to teach my children and grandchildren how to die with dignity and to give them the desire to contribute—to live life nobly based on principles." Her whole focus during the weeks and months prior to this time had been on teaching her children and grandchildren, and I know they will be inspired and ennobled by her example—as I have been—for the rest of their lives.

There are many ways to become involved in significance—within the family, with other families, and in society as a whole. We have friends and relatives whose intergenerational and extended families have rallied around them in their struggles with a Down's syndrome child, a severe drug problem, an overwhelming financial problem, or a failing marriage. The entire family culture went to work and came to the

> *There are many ways to become involved in significance—within the family, with other families, and in society as a whole.*

aid of those so involved, enabling them to reclaim their heritage and erase many psychic scars of the past.

Families can also become involved in local schools or communities to increase drug awareness, reduce crime, or assist children in families that are at risk. They can become involved in fund-raising, mentoring programs, tutoring programs, or other church or community service. Or they can become involved in significance on a higher level of interdependence—not just within the family but between families on common projects. This might include families working together in a "Neighborhood Watch" program or joining forces with other community- or church-sponsored service projects or events.

There are even some communities in the world where the entire population is involved in a massive interdependent and significant effort. One is Mauritius—a tiny, developing island nation in the Indian Ocean, two thousand miles off the east coast of Africa. The norm for the 1.3 million people who live there is to work together to survive economically, take care of the children, and nurture a culture of both independence and interdependence. They train people in marketable skills so that there is no unemployment or homelessness and very little poverty or crime. The interesting thing is that these people come from five distinct and very different cultures. Their differences are profound, yet they value these differences so highly that they even celebrate each other's religious holidays! Their deeply integrated interdependence reflects their values of order, harmony, cooperation, and synergy, and their concern for all people—particularly children.

Contributing together as a family not only helps those who benefit from the contribution, but it also strengthens the contributing family.

Contributing together as a family not only helps those who benefit from the contribution, but it also strengthens the contributing family in the process. Can you imagine anything more energizing, more unifying, more filled with satisfaction than working with the members of your family to accomplish something that really makes a difference in the world? Can you imagine the bonding, the sense of fulfillment, the sense of shared joy?

Living outside ourselves in love actually helps the family become self-perpetuating. Its very giving increases the family's sense of purpose and thus its longevity and ability to give. Hans Selye, the father of modern stress research, taught that the best way to stay strong, healthy, and alive is to follow the credo, "Earn thy neighbor's love." In other words, stay involved in meaningful, service-oriented projects and pursuits. He explains that the reason women live longer than men is psychological rather than physiological. A woman's work is never done. Built into her psyche and cultural reinforcement is a continuing responsibility toward the family. Many men, on the other hand, center their lives on their careers and identify themselves in terms of these careers. Their family becomes secondary, and when they retire, they do not have this same sense of continuing service and contribution. As a result, the degenerative forces in the body are accelerated and the immune system is compromised, and so men tend to die earlier. There is much wisdom in the saying by an unknown author, "I sought my God, and my God I could not find. I sought my soul, and my soul eluded me. I sought to serve my brother in his need, and I found all three—my God, my soul, and thee."

On the level of significance, the family becomes the vehicle through which people can effectively contribute to the well-being of others.

This level of significance is the supreme level of family fulfillment. Nothing energizes, unites, and satisfies the family like working together to make a significant contribution. This is the essence of true family leadership—not only the leadership you can provide to the family, but the leadership your family can provide to other families, to the neighborhood, to the community, to the country. On the level of significance, no longer is the family an end in and of itself. It becomes the means to an end that is greater than itself. It becomes the vehicle through which people can effectively contribute to the well-being of others.

From Problem-Solving to Creating

As you move toward your destination as a family, you may find it helpful to look at these four different levels as interim destinations on your path. The achieving of each destination represents a challenge in and of itself, but it may also provide the wherewithal to move to the next destination.

You will also want to be aware that in moving from survival to significance, there's a dramatic shift in thinking. In the areas of survival and stability, the primary mental energy focus is on problem-solving:

"How can we provide food and shelter?"

"What can we do about Daryl's behavior or Sara's grades?"

"How can we get rid of the pain in our relationship?"

"How can we get out of debt?"

But as you move toward success and significance, that focus shifts to creating goals and visions and purposes that ultimately transcend the family itself:

"What kinds of education do we want to provide for our children?"

"What would we like our financial picture to look like five or ten years down the road?"

"How can we strengthen family relationships?"

"What can we do together as a family that will really make a difference?"

DESTINATIONS

CREATING

SIGNIFICANCE

SUCCESS

STABILITY

SURVIVAL

**PROBLEM-
SOLVING**

That doesn't mean that families who have moved to success and significance don't have problems to solve. They do. But the *major* focus is on creating. Instead of trying to eliminate negative things from the family, they're focused on trying to create positive things that were not there before—new goals, new options, new alternatives that will optimize situations. Instead of rushing from one problem-solving crisis to another, they're focused on coming up with synergistic springboards to future contribution and fulfillment.

> When you're problem minded, you want to eliminate something. When you're opportunity or vision minded, you want to bring something into existence.

In short, they're opportunity minded, not problem minded. When you're problem minded, you want to eliminate something. When you're opportunity or vision minded, you want to bring something into existence.

And this is an altogether different mind-set, a different emotional/spiritual orientation. And it leads to a completely different feeling in the culture. It's like the difference between feeling exhausted from morning until night and feeling rested, energized, and enthused. Instead of feeling frustrated, mired in concerns, and surrounded by dark clouds of despair, you feel optimistic, invigorated, and full of hope. You're filled with positive energy that leads to a creative, synergistic mode. Focused on your vision, you take problems in stride.

The wonderful thing about moving from survival to significance is that it has very little to do with extrinsic circumstances. One woman said this:

We've discovered that economics really has very little to do with achieving significance as a family. Now that we have more, we're able to do more. But even in the early years of our marriage, we were able to give of our time and talents to help others. And it really united us as a family. When our children were very young, we were able to teach them the value of helping a neighbor, visiting a rest home, or taking a meal to someone who was sick. We found that these kinds of things helped define our family: "We are a family who helps others." And that made a big difference while our children were growing up. I am convinced that their teenage years were very different because of that contribution focus.

Driving and Restraining Forces

As you move from survival toward significance, you'll find that there are forces that energize you and help move you forward. Knowledge and hope will push you toward stability. Excitement and confidence drive you toward success. A sense of stewardship and a contribution vision will impel you toward significance. These things are like the tailwinds that help an airplane move more quickly toward its destination—sometimes arriving before the scheduled time.

But you'll also find there are strong headwinds—forces that tend to restrain you, to slow or even reverse your progress, to push you back, to keep you from moving ahead. Victimism and fear tend to drive you back into the fundamental struggle for survival. Lack of knowledge and a sense of futility tend to keep you from becoming stable. Feelings of boredom and escapism thwart the effort to be successful. Self-focused vision and a sense of ownership—rather than stewardship—tend to keep you from significance.

You'll notice that the restraining forces are generally more emotional, psychological, and illogical; driving forces are more logical, structural, and proactive.

Of course, we need to do what we can to power up the driving forces. This is the traditional approach. But in a force field, the restraining forces will eventually restore the old equilibrium.

Most important, we need to remove restraining forces. To ignore them is like trying to move toward your destination with your thrusters in reverse. You can put forth all kinds of effort, but unless you do something to remove the restraining forces, you'll be going nowhere fast, and the effort will exhaust you. You do need to work on driving and restraining forces at the same time, but give the

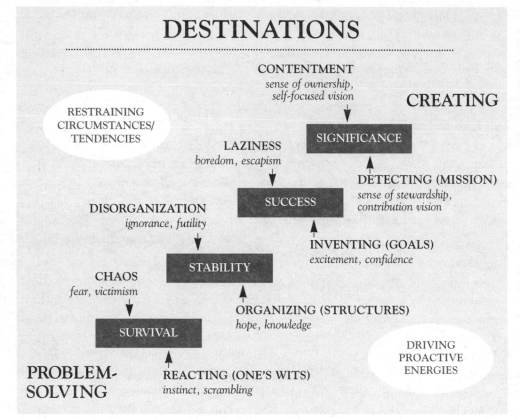

DESTINATIONS

primary effort to working on the restraining forces.

Habits 1, 2, 3, and 7 fire up the driving forces. They build proactivity. They give you a clear, motivating sense of destination that is greater than self. In fact, without some kind of vision or mission of significance, the course of least resistance is to stay in your comfort zone, to use only those talents and gifts that are already developed and perhaps recognized by others. But when you share this vision of true significance, of stewardship, of contribution, then the course of least resistance will be to develop those capacities and fulfill that vision because fulfilling the vision becomes more compelling than the pain of leaving your comfort zone. This is what family leadership is about—the creating of this kind of compelling vision, the securing of consensual commitment toward it and toward doing whatever it takes to fulfill it. This is what taps into people's deepest motivations and urges them to become their very best. Then Habits 4, 5, and 6 give you the process for working together to accomplish all those things. And Habit 7 gives you the renewing power to keep doing it.

But Habits 4, 5, and 6 also enable you to understand and unfreeze the restraining cultural, emotional, social, and illogical forces so that even the smallest amount of proactive energy on the positive side can make tremendous gains. In fact, a deep understanding of the fears and anxieties that hold you back changes their nature, content, and direction, enabling you to actually convert restraining forces into driving ones. We see this all the time when a so-called problem person feels listened to and understood and then becomes part of the solution.

Consider the analogy of a car. If you had one foot on the gas pedal and the other foot on the brake, which would be the better approach to go faster—flooring the gas pedal or releasing the brake? Obviously, the key is to release the brake. You could even lighten up on the gas pedal and still go faster as long as you got that other foot off the brake.

Similarly, Habits 4, 5, and 6 release the emotional brake (or give air) in the family so that even the slightest increase in driving forces will take the culture to a new level. In fact, there is extensive research to show that by involving people in the problems and working out the solution together, restraining forces are transformed into driving forces.[1]

So these habits enable you to work on driving and restraining forces at the same time and free you to move from survival to significance. You may find it helpful to go over the chart on the previous page with your family to get a sense of perspective, to see where you feel you are as a family, and to identify driving and restraining forces, and decide what to do about them. You may also want to use it as a tool to help your family move from a problem-solving to a creative orientation.

> *Consider the analogy of a car. If you had one foot on the gas pedal and the other foot on the brake, which would be the better approach to go faster—flooring the gas pedal or releasing the brake?*

Where Do I Begin?

Most of us have an innate desire to improve our families. Subconsciously we want to move from survival toward success or significance. But we often have a tough time. We may try as hard as we possibly can and do everything we can think of, and yet the results may be the exact opposite of the ones we want.

This is especially true when we're dealing with a spouse or a teenager. But even when we're dealing with young children, who are generally more open to influence, we wonder how to influence them in the best possible way. Do we punish? Do we spank? Do we send them to a room by themselves? Is it right to use our superior size or strength or mental development to force them to do what we want them to do? Or are there principles that can help us understand and know how to influence in a better way?

Any parent (or son, daughter, brother, sister, grandparent, aunt, uncle, nephew, niece, or other person) who really wants to become a transition person—an agent of change—and help a family move higher on the destination chart can do it, particularly if the person understands and lives the principles behind the four basic family leadership roles. Because family is a natural, living, growing thing, we'd like to describe these roles in terms of what we call the Principle-Centered Family Leadership Tree. This tree serves as a reminder that we're dealing with nature and with natural laws or principles. It will help you understand these four basic leadership roles and also help you diagnose and think through strategies to resolve family problems. (You might want to take a look at the tree on page 337.)

With the image of this tree in mind, let's take a look at the four family leadership roles and how cultivating the 7 Habits in each role can help you move your family along the path from survival to significance.

Modeling

I know of one man who loved to go hunting with his father when he was a young boy. The father would plan weeks ahead with his sons, preparing and creating anticipation for the event.

As an adult, this son told us:

I will never forget one Saturday opening of the pheasant hunt. Dad, my older brother, and I were up at 4:00 A.M. We ate Mom's big, hearty breakfast, packed the car, and drove to our designated field by 6:00 A.M. We arrived early to stake out our spot before any others, anticipating the 8:00 A.M. opening hour.

As that hour drew near, other hunters were frantically driving around us, trying to find spots in which to hunt. As 7:40 arrived, we saw hunters driving into the fields. By 7:45 the firing had started—fifteen minutes before the official start. We looked at Dad. He made no move except to look at his watch, still waiting for 8:00 A.M. Soon the birds were flying. By 7:50 all hunters had moved into the fields, and shots were everywhere.

Dad looked at his watch and said, "The hunt starts at eight o'clock, boys." About three minutes before eight, four hunters drove into our spot and walked past us into our field. We looked at Dad. He said, "The hunt starts for us at eight." At eight the birds were gone, but we started our drive into the field.

We didn't get any birds that day. We did get an unforgettable memory of a man I fervently wanted to be like—my father, my ideal, who taught me absolute integrity.

Now what was at the center of this father's life—the pleasure and recognition of being a successful hunter or the quiet soul satisfaction of being a man of integrity, a father, and a model of integrity to his boys?

On the other hand, I also know of another man who set quite a different example for his son. His wife recently said to us:

My husband, Jerry, leaves the guidance of our fourteen-year-old son Sam to me. It's been that way ever since Sam was born. Jerry has always been sort of an uninvolved observer. He never tries to help.

Whenever I get after him and tell him he should get involved, he just shrugs. He tells me he has nothing to offer, and I am the one who should teach and lead our son.

Sam is now in junior high school, and you would not believe the problems he has! I told Jerry that the next time Sam's school principal called, he would have to take the call because I've had it. That night Jerry told Sam that his mom wasn't going to help him anymore, so he'd better quit causing problems.

I got so mad when he said that, I just wanted to get up and leave. When I exploded, Jerry said, "Hey, don't blame me. You're the one who's been in charge. You've taught and led him, not me."

Who is really teaching and leading this young boy? And what is this father teaching his son? The father has tried to forfeit his influential position by stepping aside and supposedly letting his wife do the influencing. But has he not had a powerful influence as well? When Sam grows up, won't his father's actions (or lack of actions) have influenced him in profound ways?

There is no question that example is the very foundation of influence. When Albert Schweitzer was asked how to raise children, he said, "Three principles—first, example; second, example; and third, example." We are, first and foremost, models to our children. What they see in us speaks far more loudly than anything we could ever say. You cannot hide or disguise your deepest self. In spite of skillful pretending and posturing, your real desires, values, beliefs, and feelings come out in a thousand ways. Again, you teach only what you are—no more, no less.

That's why the deepest part of this Principle-Centered Family Leadership Tree—the thick fibrous root structure—represents your role as a model.

This is your personal example. It's the consistency and integrity of your own life. This is what gives credibility to everything you try to do in the family. As people see in your life the model of what you're trying to encourage in the lives of others, they feel they can believe in you and can trust you because you are trustworthy.

> *You cannot not model. It's impossible. People will see your example— positive or negative—as a pattern for the way life is to be lived.*

The interesting thing is that, like it or not, you are a model. And if you're a parent, you are your children's *first and foremost* model. In fact, *you cannot not model. It's impossible.* People will see your example—positive or negative—as a pattern for the way life is to be lived.

As one unknown author so beautifully expressed it:

If a child lives with criticism, he learns to condemn.
If a child lives with security, he learns to have faith in himself.
If a child lives with hostility, he learns to fight.
If a child lives with acceptance, he learns to love.
If a child lives with fear, he learns to be apprehensive.
If a child lives with recognition, he learns to have a goal.
If a child lives with pity, he learns to be sorry for himself.
If a child lives with approval, he learns to like himself.
If a child lives with jealousy, he learns to feel guilty.
If a child lives with friendliness, he learns that the world is a nice place in which to live.

If we are careful observers, we can see our own weaknesses reappear in the lives of our children. Perhaps this is most evident in the way differences and disagreements are handled. To illustrate, a mother goes to the family room to call her young sons to lunch and finds them arguing and fighting over a toy. "Boys, I've told you before not to fight! You work it out so each has a turn." The older grabs it away from his smaller brother with "I'm first!" The younger cries and refuses to come to lunch.

The mother, puzzled as to why her boys never seem to learn, reflects for a moment on her own handling of differences with her husband. She remembers "only last night" when they had a sharp exchange over a matter of finances. She remembers "only this morning" when her husband left for work rather disgruntled after a disagreement on plans for the evening. And the more this mother reflects, the more she realizes she and her husband have demonstrated over and over again how not to handle differences and disagreements.

This book is filled with stories that illustrate how the thinking and actions of children are shaped by what parents think and do. The thinking of the parents will be inherited by their children, sometimes to the third and fourth generations. Parents have been scripted by their parents . . . who have been scripted by *their* parents in ways that none of the generations may even be aware of.

That is why our role modeling as parents to our children is our most basic, most sacred, most spiritual responsibility. We are handing life's scripts to our children—scripts that, in all likelihood, will be acted out for much of the rest of their lives. How important it is for us to realize that our day-to-day modeling is far and away our highest form of influence in our children's lives! And how important it is for us to examine what is really at the "center" of our lives, to ask ourselves, Who am I? How do I define myself? (Security) Where do I go and what do I do to receive direction to guide my life? (Guidance) How does life work? How should I live my life? (Wisdom) What resources and influences do I access to nurture myself and others? (Power) Whatever is our "center," or the lens through which we look at life, will profoundly affect our children's thinking—whether we are aware of it and whether we want to have this influence or not.

If you choose to live the 7 Habits in your personal life, what is it that your children will learn? Your modeling will provide an example of a proactive person who has developed a personal mission statement and is attempting to live by it; of a person who has great respect and love for others, who seeks to understand them and be understood by them, who believes in the power of synergy and is not afraid to take risks in working with others to create new third-alternative solutions. You will provide a model of a person who is in a state of constant renewal—of physical self-control and vitality, continual learning, continual building of relationships, and constant attempting to align with principles.

What impact will that kind of model have on your children's lives?

Mentoring

I know a man who is very committed to his family. Even though he is involved in many good and worthwhile activities, the most important thing to him by far is to teach his children and to help them become responsible, caring, contributing adults. And he is an excellent model of all he is trying to teach.

He has a large family, and one summer two of his daughters were planning to marry. One evening when they both had their fiancés in the family home, he sat down with all four of them and spent several hours talking with them, sharing many things he had learned that he knew would help them along the way.

Later, after he had gone upstairs to get ready for bed, his daughters went to their mother and said, "Dad just wants to teach us; he doesn't want to get to know us personally." In other words, Dad just wants to dispense all this wisdom and knowledge he has accumulated through the years, but does he really know us as individuals? Does he accept us? Does he really care about us, just as we are? Until they knew that, until they could feel that unconditional love, they were not open to his influence—however good that influence might have been.

Again, as the saying goes, "I don't care how much you know until I know how much you care." That's why the next level of the tree—the massive, sturdy trunk—represents your role as a *mentor*. "Mentoring" is building relationships. It's investing in the Emotional Bank Account. It's letting people know that you care about them—deeply, sincerely, personally, unconditionally. It's championing them.

This deep, genuine caring encourages people to become open, teachable, and open to influence because it creates a profound feeling of trust. This clearly reaffirms the relationship we mentioned in Habit 1 between the Primary Laws of Love and the Primary Laws of Life. Again, only when you live the Primary Laws of Love—when you consistently make deposits in the Emotional Bank Accounts of others because you love them unconditionally and because of their intrinsic worth rather than because of their behavior or social status or for any other reason—do you encourage obedience to the Primary Laws of Life, laws such as honesty, integrity, respect, responsibility, and trust.

> *The way you fulfill your mentoring role will have a profound effect on your child's sense of self-worth and on your ability to influence and teach.*

Now, if you're a parent, it's important to realize that whatever your relationship with your children, you are their first mentor—someone who relates to them, someone whose love they deeply desire. Positively or negatively, *you cannot not mentor.* You are your children's first source of physical and emotional security or insecurity, their feeling of being loved or being neglected. And the way you fulfill your mentoring role will have a profound effect on your child's sense of self-worth and on your ability to influence and teach.

The way you fulfill your mentoring role with any family member—*but particularly with your most difficult child*—will have a profound impact on the level of trust in the entire family. As we said in Habit 6, the key to your family culture is how you treat the child that tests you the most. It is that child who will really test your ability to love unconditionally. When you can show unconditional love to that one, the other children will know that your love for them is also unconditional.

I have become convinced there is almost unbelievable power in loving another person in five ways simultaneously:

1. **Empathizing**: listening with your own heart to another's heart.
2. **Sharing** authentically your most deeply felt insights, learnings, emotions, and convictions.
3. **Affirming** the other person with a profound sense of belief, valuation, confirmation, appreciation, and encouragement.
4. **Praying** with and for the other person from the depths of your soul, tapping into the energy and wisdom of higher powers.
5. **Sacrificing** for the other person: going the second mile, doing far more than is expected, caring and serving until it sometimes even hurts.

Most often neglected of the five are empathizing, affirming, and sacrificing. Many people will pray for others; many will share. But to truly listen empathically, to truly believe in and affirm others, and to walk with them in some kind of sacrifice mode so that you are doing what they would not expect you to do—in addition to praying and sharing—reaches people in ways that nothing else can.

One of the biggest mistakes people make is trying to teach (or influence or warn or discipline) before they have the relationship to sustain it. The next time you feel inclined to try to teach or correct your child, you might want to push your pause button and ask yourself this: Is my relationship with this child sufficient to sustain this effort? Is there enough reserve in the Emotional Bank Account to enable this child to have an open ear, or will my words just bounce off as though he or she were surrounded by some kind of bulletproof shield? It's very easy to get so caught up in the emotion of the moment that we don't stop to ask ourselves if what we're about to do will be effective—if it will accomplish what we really want to accomplish. And if it won't, much of the time it's because there's not enough reserve to sustain it.

So you can make deposits into the Emotional Bank Account. You can build the relationship. You can mentor. As people feel your love and caring, they will begin to value themselves and become more open to your influence as you try to teach. What people identify with far more than what they hear is what they see and what they feel.

Organizing

You could be a wonderful model and have a great relationship with the members of your family, but if your family is not organized effectively to help you accomplish what you're trying to accomplish, then you're going to be working against yourself.

It's like the business that talks teamwork and cooperation but then has systems—such as compensation—that reward competition and individual achievement. Instead of being in alignment with and facilitating what you want to accomplish, the way you have things organized actually gets in the way.

In a like manner, in your family you may talk "love" and "family fun," but if you never plan any time together to have family dinners, work on projects, go on vacations, watch a movie, or have a picnic in the park, then your very lack of organization gets in the way. You may say "I love you" to someone, but if you're always too busy to spend meaningful one-on-one time with that person and fail to prioritize that relationship, you will allow entropy and decay to set in.

> You may talk "love" and "family fun," but if you never plan any time together, then your very lack of organization gets in the way.

Your organizing role is where you would align the structures and systems in the family to help you accomplish what's truly important. This is where you would use the power of Habits 4, 5, and 6 at the mentoring level to create your family mission statement and set up two new structures that most families don't have: dedicated weekly family times and calendared one-on-one dates. These are the structures and systems that will make it possible to carry out the things you're trying to do in your family.

Without creating principle-based patterns and structures, you will not be able to build a culture with common vision and shared values. Moral authority will be sporadic and shallow because it will be based only on the present actions of a few people. It won't be built into the culture of the family.

But the more moral or ethical authority grows and becomes institutionalized into the culture in the form of principles—both lived and structurally embodied— the less dependent you are on individual persons to maintain a beautiful family culture. The mores and norms inside the culture itself will reinforce the principles. The very fact that you have weekly family time says a hundredfold that family is truly important. So even though someone may be flaky or duplicitous and someone else may be lazy, the setting up of these structures and processes compensates for most— though not all—of those human deficiencies. It builds the principles into the patterns and structures that people can depend on. And the results are similar to those that happen when you go on a vacation: A family may have emotional ups and downs on a vacation, but the fact that they went on a vacation together and that it was renewing a tradition builds the principles into the culture. It frees the family from always being dependent on good example.

Again, in the words of sociologist Émile Durkheim, "When mores are sufficient, laws are unnecessary. When mores are insufficient, laws are unenforceable." In adapting this to the family we might say, "When mores are sufficient, family rules are unnecessary. When mores are insufficient, family rules are unenforceable."

> "When mores are sufficient, family rules are unnecessary. When mores are insufficient, family rules are unenforceable."

Ultimately, if people won't support the patterns and structures, then you'll see instability enter the family, and the family may even struggle for survival. But if these patterns become habits, they become strong enough to subordinate individual weaknesses that manifest themselves from time to time. For example, you may not begin a one-on-one or family time with the best of feelings, but if you spend the entire evening doing some fun thing together, you'll probably end with the best of feelings.

This is one of the most powerful things that I have learned in my professional work with organizations. You must build the principles into the structures and systems so that they become part of the culture itself. Then you are no longer dependent on a few people at the top. I've seen situations in which an entire top management team moved into another company, but because of the "deep bench strength" in the culture, there was hardly a blip in the economic and social performance of the organization. This is one of the great insights of W. Edwards Deming, a guru in the field of quality and management and one of the key reasons for Japan's past economic success. "The problem is not in bad people, it's in bad processes, bad structures and systems." [2]

That is why we give such energy to this organizing role. Without some basic organizing it's easy for family members to become like ships that pass in the night. So the third level of this tree—depicted by the trunk breaking out into the larger and then smaller limbs—represents your role as an *organizer*. This is where people experience how the principles are built into the patterns and structures of everyday life so that not only do you *say* that family is important but they *experience* it—in frequent meals together, family times, and meaningful one-on-ones. Soon they come to trust these family structures and patterns. They can depend on them, and this gives them a sense of security and order and predictability.

By organizing around your deepest priorities, you're creating alignment and order. You're setting up systems and structures that support—rather than get in the way of—what you're trying to do. Organizing becomes an enabler—literally transforming restraining factors into driving or enabling factors on the path from survival to significance.

Teaching

When one of our sons started junior high school, he began coming home with poor test scores. Sandra took him aside and said, "Look, I know you're not dumb. What seems to be the problem?"

"I don't know," he mumbled.

"Well," she said, "let's see if we can't do something to help you."

After dinner they sat down together and went over some of the tests. As they talked, Sandra began to realize that this boy wasn't reading the instructions carefully before taking the tests. Furthermore, he didn't know how to outline a book, and there were several other gaps in his knowledge and understanding.

So they began to spend an hour together every evening, working on reading, outlining books, and understanding instructions. By the end of the semester he had gone from 40 percent test scores to all A's and one A plus!

When his brother saw his report card on the fridge, he said, "You mean that's *your* report card? You must be some kind of a genius!"

I am convinced that part of the reason Sandra was able to have that kind of influence at that time in his life is because of her modeling, mentoring, and organizing. She placed a high value on education, and everyone in the family knew it. She had a great relationship with this son. She had spent hours and hours with him over the years, building the Emotional Bank Account and doing things he enjoyed. And she organized her time so that she could be with him to help him in this way.

These teaching moments are some of the supreme moments of family life—those incomparable times when you know you've made a significant difference in the life of another family member. This is the point at which your efforts help "empower" family members so that they develop the internal capacity and skill to live effectively. And this is at the heart of what parenting and family are all about.

> *Teaching moments are some of the supreme moments of family life—those incomparable times when you know you've made a significant difference in the life of another family member.*

Maria (daughter):

I'll never forget an experience I had with my mother many years ago when I was a teenager. My father was away on a business trip, and it was my turn to stay up late with

Mom. We made hot chocolate, chatted for a while, and then got comfortable in her big bed in time to watch a rerun of Starsky and Hutch.

She was a few months pregnant at the time, and while we were watching TV, she got up abruptly and ran to the bathroom where she stayed for a long time. After a while I realized that something was wrong as I heard her quietly weeping in the bathroom. I went in to find her with her nightgown covered in blood. She had just had a miscarriage.

When she saw me come in, she stopped crying and explained to me in a matter-of-fact way what had happened. She assured me that she was fine. She said that sometimes babies aren't fully formed the way they should be, and this was for the best. I remember taking comfort in her words, and together we cleaned up and then went back to bed.

Now that I am a mother, I am amazed at how my mother was able to subordinate what must have been heart-wrenching emotions into a learning experience for her teenage daughter. Instead of wallowing in her grief, which would have been the natural thing to do, she cared more about my feelings than her own and turned what could have been a traumatic experience for me into a positive one.

Thus, the fourth level of the tree—the leaves and the fruit—represents your role as a teacher. This means that you explicitly teach others the Primary Laws of Life. You teach empowering principles so that as people understand them and live by them, they come to trust those principles and trust themselves because they have integrity. Having *integrity* means their lives are *integrated* around a balanced set of principles that are universal, timeless, and self-evident. When people see good examples or models, feel loved, and have good experiences, then they will hear what is taught. And the likelihood is very high that they will live what they hear so that they, too, become examples and models and even teachers for other people to see and trust. And this beautiful cycle begins again.

This kind of teaching creates "conscious competence." People can be unconsciously incompetent—they can be completely ineffective and not even know it. Or they can be consciously incompetent—they know they're ineffective but don't have the internal desire or discipline to create needed change. Or they can be unconsciously competent—they're effective but don't know why. They're living out positive scripts they've been handed by others; they can teach by example but not by precept because they don't understand it. Or they can be consciously competent—they know what they're doing and why it works. Then they can teach by *both* precept and example. It's this level of conscious competence that enables people to effectively pass knowledge and skill from one generation to another.

Your role as a teacher—in creating conscious competence in your children—is absolutely irreplaceable. As we said in Habit 3, if you do not teach them, society will. And that is what will mold and shape them and their future.

Now, if you've done your own interior work so that you are modeling these

Principle-Centered Family Leadership

Four Roles

Teaching
(Empowering Principles)

Organizing
(Aligning Structure to Mission)

Mentoring
(Relationship of Respect and Caring)

Modeling
(Example of Trustworthiness)

Primary Laws of Life, if you've built relationships of trust by living the Primary Laws of Love, and if you've done the organizational work—having regular family times and one-on-ones—then this teaching will be much, much easier.

What you teach will essentially come out of your mission statement. It will be the principles and values that you have determined to be supremely important. And let me tell you here to pay no attention to people who say you shouldn't teach values until your children are old enough to choose their own. (That statement itself is a "should" statement that represents a value system.) There is no such thing as value-free living or value-free teaching. Everything is hinged and infused in values. You therefore have to decide what your values are and what you want to live by and, since you have a sacred stewardship with these children, what you want them to live by as well. Get them into the wisdom literature. Expose them to the deepest thoughts and noblest feelings of the human heart and mind. Teach them how to recognize the whisperings of conscience and to be faithful and truthful—even when others are not.

When you teach will be a function of the needs of family members, the family times and one-on-ones you set up, and those serendipitous "teaching moments" that present themselves as wonderful gifts to the parent who is watching for opportunity and is aware.

With regard to teaching, I would offer four suggestions:

1. Discern the overall situation. When people feel threatened, an effort to teach by precept—or telling—will generally increase the resentment toward both the teacher and the teaching. It's often better to wait for or create a new situation in which the person is in a secure and receptive frame of mind. Your forbearance in not scolding or correcting in the emotionally charged moment will communicate and teach respect and understanding. In other words, when you can't teach one value by precept, you can teach another by example. And example teaching is infinitely more powerful and lasting than precept teaching. Combining both, of course, is even better.

2. Sense your own spirit and attitude. If you're angry and frustrated, you can't avoid communicating this regardless of the logic of your words or the value of the principle you're trying to teach. Restrain yourself or distance yourself. Teach at another time when you have feelings of affection, respect, and inward security. A good rule of thumb: If you can gently touch or hold the arm or hand of your son or daughter while correcting or teaching and you both feel comfortable with this, you'll have a positive influence. You simply cannot do this in an angry mood.

3. Distinguish between the time to teach and the time to give help and support. To rush in with preachments and success formulas when your spouse or child is emotionally fatigued or under a lot of pressure is comparable to trying to teach a drowning man to swim. He needs a rope or a helping hand, not a lecture.

4. Realize that in a larger sense we are teaching one thing or another all the time because we are constantly radiating what we are.

Always remember that, as with modeling and mentoring, *you cannot not teach.* Your own character and example, the relationship you have with your children, and the priorities that are served by your organization (or lack of it) in the home make you your children's first and most influential teacher. Their learning or their ignorance of life's most vital lessons is largely in your hands.

How the Leadership Roles Relate to the Four Needs and Gifts

In the following Principle-Centered Family Leadership model, you will see the four roles—modeling, mentoring, organizing, and teaching. In the left column, notice how the four basic universal needs—to live (physical/economic), to love (social), to learn (mental), and to leave a legacy (spiritual)—relate to those four roles. Remember, too, the fifth need in the family—to laugh and have fun. Notice in the right column how the four unique human gifts also relate to the four roles.

Principle-Centered Family Leadership

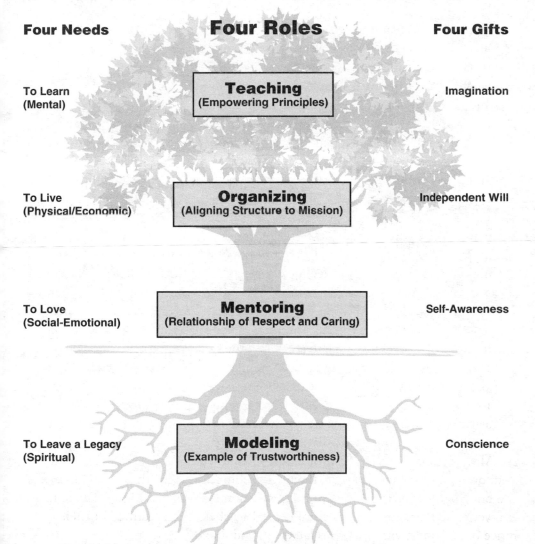

Four Needs — **Four Roles** — **Four Gifts**

Four Needs	Four Roles	Four Gifts
To Learn (Mental)	**Teaching** (Empowering Principles)	Imagination
To Live (Physical/Economic)	**Organizing** (Aligning Structure to Mission)	Independent Will
To Love (Social-Emotional)	**Mentoring** (Relationship of Respect and Caring)	Self-Awareness
To Leave a Legacy (Spiritual)	**Modeling** (Example of Trustworthiness)	Conscience

Modeling is essentially the spiritual. It draws primarily upon conscience for its energy and direction. Mentoring is essentially social and draws primarily upon self-awareness as manifested in respecting others, understanding others, empathizing and synergizing with others. Organizing is essentially the physical and taps into the independent as well as the social will to organize time and life—to set up a family mission statement, weekly family times, and one-on-ones. Teaching is primarily mental. The mind is the steering wheel of life as we are guided into a future that we create first in our minds through the power of our imagination.

In fact, the gifts are cumulative at every level so that mentoring involves conscience and self-awareness. Organizing involves conscience, self-awareness, and willpower. And teaching involves conscience, self-awareness, willpower, and imagination.

You Are a Leader in Your Family

As you look at these four leadership roles and how they relate to the four basic human needs and the four human gifts, you can see how fulfilling them well will enable you to create change in the family.

You *model*: Family members *see* your example and learn to trust you.

You *mentor*: Family members *feel* your unconditional love and begin to value themselves.

You *organize*: Family members *experience* order in their lives and grow to trust the structure that meets their basic needs.

You *teach*: Family members *hear* and *do*. They experience the results and learn to trust principles and themselves.

As you do these things, you exercise leadership and influence in your family. If you do them in a sound, principle-centered way, by modeling, you create trustworthiness. By mentoring you create trust. By organizing you create alignment and order. By teaching you create empowerment.

Like it or not, you are a leader in your family, and one way or another you are already fulfilling each of these roles.

The important thing to realize is that no matter where you are on the destination chart, *you are doing all four of these things anyway.* You may be modeling the struggle for survival, goal setting, or contribution. You may be mentoring by putting people down, "rewarding" success with conditional love, or loving unconditionally. The organization in your family may be a system of repeated disorganization, or you may have calendars, job charts, rules, or even a family mission statement. Informally or formally, you may be teaching anything from disrespect for the law to honesty, integrity, and service.

The point is that, like it or not, you *are* a leader in your family, and one way or another you are already fulfilling each of these roles. The question is *how* you are fulfilling them. Can you fulfill them in a way that will help you create the kind of family you want to create?

Principle-Centered Family Leadership

Family Member	Four Roles	Impact on Family Member
Hears/Does	**Teaching** (Empowering Principles)	Trusts Principles and Self
Experiences	**Organizing** (Aligning Structure to Mission)	Trusts Structure
Feels	**Mentoring** (Relationship of Respect and Caring)	Values Self
Sees	**Modeling** (Example of Trustworthiness)	Trusts You

Are You Managing or Leading? Doing What's "Urgent" or What's "Important"?

For many years now I have asked audiences this question: "If you were to do one thing you *know* would make a tremendous difference for good in your personal life, what would that one thing be?" I then ask them the same question with regard to their professional or work life. People come up with answers very easily. Deep inside they already know what they need to do.

Then I ask them to examine their answers and determine whether what they wrote down is *urgent* or *important* or both. "Urgent" comes from the outside, from environmental pressures and crises. "Important" comes from the inside, from their own deep value system.

Almost without exception the things people write down that would make a tremendous positive difference in their lives are important but not urgent. As we talk about it, people come to realize that the reason they don't do these things is that they're not urgent. They're not pressing. And, unfortunately, most people are addicted to the urgent. In fact, if they're not being driven by the urgent, they feel guilty. They feel as if something is wrong.

But truly effective people in all walks of life focus on the important rather than the merely urgent. Research shows that worldwide, the most successful executives focus on importance, and less effective executives focus on urgency. Sometimes the urgent is also important, but much of the time it is not.

Clearly, a focus on what is truly important is far more effective than a focus on what is merely urgent. It's true in all walks of life—including the family. Of course, parents are going to have to deal with crises and with putting out fires that are both important and urgent. But when they proactively choose to spend more time on things that are truly important but not necessarily urgent, it reduces the crises and "fires."

Just think about some of the important things that have been suggested in this book: building an Emotional Bank Account; creating personal, marriage, and family mission statements; having weekly family times; having one-on-one dates with family members; creating family traditions; working together, learning together, and worshiping together. These things are not urgent. They don't press on us in the same way as urgent matters such as rushing to the hospital to be with a child who has overdosed on drugs, responding to an emotionally hurting spouse who has just asked for a divorce, or trying to deal with a child who wants to drop out of school.

But the whole point is that by choosing to spend time on important things, we decrease the number and intensity of true emergencies in our family life. Many, many issues are talked over and worked out well in advance of their becoming a problem. The relationships are there. The structures are there. People can talk things over, work things out. Teaching is taking place. The focus is on fire prevention instead of putting out fires. As Benjamin Franklin summarized it, "An ounce of prevention is worth a pound of cure."

The reality is that most families are overmanaged and underled. But the more quality leadership that is provided in the family, the less management is needed because people will manage themselves. And vice versa: The less leadership is provided, the more management is needed because without a common vision and common value system, you have to control things and people to keep them in line. This requires external management, but it also stirs up rebellion or it breaks people's spirit. Again, as it says in Proverbs, "Where there is no vision, the people perish."

This is where the 7 Habits come in. They empower you to exercise leadership as well as management in the family—to do the "important" as well as the "urgent *and* important." They help you build relationships. They help you teach your family the natural laws that govern in all of life and, together, institutionalize those laws into a mission statement and some enabling structures.

Without question, family life today *is* a high-wire trapeze act with no safety net. Only through principle-centered leadership can you provide a net in the form of moral authority in the culture itself, and simultaneously build the mind-set and the skill-set to perform the necessary "acrobatics" required.

The 7 Habits help you fulfill your natural family leadership roles in the principle-based ways that create stability, success, and significance.

The Three Common Mistakes

People often make one of three common mistakes with regard to the Principle-Centered Family Leadership Tree.

Mistake #1: To Think That Any One Role Is Sufficient

The first mistake is to think that each role is sufficient in and of itself. Many people seem to think that modeling alone is sufficient, that if you persist and set a good example long enough, children will eventually follow that example. These people see no real need for mentoring, organizing, and teaching.

Others feel that mentoring or loving is all-sufficient, that if you build a relationship and constantly communicate love, it will cover a multitude of sins in the area of personal example and render organizational structure and teaching unnecessary, even counterproductive. Love is seen as the panacea, the answer to everything.

Some are convinced that proper organizing—which includes planning and setting up structures and systems to make good things happen in relationships and in family life—is sufficient. Their families may be well managed, but they lack leadership. They may be proceeding correctly but in the wrong direction. Or they're full of excellent systems and checklists for everybody but have no heart, no warmth, no feeling. Children will tend to move away from these situations as soon as possible and may not desire to return—except perhaps out of a sense of family duty or a strong spiritual desire to make some changes.

Others feel that the role of parents is basically to teach by way of telling and that explaining more clearly and consistently will eventually work. If it doesn't work, it at least transfers responsibility to the children.

Some feel that setting the example and relating—in other words, modeling and mentoring—are all that is necessary. Others feel that modeling, mentoring, and teaching will suffice, and organizing is not that important because in the long run, it's relationship, relationship, relationship that really counts.

This analysis could go on, but it essentially revolves around the idea that we don't really need all four of these roles, that only one or two is sufficient. But this is a major—and a very common—mistake. Each role is necessary, but absolutely insufficient without the other three. For example, you might be a good person and have a good relationship, but without organization and teaching, there will be no structural and systemic reinforcement when you are not present or when something happens that negatively affects your relationship. Children need not only to see it and feel it but also to experience it and hear it—or they may never understand the important laws of life that govern happiness and success.

> *Just as the roots of the tree bring nutrients and life to every other part of the tree, so your own example gives life to your relationships, to your efforts to organize, to your opportunities to teach.*

Mistake #2: To Ignore the Sequence

The second mistake, which is even more common, is to ignore the sequence: to think that you can explicitly teach without having the relationship; or that you can build a good relationship without being a trustworthy person; or that verbal teaching is sufficient and that the principles and laws of life contained in this verbal teaching do not need to be embodied into the patterns and process, the structures and systems of everyday family life.

But just as the leaves on the tree grow out of the branches, the branches grow out of the limbs, the limbs grow out of the trunk, and the trunk grows out of the roots, so each of these leadership roles grows out of those that precede it. In other words, there is an order here—model, mentor, organize, teach—that represents the true inside-out process. Just as the roots of the tree bring nutrients and life to every other part of the tree, so your own example gives life to your relationships, to your efforts to organize, to your opportunities to teach.

Truly, your modeling is the foundation of every other part of the tree. And every other level is a necessary part of those that grow out of it. Effective family leaders recognize this order, and whenever there's a breakdown, use the sequence to help diagnose the source of the problem and take the steps necessary to resolve it.

In Greek philosophy human influence comes from *ethos, pathos, logos*. *Ethos* basically means credibility that comes from example. *Pathos* comes from the relationship, the emotional alignment, the understanding that is taking place between people and the respect they have for one another. And *logos* deals with logic—the logic of life, the lessons of life.

As with the 7 Habits, the sequence and the synergy are the important things. People do not hear if they do not feel and see. The logic of life will not take root if you don't care or if you lack credibility.

Mistake #3: To Think That Once Is Enough

The third mistake is to think that when you have fulfilled these roles once, you don't have to do them anymore—in other words, to look at fulfilling these roles as an event rather than as an ongoing process.

Model, mentor, organize, and *teach* are present-tense verbs that must continually take place. They must go on day in and day out. Modeling or example must always be there, including the example of apologizing when we get off course. We must continually make deposits in the Emotional Bank Account because yesterday's meal does not satisfy today's hunger, especially in family relationships where expectations are high. Because circumstances are constantly changing, there is always the role of organizing to accommodate that changing reality so that the principles are institutionalized and adapted to the situation. And explicit teaching must constantly go on because people are continually moving from one level of development to another, and the same principles apply differently at different levels of development. In addition, because of changing circumstances and age and stage realities, new principles apply and come into play that must be taught and reinforced.

In our own family we've discovered that each child represents his or her own unique challenge, unique world, and unique needs. Each represents a whole new level of commitment and energy and vision. We even sensed with our last child—out of nostalgia for the past glorious years of raising a family—a tendency to overindulge. Perhaps this comes from our own need to be needed, even though our mission statement focuses on producing independence and interdependence.

Joshua (son):

Being the youngest of nine has its advantages. The older kids are always complaining and moaning to Mom and Dad that I'm spoiled and get away with murder. They say that

Mom and Dad aren't half as strict as they used to be, that I don't have to work and slave like they did. They ask, "What do you do anyway besides pick up your room and take out the garbage?"

They tell me that when they were growing up, it was harder to become an Eagle Scout, their schoolteachers were meaner and tougher, and Mom and Dad weren't nearly as well off. They complain that while they have to stay home and put food on the table, I get to go on trips. The boys say they used to lift weights and work out and have muscles, but now they have to be responsible—and that's why they can't beat me in a game of tennis or basketball anymore. They say I'd better buckle down and get straight A's if I want to get into a good college, and I'll never go to graduate school if I read Cliffs Notes instead of doing my own thinking. They tell me that's why I should listen to their advice and not make the same mistakes they did. They also say for sure I'll get to go "pro" in whatever sport I choose because they've all offered to train me. And if I just do what they say, my life will be a lot easier than they had it.

Even as I write this book, I find myself increasingly grateful for the significance of the airplane metaphor and the opportunity to constantly change and improve and to apply what I'm trying to teach. This has been a forceful reminder to me that we need to keep on keeping on, to endure to the end and respect the laws that govern growth, development, and happiness in all of life. Otherwise, we become like the well-intended person who, seeing a butterfly struggling to come out of its cocoon, wildly swinging its wings to break the one small tendon that holds it to the old form, the old structure, out of a spirit of helpfulness takes a penknife and cuts the remaining tendon. As a result, the butterfly's wings never fully develop and the butterfly dies.

So we must never think that our work is done—with our children, our grandchildren, even our great-grandchildren.

Once in the Florida Keys I spoke to a group of extremely wealthy retired couples about the importance of the three-generation family. They acknowledged they had essentially compartmentalized their sense of responsibility to their grown children and their grandchildren. Family involvement was not the central force in their lives; it was an occasional "holidays only" guilt reliever justified by the rationale of helping the kids to become independent from them. But as they opened up and leveled, many acknowledged their sadness in this compartmentalization, even abdication, and resolved to become engaged with their families in a number of new ways. Helping our children become independent is important, of course, but this kind of compartmentalized attitude will never create the intergenerational family support system that is needed today to deal with the onslaught of the culture on the nuclear family.

Families often get caught in one of two extremes. Either they become too enmeshed—that is, too emotionally dependent upon one another (and perhaps socially, financially, or intellectually dependent as well)—or, perhaps through fear of dependence, they become too detached, too independent. This is actually a kind of counter/dependence. Sometimes families cultivate independent lifestyles that have the appearance of interdependence even though deep within, there is profound dependence. Usually, you can distinguish between such dependence and true interdependence by listening to the language; people are either in a blaming and accusing mode, or they focus on the future and opportunities and responsibilities.

Only as family members really pay the price by winning the private victory and producing a genuine and balanced independence can they begin to work on the issues of interdependence. With regard to our own intergenerational family, Sandra and I have concluded that the responsibility of being grandparents is secondary to that of being parents. In other words, we have defined our primary job as that of affirming our own children and the job they're doing with their children. That clear value gives us direction in our involvement with our married children and their families. We are convinced that grandparents must never become anesthetized by the "retirement" mind-set into thinking that there is no longer a vital need for family involvement. You never "retire" from the family. There is always a need for providing ongoing support and affirmation, for being at the crossroads, for building a sense of vision of what the intergenerational family is about.

Even when the children are out of the nest, parents need to recognize their children's need for affirmation of their roles as parents and of how well they're doing; they need to recognize their grandchildren's need to have special time with their grandmother and grandfather, both collectively and one-on-one. In this way they serve as another source of reinforcing the teachings given in that home or help compensate for temporary deficiencies in the home.

> You never "retire" from the family.

The opportunities for intergenerational love and support and for creating a legacy only keep growing as your posterity keeps growing. And regardless of your age, you can always be that "someone" who the best research shows is vital to healthy, happy children and grandchildren—someone who is absolutely, positively, unconditionally "crazy" about them.[3] A grandparent is uniquely able to do that.

Sandra and I feel a tremendous obligation toward each one of our nine children and their spouses and our (so far) twenty-seven grandchildren. We look forward to continuing a sense of stewardship and responsibility toward more grandchildren and toward the fourth generation, the great-grandchildren. We hope we'll even be around long enough to help raise the great-great-grandchildren.

The first line of defense must always be the family—the nuclear family, the intergenerational family, and the extended family. So we must never think our modeling, mentoring, organizing, and teaching is done.

The Trim Tab Factor

This journey from survival to significance can seem overwhelming at times. It may seem as though there's too much to do. The gap between the real and the ideal may seem huge. And you're only one person. Just how much can one person really do?

One of the most helpful images to have of yourself in your family is that of a trim tab—the small rudder that moves the big rudder and eventually changes the entire direction of the plane.

I'd like to suggest a single, powerful image for the transition person to keep in mind.

Airplanes and ships have a small surface often called the *trim tab*. When this trim tab is moved, it moves a larger surface that acts as a rudder and affects the direction of the ship or plane. While it takes a long period of time to turn a big ocean liner 180 degrees, a plane can be turned quite rapidly. But in both cases it takes that small trim tab to make it happen.

One of the most helpful images to have of yourself in your family is that of a trim tab—the small rudder that moves the big rudder and eventually changes the entire direction of the plane.

If you are a parent, you are obviously a trim tab. In you lies the power to choose, to commit. Commitment is the gear that connects vision to action. If commitment is not there, actions will be governed by circumstance instead of vision. So the first and most fundamental requirement out of which everything else emerges is to make a total commitment to yourself and to your family, including a commitment to live the 7 Habits. Interestingly, this total leadership commitment, or TLC, also stands for "tender, loving care."

Though parents play the primary leadership role, we have also seen many others—sons, daughters, aunts, uncles, cousins, grandparents, and foster parents—represent the trim tab in their families. They have brought about fundamental change and improvement in the family culture. Many have been the real transition figures. They have stopped the transmission of negative tendencies from one generation to another. They have transcended genes, programming, conditioning, and environmental pressures to begin anew.

One man who came from a background of welfare and abuse said this:

All through high school I had this desire to go to college. But Mom would say, "You can't do that. You're not smart enough. You're going to have to be like everyone else and go on welfare." It was so discouraging.

But then I'd spend the weekend with my sister, and through her I was able to see that there was more to life than just living on welfare and receiving food stamps. She was able to show me that by the way she lived.

She was married. Her husband had a nice job. She worked part-time when she wanted to—she never had to. They lived in a nice neighborhood. And it was through her that I was able to see the world. I'd go on camping trips with their family. We did a lot of things together. Through her I got the thirst for a good life. I thought, This is what I want to do. This is how I want to be able to live. And I can't do that on welfare.

She's had a profound influence on my life over the years. Because of her I had the courage to move out west, to go to school, to make something more of my life. Even now we travel back and forth to see each other once a year. We do a lot of talking, a lot of confiding in each other, a lot of sharing of dreams, aspirations, and goals in life. Having and being able to renew that relationship has been a really great thing in my life.

Another husband and father who became an agent of change himself reflected on the agent of change in his life:

When I was nine years old, my parents divorced. My dad left my mom with seven children from seventeen down to one and a half. He was an alcoholic and was not supportive emotionally or financially to the family. He never paid alimony or child support. The year after my dad left, my brother left for the Navy. So I was there at home with five sisters and a mom. I guess that is why I'm kind of crazy. I can hang wallpaper better than I can work on an engine. At any rate, I didn't have much of a father's influence in my life.

When I married Cherlynn, I was exposed to a completely different family situation. Her dad was a very strong role model. He was very involved with his children. He devoted tremendous time and energy to them. He encouraged them to set educational and other important goals. He planned family vacations. He called everyone together for family prayer. When there were problems, he hung in there and resolved them in true win-win ways.

This man was such a strong, active participant in the family's rearing that it left an indelible impression on me. Here was a family that was turning out really well, and I recognized that this father had a big influence on that. So I became something of a sponge—just watching everything, observing, and being very impressed. Without question, Cherlynn's father has been the largest role model in my life.

Can you see the influence these transition people—these agents of change, these "trim tab" people—have had? Even when there's no need to overcome a negative past but just to build a positive future, trim tab people can make a profound difference.

The truth is that each of us belongs to a family, and each has the power and the capacity to make a tremendous difference. As author Marianne Williamson has said:

Our deepest fear is not that we are inadequate. Our deepest fear is that we are powerful beyond measure. It is our light, not our darkness, that most frightens us. We ask ourselves, Who am I to be brilliant, gorgeous, talented, fabulous? Actually, who are you not to be? You are a child of God. Your playing small doesn't serve the world. There's nothing enlightened about shrinking so that other people won't feel insecure around you. We are all meant to shine, as children do. We were born to make manifest the glory of God that is within us. It's not just in some of us, it's in everyone. And as we let our own light shine, we unconsciously give other people permission to do the same. As we're liberated from our own fear, our presence automatically liberates others.[4]

This truly represents the fullness of the human condition and nature—to see in ourselves such capacity that we can transcend our own history and provide leadership for our families, that we can lead our families into becoming catalysts who provide leadership in society as well.

Letting Go

I will never forget the first experience I had rappelling down a mountain. The cliff was probably 120 feet high. I watched as several others were trained to rappel and then did it. I saw them reach the safety of waiting arms and receive the cheers of the people at the bottom.

But when it came to my turn, all my intellectualization went into my stomach, and I experienced sheer terror. I was supposed to walk backward off the cliff. I knew there was a safety rope around me in case I should black out. In my mind I could see the other people who had done it successfully. I had an intellectual understanding of the whole situation and an intellectual sense of security. I was even one of the instructors—not dealing with the technical side but with the social, emotional, and spiritual sides. And forty students were looking to me for leadership and guidance. Nevertheless, I was terrified. That first step off the cliff was the moment of truth, the paradigm shift from faith in my comfort zone to an intellectual, physical system of ideas and ropes. As terrifying as it was, I did it—as did others. I arrived safely at the bottom, invigorated by the success of meeting the challenge.

I can't think of an experience that better describes the feeling of some who may struggle with the ideas in this book. Perhaps you may feel this way. The idea of a family mission statement and of having a weekly family time and regular one-on-one bonding experiences may be so far out of your comfort zone that you just can't imagine how you could do it even though it makes intellectual sense to you and you really want to do it.

All I would like to say to you is "You can do this!" Take that step. As the expression goes, "Put your money in your left hand and your guts in your right hand and jump."

I know we've covered a lot of material in this book. But do not let it overwhelm you! If you will just start where you are and keep working, I promise you that unbelievably wonderful insights will come. The more you live these habits, the more you will see how their greatest power is not in the individual habits but in the way they work together to create a framework—or a sort of mental map—that you can apply in any situation.

Consider how helpful an accurate map is in helping you reach any destination. An inaccurate map, on the other hand, is worse than useless—it's misleading. Imagine trying to reach a destination in the United States when all you have to go by is a map of Europe. You might try harder, but you'd be lost twice as fast. You might think positively and end up being cheerful, but you would still be lost. The bottom line is that, assuming this is the only source of information you have, it's very unlikely you would ever reach your destination.

In working with families, there are at least three common misleading maps:

1. **The "advice from others" map.** Projecting our own experience onto other people's lives is a common thing to do. But think about it: Would your glasses work for someone else? Would your shoes fit someone else's feet? In some cases, yes, but most often, no. What works in one situation does not necessarily work in another.

2. **The social values map.** Another common map consists of theories that are based on social values rather than principles. But as we saw in Habit 3, social values are not necessarily the same as principles. For example, if you love a child based on his or her behavior, you may manipulate that behavior in the short run. But the child learns to win love by good behavior. Can that possibly bring good results over time? And does it give a realistic picture of what "love" really is?

3. **The "deterministic" map.** One of the most subtle of all paradigms is the map that is based on deterministic assumptions. The picture it creates is that essentially we are victims of our genes and circumstances. People who live with this map tend to speak and think in terms such as these:
   "That's just the way I am. There's nothing I can do about it."
   "My grandmother was like that, my mother was like that, and so am I."
   "Oh, that character trait comes from my father's side of the family."
   "He makes me so mad!"
   "These kids are driving me crazy!"
   The deterministic map gives a skewed picture of our own deep inner nature, and it denies our fundamental power to choose.

Now these and other maps are at the root of many of the things we think and do in the family. And as long as we have these maps, it is very difficult for us to act outside them.

To illustrate, one time when I spoke to a large group of people, my mother was in the audience. She sat up close to the front, and she became very upset during my speech because two people in the front row kept talking. She felt it was inconsiderate—and even insulting—to her son, and she fretted over what she considered rude and inappropriate behavior.

At the end of the speech she went up to another person who had been sitting in the front row and began to comment rather heatedly on the situation. The other person responded, "Oh, yes! That woman is from Korea, and the gentleman is her interpreter."

My mother was totally chagrined. Suddenly she saw the whole thing differently. She was ashamed and embarrassed about her judgmental attitude. And she realized that she had lost much of what was offered in the presentation because of it—all because of a wrong map.

Throughout the speech she may have tried to think more charitably toward those two people in the front row. Afterward, she may even have tried to interact with them in positive ways. But as long as her "map" said that they were being rude and discourteous, any effort to simply change her attitude or her behavior would have brought minimal results. It wasn't until she got a more accurate map that she was able to effect a change in herself and in the situation.

The point is that we all act based on our maps. And if we want to create change in our lives and in our families, it's not enough to focus on attitudes and behaviors. We have to change the map.

Outside-in will no longer work. Only inside-out will work. As Einstein put it, "The significant problems we face cannot be solved at the same level of thinking we were at when we created them." The real key is in learning and using a new way of thinking—a new, more accurate map.

Experiencing the 7 Habits Framework

Next to the emotion of hope and resolve, I would like you, the reader, to take from this book an appreciation of the usefulness and power of the 7 Habits map or framework as a whole in understanding and in resolving any family problem you may have. The key is not in any particular habit or any particular story, however fascinating, or any particular practice, however well it has worked for others. The key is in learning and using this new way of thinking.

You might well ask, "But how can a single approach possibly deal with every conceivable situation—with the challenges of a large growing family, a childless couple, a single-parent family, a blended family, grandparents and grown siblings?" You might also ask, "Can a single approach work in different nations, different cultures?"

The answer is: It can—*if* it is based on universal needs and universal principles.

The 7 Habits framework is based on a principle-centered approach to fulfilling our needs—physical/economic, social, mental, and spiritual. This framework is simple but not simplistic. As Oliver Wendell Holmes said, "I wouldn't give a fig for the simplicity on this side of complexity, but I would give my right arm for the simplicity on the far side of complexity." The 7 Habits approach is simplicity on the far side of complexity because all the habits are based on universal principles, organized inside-out, to be adapted to any situation by the individuals involved. It addresses both the acute and the chronic problems—both the felt pain and the underlying cause. The 7 Habits approach is not heavy academic theory, nor is it a bunch of simplistic success formulas. It truly is a third alternative in family literature.

To illustrate how you can apply this framework, let me share with you two stories of people who did so successfully in very different situations. As you read these stories, watch for instances where the people involved begin to use the 7 Habits—either to understand or to resolve their concern.

One woman shared this experience of a crisis she had in her marriage:

My husband and I have always had a really volatile marriage. We're both extremely stubborn people who know exactly what we want and are determined to get it at all costs.

About a year and a half ago, we hit an absolute wall. Three years earlier, Jeff had informed me that he was going to graduate school—across the country in Pennsylvania, no less. I was not happy with that at all because I had a promising career, we had just purchased a home, my family all lived nearby, and I was as happy as a clam right where I was.

So I dug in my heels and resisted ferociously for about six months. Finally I decided, Well, I'm married to this guy, so I guess I'll go with him. I followed him, resentfully, across the country to Pennsylvania. I supported him financially for the next two years, but that's about it. I was very grumpy about being there. I'm not much of an easterner, so it took me quite a while to get accustomed to living in Pennsylvania. I had no friends and no family there. I had to start all over. And I totally blamed Jeff for how miserable I was because it had been his idea to drag me there.

When Jeff finally graduated, I said, "Okay, I've been working all this time, and now it's your turn to start looking for a job." He dutifully went about the normal process of job hunting, applying all over the country and going on interviews. But things just weren't panning out for him, and he was miserable.

And I didn't even care that he was miserable. I just wanted him to find a job somewhere—anywhere—and get me out of this hick college town.

Off and on he tried to talk with me about his feelings. He'd say, "You know, Angie, what I'd like to do is start my own business. I don't really want to work for somebody else."

And I said, "You know what? I really don't care. We're in debt for school. We have no equity. You need to get a job and support us. I want to have more children. I want to settle down. I want to stay in one place for a while, and you're not making that happen for me." Finally, I had just had it with his not being able to decide what he wanted to be when he grew up. I got really frustrated and went out west to visit my parents.

While I was there, I decided to interview for a job. And I got it. I called Jeff and said, "You're not getting a job, so guess what I did. I went out and got a job because I wanted to." I worked at this job for about three months. During this time I was exposed to the 7 Habits.

Jeff finally decided to come out and talk things over. We were so at odds with each other. He was living in Pennsylvania, and I was living in Utah. We barely spoke to each other. We had no home. Everything we owned was in storage. We had a child. We had come to this crisis point: Were we going to be married or were we going to barrel through our lives separately?

We went to dinner the night he arrived, and I thought, I'm going to try this. I'm going to think win-win if it kills me. I'm going to try to synergize if it's the last thing I do.

I explained some of these things to Jeff, and he agreed to try it. For the next four or five hours we sat in the restaurant talking things over. We started making a list of what we really wanted from our marriage. He was surprised to find that what I really wanted was stability, that I didn't care so much if he had a normal job, but a normal job was the way that I perceived stability.

"If I can give you stability and open my own business, would that be acceptable to you?" he asked.

I said, "Sure."

"If I were able to do this and you were able to find work that you enjoy and live in a part of the country that you enjoy, would that be good for you?"

Again I said, "Sure."

Then he asked, "Do you not like working? Is that why you keep telling me to get a job?"

And I said, "No. I actually love working, but I don't like feeling that it's all my responsibility."

We went back and forth, and we hammered all these things out. We walked out of the restaurant that night with a list of shared, clearly defined expectations. We wrote them down because we were afraid we wouldn't commit to our plan if we didn't have it in writing.

Last September, on the one-year anniversary of that dinner, Jeff pulled out the list, and we took inventory of what had happened.

He had opened his own business, which is flourishing. It's still a huge struggle. He sometimes works twenty hours a day, and I've had to keep mum about the debt we've incurred to get it started. But the business has actually paid for itself, and we're already making significant progress in getting out of debt.

I came to consider my own job more seriously—in part because of the risk involved in

Jeff's setting up his own business. But I also came to enjoy my work. I was promoted several times and finally found exactly what I like to do.

We bought a home. In fact, we discovered we'd done everything on the list. For the first time in our lives, I feel that we're stable. And I'm happy. It all began on that night when we sat down determined to practice Habits 4, 5, and 6.

Did you notice how this woman made the proactive choice (Habit 1: Be proactive) to face the challenge in her marriage? Even though it was difficult, she decided to practice Habits 4, 5, and 6 (Think win-win; Seek first to understand, then to be understood; Synergize). She explained the process to her husband, and together they created a list of what they really wanted from their marriage (Habit 2: Begin with the end in mind).

Notice how they started to think in terms of mutual benefit (Habit 4: Think win-win) and moved toward mutual understanding (Habit 5: Seek first to understand, then to be understood). As they talked back and forth and each became more open, they made more and more discoveries about how the other felt inside. They hammered out the issues and finally left the restaurant with a list of shared expectations (Habit 2: Begin with the end in mind). Later, they reconnected with that list and evaluated their progress (Habit 7: Sharpen the saw).

Can you see how this couple used the 7 Habits framework to create positive change in their marriage and in their lives?

Let's look at another example. A single mother shared this experience of going through the disability and death of her husband.

Five years ago my husband, Tom, was in an accident that left him paralyzed from the neck down. At that point any future planning stopped for us. We had no focus on the future. We weren't sure there would even be a future. The only focus we had was on Tom's survival from day to day.

Just when we would begin to feel secure in his progress, he would go back into the hospital again. This happened about every six months. And these weren't short hospital stays. He would be there for four to eight weeks at a time. During those stays, any progress he'd made would generally fade, and he'd have to start developing what little skills he had all over again.

It was like being on a roller coaster every minute. You knew you were going over the edge, but you never knew when. There was nothing to hold on to. We knew that the accident meant a shorter life expectancy for Tom, but no one could tell us what that meant. It could be an hour, a day, a year, ten years. We lived in a timeless world waiting for the next shoe to drop.

It was during this time that I changed jobs. The environment I had come out of was one where if you weren't working sixty hours a week and your work wasn't first, you weren't working hard enough or smart enough or fast enough. And suddenly I found myself in an environment where Habit 3 (Put first things first) was the rule of thumb. In this environment, I was told, "You decide what's first. Not only can you decide what's first, but you can make it first in your life."

It was very clear that Tom's life had a very limited time frame, and I realized that his quality of life was a real priority for me. And suddenly I had been given permission to put him first.

So after work I would go home and spend time with Tom. Sometimes I'd take him places. Sometimes we'd just sit and hold hands or watch TV. But I didn't have to worry about whether I was working hard enough or smart enough or fast enough. Before, I would run home, feed him, and hurry to get everything done before I had to get back to work the next day. My time with him had been very, very limited. But now that I found I could make him the priority he was in my life, I actually spent the most incredible quality time with him. We talked about his death. We planned his funeral. We talked about our life. Mostly we talked about the things we shared and how much we had enriched each other's lives. We developed a bond in our relationship during those last six months that went far beyond anything we had ever gained in our lifetime before.

The mission statement I wrote during that time contained this phrase: "I will serve the world one person at a time." And for six glorious months Tom was the person I served. Tom was very clear what his mission was: to make sure that whatever hardships he had to face he faced with dignity and that he was to find the best learning from his experience and share it with others. He felt that part of his purpose in life was to be a role model for his sons, to make sure they knew that whatever life deals you is something to learn from.

Tom's death gave us, as a family, a sense of freedom. And my mission statement continued to give me a sense of direction. It was hard. After dedicating every moment of my life to my husband, I was left with a terrible void. But suddenly there was time that needed to be spent with children who were also facing a critical time in their lives. And that mission statement gave me permission to spend time in the healing process that all of us needed. During the next few months that "one person" I had determined to serve sometimes became the children; at other times it was myself.

I have found as a single parent that when I remember to focus on my children, when I remember that my role as a mother is my most important role each day, I don't have any problem making my children the first things in my life. And that has given me something I never had from my own family. It's given me the opportunity to spend time with my kids and make sure as we go along that I share with them the experiences and values and principles that have helped me through my darkest hours. I can do that without pulling away from anything else in my life. I can still work hard, and my work doesn't suffer because I'm constantly nurturing and being nurtured by the most important relationships in my life.

Notice how this woman began to use Habit 3 (Put first things first) to organize around her real priorities. Notice how she and her husband talked and began to understand each other's deepest thoughts and feelings (Habit 5: Seek first to understand, then to be understood). Notice how they both practiced Habit 2 (Begin with the end in mind) by creating their mission statements, which gave each of them a tremendous sense of purpose during this difficult time. And notice how this woman's mission statement continued to give her strength even after her husband died.

Notice her sense of purpose and service orientation in dealing with her children (Habit 2: Begin with the end in mind) and her proactive decision to spend much-needed time with them (Habit 3: Put first things first). Notice, too, the spirit of renewal (Habit 7: Sharpen the saw) and her comfort in spending time with herself and her children in healing.

Even in the midst of her struggles, this woman became a transition person, an agent of change. Instead of passing on the kind of treatment she had received from her own parents, she proactively chose to give her children a legacy of love.

Now, even though these situations are different, can you begin to see how the 7 Habits framework can address both effectively?

Again, the greatest power of this framework is not in each habit individually but in how they work together. In their synergy they create a whole—a powerful, problem-solving framework—that is even greater than the sum of its parts.

Applying the 7 Habits Framework in Your Own Situation

I'd like to invite you now to consider a family challenge that you have and to see how you might apply this framework in your situation. I've included a worksheet on the following page to make it easier. I suggest that if you develop the habit of going through this or a similar process with each of your family challenges, you will find your family becoming more and more effective because you will be accessing and integrating the principles that govern in all of life.

And as each challenge brings you back to these underlying principles and as you see how they play out in each situation, you will begin to recognize their timeless, universal nature and to really understand them—almost for the first time. As T. S. Eliot has said, "We must not cease from exploration. And the end of all our exploring will be to arrive where we began and to know the place for the first time."[5]

You probably will also discover that one of the most significant benefits (aside from the fact that it works) is that you will have a language with which you can communicate more effectively what's happening inside your family. In fact, this is one of the things I hear most often from families who are working with the 7 Habits.

The 7 Habits Family Worksheet
Applying Principles to Your Challenges

You are the expert in your life. Take any challenge you are dealing with and apply the 7 Habits to develop a response that is true to principles. You may decide to carry out this exercise with another family member or a helpful friend.

The situation: What is the challenge? When does it occur? Under what circumstances?

	Questions to ask yourself	**Ideas you have for using the 7 Habits to respond to your challenge**
Habit 1: Be Proactive	Am I taking responsibility for my actions? How am I using my pause button to act based on principles instead of just reacting?	
Habit 2: Begin with the End in Mind	What is my end in mind? How could a personal or family mission statement (or working on one) help?	
Habit 3: First Things First	Am I doing what matters most? What can I do to better focus? How can weekly family time or one-on-ones help?	
Habit 4: Think "Win-Win"	Do I really want everyone to win? Am I open to seeking a third-alternative solution that will benefit everyone?	
Habit 5: Seek First to Understand . . . Then to Be Understood	How can I more earnestly seek to understand others? How can I exercise courage and consideration in expressing my own view?	
Habit 6: Synergize	How and with whom can I interact creatively to come up with a solution to this challenge?	
Habit 7: Sharpen the Saw	How can I engage in personal and family renewal so that we can all bring our best energy to this challenge?	

One husband and father said this:

I think one of the most important things that has come out of being exposed to the 7 Habits is that we now have a common language to talk about things on a higher level. The language used to be slamming doors or walking out or yelling something in a rage. But now we can talk. We can express ourselves when we feel anger or pain. And when we use words like "synergy" or "Emotional Bank Account," our kids understand what we're talking about. And that's really important.

One wife said this:

The 7 Habits have made us a lot more teachable, more humble. They are a part of every-thing we do every day. If I say something unkind to my husband, he'll just remind me that it was a withdrawal, not a deposit. Those words are part of our conversation, and so we can acknowledge it. We don't get into a fight about it or suffer in silence with hurt feelings over it. It's a way to put things that isn't hostile or volatile. It's subtle and kind.

A woman who was recently married said this:

With the 7 Habits there's an actual language and a framework. Now I can recognize "Oh, yes, we're thinking win-win here" or "Yes, this is a proactive choice we can lovingly make together" or "Yes, we dis-agree, but I really do want to understand what you're believing and say-ing. It's truly important to me, and I'm convinced that we will come up with a third alternative that is going to be much better than my own monovision on the subject."

> *Becoming a transition person or a transition family probably takes courage more than anything else.*

Truly, the 7 Habits framework will give your family a new language and a new level of communication. It will also empower you to become a transition person, an agent of change, in any situation.

Making "Courage" a Verb

As the rappelling experience I shared earlier suggests, becoming a transition person or a transition family probably takes courage more than anything else. Courage is the quality of every quality at its highest testing point. Take any quality or virtue you can think of—patience, persistence, temperance, humility, charity, fidelity, cheerfulness, wisdom, integrity. Go as far as you can go with that quality until the resisting forces push back and the whole environment is discouraging. At that very moment courage comes into play. In a sense you didn't need courage until that moment came because you were carried by the momentum of the circumstance.

In fact, it's because of *discouraging* circumstances that you exercise courage. If the circumstances and people surrounding you are *encouraging*—if they put courage *into* you—then you can often be carried by the energy of their influence. But if they are *discouraging*—if they draw courage *out* of you—then you need to draw courage from within.

If you will recall, in Habit 3 we talked about how forty to fifty years ago society was *encouraging* to the family. Therefore, successful family life took less commitment and prioritization from within because those things were instilled from without. But today the environment is *discouraging*, so much so that the very hallmark of transition people and transition families today is inner courage. It takes tremendous personal and also family courage today to create an encouraging and nurturing home environment in the midst of the wider, discouraging environment of society.

But we can do it. Perhaps we ought to turn "courage" into a verb so that we can clearly understand that it lies in our power, that we can make it happen. We could say, "I *couraged* myself through that struggle. I *couraged* myself into synergy. I *couraged* myself into seeking first to understand." Just as *forgive* is a verb and *love* is a verb, we could make *courage* a verb. It's something that lies in our power. That very thought is encouraging. That very thought strengthens the heart and gives one bravery. When you combine that thought with the vision of what your family can be, it can energize and excite you. It's compelling. It drives you.

> *One of the best parts of being a family is that you can encourage one another. You can believe in one another. You can affirm one another.*

One of the best parts of being a family is that you can encourage one another. You can put courage into one another. You can believe in one another. You can affirm one another. You can assure one another that you are never going to give up, that you see the potential, and that you are acting in faith based on that potential rather than on any particular behavior or circumstance. You can be bold and strengthen one another's hearts and minds. You can weave a strong and secure safety net of *encouraging* circumstances in the home so that family members can cultivate those kinds of internal resiliencies and strengths that will enable them to deal with the *discouraging*, anti-family circumstances outside.

"Sweet Love Remembered"

A short while before my mother died, I opened a love letter from her on a plane flying to some speaking engagement. She wrote such letters frequently even though we talked daily on the phone and visited personally every week or so. Private, effusive letters were her special form of expressing affirmation, appreciation, and love.

I remember reading her letter and feeling the tears roll off my cheeks. I remember feeling a little embarrassed, a little childlike, a little ashamed for being so vulnerable. Yet I felt so warmed and nurtured and treasured. I thought, Everyone needs a mother's love and a father's love.

When Mother passed away, we put on her tombstone a line from one of Shakespeare's great sonnets: "For thy sweet love remembered, such wealth brings . . ."

I would encourage you to read this sonnet slowly and carefully. Let your imagination fill in the richness and meaning of each phrase.

When in disgrace with fortune and men's eyes
I all alone beweep my outcast state,
And trouble deaf heaven with my bootless cries,
And look upon myself and curse my fate,
Wishing me like to one more rich in hope,
Featured like him, like him with friends possessed,
Desiring this man's art and that man's scope,
With what I most enjoy contented least.
Yet in these thoughts myself almost despising,
Haply I think on thee, and then my state,
Like to the lark at break of day arising
From sullen earth, sings hymns at heaven's gate:
For thy sweet love remembered, such wealth brings,
That then I scorn to change my state with kings.

All of us can be our children's and grandchildren's "sweet love remembered." Can anything be more important or more significant than that?

As with many of you parents, Sandra and I have shared supernal, marvelous, spiritual experiences with the birth of each of our children—particularly the last three when fathers were permitted to be present in the delivery room—and also when we were invited to be with our daughter Cynthia at the birth of her sixth child.

Our children were born before the modern-day miracle of the epidural was commonplace. I remember once when Sandra was in the last stages of labor with no anesthetic, she asked me to help her breathe correctly. She had been trained in this breathing technique during fourteen special preparation classes we had attended together at the hospital. As I encouraged and tried to model, Sandra said that all her instincts were to breathe opposite to the training given and that she had to "discipline herself and really focus to do it right." She also said I was clueless as to what she was really experiencing although she valued my intention and effort.

As I saw Sandra go into the "valley of the shadow," I felt an inexpressible, overwhelming love and reverence for her—in fact, for all mothers, for their many acts of sacrifice. I came to feel that all truly great things are born of sacrifice and that only through sacrifice—focused, dedicated parental sacrifice—can a truly good family come into being.

Through it all and despite the fact that we're off track 90 percent of the time, I am absolutely convinced that the highest role and the most important stewardship we could ever have is that of mother or father. As my own grandfather, Stephen L Richards, said—and his words have impacted me powerfully over the years with regard to my own role as husband and father—"Of all the vocations that men may pursue in this life, no vocation is fraught with as much responsibility and attended with as much boundless opportunity as the great calling of husband and father. No man, whatever his accomplishments may be, can, in my judgment, be said to have achieved success in life if he is not surrounded by his loved ones."

The Union of Humility and Courage

After a lifetime of study, Albert E. N. Gray made a profound observation in a speech titled "The Common Denominator of Success." He said, "The successful person has the habit of doing the things unsuccessful people don't like to do. They don't like doing them either, but they subordinate their disliking by the strength of their purpose."[6]

As leaders in your family, you have a very strong and worthy purpose. And that purpose—that sense of destination—will motivate you to have courage and to subordinate your fears and your discomfort in starting some of the things you learned about in this book.

In fact, *humility* and *courage* could be compared to the mother and father of a metaphorical family we all have within us. It takes humility to recognize that principles are in control. It takes courage to submit to principles when the social value systems go in another direction. And the child of the union of courage and humility is *integrity*, or a life that is integrated around principles. The grandchildren are *wisdom* and *an abundance mentality*.

These are the things that enable each of us—as individuals and as families—to have hope even when we get off track and to keep coming back time and time again. We must always remember that there are "true north" principles that govern unerringly, that we have the power of choice to apply those principles in our own situation, and that our destination can be reached.

Even with all the struggles inherent in family life, there is no effort that brings richer rewards, sweeter treasures, and deeper satisfactions. With all the energy of my soul, I affirm that despite its challenges, family life is worth all the effort, sacrifice, giving, and long-suffering. And there is always a brightness of hope.

I once watched a television program where two prisoners independently expressed how unfeeling they had become as a result of their incarceration; they had reached a point where they no longer cared about anyone and were no longer influenced by anyone else's pain. They told how completely selfish they had become, how totally wrapped up they were in their own lives, how they essentially saw people as "things" that either helped them get what they wanted or kept them from getting it.

Both of these men were given an opportunity to learn more about their ancestors. They became acquainted with how their parents, grandparents, and great-grandparents had lived their lives—their struggles, triumphs, and failures. In their interviews, both prisoners spoke about how enormously meaningful this had become to them. Realizing that their ancestors also had challenges and struggled to overcome them caused something to happen inside the prisoners' hearts. They began to see others differently. Each began to think, Even though I have made terrible mistakes, my life is not over. I'm going to make my way through this, and like my ancestors, I'm going to leave a legacy that my descendants will be able to see. It doesn't even matter if I never leave prison. They will have my history and my intentions. They will better understand the way I lived my life here. These men—sitting there in their orange prison suits, all the hardness gone from their eyes—had found conscience and hope. It came from coming home, from finding out about their ancestors—their family.

> We never know when human beings will be inspired to reach into the depths of their soul and exercise their most precious gift of life: the freedom to choose to finally come home.

Everyone has a family. Everyone can ask, "What is my family legacy?" Everyone can seek to leave a legacy. And I personally believe that even beyond our own influence and the strength of our family, we have the ability to tap into a higher form of influence: the power of God. If we continue in faithfulness—never giving up on wayward sons or daughters but doing everything in our power to reach them and continually offering a prayer of faith—God may take a hand in the situation in His way and in His time. We never know when human beings will be inspired to reach into the depths of their soul and exercise their most precious gift of life: the freedom to choose to finally come home.

God bless you in your effort to create a beautiful family culture. And God bless your family. As I quoted in Chapter 1:

> There is a tide in the affairs of men,
> Which, taken at the flood, leads on to fortune;
> Omitted, all the voyage of their life
> Is bound in shallows and in miseries.
> On such a full sea are we now afloat,
> And we must take the current when it serves,
> Or lose our ventures.

Some of the most cherished moments in my life have come fairly frequently when disembarking a plane. I would see a loving family waiting there for a family member who had been away and was coming home. I would stop and watch and feel. As these loved ones embraced one another, with tears of joy and gratitude and reuniting showing their precious caring and true wealth, my eyes also moistened and my heart longed to come home. They—and I—were all reaffirmed once again in the truth that life is really about coming home.

SHARING THIS CHAPTER WITH ADULTS AND TEENS

Moving to Higher Destinations

- Review the material on pages 316–321. Identify the four levels—survival, stability, success, and significance—and discuss the main characteristics of each level. Ask family members: Where are we as a family? What is our desired destination?
- Discuss the statement: "Contributing together as a family not only helps those who benefit from the contribution, but also strengthens the contributing family in the process."
- Review the material on pages 321–325. Talk together about the idea of being *problem minded* (foot on the brake) versus being *opportunity minded* (foot on the gas). Ask family members: How can we remove restraining forces so that driving forces will move us forward?

Leadership in the Family

- Review the material that describes the Principle-Centered Family Leadership Tree (pages 326–336). Discuss the four leadership roles: modeling, mentoring, organizing, and teaching. Talk about the main characteristics of each role. Ask the following questions:
  —Why is being trustworthy important to modeling?
  —Why is building trust a vital part of mentoring? How can the idea of the Emotional Bank Account help build trust?
  —Why does planning and organizing play such a significant role in family influence and leadership? What is the principle of alignment and how is it applied here?
  —Why is teaching important in the family? How does the principle of empowerment work?
- Discuss the three common mistakes with regard to principle-centered family leadership (pages 341–345).
- Review the difference between discipline and punishment. You may want to refer back to Habit 4, pages 197–198. Ask: How can principle-centered leadership help us discipline without punishing?
- Discuss the trim tab factor (pages 346–348), letting go (pages 348–350), courage (pages 357–358), and humility (page 360). Talk about how these ideas relate to family guidance and child development.
- Consider together: Are we managing or leading in our family? What is the difference?
- Discuss the statement: "Whether you realize it or not, you *are* a leader in your family!" Why is this statement true?

SHARING THIS CHAPTER WITH CHILDREN

"We are kind to others and try to help them"

- Discuss the following situations:
  1. Amy asked her dad to help her with her homework. He was tired, but he smiled and helped anyway.
  2. Adam wanted to play with his toy car, but his twin brother was playing with it. Mom asked Adam, "Couldn't your brother play with it just a little longer?"

  Ask: What happens when family members are kind and unselfish with one another? How do family members feel?
- Write the name of each family member on a slip of paper and put all the slips in a box. Have family members draw names without letting anyone else know whose name they have. Encourage everyone to be kind and helpful toward the person whose name they drew throughout the coming week and to notice how it makes them feel.
- Tell the following story:

  Sammy stood looking out the window, watching the rain pouring down. He heard a crying sound coming from outside. He listened very carefully. He tried to see through the glass, but it was raining too hard to see clearly. He quickly went to the front door and opened it. On the doorstep was a little brown kitten, soaking wet and meowing over and over again. Something inside Sammy swelled up at the sight of that little wet animal. He gently picked up the kitten and felt it shivering. He held the kitten tightly next to his chest and walked into the kitchen. Sammy's sister put some clean rags in a little box. She dried off the kitten. She put some milk in a saucer. Sammy sat down beside the box and put his hand on the kitten to warm it. It stopped shivering. Sammy felt warm and good. "I'm so glad we heard the kitten," Sammy said. "Maybe we saved his life."

  Ask family members: How did Sammy feel about the kitten? Responses may include: He felt sorry for it because it was wet and cold. He wanted to be kind and help it. It made him feel good to be kind and want to help.
- Share stories from your personal or family experience of times when you or others showed kindness and helped others. Share how it made you feel. Help children think of ways they can help others who are outside the family. Encourage them to follow through during the week. Have them share their feelings.
- Involve younger children in service projects that you perform for neighbors, friends, and community. As you model an abundance mentality, your children will grow up to be sharing, contributing adults who truly have an interest in the welfare of others.

NOTES

A Personal Message

1. Commencement address by Barbara Bush to the 1990 graduating class at Wellesley College (Wellesley College Library, Wellesley, Mass.), pp. 4–5.

You're Going to Be "Off Track" 90 Percent of the Time. So What?

1. Leo Tolstoy, *Anna Karenina* (London: Oxford University Press, 1949), p. 1.
2. Governor Michael Leavitt of Utah, presented in a teleconference on the Governor's Initiative for Families Today, March 1997.
3. *Monthly Vital Statistics Report*. U.S. Department of Health and Human Services: National Center for Health Statistics, vol. 44, no. 11(S), June 24, 1996.
4. U.S. Bureau of the Census, as published in the *Statistical Abstracts of the U.S.*, October 1996, p. 99.
5. U.S. Bureau of the Census, *Current Population Reports*, pp. 23–180, and National Center for Health Statistics, *Advance Data from Vital and Health Statistics*, no. 194.
6. National Center for Health Statistics, Mortality Statistic Branch: *Vital Statistics of the U.S.*: 1975–1990, vol. 2.
7. U.S. Department of Education, *The Condition of Education*. The Office of Educational Research and Improvement, 1996.
8. F. Byron Nahser and Susan E. Mehrtens, *What's Really Going On?* (Chicago: Corporantes, 1993), p. 12.
9. U.S. Bureau of the Census, *Current Population Reports*, pp. 23–180, and National Center for Health Statistics, *Advance Data from Vital and Health Statistics*, No. 194.
10. *Congressional Quarterly* as cited in William Bennett, *Index of Leading Cultural Indicators* (New York: Simon & Schuster, 1994), p. 83.
11. U.S. Bureau of the Census, as published in the *Statistical Abstracts of the U.S.*, October 1996, p. 99.
12. Robert G. DeMoss, Jr., *Learn to Discern* (Grand Rapids, Mich.: Zondervan Publishing House, 1992), pp. 14, 53.
13. Alfred North Whitehead, "The Rhythmic Claims of Freedom and Discipline," in *The Aims of Education and Other Essays* (New York: New American Library, 1929), p. 46.
14. Robert Frost, "The Road Not Taken," in *Selected Poems of Robert Frost* (New York: Holt, Rinehart, and Winston, 1963), pp. 71–72.
15. William Shakespeare, *Julius Caesar* (New York: Penguin Books, 1967), act 4, scene 3.

Habit 1: Be Proactive

1. M. Scott Peck, *The Road Less Traveled* (New York: Simon & Schuster, 1978), p. 83.
2. Questionnaire originally published in Stephen R. Covey, A. Roger Merrill, and Rebecca R. Merrill, *First Things First*. (New York: Simon & Schuster, 1994), pp. 62–63.
3. The phrase "Know thyself" is traditionally reported to have been given by the oracle at

Delphi and was inscribed on the entrance to the temple. See *Early Socratic Dialogues/Plato*, edited with a general introduction by Trevor J. Saunders (New York: Penguin, 1987).

4. This quote is attributed to Saint Francis of Assisi and has served as an inspiration to thousands through the programs of Alcoholics Anonymous.

5. Glen C. Griffin, M.D., as featured in *It Takes a Parent to Raise a Child*. Used by permission.

6. Joseph Zinker, "On Public Knowledge and Public Revolution," as quoted in Leo Buscaglia, *Love* (New York: Fawcett Crest, 1972), p. 49.

Habit 2: Begin with the End in Mind

1. Victor Frankl, *Man's Search for Meaning* (New York: Pocket Books, 1959), p. 98.

2. Benjamin Singer, "The Future-Focused Role-Image," in Alvin Toffler, *Learning for Tomorrow: The Role of the Future in Education* (New York: Random House, 1974), pp. 19–32.

3. See Andrew Campbell and Laura Nash, *A Sense of Mission* (Reading, Mass.: Addison Wesley Longman, 1994). See also James Collins and Jerry Porras, *Built to Last: Successful Habits of Visionary Companies* (New York: HarperCollins, 1996).

4. Benjamin Franklin, "Franklin's Formula for Successful Living—Number Three," *The Art of Virtue* (Eden Prairie, Minn.: Acorn Publications, 1986), p. 88.

Habit 3: Put First Things First

1. Rabindranath Tagore, *101 Poems* (New York: Asia Publishing House, 1966).

2. Mary Pipher, *The Shelter of Each Other* (New York: Grosset/Putnam Books, 1996).

3. Ibid., pp. 194–195.

4. Urie Bronfenbrenner as quoted in Susan Byrne's interview, "Nobody Home: The Erosion of the American Family," *Psychology Today*, May 1977, pp. 41–47.

5. John Greenleaf Whittier, *Maud Muller* (New York: Houghton, Mifflin, 1866).

6. Robert G. DeMoss, Jr., *Learn to Discern* (Grand Rapids, Mich.: Zondervan Publishing House, 1992), p. 52.

7. Ibid., p. 14.

8. Arlie R. Hochschild, *The Time Bind* (New York: Metropolitan Books, 1997).

9. United States Supreme Court, *Zablocki v. Redhail*, no. 76-879; January 1978.

10. Wendell Berry, *Sex, Economy, Freedom, and Community: Eight Essays* (New York: Pantheon Books, 1993), pp. 125, 137-139.

11. Ibid., p. 139.

12. Betsy Morris, review of Arlie R. Hochschild, *The Time Bind*, in *Fortune*, May 1997.

13. U.S. Department of Commerce, Bureau of the Census, "Current Population Reports," 1994.

14. Eve Arnold, "In God We Trust: Testing Personal Faith in a Cynical Age," *U.S. News & World Report*, April 4, 1994, p. 56.

15. John Robinson and Geoffrey Godbey, *Time for Life* (Pennsylvania State University Press) as reviewed in *Newsweek*, May 12, 1997, p. 69.

16. Marilyn Ferguson, *The Aquarian Conspiracy: Personal and Social Transformation in the 1980's* (New York: St. Martin's Press, 1980), p. 356.

17. Quoted from a speech given by author Stanley M. Davis at a conference in Asia in which we both participated.

18. U.S. Department of Justice, *Strengthening America's Families: Promising Parenting and Family Strategies for Delinquency Prevention* (Office of Justice Programs, 1992).

19. Alexander Pope, *The Best of Pope* (New York: The Ronald Press Co., 1940), pp. 131–132.
20. Attributed to scholar, researcher, and psychologist Victor Cline.
21. Edward Gibbon, *The Decline and Fall of the Roman Empire*, in *Great Works of the Western World*, vol. 37–38 (Chicago: Encyclopedia Britannica, 1990).
22. F. Byron Nahser and Susan E. Mehrtens, *What's Really Going On?* (Chicago: Corporantes, 1993), p. 11.
23. William Doherty, *The Intentional Family: How to Build Family Ties in Our Modern World* (New York: Addison-Wesley, 1997), p. 10.
24. Patricia Voydanoff, "Economic Distress and Family Relations: A Review of the Eighties," *Journal of Marriage and the Family*, 52 (November 1990), p. 1102. See also Lynn K. White, "Determinants of Divorce: A Review of Research in the Eighties," *Journal of Marriage and the Family*, 52 (November 1990), p. 908.
25. This quote is attributed to both John Glenn and Neil Armstrong.
26. James B. Stockdale, *A Vietnam Experience: Ten Years of Reflection* (Stanford: Hoover Institution, Stanford University, 1984), p. 94.

Habit 4: Think "Win-Win"

1. J. S. Kirtley and Edward Bok, *Half Hour Talks on Character Building by Self-Made Men and Women* (Chicago: A. Hemming, 1910), p. 368.
2. Michael Novak, "The Family Out of Favor," *Harper's Magazine*, April 1976, pp. 39, 42.
3. Catherine Johnson, *Lucky in Love: The Secrets of Happy Couples and How Their Marriages Thrive* (New York: Viking Penguin, 1992).
4. Frederick Herzberg, *Work and the Nature of Man* (New York: World Publishing Co., 1966), pp. 71–91.

Habit 5: Seek First to Understand . . . Then to Be Understood

1. The books and authors mentioned here are as follows:
   Deborah Tannen, *You Just Don't Understand: Men and Women in Conversation* (New York: Ballantine Books, 1990).
   John Gray, *Men Are from Mars, Women Are from Venus* (New York: HarperCollins, 1992).
   Carl Rogers, *On Becoming a Person* (Boston: Houghton Mifflin, 1961).
   Thomas Gordon, *Parent Effectiveness Training* (New York: New American Library, 1975).
   Haim Ginott, *Between Parent and Child* (New York: Macmillan, 1970). See also
   Haim Ginott, *Between Parent and Teenager* (New York: Macmillan, 1969).
2. Gordon B. Hinckley, "What God Hath Joined Together," *Ensign*, May 1991, p. 72.
3. C. S. Lewis, *Mere Christianity* (New York: Macmillan, 1952), pp. 109–10.
4. Note: Many helpful informational pamphlets can be found through your local health department, your doctor's office, or the government. Also, we recommend the following as excellent references for those wanting to know more:
   Arlene Eisenberg, Heidi E. Murkoff, and Sandee E. Hathaway, *What to Expect the First Year* (New York: Workman Publishing, 1989).
   ———. *What to Expect the Toddler Years* (New York: Workman Publishing, 1994).
   Penelope Leach, *Your Baby and Child* (New York: Knopf Publishing, 1989).
   T. Berry Brazelton, *Touchpoints* (Reading, Mass.: Addison Wesley Longman Publishing, 1992).

Habit 6: Synergize

1. Victor Cline, *How to Make Your Child a Winner* (New York: Walker and Company, 1980), pp. 216–226, and Victor Cline, Roger Croft, and Steven Courrier, "Desensitization of Children to Television Violence," *Journal of Personal and Social Psychology*, vol. 27 (3), September 1973, pp. 360–63.
2. See Larry Tucker, "The Relationship of Television Viewing to Physical Fitness," *Adolescence*, vol. 21 (89), 1986, pp. 797–806.
3. See *Report on Television and Behavior* by the National Institute of Mental Health (Washington, D.C., 1982). See also Susan Newman, "The Home Environment and Fifth Grade Students' Leisure Reading," *Elementary School Journal*, January 1988, vol. 86 (3), pp. 335–43.
4. Ibid., *Report on Television and Behavior*.

Habit 7: Sharpen the Saw

1. Richard L. Evans, *Richard Evans' Quote Book* (Salt Lake City: Publishers Press, 1971), p. 16.
2. Marianne Jennings, "Kitchen Table Vital to Family Life," *Deseret News*, February 9, 1997. Reprinted with permission.
3. Dale Johnson, "Sex Differences in Reading Across Cultures," *Reading Research Quarterly*, vol. 9 (1), 1973.
4. CNN/*USA Today*/Gallup Poll (Princeton, N.J., December 16–18, 1994).
5. David G. Myers, *The Pursuit of Happiness* (New York: William Morrow & Company, 1992), pp. 177–204.
6. C. S. Lewis, *Mere Christianity* (New York: Macmillan, 1976), pp. 164–65.
7. You might want to read the following:
   Frank Walters, *Book of the Hopi* (New York: Ballantine, 1963).
   James Allen, *As a Man Thinketh* (Salt Lake City: Bookcraft, 1983).
   Henry David Thoreau, *Walden* (New York: Carlton House, 1940).
   William Bennett, *The Book of Virtues* (New York: Simon & Schuster, 1993).
   Jack Canfield and Mark Victor Hansen, *Chicken Soup for the Soul* (Deerfield Beach, Fla.: Health Communications, 1993).

From Survival . . . to Stability . . . to Success . . . to Significance

1. Kurt Lewin, *Field Theory in Special Science* (New York: Harper, 1951), p. 183.
2. W. Edwards Deming, *Out of the Crisis* (Cambridge: Massachusetts Institute of Technology, 1982), pp. 66–67.
3. Urie Bronfenbrenner, as quoted in Susan Byrne's interview, "Nobody Home: The Erosion of the American Family," *Psychology Today*, May 1977, pp. 41–47. See also a study by E. E. Maccoby and J. A. Martin, "Socialization in the Context of the Family: Parent–Child Interaction," in P. H. Mussen (ed.), *Handbook of Child Psychology*, vol. 4 (New York: John Wiley, 1983), pp. 1–101.
4. Marianne Williamson, *A Return to Love* (New York: HarperCollins, 1992), p. 165.
5. *The Complete Poems and Plays of T. S. Eliot* (London: Faber and Faber, 1969), p. 197.
6. Albert E. N. Gray, "The Common Denominator of Success," a speech given at the Prudential Insurance Company of America (Newark, New Jersey, 1983).

GLOSSARY

Abundance mentality: The view that there is more than enough to go around for everybody.

Agent of change: A person who brings about change in a relationship or situation.

Big rocks: Those activities that are the most important priorities in our lives.

Circle of Concern: All matters that a person or family is concerned about.

Circle of Influence: Those things that a person or family can directly impact.

Compass: A person's internal guidance system consisting both of principles and the four human gifts.

Conscience: An inner sense of what is right and wrong.

Driving force: Something that motivates, excites, and inspires us and our family.

Effective family: A nurturing, learning, enjoyable, contributing, and interdependent family.

Emotional Bank Account: The amount of trust or the quality of a relationship with others.

Entropy: The tendency for things to deteriorate or fall apart.

Faithful translator: One capable of truly reflecting the content and feeling of another's comments.

Family culture: The climate, character, spirit, feeling, and atmosphere of the home and family.

Family mission statement: A combined, unified expression from all family members of what the family is all about, what family members want to do and be, and the principles that will guide the family's flight plan.

Family time: Weekly time set aside to be together as a family.

Four human gifts: See *Self-awareness*, *Conscience*, *Imagination*, and *Independent will*.

Framework/Paradigm: Our perspective or map or the way we think about and see things.

Habit: An established pattern or way of thinking and doing things.

Imagination: The ability to visualize something in our mind beyond the present reality.

Independent will: The ability to choose and act on our own inner imperatives and determinations.

Inside-out: Initiating change by changing self rather than trying to change others.

Leadership Influence: See *Modeling*, *Mentoring*, *Organizing*, and *Teaching*.

Mentoring: Relating to another individual in a one-on-one, personal, and helpful way.

Modeling: Setting a principle-based pattern for another person to follow.

Nuclear family: The core or essential family around which the extended family (grandparents, aunts and uncles, cousins) is grouped.

One-on-one bonding time: Regular time set aside to have meaningful, relationship-building interactions.

Opportunity minded: Being focused on bringing something into existence.

Organizing: Creating order and systems to help accomplish what is valued by the family.

Outside-in: Influenced more by external surroundings than internal commitments.

Paradigm/Framework: Our perspective or map or the way we think about and see things.

Pause button: Something that reminds us to stop, think, and act in a better way.

Primary Laws of Life: The basic principles or natural laws of effectiveness that govern in all of life.

Primary Laws of Love: Natural laws that affirm the inherent worth of people and the power of unconditional love.

Principles: Universal, timeless, self-evident, natural laws that govern in all of life's human interactions.

Proactive: Being responsible for our own choices; having the freedom to choose based on values rather than moods or conditions.

Problem minded: Being focused on eliminating something. Compare with *Opportunity minded*.

Restraining force: Pressure that hinders or prevents us from achieving our goals.

Scarcity mentality: A mind-set of competition and being threatened by others' successes.

Self-awareness: The ability to stand apart and examine our own thoughts and behaviors.

Sharpening the Saw: Renewal, rejuvenation, and re-creation of one's spiritual, mental, social-emotional, and physical self and family.

Significance: A condition in which the family has developed a beautiful family culture and is making a larger contribution both inside and outside of the family.

Social will: The norms and the moral or ethical force created by the culture of the family.

Stability: A condition in which the family is predictable, dependable, and functional with basic structure and organization, and has some communication and problem-solving ability.

Stewardship: Something we are entrusted with.

Success: The condition in which the family is accomplishing worthy goals, feels genuine happiness, has fun and meaningful traditions, and is serving one another.

Survival: A condition in which the family is struggling physically, economically, socially, emotionally, and spiritually to live and love at the minimum day-to-day existence level.

Synergy: The result of two or more people producing together more than the sum of what they could produce separately (one plus one equals three or more).

Teaching: Intentionally sharing with, explaining to, and informing other people.

Transcending ourselves: Overcoming past negative scripting and becoming the creative force in our own lives.

Transition person: One who stops negative tendencies and cycles and becomes an agent of change.

Trim tab: A person who influences and helps set the direction of the family, like the rudder of a ship.

Win-win agreement: A shared expectation and commitment regarding desired results and guidelines.

PROBLEM/OPPORTUNITY INDEX

As I've said, the power of the 7 Habits is not in the individual habits but in how they work together as a whole. Nevertheless, you may find some material more directly applicable and helpful in dealing with specific questions or concerns. This index has therefore been designed as a resource to help you access material that deals directly with specific problems and opportunities.

I've divided this index into six areas: personal, marriage, family, parenting, intergenerational and extended family, and societal issues. CAPITALIZED entries represent entire chapters or sections that either completely include or introduce the referenced material. *Italicized* entries represent stories (which are also *italicized* in the book if they're told by someone else, or are in normal text if they're told by me). Entries in normal text refer to ideas on the specified pages.

It's my hope that this index will help you refer more quickly to the material that will help with your challenges.* In addition, I suggest that, as with any challenge, you go through the 7 Habits Family Worksheet on page 356.

---

*For additional help, reference the Problem/Opportunity Index in *The 7 Habits of Highly Effective People* (London: Simon & Schuster, 1992).

PARENTING

Although I recognize that many single parents must deal with these issues alone, I've used "we" in the following questions to acknowledge the value of synergy as well as proactivity, and to encourage synergy when appropriate— whether it be with a spouse, an extended family member, or an interested friend.

INDEX

A

abandonment, 57–58
abortion, 108, 271–72
abuse, child, 12, 15, 100, 130
"acting out," 208
active aggressive personality, 83
Adams, Abigail, 286, 287
Adams, John, 286, 287
"advice from others" map, 349
"aha!" experience, 237
AIDS, 261
alcoholism, 17, 100, 108, 131
allowance, 190–91, 194
Alternative Learning Center (ALC), 107
anger, 29, 44, 66, 97, 210, 213, 220–22, 233
animals, 31, 32, 34
Anna Karenina (Tolstoy), 15
Apollo 11 mission, 149–50
apologies:
    for bad temper, 10
    conscience and, 54
    as emotional deposit, 52–54, 64
    imagination and, 54
    for judgmental behavior, 13–14, 210, 230
    proactivity and, 43
    reactivity and, 28
    self-awareness and, 54
    synergy and, 248
    will and, 54
approval, 30, 51, 61, 63, 330
Aquarian Conspiracy, The (Ferguson), 125
architecture, 144
Argentina, 164
arguments, 170, 171, 178, 179–81, 183
autobiography, personal, 171, 218, 225, 229, 245

B

baby-sitters, 120, 143, 266
bedtime, 256
begin with end in mind (Habit 2), 70–111
    adult applications of, 110
    child applications of, 111
    destination defined by, 67, 71–73, 77–78, 83–84, 114, 197
    long-range goals in, 100, 180, 328
    for mission statement, *see* mission statements
    planning and, 162
    priorities in, 73, 74–75, 102–4
    problem-solving scripts for, 83
    synergy and, 250, 264
    teaching of, 144
    teen applications of, 110
    things created twice and, 72, 110, 133, 144
    vision in, 72–73, 278
behavior:
    changing of, 233–35
    identity vs., 233

judgmental, 13–14, 210, 230
    negative, 29–30, 104, 106–8, 197, 233
    principles vs., 128
    understanding and, 209, 233
Berry, Wendell, 122, 123
Bible, 53, 73, 104, 208, 301, 341
birthdays, 291–93
"blind spots," 233, 235
Bok, Edward, 181
bonding:
    activities for, 26, 121, 320
    in childbearing, 172
    with children, 26, 121, 154–57, 168
    as "completely present," 151–52
    Emotional Bank Account and, 159, 160, 264
    in marriage, 152–54
    one-on-one, 18, 113, 115, 331, 336, 340, 345, 348
    planning for, 157, 159, 160–63
    as priority, 160–63, 164, 165, 167
    as process, 22
    renewal and, 279, 280, 281, 288, 306, 310, 311
    synergy in, 78–79, 95, 273
    teaching and, 159–60
    trust and, 157–59
    understanding and, 222
brain:
    imprinting by, 95
    left vs. right, 252–55
Bronfenbrenner, Urie, 119
Brownlee, Shannon, 117–18
Bush, Barbara, 2

C

calendars, 142, 143n, 162
camping, 288
careers:
    divorce and, 276
    family vs., 103, 114–19, 121–22, 134, 135, 320–21
    marriage vs., 276
change:
    agents of, 7, 15, 19, 32–33, 46, 48–49, 67, 100, 101, 102, 134, 181, 325–26, 346–48, 355, 357
    cultural, 131–32, 134–36
    forgiveness and, 60–61
    from inside out, 15, 44, 46, 48, 66, 100, 107, 117
    principles and, 155
    results of, 150–51
    social, 17–18, 133–37, 164
cheating, 158–59
children:
    abuse of, 12, 15, 100, 130
    accountability of, 95, 282
    bonding with, 26, 121, 154–57, 168
    children as teachers of, 187
    commitment to, 62–63, 99, 119–20
    custody of, 217–20
    developmental stages of, 175, 187–88, 208, 240–43
    dissatisfaction of, 184

ABOUT THE AUTHOR

Stephen R. Covey, husband, father, and grandfather, is an internationally respected leadership authority, family expert, teacher, organizational consultant, founder of the former Covey Leadership Center, and co-chairman of Franklin Covey Company. He has made teaching Principle-Centered Living and Principle-Centered Leadership his life's work. He holds an MBA from Harvard and a doctorate from Brigham Young University, where he was a professor of organizational behavior and business management, and also served as director of university relations and assistant to the president. For more than thirty years he has taught millions of individuals and families and leaders in business, education, and government the transforming power of principles or natural laws that govern human and organizational effectiveness.

Dr. Covey is the author of several acclaimed books including *The 7 Habits of Highly Effective People*, which has been at the top of the best-seller lists for over seven years. More than ten million copies have been sold in twenty-eight languages and seventy countries. His books *Principle-Centered Leadership* and *First Things First* are two of the best-selling business books of the decade.

Dr. Covey and other Franklin Covey authors, speakers, and spokespersons, all authorities on leadership and effectiveness, are consistently sought by radio and television stations, magazines, and newspapers throughout the world.

Among recent acknowledgments, Dr. Covey has received the Thomas More College Medallion for continuing service to humanity, the Toastmaster's International Top Speaker Award, *Inc.* magazine's National Entrepreneur of the Year Lifetime Achievement Award for Entrepreneurial Leadership, and several honorary doctorates. He has also been recognized as one of *Time* magazine's twenty-five most influential Americans.

Stephen, his wife, Sandra, and their family live in the Rocky Mountains of Utah.

ABOUT FRANKLIN COVEY

Stephen R. Covey is co-chairman of Franklin Covey Company, a four-thousand member international firm devoted to helping individuals, organizations, and families become more effective through the application of proven principles or natural laws. In addition to working with and creating products for individuals and families, the company's client portfolio includes eighty-two of the Fortune 100 companies, more than two-thirds of the Fortune 500 companies, thousands of small and midsize companies, and government entities at local, state, and national levels. Franklin Covey has also created pilot partnerships with cities seeking to become principle-centered communities, and is currently teaching the 7 Habits to teachers and administrators in more than three thousand school districts and universities nationwide and through statewide initiatives with education leaders in twenty-seven states.

The vision of Franklin Covey is to teach people to teach themselves and become independent of the company. They encourage organizations to be family friendly, and they teach skills and provide products to help people balance work and family life. To the timeless adage by Laotzu: "Give a man a fish and you feed him for a day; teach him how to fish and you feed him for a lifetime," they add: "Develop teachers of fishermen, and you lift all society." This empowerment process is carried out through programs conducted at facilities in the Rocky Mountains of Utah, custom consulting services, personal coaching, custom on-site training, and client-facilitated training, as well as through open enrollment workshops offered in over three hundred cities in North America and forty countries worldwide.

Franklin Covey has more than seven thousand licensed client facilitators teaching its curriculum within their organizations, and it trains in excess of 750,000 participants annually. Implementation tools, including the Franklin Day Planner, the 7 Habits Organizer, and a wide offering of audio- and videotapes, books, and computer software programs enable clients to retain and effectively utilize concepts and skills. These and other family products carefully selected and endorsed by Franklin Covey are available in more than one hundred Franklin Covey 7 Habits Stores throughout North America and in several other countries.

Franklin Covey products and materials are now available in twenty-eight languages, and their planner products are used by more than fifteen million individuals worldwide. The company has over twelve million books in print, with more than one and a half million sold each year. *Business Week* lists Dr. Covey's *The 7 Habits of Highly Effective People* as a number one best-selling trade business book of the year and its *First Things First* time management book as a number three.

For information on the Franklin Covey 7 Habits Store or International Office closest to you, or for a free catalog of Franklin Covey products and programs, call or write:

Franklin Covey Organisation Services Ltd
4 Berghem Mews
Blythe Road
London W14 0HN
Tel: (44-171) 602 6557
Fax: (44-171) 602 2166

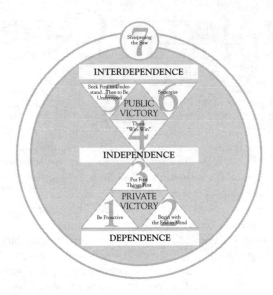

The 7 Habits of Highly Effective Families

Habit 1: Be Proactive
Families and family members are responsible for their own choices and have the freedom to choose based on principles and values rather than on moods or conditions. They develop and use their four unique human gifts—self-awareness, conscience, imagination, and independent will—and take an inside-out approach to creating change. They choose not to be victims, to be reactive, or to blame others.

Habit 2: Begin with the End in Mind
Families shape their own future by creating a mental vision and purpose for any project, large or small. They don't just live day to day with no clear purpose in mind. The highest form of mental creation is a marriage or family mission statement.

Habit 3: Put First Things First
Families organize and execute around their most important priorities as expressed in their personal, marriage, and family mission statements. They have weekly family times and regular one-on-one bonding times. They are driven by purpose, not by the agendas and forces surrounding them.

Habit 4: Think "Win-Win"
Family members think in terms of mutual benefit. They foster support and mutual respect. They think interdependently—"we," not "me"—and develop win-win agreements. They don't think selfishly (win-lose) or like a martyr (lose-win).

Habit 5: Seek First to Understand . . . Then to Be Understood
Family members seek first to listen with the intent to understand the thoughts and feelings of others, then seek to effectively communicate their own thoughts and feelings. Through understanding, they build deep relationships of trust and love. They give helpful feedback. They don't withhold feedback, nor do they seek first to be understood.

Habit 6: Synergize
Family members thrive on individual and family strengths so that, by respecting and valuing one another's differences, the whole becomes greater than the sum of the parts. They build a mutual problem-solving and opportunity-seizing culture. They foster a nurturing family spirit of loving, learning, and contributing. They don't go for compromise ($1 + 1 = 1^{1}/_{2}$) or merely cooperation ($1 + 1 = 2$) but creative cooperation ($1 + 1 = 3$ . . . or more).

Habit 7: Sharpen the Saw
The family increases its effectiveness through regular personal and family renewal in four basic areas of life: physical, social/emotional, spiritual, and mental. They establish traditions that nurture the spirit of family renewal.

FRANKLIN COVEY COMPANY®, GLOBAL OFFICES

**Franklin Covey Company
Australia**

Ground Floor, Fujitsu House
159 Coronation Dr.
Milton, QLD 4064
Tel: (61-7) 3259-0222
Fax: (61-7) 3369-7810
australia@covey.com

**Covey Leadership Center
Bermuda**

4 Dunscombe Rd.
Warwick, Bermuda WK08
Tel: (441) 236-0383
Fax: (441) 236-0192
bermuda@covey.com

**Covey Leadership Center
Brazil**

Ave. Brig. Faria Lima 2003
Cj. 1301-1302
CEP Sao Paulo, Brazil 01451
Tel/Fax: (55-11) 815-7797
brazil@covey.com

Franklin Covey Europe

Grant Thornton House
46 West Barr Street
Banbury
Oxon OX16 9RZ
Tel: (44-1295) 274 100
Fax: (44-1295) 274 101

**Covey Leadership Center
Indonesia**

J1. Bendungan Jatilihur 56
Bendungan Hilir
Jakarta, Indonesia 10210
Tel: (62-21) 572-0761
Fax: (62-21) 572-0762
indonesia@covey.com

**Covey Leadership Center
Ireland**

5 Argyle Square
Donnybrook
Dublin 4, Ireland
Tel: (353-1) 668-1422
Fax: (353-1) 668-1459
ireland@covey.com

**Covey Leadership Center
Japan**

Ogimura Bldg. 7F
2-4-11 Kudan Minami
Chiyoda-Ku, Tokyo 102, Japan
Tel: (81-3) 3264-7401
Fax: (81-3) 3264-7402
japan@covey.com

**Franklin Covey Company
Japan**

Seibunkan Building 3F
Iidabashi 1-5-9
Chiyoda-ku Tokyo 102
Tel: (81-3) 3234-4025
Fax: (81-3) 3238-1696
CS/Retail: (81-3) 5276-5207

**Covey Leadership Center
Korea**

6F 1460-1 Seoyang Bldg
Seocho-Dong
Seocho-Ku
Seoul, 137-070 Korea
Tel: (82-2) 3472-3360/3, 5
Fax: (82-2) 3472-3364
korea@covey.com

**Covey Leadership Center
Latin America/Caribbean**

107 N. Virginia Ave.
Winter Park, FL 32789
Tel: (407) 644- 4416
Fax: (407) 644-5919
latinamerica@covey.com

Argentina Office

Corrientes 861, 5to. Piso
2000 Rosario, Argentina
Tel/Fax: (54-41) 408-765
argentina@covey.com

Chile Office

Ave. Presidente Errazuriz
#3328 Las Condes
Santiago, Chile
Tel: (56-2) 242-9292
Fax: (56-2) 233-8143
chile@covey.com

Colombia Office

Calle 90 No. 11 A-34, Oficina 206
Santa Fé de Bogotá, Colombia
Tel: (57-1) 610-0396/0385
Fax: (57-1) 610-2723
colombia@covey.com

CLC Curacao

Ajaxway 3
Curacao, Netherlands Antilles
Tel: (599) 9-371284/1286
Fax: (599) 9-371289
curacao@covey.com

Panama

Via Ramón Arias, El Carmen
Oficentro Ropardi, Oficina 1G
Panamá 1, Republica de Panamá
Tel: (507) 223-3341/7671
Fax: (507) 269-2978
panama@covey.com

*For all Latin American countries
not listed, please contact CLC Latin
America Headquarters.*

**Covey Leadership Center
Malaysia/Brunei**

J-4, Bangunan Khas
Lorong 8/1E
46050 Petaling Jaya
Selangor, Malaysia
Tel: (60-3) 758-6518
Fax: (60-3) 755-2589/758-6646
malaysia@covey.com

**Covey Leadership Center
Mexico**

José Ma, Rico 121-402
Colonia del Valle
03100 México D.F. Mexico
Tel: (52-5) 524-5804
Fax: (52-5) 524-5903
mexico@covey.com

**Franklin Covey Company
Mexico**

Edificio Losoles D-15
Avenida Lazaro Cardenas
#2400 Pte.
San Pedro Garza Garcia
NL 66220
Mexico
Tel: (52-5) 363-2171
Fax: (52-5) 363-5314

**Franklin Covey Company
Middle East Region**

3507 North University Ave.
Suite 100
Provo, Utah 84605-9008
Tel: (801) 496-5036
Fax: (801) 496-5195
middleeast@covey.com

**Covey Leadership Center
New Zealand**

111 Valley Road
Mount Eden
Auckland, New Zealand
Delivery address
Private Bag 56 907
Dominion Road
Auckland, New Zealand
Tel: (64-9) 623-2917
Fax: (64-9) 630-1250
newzealand@covey.com

**Covey Leadership Center
Nigeria**

Plot 1664 Oyin Jolayyemi st
(4th floor)
Victoria Island, Nigeria
Tel: (234-1) 823-270
Fax: (234-1) 262-2706
nigeria@covey.com

**Covey Leadership Center
Philippines**

Atenco Univ.-C.G.B.
Loyola Heights
Quezon City, 1108 Philippines
Tel: (63-2) 924-4490
Fax: (63-2) 924-1869
philippines@covey.com

**Covey Leadership Center
Puerto Rico**

Edif. Banco Coop. Plaza
Suite 601-B
623 Ave. Ponce de Leon
Hato Rey, PR 00917
Tel: (787) 754-7436/7441
Fax: (787) 751-3840
puertorico@covey.com

**Covey Leadership Center
Singapore, Hong Kong,
Taiwan, China**

19 Tanglin Road, #05-18 Tanglin
Shopping Ctr., Singapore 247909
Tel: (65) 838-8638
Fax: (65) 838-8618 or 8628
singapore@covey.com

**Franklin Covey Company
International Asia, Inc.**

Room 1803
Tung Wai Commercial Building
109-111 Gloucester Road
Wanchai, Hong Kong
Tel: (852) 2541-2218
Fax: (852) 2544-4311

**Franklin Covey Company
Taiwan**

7F-3, No. 9, 1/F, Admiralty Centre
Tower 1
18 Harcourt Road
Hong Kong
Tel: (886) 2731-7115
Fax: (886) 2711-5285

**Covey Leadership Center
Southern Africa**

18 Crescent Road
Parkwood 2193
Johannesburg, South Africa
Tel: (27-11) 442-4589/4596
Fax: (27-11) 442-4190
southernafrica@covey.com

Cape Town Office
20 Krige Street
P.O. Box 3117
Stellenbosch 7602
South Africa
Tel: (27-21)886-5857
Fax: (27-21) 883-8080
gcloete@covey.com

**Covey Leadership Center
Thailand**

thailand@covey.com

**Covey Leadership Center
Trinidad/Tobago**

#23 Westwood St.
San Fernando
Trinidad, West Indies
Tel: (868) 652-6805
Fax: (868) 657-4432
trinidad&tobago@covey.com

**Franklin Covey Organisation
Services Ltd
United Kingdom**

4 Berghem Mews
Blythe Road
London
W14 0HN
Tel: (44-171) 602 6557
Fax: (44-171) 602 2166

**Covey Leadership Center
Venezuela**

Calle California Con Mucuchies
Edif. Los Angeles, Piso 2,
Ofic. 5-6B, Las Mercedes
Caracas, Venezuela
Tel: (58-2) 993-8550
Fax: (58-2) 993-1763
venezuela@covey.com

THE 7 HABITS OF HIGHLY EFFECTIVE PEOPLE
Powerful Lessons in Personal Change

Stephen R. Covey

'This book has the gift of being simple without being simplistic'
M. Scott Peck, author of *The Road Less Travelled*

In *The 7 Habits of Highly Effective People* Stephen R. Covey presents a
holistic, integrated, people-centred approach for solving personal and
professional problems. With penetrating insights and pointed anecdotes,
Covey reveals a step-by-step pathway for living with fairness, integrity,
honesty and human dignity – principles that give us the security to adapt
to change, and the wisdom and power to take advantage of the
opportunities that change creates.

'Fundamentals are the key to success. Stephen Covey is a master of them.
Buy his book, but most importantly, use it!'
Anthony Robbins, author of *Unlimited Power*

0684858398   £10.99
Also on audio read by Stephen Covey – 0671853236   £8.99

PRINCIPLE-CENTRED LEADERSHIP
A Philosophy for Life and for Success in Business.

Stephen R. Covey

Principle-Centred Leadership will help solve these dilemmas – and many others:

How do we achieve a wise and renewing balance between work and family in the midst of constant pressures and crises?

How do we unleash the creativity, talent and energy of the vast majority of the work force, whose jobs neither require nor reward such resources?

How can we have a culture characterised by change, flexibility, and continuous improvement and still maintain a sense of stability and security?

How can we realise that the choice between hardball 'tough' management and softball 'kind' management is transcended by a third alternative that is both tougher and kinder?

How do we create team spirit and harmony among people and departments that have been criticising and attacking each other for years?

How do we get people and culture aligned with strategy, so that everyone in an organisation is as committed to the strategy as those who formulated it?

068485841X   £10.99
Also on audio read by Stephen Covey – 0671755455   £8.99

FIRST THINGS FIRST

Stephen R. Covey, A. Roger Merrill with Rebecca R. Merrill

In the first real breakthrough in time management in years, Stephen R.
Covey and A. Roger Merrill apply the insights of *The 7 Habits of Highly
Effective People* to the daily problems of people who must struggle with
the ever-increasing demands of work and home-life. Rather than
focusing on time and change, Covey and Merrill emphasise relationships
and results. And instead of efficiency, they emphasise effectiveness.

First Things First shows:

Why your previous attempts to manage time failed.

How to overcome the tremendous gravity of habit.

What the connections are between time management and money
management.

How to turn your resolutions into reality.

How to delegate without losing control.

Where the winners really spend their time.

How to rediscover your power and passion.

How to lead your life, not just manage your time.

With the wisdom and insight that has made *The 7 Habits of Highly
Effective People* a massive international bestseller, *First Things First* will
empower you to define what is truly important; to accomplish worthwhile
goals; and to lead rich, rewarding and balanced lives.

0684858401   £10.99
Also on audio read by Stephen Covey – 0671853228   £8.99

DAILY REFLECTIONS FOR HIGHLY EFFECTIVE PEOPLE

Stephen R. Covey

As a succinct introduction to Dr. Covey's revolutionary thinking or as a reminder of key principles, *Daily Reflections* provides an inspirational recharge that will bring you closer to a holistic sense of personal effectiveness and purpose.

0671887173   £4.99
Also on audio read by Stephen Covey – 0671900196   £8.99

*For a complimentary self-scoring survey to help you evaluate your current family culture, call (44) (0)870 600 0226 or visit www.franklincovey.com on the Internet.

*For additional examples of family mission statements and a worksheet to help you develop your own, call (44) (0)870 600 0226 or visit www.franklincovey.com on the Internet.

*For information about the *7 Habits of Highly Effective Families* calendar, call (44) (0)870 600 0226 or visit www.franklincovey.com on the Internet.

*For complimentary samples of the roles and goals worksheet from the 7 Habits Organizer, call (44) (0)870 600 0226 or visit www.franklincovey.com on the Internet.

*For additional help, reference the problem/Opportunity Index in *The 7 Habits of Highly Effective People* (London: Simon & Schuster 1992).

Franklin Covey Europe Ltd
Grant Thornton House
46 West Bar Street
Banbury
Oxfordshire
OX16 9RZ
Tel: (44) (0)1295 274100
Fax: (44) (0)1295 274101

To learn more about how Franklin Covey can impact your personal and professional life and the performance of your organization call (44) (0)1295 274100 and ask to speak to a client representative.

All of these titles are available, or can be ordered from your local bookstore. If difficulties are encountered, it is possible to buy through mail-order:

CODE	TITLE	PRICE	QUANTITY REQUIRED	TOTAL PRICE
BEPB7HB	7 Habits Book	£10.99		
BEPB1ST	First Things First book	£10.99		
BEPB8CL	Principle-Centred Leadership book	£10.99		
BEPBDAI	Daily Reflections book	£4.99		
	7 Habits . . . Families book	£10.99		
AE1S7HB	7 Habits audio	£8.99		
AE1SLIV	Living the 7 Habits audio	£8.99		
AE1SIST	First Things First audio	£8.99		
AE1S8CL	Principle-Centred Leadership audio	£8.99		
AE1SDAI	Daily Reflections audio	£8.99		
			p&p (£1.60 per book, 50p per tape)	
			Grand total	

Send your order to Franklin Covey Organisation Services Ltd, 4 Berghem Mews, Blythe Road, London W14 0HN. Alternatively call (44) 0171 602 6557 to place your order, but please be ready to quote the relevant code number(s) for the item(s) you require. Mastercard, Visa and American Express are accepted. You can also fax your order on (44) 0171 602 2166.

For a full list of the many business and positive development books and tapes available from Simon & Schuster, please write to Simon & Schuster Business Books, Africa House, 64-78 Kingsway, London WC2B 6AH, United Kingdom.